LITERATURE IN THE ROMAN WORLD

Literature in the Roman World

Edited by Oliver Taplin

OXFORD
UNIVERSITY PRESS

OXFORD
UNIVERSITY PRESS

Great Clarendon Street, Oxford OX2 6DP

Oxford University Press is a department of the University of Oxford.
It furthers the University's objective of excellence in research, scholarship,
and education by publishing worldwide in

Oxford New York

Athens Auckland Bangkok Bogotá Buenos Aires Cape Town
Chennai Dar es Salaam Delhi Florence Hong Kong Istanbul Karachi
Kolkata Kuala Lumpur Madrid Melbourne Mexico City Mumbai Nairobi
Paris São Paulo Shanghai Singapore Taipei Tokyo Toronto Warsaw

with associated companies in Berlin Ibadan

Oxford is a registered trade mark of Oxford University Press
in the UK and in certain other countries

Published in the United States
by Oxford University Press Inc., New York

© Oxford University Press 2000

First published 2000

First issued as an Oxford University Press paperback 2001

British Library Cataloguing in Publication Data

Data available

Library of Congress Cataloging in Publication Data

Data available

ISBN 0–19–289301–7

1 3 5 7 9 10 8 6 4 2

Typeset by RefineCatch Limited, Bungay, Suffolk
Printed in Spain by Book Print S.L.

Contents

LATIN LITERATURE

Preface

This is not just another collection of piecemeal essays: it is an attempt at an overview of a wide expanse of literature from a fresh perspective. The contributors have between them tried to survey all the major productions of ancient Latin literature (though inevitably some works are more fully covered than others). It is all the more remarkable that without exception they have been so prompt and responsive that the book has kept to its schedule—a rare feat! I wish to thank all for their good humour, flexibility, punctuality, and for their patience with my handwriting.

The relatively smooth and rapid progress of this book also owes much to the excellent team at Oxford University Press, especially George Miller, the editor who launched the project, and Shelley Cox, who skilfully piloted it over the waves to harbour. Ali Chivers has done sterling work on the production, especially on the division of the orginal single volume into two parts. I would also like to thank Ela Harrison, Mary Lale, and Mary Worthington for their efficient and intelligent work on various stages of the voyage. Many of the contributors are mutually indebted to each other for advice and help. One or other of us would also like to thank Ed Bispham, Jane Chaplin, Roger Crisp, Andrew Garrett, Mark Griffith, Edith Hall, Rachel Jacoff, Sandra Joshel, Bob Kaster, Tony Long, Kathleen McCarthy, Donald Mastronarde, Kathryn Morgan, Robin Osborne, Tony Woodman.

I have encouraged the contributors to quote liberally and try to give a taste of the literature they are discussing. All translations are by the author of the chapter in question, unless indicated otherwise. (Complete translations have been recommended in the section on Further Reading.)

The situation with the spelling of proper names is not so straightforward. Since this book deals with both Greeks and Romans and with their interactions, I have insisted that Greek names should be transcribed direct rather than into their more traditional Latin spelling. We have, however, kept the traditional spelling for names from both languages which are very familiar in their Englished form (such as Homer, Virgil, Athens, Rome, Oedipus (actually the Latin!), Hadrian etc, etc). The dividing line round this category is inevitably arbitrary (thus Ithake yet Attica, for example). Furthermore, when Greek names are being used in Roman or Latin contexts they are Latinized; when they are turned into adjectives they are Englished (eg callimachean, aeolic). This is an issue on which it is impossible to please everyone—indeed it is probably impossible to please anyone.

With the book as a whole we hope it will prove the reverse.

Oliver Taplin
Oxford
March 2001

List of illustrations

List of maps

Notes on contributors

OLIVER TAPLIN is Professor of Classical Languages and Literature at Oxford University, where he is a Tutorial Fellow at Magdalen College. He is also co-director (with Edith Hall) of the Archive of Performances of Greek and Roman Drama. His books include *Homeric Soundings* (Oxford, 1992) and *Comic Angels* (Oxford, 1993). He maintains the importance of reaching wider audiences, and has collaborated with various productions in radio, television, and the theatre.

CATHERINE CONNORS is Associate Professor of Classics at the University of Washington, Seattle, and the author of *Petronius the Poet: Verse and Literary Tradition in the Satyricon* (Cambridge, 1998).

MICHAEL DEWAR studied French and classical literature at Oxford, and now teaches Classics at the University of Toronto. He has published books on Statius and Claudian, and a number of articles on Latin poets ranging from the age of Augustus to the sixth century.

PHILIP HARDIE is a University Reader in Latin Literature at Cambridge, and a Fellow of New Hall. He specializes in Latin poetry of the Augustan and early imperial periods, and his publications include *Virgil's Aeneid: Cosmos and Imperium* (Oxford, 1986) and *The Epic Successors of Virgil: A Study in the Dynamics of a Tradition* (Cambridge, 1993).

CHRISTINA S. KRAUS studied at Princeton and Harvard and taught in New York before coming to the UK. After three years at University College London she moved to Oxford, where she is Fellow and Tutor at Oriel College. She has written on Greek tragedy, Latin prose style, and Roman historiography, and is the editor of *The Limits of Historiography* (Brill, 1999).

MATTHEW LEIGH was formerly lecturer in Classics and Ancient History at the University of Exeter and is now Tutorial Fellow at St Anne's College, Oxford. He is the author of *Lucan: Spectacle and Engagement* (Oxford, 1997), and is currently working on the culture of Republican Rome.

LLEWELYN MORGAN is Teaching Fellow in Classics at Brasenose College, Oxford. He previously taught in the Republic of Ireland. He has published on republican and early imperial Roman literature, and is particularly interested in the diverse ways in which the Roman civil wars were discussed and validated in contemporary poetry and prose. His *Patterns of redemption in Virgil's Georgics* (Cambridge) was published in 1999.

Timeline of chapters

BCE

CE

750 650 550 450 350 250 150 50 50 150 250 350 450 550

1 Beginnings of Latin literature

2 Earlier prose literature

3 Poetry of late republic

4 Poetry 44–19 BCE

5 Poetry 19 BCE – Tiberius

6 Later prose literature to c.120

7 Imperial epic

8 Imperial leisure literature

9 Later Latin literature

Introduction

OLIVER TAPLIN

The public is the manure round the roots of every artistic growth.

(Cesare Pavese)

This book is for those who know a little and would like to know more about the literature which was written or composed in ancient Latin. It grows from a fundamental sense that this literature still has something significant to offer at the beginning of the third millennium—indeed, that some of the works still stand among the most worthwhile achievements of human creativity from any place or time. At the same time our access to them is not simple or direct. The approach taken here is at root historical: it looks, that is, at the literature within the world that first produced it. The focus, though—and this is what makes it distinctive from most previous overviews or surveys—is on the receivers of the literature, the public, readers, spectators, and audiences. The six contributors are various in their specializations and methodologies, but are united in the belief that it is valuable to ask who these works of literature were for. What did those people think they were getting from their literature; why did they give it their time and attention? For all our differences, we hold that our present appreciation of Roman literature can be informed and influenced by consideration of what it was originally appreciated for. The past, for all its alienness, can affect and change the present.

There is a kind of eternal triangle of elements or parties involved in any instance of literature: these are conventionally labelled Author, Reader, and Text. *Maker* may be a preferable word to 'author' because it comes without the controversial associations of, for example, 'authority' or 'intention'. Similarly *Receiver* has advantages over 'reader' since it includes audiences, spectators, and so forth. It is obvious, once you think about it, that literature does not necessarily have to be written down, and that it can be appreciated in other ways as well as being read; and this was actually far more the case in the ancient Roman world than it is in the modern era. As for the third element—the text, the words—this is clearly distinct from the other two, because, although it is conveyed through human-produced agency or technology (printed book, recitation, or whatever), it is not a sentient person. And by making the receivers our focus, it becomes obvious that there is bound to be a dynamic, an interaction, between the three elements rather than a static isolation of any one.

Claims for other parties might be made, and have been made, outside this triangle. The literature might be, for example, the creation of god or an oracle or a 'found poem'. But these are all, surely, subsidiary variations on the maker. Similarly with variant receivers such as god (again) or the universe or animals or an inanimate object. So peculiar exceptions who get wheeled out, like Orpheus, who performed for wild creatures, or Emily Dickinson, who kept her poems to herself, do not invalidate the basic claim that it takes an audience, receivers, to make literature. If Dickinson had never been discovered, her poems would not have become literature.

Most previous surveys and histories of literature have made either the authors or the texts their primary focus. It has been traditional to document the authors' biographies, the sequence of their mental lives, their interests, priorities, and beliefs, as revealed by external evidence, and as implied within their works. This kind of approach, which tends to put the fascination of creative genius in the spotlight, usually supposes that the lives of the authors somehow *explain* their literature. But is individual genius any more than a cipher as long as it is without surroundings, without circumstances of production, social context?

The approaches of some more recent literary theories, on the other hand, have tended to regard the texts as the only proper, or even possible, subject of attention. The texts have obligingly delivered meanings which 'anticipate' contemporary preoccupations with indeterminacy, the destabilization or fragmentation of conceptual monoliths, or the exposure of the operations of power through language. But these strategies should also leave room for approaches that treat the original production and communication of the texts as a valid subject for a kind of history. The fact that the history we can reconstruct is bound to be, to a greater or lesser extent, partial, speculative, and selective does not make it emptily arbitrary, merely or purely a construct. The first audiences of this literature did once live, and did once give their attention to the works.

In this interaction nearly all makers of literature want, and go out of their way to seek, an appreciative public: they desire attention and 'success'. There may be many ways of measuring that success; and it is not necessarily a matter of the numbers of the appreciative public. Artists often seek (or claim to seek, at least) the approval of only the select few—this is quite a common pose in the Roman world. Nor are celebrity or prosperity necessarily invariable criteria; and money is by no means the only possible reward. Sometimes success only comes posthumously, but makers prefer to have their appreciative public (and their rewards!) within their lifetimes. Correspondingly, a good proportion of those people who have the opportunity have been happy to give some of their time and resources to the benefits of literature, to become receivers, that is. The formative experience of listening to stories in childhood is undoubtedly very important here. Whatever the roots of the phenomenon, the public is generally on the look-out, perhaps surprisingly ready to be persuaded that paying attention to literature might be worth their time and trouble.

Throughout most of the history of most literatures the interaction between artist and public has, then, been by and large reciprocal, mutually beneficial. There has been a kind of *symbiosis*. The preferences and responses of the receivers have been assimilated by the makers, who have tried to meet them. And the makers, in their turn, have affected their audiences, have pleased them, and have led them to see things that were not already familiar and respectable. The maker looks to the public for attention and appreciation: the public expects some kind of benefit or gratification. Just what those hoped-for benefits were or are is elusive and shifting; and they are one of the major concerns of this book.

And yet, apparently in contradiction to this productive symbiosis, it is widely believed that most artists—or at least the great ones—suffer a flawed and difficult interaction with their contemporary public. Creative individuals are supposed to be alienated, ahead of their times, temperamental, tortured; and their potential public fails to recognize the genius in their midst. Audiences are characterized, on the other hand, as vulgar, fickle, conservative, complacent; they do not see what is good for them. This is one reason why so much emphasis has usually been put on makers and so little on receivers: the public is seen as irrelevant, and even obstructive, to genius. What is more this 'romantic' picture of the mismatch between the creative artist and the unappreciative public was familiar in the Roman world. The fascination with the creative misfit goes back as far as anything like literary history can be traced—though it must be pointed out that Greek and Roman literary biographies were far more overt than their modern counterparts in the invention of attractive fictions. From early days the poet was often seen as a lonely genius driven by creativity despite an unappreciative public: Euripides, and even the blind itinerant Homer, are archetypal examples. Behind this lurks a deep-seated desire for the prophet or genius to be a marginalized, tortured figure. Some great price must be paid for superhuman talent. Also, the later readers, who so love the stories of the unrecognized prodigy, can bask with hindsight in the complacent satisfaction of knowing better. We lavish on Mozart or Hopkins or Van Gogh the recognition that their contemporaries were too stupid to give. Yet how often has the creative maker really worked without *any* encouragement or appreciation, without any public?

Hand in hand with this segregation of the individual genius from the mass of receivers goes a certain condescension and snobbishness—which can be seen already in Plato—towards the public of art, especially large popular bodies of receivers. This is another of the main reasons, I suspect, why they have been largely excluded from most accounts of literature. How could the crude people of that bygone age have appreciated the subtlety and complexity of the (our) literature? The artistry is too fine, the ambiguity too far-reaching, to be dragged down by mass appreciation. It needs the greater sophistication and insight and theoretical awareness of a later age (ours, of course) to see its true quality, to create meaning for it. There is often a taint of this superior self-promotion in recent academic writing.

It is bound to be true that we read very differently from the original receivers, but that does not necessarily mean that we read better. In fact, there is a disturbing presumptuousness about supposing that we can interpret and appreciate *better* than the audience that the literature was made for. The work was in a real sense made to their specifications—the carpenter built the house for them to live in. The literature came into existence in their world, in their language, society, and mental landscape. It might well be argued that, if we find any society in the past which has produced a particularly rich crop of creative achievements, then we should be asking what it was about the people of that time, the receivers and their symbiosis with their makers, that stimulated the productivity. We should be looking to them for ideas, not treating them with condescension.

Any work of literature that has stood the test of time has, by definition, been appreciated by many later receivers as well as the original public who had it fresh-minted from the maker. It has been the achievement of Reception Studies, especially in the last third of the twentieth century, to emphasize that all those many receptions are still of interest; and that many, if not all, of them contribute to our contemporary interpretation of the work. But the fact that a work of literature has survived across the centuries, and has been valued or devalued in various ways as time goes by, does not alter another fact: that it was once new, that before a certain time and context it did not exist, and that afterwards it did. Some theories have led to the claim that the genesis of the work in the symbiosis between maker and receivers is of no special interest (the term 'the originary fallacy' has been coined). But this volume takes the more historically minded view that the contextual genesis is bound to be particularly suggestive for our modern interpretation. To deny this is like digging up an artefact and having no curiosity about why anyone wanted to have that artefact in the first place.

So we believe that audiences and readers matter; that without them creative makers do not make. We do not believe that art is solely for art's sake: we believe that it is, and always has been, for people. And we do not believe that art is created in a vacuum, or in the isolated crucible of the unique mind. To have the potential to outlast its original public, it must have had an original public. Who were they? And what did they think that their literatures were for?

A sketch of the territory

Through this book we are talking of a span of time that extended for well over five hundred years, from roughly 250 BCE to even more roughly 500 CE. We are also talking about a geographical area greater than modern Europe, which spread, at one time or another, from Tunis to York to Budapest, from the Black Sea to the Dead Sea, from the Rhône to the Nile to the Euphrates. And the edges and limits of these times and places are quite indistinct; they are not neatly demarcated by frontiers and significant battles. It is often implied, and occasionally asserted, that the 'The Classical World' (or 'The Ancient World') has some special, stable unity: this is a myth.

On the other hand, we can, for the purposes of this volume, circumvent many difficult problems of military and administrative history, and of acculturation and ethnicity. The worlds in question are made up of the people who heard, watched, and read literature. What 'the Roman World' means here is, in effect, the primary receivers of Latin literature.

It seems best to 'plot' the people we are talking about against the two basic axes of Time and Place. Although there are other ways of 'locating' people historically, this will still make for the clearest introduction. The points that I plot against these axes will all have the making and receiving of literature primarily in mind; and they are, of course, highly summary and selective. What follows is, then, a kind of small-scale map of the literary lands that the rest of this book will be visiting in more detail.

During the five 'golden' centuries of breathtaking creativity in the Greek world from about 750 to 250 BCE, there was no literature to speak of in the as yet only incipient Roman world—at least if there was we know nothing of it. It would be misleading, though, to picture Rome as a backwoods village of wild men. During the 500s BCE, when Rome was first becoming dominant over the surrounding fellow Latin towns, the city itself, as archaeology has revealed, was quite developed and cosmopolitan, and even had some literacy. But it was to be a long time before any memorable literature came onto the scene: the Romans were, it seems, too busy developing a sense of national identity, working out a powerful social system, and subduing an ever-increasing area by military conquest or by dominating treaties. By 300 Rome was the greatest power in Italy: her expansion took in not only Etruscans, Umbrians, Samnites, and a host of other Italian tribes, but also the highly developed Greek cities round the southern coasts. The last to succumb was the great artistic centre of Taras (Latin: Tarentum) in 272; Sicily, a focus of Greek civilization for nearly 500 years, was added before long.

One reason, it may be, why Rome did not nurture a Latin literature sooner was that there was such a mature concentration of awe-inspiring Greek civilization on the doorstep. The nearest substantial Greek city, Neapolis (Naples) was little over 200 kilometres away. A high-quality Roman road, the Via Appia, had reached there before 300 (and it was extended to Taras before long). So if a Roman wanted to watch or listen to a Greek performance, it was not a long journey; and it may well be that Greek touring artists visited Rome. Once a Roman learned Greek, the whole literary heritage was opened—and it must have seemed above emulation, inimitable, far beyond reach in simple Latin.

Once the Romans had overcome the threat of the Carthaginians under Hannibal in the late 200s, the ensuing expansion of power and wealth was

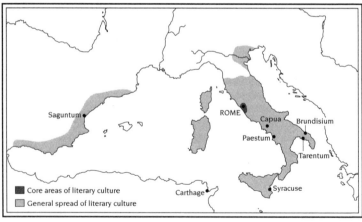

The world of Latin literature: c.150 BCE

stunning: northern Italy, southern Spain, mainland Greece, and central North Africa had all come under Rome by 146 BCE. As the Greek historian Polybios, who spent much of his life at Rome, observed, this one city had become the greatest power in the Mediterranean world in the space of some fifty years. It is from around this period that Roman literature emerges (Ch. 1). The early makers mostly came from the Greek parts of southern Italy, and learned Latin as a second or a third language (meanwhile a Roman wrote local history in Greek). And it was these poets who superimposed Greek metrics on the Latin language, a foreign surcharge that would persist for over 500 years. The turning of the prestige art-forms of tragedy and comedy into Latin was a crucial landmark; and the comedies of Plautus and Terence are the first complete works of Latin literature to survive. In the same era as them Ennius composed the first national epic of Rome, in the style and metre of Homer. Clearly there was a public, even if composed mainly of rich aristocrats, for these Latin transformations of Greek literature, and for crafted political rhetoric also. It is a great pity that, apart from the comedies, only a mass of tiny fragments of Latin literature survive from before about 70 BCE.

This preparation of the ground, so to speak, continued through the first half of the first century. Further territorial expansions into the Greek world in Asia Minor and the Near East continued, to culminate in the addition of the Egypt of the Ptolemies (last queen—Kleopatra) in 30. The cultural aspirations of the Roman aristocracy are reflected in the way that they brought larger and larger numbers of Greek intellectuals, especially philosophers and poets, to Rome and to their luxury villas in Italy. Some of these were slaves, others were a kind of mobile intellectual labour force. At the level of public display, grand theatres and libraries now began to be built at last: the most powerful city in the world wanted to become the centre of the cultural world also.

In the middle of the first century BCE Cicero and his contemporaries greatly developed the power of prose in Latin, rhetorical, academic, and historical (Ch. 2). New movement in poetry owes much to two remarkable and contrasted makers, who may well have been composing for the same group of receivers (though they never name each other): Lucretius and Catullus (Ch. 3). Catullus clearly sees himself as belonging to a group of fashionable, mutually admiring literary people, who agree in despising poets who are too conventional to be daring. The public for Lucretius and Catullus was evidently an élite, mainly the 'idle rich' of the metropolis. But their larger importance is that, through the symbiosis between them and their receivers, however exclusive, a new facility and subtlety in the handling of the Latin language, and in its exploitation of the Greek metrics, was developed. Latin literature had become significantly and distinctively Roman as well as Greek.

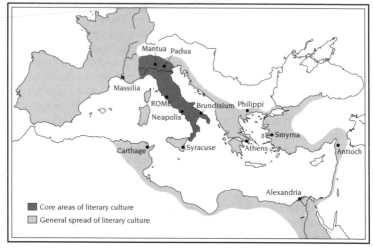

The world of Latin literature: c.27 BCE

Core areas of literary culture
General spread of literary culture

It is hard to say whether the horrific upheavals and civil bloodshed in the 40s, centred on the assassination of Julius Caesar, were more a kind of suppression to creativity or a stimulus. Either way, once Octavianus and his associates—and eventually Octavianus as monarch, with the title Augustus—had reimposed relative peace and security, there was an extraordinary literary flood. At least half of the top ten in any standard canon of Latin literature were active in the half-century from 40 BCE to 10 CE (Chs. 3 and 4). They and their public were aware that they were living through a great flowering, which was turning Latin into the language of a great literature in its own right, a literature which would survive as long as mighty Rome herself.

Virgil only lived to the age of 51, yet already in his lifetime he was seen as a great 'classic'. His poetry spread through the Roman world, and was, far more than any other, reflected in art-works, and even in graffiti. Augustus' agent for literature, Maecenas, made sure that Virgil and other talented poets were comfortable, and that they were given recognition. Many of the élite at Rome have an ode by Horace addressed to them. And Augustus himself commissioned a celebratory poem from Horace for his big jubilee in 17 BCE. Conversely, when Augustus decided that Ovid was a bad thing, he attempted to have his poetry totally suppressed. It tells us something about the dissemination of literature that (fortunately) he failed.

This was undoubtedly a highly élitist society; and presumably literature did not filter far down the social scale beyond the rich and powerful. But the public for literature was spreading: libraries were being built at Rome and other major cities; and there was by now a substantial book trade. The first stone theatre at Rome was built as late as 55 BCE; but over the next two centuries theatres were constructed in towns throughout the empire. Rome was, however, the unique centre of the Roman world. And no doubt this one city—an unprecedentedly vast city of over a million inhabitants—accounted for the core reception of virtually all Latin literature. This is very different from the widespread Greek scene.

Another limitation on the potential public was that Latin was never imposed on the empire, outside Italy that is, except as the language of administration and of the law. Thus, there are over fifty times as many Greek literary papyri from Egypt than there are Roman. Of the forty or so examples of Latin literature proper that have been excavated, half are of Virgil, trailed next by Cicero and by the historian Sallust. But it is worth remembering that Latin-speaking soldiers were stationed all over the empire; and that tens of thousands of Romans and Italians were settled in colonies the length and breadth of the provinces, from Merida (in remote Spain) to Cologne (Köln, Latin *Colonia*) to Beirut to Caesarea (one in Palestine, another in Algeria, and several others). A totally unpredictable reminder that we should not over-restrict the scope of the Roman literary world turned up in 1979. At a briefly held frontier fort far up the Nile excavators found a papyrus scrap written in the 20s BCE: it turned out to contain poems by Virgil's friend and contemporary Cornelius Gallus (see illustration on p. 53).

The maturing of Latin literature during the rule of Augustus was so fertile that the standard periodization of literary history has tended to cut it off from what followed, most obviously by applying the labels Golden and Silver. This is more misleading than helpful. Although the security of the lives of the makers became less stable, especially under Nero (50s and 60s CE), it can be argued that the great age of Latin literature continued for another 120 years (Chs. 6, 7, 8). At the same time, it cannot be denied that more memorable literature was produced during the insecure times of the Julio-Claudian dynasty in the first century than in the celebrated prosperity and patronage of the arts under Trajan and Hadrian in the second. In its own way the first century CE can claim to be another, related but different, 'golden age', emulating that of the first century BCE.

But from now on the slope of the terrain is intermittently downhill. One might trace the beginnings of the end of the Roman world, and of the Greek world under the Romans, right back to the death of the philosophical emperor

Marcus Aurelius in 180 CE. The usual kind of imperial and military history is told in terms of endless complicated power struggles and frontier wars; but the less extended and less contested worlds of literature were not in such turmoil, as the thousands of texts from the rubbish tips of Oxyrhynchos remind us. In both the Roman and the Greek worlds various interesting, and occasionally surprising, works emerge from the highly professionalized culture of the rhetoric schools. The recent repudiation of an established canon of 'Classics' has led to some interesting revaluations of the productions of this long, less brilliant era (Ch. 9).

The Western, Latin half of the empire, based on Rome, and the Eastern Greek half, based on Byzantion (which was to become Constantinople, and then Istanbul) sporadically but inexorably grew apart. Yet the long twilight of the world of 'classical' literature was not so dissimilar throughout both. The pressure of new assertive powers, such as those of the Goths, the Vandals, and the Arabs, set up great whirlpools of insecurity. And the encroachment, and eventually triumph, of the absolute faith of Christianity, which also meant the growing importance in education of monks and clerics, was going to bring an end—as we can now see with hindsight—to the kind of pluralism that had been essential to Greek literature and to its Latin offspring (Ch. 9). One can pin-point key moments in the chronic debilitation of the 'classical' world, such as the official adoption of Christianity by the Roman authorities in 312, the first sack of the city of Rome in 410, the closure of the philosophy schools in Athens in 529, but this tends to hide the long, sporadic process. The overall effect was this: in 300 CE literature was still being widely read and copied, even though not a great deal was being created; by 550 CE, in the West entirely, and in the East largely, a literary 'dark age' had closed in. No one could claim that more than minimal literature was being made any more; and the vast quantities, from the tedious to the sublime, that had been created and disseminated during the previous 1,250 years was being neither read nor copied. By the time when, two or three hundred years later, there were, in their very different ways, literary revivals—in the West under Charlemagne and in the East under the emperors of Byzantion—the great bulk of both literatures had been irrecoverably lost—rotted, discarded, or burnt.

The twin sagas of how what survived of Greek and Roman literature did survive, separately until about the 1300s, and then in the reunion of the Renaissance, is another story. Most of the literature that was recopied by 900 CE has survived until today, though not all—there were further bottlenecks and bonfires. All but one of the poems of Catullus came through these hazards in only one copy, and it should not be forgotten how much failed to make it. The productions of many major makers did not survive at all except in tiny

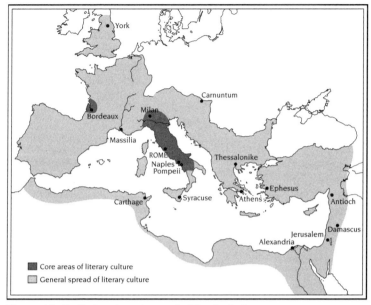

The world of Latin literature: 1 CE–end of the classical era

fragments quoted in other works; hardly anyone's *œuvre*, however great, has come through in its entirety. Whatever reached the era of the printed book, however, still exists today in multiple copies—and in electronic form. The 'Literature' of this volume means inevitably the literature which has survived down to today, but it is worth remembering that this is very far short of being co-extensive with the literature which was known to its early receivers.

Latin literature has survived as texts, as the copied written records of the crafted words of its makers. It has not survived with any of their nurturing context; the dry core has been conserved without the surrounding appreciation of its receivers. It is rather like the survival of the skeleton of what was once a human who lived a life. The symbiotic creation and appreciation of the text, like the living body of the skeleton and its personal and social context, have to be painstakingly reconstructed, often (inevitably) with a fair degree of speculation. But without that original symbiosis of maker and public the literature would never have come into being in the first place. It is the mission of this book to say something about those shadowy, mostly nameless, publics of our great (though depleted) treasury of ancient Latin literature. To come alive in our far distant, far different worlds, the texts need the revivification of the audience, the readers and listeners who farmed and cultivated their growth. To develop the vivid image from the Italian poet, Cesare Pavese: although they are now rotted away, they were essential to the growth of the flowers we still pick and the fruit we still relish.

Latin Literature

The Roman World: chief places mentioned in the text

DACIA

MOESIA

Tomis

BLACK SEA

ARMENIA

ACEDONIA Philippi Adrianople Byzantium
Thessalonike   BITHYNIA

ACHAEA   Pergamum
                      ASIA   CILICIA
         Ephesus
Corinth   Delos   Antioch
    Athens   PARTHIA

              Rhodes

                                    Damascus

                                    SYRIA

                      Jerusalem

CYRENAICA   Alexandria

         AEGYPTUS   ARABIA

                   R. Nile

1 | Primitivism and power: The beginnings of Latin literature

MATTHEW LEIGH

To later Latin critics the very earliness of the earliest phase of Latin literature is bound up with the perception of its primitivism and the image which they have of their predecessors is strikingly visual in form. The dominant metaphor is that of the barbershop: to Cicero and Quintilian, the prose-style of Cato the Elder is rough or hairy, to Gellius it is unkempt; to Ovid and Propertius, the verse of Ennius is shaggy or hirsute. A proper modern style is therefore neat, restrained, and tasteful. An excessive pursuit of innovation prompts talk of perfumes, ringlets, and curling-tongs.

Consider the implications of the tonsorial metaphor. When the satirist Juvenal, writing in the late first and early second century CE, evokes the life of man in the golden age, he houses him in caves, makes him sleep on skins and straw and gives him a wife hairier than her acorn-belching husband. To Juvenal, therefore, hairiness can be a marker of absolute primitivism. To Marcus Terentius Varro (cf. p. 37), a century and a half before him, the picture is more complex. He adduces that there were no barbers in early Rome from the fact that all the statues of the men of this time have long hair and beards and adds that the first barbers were brought to Rome from Sicily at the start of the third century by one T. Ticinius Mena. Ancient Sicily was a profoundly Greek culture and it is clear that Varro understands the introduction of shaving as a stage in the Hellenization of Roman culture. Pliny the Elder implies much the same when he states that the great general and statesman Scipio Aemilianus was the first Roman to adopt the practice of daily shaving. As will be seen, he too had a major role in the cultural development of Rome in the late second century.

There is a significant paradox to be drawn from this pattern. Both Cato and Ennius will play a major part in accounts of Roman culture in this period. Neither, it may safely be assumed, lived in a cave—they are not Juvenal's absolute primitives. Yet their response to accusations of shagginess or unshavenness of style might well have been very different. When Horace talks of 'unshaven

Cato' the idea which he seeks to encode is that of the rigorous morality and austere life-style to which he devoted himself. Ostentatiously to have worn a long beard would have been entirely in tune with Cato's public stance of strident political and cultural Hellenophobia. The archaizing tendency in all that Cato did would have had little trouble accommodating imputations of artistic shagginess were that seen as proof of his freedom from all Greek corruption. To Ennius, however, the very implication would have provoked horror. For all that he becomes the epic voice of Roman success in arms, Ennius is only too aware of the Greek culture in which he was raised, of his profound debt to Greek literary forms and models. He takes intense pride in his own artistic modernism, parades the Greekness of this modernism, and mocks his own 'primitive' predecessors for their dependence on native Italian forms (cf. pp. 10–13).

Another author who is perceived as unrefined is the great comic writer Titus Maccius Plautus (c.254–184 BCE). In the twenty-one extant comedies of Plautus we have the first complete Latin works of all and the most extensive of any writer in this early period. The judgement of Horace on his work is also a judgement on his audience—no concern for artistic coherence as long as the play is a commercial success:

> Comedy is thought to be no sweat, its subject
> drawn from every day, but it's all the tougher
> the less it is indulged. Look at Plautus
> and how he sustains the role of the young Romeo,
> the watchful pa, the tricky pimp,
> see what an antiquated hick he is among his tricky parasites,
> with how loose a slipper he races round the stage,
> he's striving just to bank his fee, no matter
> whether the play should stand or fall after that.
> (Horace, *Epistles* 2. 1. 168–76)

The audience which gives him his success without worrying about the defects of his artistry is clearly not as sophisticated as it might be. The insinuation has stuck and Plautus is often dismissed as slipshod, his public as 'groundlings'. On closer inspection, however, it will be found that he remains well ahead of his critics and that his audience are a little more knowing than might be inferred.

Plautus frequently parades the fact that his drama is adapted from an original in Greek New Comedy. In doing so he positively embraces the implication that he has debased his model by stating that he has translated it into barbarian. The criticisms of the Greek-speaking snob are not deflected, they are made part of the comic experience. If anyone had called Plautus shaggy to his face, he would have bought the biggest possible wig and made a joke out of it. As for his audience, the best thing that we can do is to be ready to divest ourselves of any prejudices, and be as prepared to be surprised by them as they were by him.

The prologue of the *Poenulus* or *Little Carthaginian* is the best antidote to any complacent assumptions about Plautus or his audience. Two factors must particularly be emphasized. The first is the level of literary sophistication which we must assume in author and audience. This is an issue from the very opening lines of the play:

> I am inclined to translate the *Achilles* of Aristarchus;
> I'll take my beginning from that tragedy.
> Pray silence and be quiet and pay heed,
> the general . . . manager bids you listen.
> (Plautus, *The Little Carthaginian* 1–4)

The audience have flocked to hear a comedy by Plautus but they will require rather more theatrical knowledge than one might expect. Aristarchos wrote his *Achilles* around 450 BCE and wrote it, of course, in Greek. At some point in the early second century BCE, Ennius adapted it for the Roman stage and Plautus is plainly parodying the speech of a herald not from Aristarchos but Ennius. Yet he does not mention Ennius at all. For this joke to work, therefore, his audience must both identify the parody of a noted scene from Ennius and know enough of the literary filiation of his work to explain the attribution to Aristarchos.

Parody, meanwhile, requires an ear familiar with the resonances of the work parodied. How far this process continues in the prologue remains uncertain but there is a clear interruption at the end of the fourth line: 'Pray silence be quiet and pay heed, the general . . . manager bids you listen.' The general could be one of the Greek commanders at Troy and the words those of his herald—of a Talthybius to his Agamemnon—but Plautus coins his own adjective (*histricus*) and the general of tragedy suddenly becomes the general manager of a company of actors. The audience laughs because it knows the high tone of the tragic genre, can recognize its imitation and engage with the bathetic return to professional theatrical reality which subverts it.

The evidence of this passage would suggest that Plautus plays to a surprisingly sophisticated and dexterous audience. Other considerations might also lead us to believe that they are also rather more tolerant than might have been imagined. The prologue-speaker reveals the details of the plot. The action is set in Kalydon in Aitolia but the family whose vicissitudes it recounts are Carthaginian: two daughters stolen away with their nurse when 4 and 5 and sold into prostitution, their cousin who was kidnapped at 7, and their father, Hanno, who roams the Mediterranean in the hope of finding them. When the speaker comes to describe the father, it is noteworthy that he does so in such a way as to suggest that there are some things which his audience just must know about Carthaginians:

> But the Carthaginian father of the girls, ever since he lost them,
> has been hunting for them high and low over land and sea.
> Every time he gets into a town, straightaway
> he looks up all the tarts wherever each one lives;
> he pays his cash, books a night, then asks where
> the girl is from, which land, whether she was captured or kidnapped,
> in what rank she was born, who her parents were.
> So cleverly and cunningly does he hunt his daughters.
> And he knows every language and knowingly pretends
> he doesn't know: a perfect Carthaginian. What more need I say?
>
> (Plautus, *The Little Carthaginian* 104–13)

Yet what is it that this audience knows about Carthaginians and how is this to aid interpretation of the play?

At some point in the middle or end of the 300s, the Greek comedians Alexis and Menander both wrote comedies called *Karchedonios* or *The Carthaginian*. In the mixed-up world of Mediterranean trade and travel this title was perhaps no more significant than *The Girl from Perinthos* or any number of other equivalent forms. Yet for a Roman audience of the late third or early second century the very word Carthaginian could scarcely fail to conjure up the most painful of associations. How many had witnessed Hannibal and his army at the walls of Rome? How many had seen service in the Second Punic War? The trauma of Hannibal, the hateful memory of the faithless, treaty-breaking, Rome-hating enemy was kept alive for generations afterwards. To allude to 'the perfect Carthaginian' would seem therefore to play on just such a collective understanding. These very lines have even been cited as part of a litany of anti-Carthaginian prejudices which any Roman reader would have to carry with her and impose on the complex and suffering figure of Virgil's Dido. Yet Plautus' Hanno is not at all what he might be assumed to be. The very title under which this play is transmitted, *The Little Carthaginian*, is itself reassuring: the feared enemy is now far enough in the past to be patronized, his wounded dignity a source of gentle humour, his rediscovery of his daughters the happy ending of the tale. This gentleman's skill with languages, moreover, is not quite of the sort for which the bogeyman was loathed. It is likely that, in the contested areas of Sicily and Greek southern Italy, the Carthaginians were found to be much more adept in the local Greek language than their Roman enemies; but they are damned in some of our sources as *bilingues*, not because they were bilingual but because of their faithlessness, because they ever spoke with forked tongue.

Plautus calls on his audience's knowledge of what makes a 'perfect Carthaginian' but then treats them to something very different. When Hanno does use his skill in languages it is only in order to rescue his daughters. There is a truly faithless villain in this drama but it is the Greek pimp Lycus. Hanno's linguistic dexterity is as much as anything a mirror for that of Plautus himself, who translates from Greek into Latin and, for good measure, throws in an extended passage of what may well be genuine Punic but is no less comical for all that.

The audience flock to laugh at Plautus' plays and to celebrate the reunification of a dispersed family, even a Carthaginian one. The prologue reminds them of their prejudices about Carthaginians, the drama subverts them. They still cheer. We will do well to assume as little as possible in advance about the literary sophistication and the political preconceptions of those people who took Plautus to their hearts.

What was a proper Roman of the middle Republic like? Marcus Porcius Cato the Elder (234–149 BCE) could have told you. A proper Roman was not of the city at all, but a child of the land, hardy and thrifty, a man of few words, a stout soldier, religiously devout, well fed on indigenous Italian fare and kept healthy by traditional local medicine. Cato made his own contribution to the development of Roman literature, propounding his cranky vision in anything from farming manuals to published speeches, and on to the earliest work of Latin prose history, the *Origines*. His baleful charisma endures, his campaign to refashion Rome in his own image as successful today as ever. Nowhere is he more successful than in his hijack of the debate surrounding the famous *Lex Oppia* and its ban on female ornament. Discussions often go no further than recording the opinions offered by Cato in its defence as proof of the austerity of Roman morality in the period. That this was only ever a wartime emergency measure, that Cato's opposition to its repeal was intended to make such conditions permanent, that Livy offers a version of the speech of the senior magistrate for the year urbanely refuting his claims, that Cato was defeated and the law repealed all seems to get lost along the way.

When Cato took to writing history, he invented Rome's original identity: that which ever had been ever should be. The self-servingly antiquated perspective of this farmer-soldier-politician was suddenly bolstered by an array of myth-historical predecessors, his vision of what was truly Roman authenticated by the discovery that he was not a freak but the last representative of a long and noble tradition. Yet it must be emphasized that this was a fundamentally reactionary vision. By this I mean not just that it was stridently old-fashioned, but rather that it was a conception of Romanity whose genesis lay in reaction to and distress at the inevitable changes overtaking a city-state already controlling the Italian peninsula and gradually advancing to a much wider empire. The pernicious fictions purveyed by Cato were perforce opposed. That part of Roman society which could see no harm in acquiring a Greek literary education or filling its houses with the statuary of a plundered world was reassured by rival inventions which asserted that their city was a Greek foundation, and that many of their cults were the creation of the greatest of Greek heroes, Hercules. If the uncouth and warlike Romulus was to be the first king of Rome, then no less importance should be attached to his successor Numa, who taught the people law and religious observance, who conversed with the Greek mage Pythagoras and effectively refounded the city in his own distinctly Hellenic image.

Nowhere was the new cosmopolitanism of Roman culture more apparent than in the world of the arts. The one factor, indeed, which links all the great creators of Roman literary culture is the fact that they do not come from the city itself. In comedy, for instance, the two authors whose plays have been transmitted in complete form to us are those of Plautus, a native of Sarsina in Umbria, and of Terence, a former Carthaginian slave freed by his noble patron Terentius Lucanus.

In this same period, three further writers distinguished themselves by their ability to compose works in epic poetry, tragedy, and comedy all at once. Of these, the oldest, Livius Andronikos, was a Greek slave freed by a member of the Roman *gens Livia* (hence his name, half-Greek, half-Roman); Naevius a Roman citizen from Capua near Naples; Ennius a native of Rudiae (a small town between Brindisium and Tarentum) which Strabo calls Greek but where he also learned Oscan. Like Plautus and Hanno he was noted for his trilingualism. Of these authors only Naevius is likely to have been born into the citizenship, and even his Campanian upbringing can hardly have failed to expose him to cultural influences very different from what a Catonian could have taken for authentically Roman. Likewise, anyone reading the first epic, the *Odyssia* of Livius Andronikos, could not help but be struck by its cultural hybridity: the poem is composed in the indigenous Latin metre, the Saturnian, the hero of the poem is given the Latin name Ulixes, but the work preserves the Greek title of the Homeric epic which it translates. The mixture of Greek and Roman elements even extends to the name of the author himself. By contrast, the readers of the *Bellum Poenicum* of Naevius and the *Annales* of Ennius will have been confronted with a literary form which has now been adapted to narrate the myths of their nation's origins and to describe the specifically Roman historical experiences of the First and Second Punic Wars. Yet even here the cultural standard is Greek. Ennius mocks Naevius for composing in the Saturnian and implicitly prides himself on fitting the Homeric hexameter to the Latin tongue. He no longer seeks his inspiration from the Latin Camenae but rather from the Greek Muses; and from the Greek he coins the terms *poemata* to describe his verses and *poeta* for himself. Pride in native military achievement and embarrassment at indigenous cultural forms are inextricably intertwined.

Ennius in the schoolroom

How is the audience for early Roman epic to be imagined? An important element here is the tendency of aristocratic generals and politicians to keep authors in their personal retinue. Quintus Ennius (239–169 BCE) is said to have been brought to Rome by none other than Cato the Elder in 204 BCE. He later followed the consul M. Fulvius Nobilior on campaign in Aitolia in 189 BCE and composed the celebratory drama, the *Ambracia*, in his honour. The vengeful Cato delivered an oration damning Fulvius for taking poets with him to his province. Though Ennius marks the closure of the fifteenth book of his *Annales* and its account of the very same Aitolian campaign as the end of his narrative, he was later induced to add three further books and to take the story up to the Istrian and Macedonian Wars and around the year 171 BCE. Pliny the Elder attributes the addition of the sixteenth book to Ennius' admiration for one T. Aelius Teucer but it is hard to imagine that he would have felt such overwhelming esteem for one who could offer no further inducement.

If early Latin epic is made in a culture of patronage and perhaps finds a first audience at recitations in the household of the patron, it still remains to explain how it attains to a much wider audience. Here again, an important role seems to have been played by M. Fulvius Nobilior, who brought back from his Ambracian campaign the statue group which formed the centre-piece of the Temple of Hercules of the Muses dedicated in 179 BCE. While the first evidence for the association of this temple with the College of Poets concerns an event towards the very end of the life of the tragedian Accius (*c.*170–88 BCE) around the year 90 BCE, it is very possible that this guild met here to listen to recitations from the beginning. Evidence in Livy and Festus for a College of Scribes and Actors meeting in the Temple of Minerva on the Aventine in the late third century BCE would support such an inference.

Yet it is as a published text that the epic of Ennius must finally have reached its widest public. So it is important to consider the implications of the claim that Ennius established himself on the Aventine and pursued the profession of *grammaticus* or teacher. For the canonical status of the *Annales* in all Roman culture up to the time of Catullus and Lucretius must reflect the practices of the schoolroom, the rote learning and recitation of generations of pupils. There remains extant not one serious epic poem between Ennius and the *De rerum natura* of Lucretius in the 50s BCE (cf. Ch. 3, pp. 55–65). Such poems were composed, but none even threatened to displace the *Annales*. Where fragments and brief quotations of works such as the *Bellum Istricum* of Hostius are found, they show no significant advance in style or content from the work of Ennius and suggest only a reverent reproduction of the master they have been taught to admire. To Marcus Tullius Cicero, Ennius was 'the second Homer'. To Roman schoolboys he must have dominated the literary curriculum in the manner of Shakespeare in England or Manzoni in Italy.

Yet what was the vision of their nation's history which the *Annales* presented to the youth of Rome? When all that is left of a seventeen-book epic is something short of six hundred lines of verse, and none of these fragments lasts longer than twenty lines, it is rash to make any too confident pronouncements. Yet a clear indication of the ennobling character of some of Ennius' verse may be drawn from episodes such as the description of the solitary resistance of a stalwart subaltern in the Istrian War:

> From all sides like rain the spears fell on the tribune;
> they pierce his shield, the boss rings with the tips,
> the helmet with a brazen din; yet no man can
> tear his body with the steel, press from all sides though they may.
> At every moment he breaks and brandishes the spears abundant.
> Sweat covers all his body and he labours much,
> nor is there time for him to breathe: with winged steel
> the Istrians were pressing him, casting spears from their hands.
> (Ennius, *Annals* 391–8, trans. Skutsch)

The solitary warrior holding off the foe has a powerful appeal at Rome; for this we need think only of the myth of Horatius Cocles on the bridge. Cato himself had found another heroic military tribune in his contemporary Q. Caedicius, and in the *Origines* he celebrates his resistance as the equal of that of Leonidas and the 300 holding the pass at Thermopylai. Ennius is doing much the same. He too chooses a middle-ranking officer—the military tribune and the centurion are specifically charged with the task of holding the line, of organizing and sustaining the resistance of their legion—and he too colours this action with an unmistakable heroic tint. For we possess these lines only thanks to the late Latin author Macrobius, who notes explicitly the lines of Homer which inspire Ennius' verse. From books 13 to 16 of the *Iliad* there is scarcely a moment when Hektor and the Trojans are not just about to set fire to the ships of the Greeks and drive the invader back into the sea, scarcely a moment when the massive, immobile Aias (Latin 'Ajax'), the 'rampart of the Greeks', does not stand firm with his giant shield of seven ox-hides and hold them at bay. Ennius adapts the lines which mark the very culmination of Aias' resistance but he transfers them not to one of the great generals of Rome but to a figure of far lower rank and lesser name, to one who lives and fights in a very different world but who can, by his example, turn his indomitable legion into an Aias for the modern world.

Other passages are more complex. In one which is recorded by Cicero, gold is refused as a ransom and the enemy challenged to the test of *virtus*, of martial courage. Yet those bearing gold are the Romans, and the speaker who twice invokes the quality which the martial nation held most dear is none other than the great Greek general and self-proclaimed descendant of Achilles, King Pyrrhos. A further passage, 'Blunted back were spears that clashed against oncoming spears', is quoted by an ancient commentator as the inspiration for the opening lines of Lucan's despairing poem of civil war, the *Pharsalia*. Does Lucan take a stirring line from Ennius' account of war in Spain and turn it to negative effect? Both Romans and Spaniards are said to have used the particular type of spear described, so this is quite possible. Alternatively, we may look to Livy and his account of the Latin wars where Rome fought a foe so like her in military equipment and organization as to make the combat feel like a form of civil war. Perhaps Lucan finds a first expression of his pained consciousness in a darker section of Ennius' poem.

Latin literary scholars are well used to searching for difficult and potentially troubling messages in the national poetry of Virgil. To do so in the works of 'shaggy Ennius', the primitive epic forefather affectionately constructed by the self-consciously refined Augustans, may seem captious. Yet Ennius himself is determined to project an image of modernity and sophistication, and to purvey a vision of the *Annales* as without nuance or reflection is to risk falsifying the importance of the poem for the generations of readers raised on it. Perhaps the most famous line of the entire work is one recorded by Cicero in his *De re publica* (On the State): 'On manners and on men of good old time stands firm the Roman state.' It has been noted that the initial letters of the first four words of this verse (*moribus antiquis res stat Romana virisque*) spell out Mars, at times the god of war and at times its metonym. The ancient customs and men are thus the ways of war and the warriors who sustain them. Which martial culture could not adopt this line for itself? How many young warriors from Pydna to Passchendaele have not had it drilled into them? Yet this tells us nothing of how it was actually understood by the readers of the *Annales*. A precious clue is, however, preserved in the eighth book of the histories of Livy. Here, a father chastises his son with the complaint that 'as far as in you lay, you have broken the military discipline by which the Roman state has stood unshaken until this day' (*quantum in te fuit, disciplinam militarem, qua stetit ad hanc diem Romana res, solvisti*). That father is T. Manlius Torquatus. Livy tells us that he was the son of L. Manlius Imperiosus, and that the father obtained his name from his imperious treatment of others, most notably his close relations. The young Manlius Torquatus is kept from the family home, the city, and the forum and consigned to a gaol or workhouse by his father, and all for the simple reason that a defect in his speech and his perceived stupidity render him an embarrassment. He endeavours to win back his father's affection by heroic endeavour when the latter is arraigned by the tribunes but only finally achieves glory when accepting the challenge of single combat against a giant Gaul, slaying him and stripping him of the chain or torque from which he gains his name. Now, a generation later, his own son has sought to impress his father by an act of heroic bravery. Yet the son has done so in violation of the order that no soldier may engage the enemy without the strict instructions of the general: to make an example of this violation of discipline, Manlius Torquatus executes his own son. The severity of his deed does much to restore discipline and is not without benefit to the cause, but it is also repulsive to the Romans who witness it; and 'Manlian commands' become proverbial in Rome for excessive severity in the exercise of power. If our one-line fragment of Ennius is spoken by T. Manlius Torqautus and comes from the same speech as Livy records, then the message it conveys to the schoolboy readers of the *Annales* is far more complex than the decontextualized tag might imply. To learn about the nature of fatherhood and the proper exercise of authority may be just as valuable as to be taught to hold the line.

Theatre and festival

If it is hard to imagine a mass audience for epic outside the classroom, the opposite is true for tragedy, historical drama, and comedy. In the Athens of the fifth and fourth century, the great dramatists composed primarily for contests held at two civic festivals lasting a total of only six days a year. It is therefore a phenomenon of central importance that the Rome of the late third and early second century saw a veritable explosion of such annual festivals, from the Ludi Romani in 240 BCE to the Ludi Plebeii around 220, the Ludi Ceriales some time before 201, the Ludi Apollinares from 212, the Ludi Megalenses in 204, and the Ludi Florales perhaps first held in 240 and an annual festival from 173 onwards. Each of these festivals seems to have begun in fulfilment of a vow or in celebration of a specific occasion, and each appears to have followed the pattern of a day or days set aside for theatrical games or *ludi scaenici* followed by

FESTIVALS AND HOLIDAYS. An extract from a calendar compiled c.25 CE. In the Roman world there was no regular pattern of rest days, and religious festivals, which included the celebration of athletics and theatre, provided opportunities for holidays. On this calendar they are marked LUDI.

a shorter period of circus games or *ludi circenses*. By the time of the Augustan calendar, no fewer than forty-three days a year were devoted specifically to theatrical games at Rome. Even if this constituted a considerable advance on the mid-Republican period and even if certain events, in particular the Ludi Florales, were devoted to erotic mime and sub-literary indecency, this still represents a thriving theatrical culture. When one adds in the frequency with which these festivals might be subject to the religious obligation of reperformance or *instauratio,* and notes the propensity of Roman aristocrats intermittently to put on theatrical shows at the dedication of temples, at funerals, at triumphs or in payment of a vow for victory in battle, it is possible to wonder whether the phenomenon of the 'resting' actor was ever seen at all in the Rome of this period. No surprise perhaps that the great writers for the Roman stage from Livius to Accius were almost all active in the third and second centuries.

Where there is evidence for the first performance of a Roman drama of this period, the context is always a festival of one sort or another. For serious drama the best documentation is that provided for the *praetexta* or Roman historical drama (named after the *toga praetexta,* worn by senators). Many of the examples recorded celebrated recent events and were composed for one of the special non-recurring festivals in payment of a vow, at a triumph or a funeral. The whole enterprise reeks of self-promotion. As for *tragoedia*, the adaptation into Latin of Greek mythological tragedy, an interesting example is the *Thyestes* of Ennius which was performed at the Ludi Apollinares of 169. Unlike most plays with this title, this is not about the Thyestean feast but its aftermath, the exile of Thyestes in Thesprotia and his return to Argos to overthrow his brother Atreus. A notable element in Latin accounts of this part of the myth is the advice of the oracle of Apollo to Thyestes, and such an episode would have involved a felicitous harmony between festive context and dramatic content.

It would be satisfying to detect such a relationship between the *Eunuch* of Terence and its performance at the Ludi Megalenses of 161, for the cult of the Great Mother was the preserve of her eunuch priests, the Galli; but the *Girl from Andros*, the *Self-Tormentor*, and the *Mother-in-law* were also put on at the same festival in 166, 165, and 163 and none of these overtly thematizes the problem of castration. It is also worth thinking about the interaction between the themes of the *Brothers* and the traditions surrounding the life of L. Aemilius Paullus Macedonicus, at whose funeral games it was performed in 160. This drama which infuses discussion of whether to raise children strictly or with indulgence with the language of forgiveness (*clementia*) and of the power of the ruler (*imperium*) is peculiarly appropriate for a man who achieved almost as much fame for his humanity to his defeated enemy as he did for finally conquering the homeland of Philip and Alexander. For Plautus the evidence is more sketchy but it is relevant that his masterpiece, the *Pseudolus*, was performed at the Ludi Megalenses of 191, a particularly auspicious occasion since that year also saw the dedication of the Temple to Flora and the Great Mother. The only other drama for which we have a date is the *Stichus*, which was put on at the Ludi Plebeii of 200, games which were reperformed in their entirety three times in just one year. It has been suggested that this *instauratio* was induced by public zeal for Plautus' comedy. There is no ancient evidence to support this hunch but, were it correct, it would tell us a good deal about the power of audiences in this period.

It is not easy to account for the popularity of Greek mythological tragedy in the early years of the Roman theatre. In comedy, it is possible to analyse the process of adaptation involved in the presentation of Greek New Comedy at Rome. It is clear, for instance, that nobody attempted to Romanize the exuberant fantasies or contemporary political humour of Aristophanes, and the other masters of fifth-century Old Comedy. Rather, the pieces which won such favour with Roman audiences were those which adapted the domestic, bourgeois New Comedy of late fourth- and early third-century authors such as Menander, Diphilos, and Philemon. Some ancient critics praised Menander in particular for his naturalism, for the mirror which he held up to life. When he presented an Athenian youth on the stage he wore clothes which had been subject to some degree of stylization but which were not dissimilar to those typical of his class in the world outside the theatre. In a Roman palliate comedy (named after the *pallium*—Greek-style cloak, to designate the Greek origins of the genre, contrasted with partly Roman 'togate' comedy), every time a character refers to 'my *pallium*' he is also drawing attention to his theatrical costume, to the marker of the burlesque national identity which he has embraced. Plautus veritably proclaims the Greekness of his comic world, even to the extent of having his characters make comments about Romans as barbarians. Yet for tragedy there is no obvious reason to want to create the same ironic distance from the form in which the author has chosen to compose. When Livius wrote his *Achilles* and his *Tereus*, Naevius his *Lycurgus* or Ennius *Medea*, their efforts at Greek high culture in Latin must have been free of all the self-conscious ethnic play which characterizes Plautine comedy. In a later period it is evident that the audiences of Accius in particular were accustomed to treat the theatre as a political forum, to respond to significant intonations from the actors, to identify contemporary politicians behind the masks of the tragic heroes, and to boo Caesar as a Tereus or weep for the exiled Eurysaces as a Cicero, but there is no record of anything of the sort in the very early years.

The fact which remains is that tragedy was a continuing success at Rome for at least two centuries. Even when no great creative talent emerged to replace the aged Accius after his death around 88 BCE, his plays continued to be revived throughout the period of the late Republic. If Cicero is anything to go by, then the tragedies of Accius, Pacuvius, and even Ennius provided a powerful armoury of allusions and quotations for dialogues, works of philosophy, and speeches. Nor would it be appropriate to think of Roman tragedy as a highbrow pursuit which attracted only the limited audiences who frequented the tragic recitations of the imperial salons. If so, it is hard to imagine quite why popular comedy, particularly that of Plautus, should be so full of parodies of the tone and content of the tragic drama. We have already seen an extreme example of this in the prologue of the *Little Carthaginian* (pp. 6–8 above), but the practice is widespread.

Imagine the impact of attending the first performance of Plautus' *Amphitryon*. Gone are the two bourgeois houses and the city street of New Comic tradition, in its place the palace and courtyard of the royal family of Thebes. Mercury comes forth—and there must still be some recognizable part of Mercury in him—but this time the messenger of the gods is dressed in the guise of a comic slave. The conflicting visual signals which setting and costume send out are then embraced in a crucial section of Mercury's speech:

> Now, first of all, I'll tell you what it is I have come to ask of you,
> then I'll let you know the plot of this tragedy.
> What? You frown, because I said this
> would be a tragedy? I'm a god, I'll change it.

> This same play, if you wish, I'll turn from
> tragedy to comedy and never change a single verse.
> Do you want me to, or not? But that was a bit thick of me,
> I who am a god pretending not to know you want it.
> I quite appreciate your feelings on this matter:
> I'll mix it up; it can be a tragicomedy.
> After all, I don't think it would be right to
> make it 100 per cent; comedy, with kings and gods on stage.
> What then? Since there's a slave involved as well,
> I'll do just as I said and make it a tragicomedy.
>
> (Plautus, *Amphitryon* 50–63)

The drama which follows teeters constantly on the verge of madness, loss of identity, violence towards kin and the other staples of Attic tragedy. Appropriately for a drama set in the palace of Thebes, it engages repeatedly with the central themes of two other works describing the destruction of the royal family of that city: *Bakchai* and *Hercules Mad* of Euripides. It appeals, in other words, to a public with a highly developed theatrical consciousness. Later writers like Molière and Dryden have refashioned the *Amphitryon* by emphasizing its comedy; others, most importantly Kleist, respond to the potential darkness of its vision. It is a marker of the low esteem under which Plautus labours that a critic of a recent London production of Kleist's *Amphitryon* credited the German playwright with taking Plautus' frothy comedy and turning it into a tragicomedy. Yet it was Plautus who coined the term 'tragicomedy', and it was surely the pleasure which his audience took in tragedy and the sophisticated understanding of the form which they possessed which made it possible for the *Amphitryon* to be.

A mirror to the audience

There is no doubt a danger in identifying the most sophisticated manifestations of Plautine comic technique and drawing from these generalizing inferences about the cultural awareness of the audience as a whole. The value of certain jokes to those who get them is only heightened by the consciousness that there are others watching who are left entirely bemused. Yet it is surely better to discover the audience of Roman drama through what the evidence of the text suggests that the writers thought it possible to convey than to cling to a dogmatic assumption of primitivism and then hack away at the text in order to make it banal enough to conform to this assumption (though this has not been an uncommon practice among experts). Another phenomenon, which underlies all the modern editions of the comedies is the excision of great swathes of text which are condemned for their repetition and reduplication of previous information. What emerges is decidedly neater than what is contained in the manuscripts but it is uncertain whether it is actually any closer to an authentic Plautine script. What may seem like tedious repetition to the modern reader of a text (or even to the modern audience in an indoor theatre with near-perfect acoustics) may have been a vital resource to the second-century actor struggling to make himself heard to a potentially restless festive crowd from a temporary wooden stage with only the sky as a roof.

The audience of Plautus should be sought in the plays of Plautus, not imposed from outside: and that audience is a constant presence in the dramas themselves. The poets and chorus of Greek Old Comedy frequently step out of their roles and address the theatrical audience directly on issues of dramatic technique, rivalry between authors, and the competition between the plays on show, but they do so in the formal section of the drama known as the parabasis. Menandrean New Comedy features a range of divine prologue-speakers who address the audience directly and sketch out the plot of the drama to follow; characters in Menander occasionally recount some off-stage incident to the audience and address them as 'Gentlemen'. Terence in turn will adopt the prologues of Menander, but eliminate all expository content in favour of literary criticism and polemic against competitors. None of these writers, however, comes close to the intense interaction between actor and audience which typifies Plautine comedy.

The tendency of characters to speak 'outside the comedy' is condemned as a particular failing of Plautus by the late grammarian Evanthius, and Terence is praised for his avoidance of this mode. Yet Evanthius is a textualist by profession and his knowledge of Plautus is acquired in the library, not the stalls. This is not to say that the far greater naturalism of Terence and Menander is not theatrically effective in its own way, just that the particular mode which Plautus represents loses far more of its impact without an audience, without a theatre. For the Plautine actor, the stage on which he takes his stand is both an Athenian street and the space in which a theatrical performance takes place. When that actor enters a house or departs for the country or the port, he revels in the fact that he is also leaving the stage for the changing-room; what the actor wears is always costume before it is dress; the edge of the stage is not an invisible boundary over which the actor must never step but a garden wall across which the actor gossips and flirts with the public as if they were neighbours; conversations between two characters pullulate with knowing asides to the audience.

Naturalistic theatre seeks to submerge the identity of the actor in that of the character played and the theatrical space in the world represented; Plautus does not dispense with this illusion, but its function in Plautus is as an idea, a possibility, and as a reflection of what the characters on stage are doing. The idea of acting is often expressed in Latin through verbs of simulation (*simulare*, *dissimulare*). In Plautus, the theatrical event is therefore reproduced in microcosm as characters use the same verbs to express the intention to present themselves to an unwitting third party as that which they are not: the slave-hero of the *Pseudolus* deludes Harpax the representative of the boastful soldier by taking on the part of the pimp's doorkeeper; the courtesan Acroteleutium in the *Boastful Soldier* snares the infinitely vain warrior with the pretence that she is the lustful young wife of the venerable Periplectomenus.

The inevitable accompaniment of the adoption by characters of a separate identity in order to effect a deceit is the employment of a disguise. Again, this allows Plautus to offer another microcosm of the theatrical experience. For the disguise worn by the characters is never clothing (*vestis*), always costume (*ornamenta*). In the *Three-Bob-Day* (*Trinummus*), the disguised swindler makes it clear that he has obtained his costume from none other than the *choragus*, that is to say the props manager commissioned by the magistrates to supply costumes for the play. The slave hero of the *Persian Girl*, Toxilus, instructs Saturio to bring the girl in outlandish, foreign costume and advises him to secure it from the *choragus*; when she returns, we are told that she has learned her lines better than any tragic or comic actors are wont to do. The constant changes of costume and identity undertaken by the hero of the *Curculio* prompt the *choragus* actually to come on stage and express his despair at ever recovering what has been borrowed.

Compare all this with the *Eunuch* of Terence. Here the disguise adopted by Chaerea has a double function. Within a play which generally eschews the self-conscious theatricalization of the Plautine stage, the clothes put on by Chaerea are the proper garb of one character, the eunuch Dorus, before they ever become the disguise of the youthful deceiver. And the paradox is that they fit Chaerea much the better. It is Chaerea who really looks like a high-class present for a high-class courtesan; Dorus is only mangy and unattractive, scarcely fit to put his own outfit on. I cannot think of a single Plautine disguise which starts the play as the dress proper to another character. This distinction between the method of the two playwrights is subtle, but telling.

Procedures of this sort give a central position to the experience of the audience. If it is the actor who supplies the experience of having perpetrated a deceit, it is the audience, who believed him to be the character he represented, who know what it is to have been taken in. Similarly, the play often appeals to the immediate experience of the audience by establishing a festive context for the events which are taking place on stage. In the *Pseudolus* of Plautus and the *Self-Tormentor* of Terence, the characters find themselves on the evening of or before the festival of Dionysos, and both plays involve a party inside one of the private houses on the stage. In the *Persa* and the *Stichus*, Plautus has his slaves freed long enough from the authority of their masters to celebrate an informal Eleutheria or festival of freedom. In the *Casina*, the prologue speaker proclaims that the games (*ludi*) are on and that an Alcedonia is being celebrated in the forum. The name of this particular fictive festival refers to the time of the year when the sea is so calm that the halcyon makes its nest upon the waves, expressing the abandonment of workaday concerns in favour of the spirit of play. No surprise perhaps that some of the most common terms for the playing of a trick by one character on another turn on the same key-word *ludus* and invoke the idea of making a game out of one's victim (*illudere*, *ludos facere*, *ludificari*). More troubling to consider the location of so many of the acts of sexual violence, on which numerous comedies turn, in the drunken, nocturnal licence of the Cerealia or Adonia. Is this part of what the audience associate with their experience of festival? If so, do their misadventures always resolve themselves into the happy endings which comedy is generically obliged to supply?

Terence: The invitation to join the coterie

Terence (in full: Publius Terentius Afer) knows how to make his audience think through these problems. The world of his dramas (185–159 BCE) is undoubtedly more naturalistic and less theatricalized than that of Plautus, but those moments where his works reflect the dramatic and comic process which has created them can often have a significant impact. In the *Eunuch*, Chaerea commits a rape by daylight, when sober, and without any festival as a cover for his deeds. He is 16 years old and not even out of the period of military service after which a Terentian hero might well turn to the high life. His arrival on stage entirely smitten with his future victim prompts the slave Parmeno to muse that the madness of a passionate Chaerea will make the activities of his elder brother look like a game and a joke (*ludum iocumque*). Yet Parmeno takes the girl for a prostitute and decides to educate Chaerea in the ways of this class by sneaking him into the house of the courtesan Thais and urging him to 'take your food with her, be near her, touch her, play with her, sleep by her'. Parmeno never means Chaerea to do anything like what he actually does. What then is to be made of the emergence of the distressed maid Pythias? She recounts the rape to the audience and complains that Chaerea has made a mockery of the girl, that the women of the house have been laughed at in unworthy ways. When Chaerea returns, she assumes that he must mean to laugh at them all over again. Is this then funny, a fit subject for laughter? Were Chaerea to think of his rape as getting the laugh over his victim, what would that mean to the audience?

Terence uses the language proper to the experience of the comic audience in order to frame the questions implied. Even more striking is the way that the same terms recur at the close of the drama. Is the question answered or the problem put forward again? Pythias has blamed Parmeno for suggesting the plan to Chaerea and complains again of being mocked. Yet she will not go unavenged. Rather, she in turn performs a trick on Parmeno by pretending that Chaerea is receiving an adulterer's punishment, causing the slave to warn the boy's aged father Laches, who therefore bursts into the house of Thais. The result is a joke which, as she puts it, she alone got. Pythias therefore celebrates and assures Parmeno that she cannot tell him what *games* he provided indoors. Now it is Parmeno's turn to complain that he is being laughed at. There is something deeply uncomfortable about this process. The reciprocity whereby I laugh at you and then you at me and we both go off hand in hand is too neat and schematic. It makes us think that it is all over, that one level of conflict has been resolved. But it does so by inviting us to imagine that a foolish jape with an old man and a slave is in some sense commensurable with a rape, when any rational judgement would tell us that they belong to entirely separate scales. The process which began by helping us frame the question 'Is Rape Funny?' closes by telling us that rape can somehow be accommodated within a process of comic exchange. But can it? The audience of the *Eunuch* have come to be entertained and to laugh, but it is not obvious that they find in the laughter of Pythias the perfect reflection of their aspirations.

Much of the appeal of Terence's comedy is cerebral. Yet it is worth bearing in mind that this same *Eunuch* earned Terence the unprecedented fee of 8,000 sesterces, and that its first performance was received with such acclaim that it was reprised that very day. Terence the success, the crowd-pleaser does not feature very prominently in literary histories and he has only himself to blame for it. The fault lies with the two prologues which accompany another of Terence's works, the *Hecyra* or *Mother-in-law*, both of which tell of calamitous events at the first two attempts to put on the play. No more famous tale of artistic disaster has come down from antiquity. According to the first prologue, the première could not be seen or heard because the people became captivated by the counter-attraction of a rope-dancer. The second prologue is rather more elaborate. The speaker now is the great actor-manager L. Ambivius Turpio and his stated resolution is to show the same persistence in backing Terence as once he did with the great Caecilius Statius (c.225–168 BCE). This is how he tells the tale of the initial failure of the play:

> Now as for what I seek for my own sake, your benevolent attention please.
> I bring you the *Mother-in-law*, a play I have never been allowed
> to perform in silence; so cruelly has disaster dogged it.
> Your understanding will ease that disaster,
> if it will give assistance to my zeal.
> The first time I started to perform it, the boasting of boxers,
> (and the eager expectation of a rope-walker to boot)
> the gathering of fans, the din, the shouting of women,
> drove me off the stage ahead of time.
> I decided to follow my old method of
> experiment with a new play: I put it on again.
> For the first act they loved me; when the story went around
> that gladiators were next on, the crowd rushed in,
> rioted, shouted, fought for a place.
> Now there is no disturbance: peace and quiet reign:
> I am granted the time to act; you are given
> the chance to add some splendour to the theatrical games.
> As much as you can, let not the art of the muses
> fall into the hands of the few; make your authority
> favour and aid my authority.

(Terence, *The Mother-in-law* 28–48)

Much has been made of this story. Some dismiss it as a charming fiction; others assume that the other less elevated attractions deprived Terence of the attention of his audience and that they rushed off to wherever they were being held. Others rightly point out that the real trouble only starts when word gets round that boxers and gladiators are due to *follow* the performance of the *Mother-in-law* and on the same stage. In other words, what actually goes wrong is that the refined entertainment on offer is drowned out by the fight for seats as grapple-fans and aesthetes come to blows. Even when aesthetes are foolish enough to involve themselves in such disputes, it tends to be the grapple-fans who win.

A later source assures us that the third performance of the *Mother-in-law* was a hit. Its popularity may not have matched that of the *Eunuch*, perhaps, but a success it was for all that. How then are we to reconcile these protestations of failure on the part of the author with what seem to be the facts of his actual good fortune? The answer surely is that Terence has constructed a comic personality for himself. His comedies display a genuine subtlety and intellectual refinement and they eschew the most physical and farcical elements of Plautus.

There are not the burping, drunken slaves of *Pseudolus* and *Stichus* or the piggy-back riding with which the *Asinaria* concludes. The best way then to see off the inevitable accusations of élitism is to embrace them and make a joke out of them. The audience which stays with the *Mother-in-law* until the very end can identify itself with the culturally refined and against the boorish mob.

The same procedure is apparent in other Terentian prologues. In the *Phormio*, for instance, a 'malevolent old poet' is said to complain that Terence's previous plays are slender in language and lightweight in composition (*tenui . . . oratione et scriptura levi*). A century later, Cicero will characterize the stylistically ultra-refined speeches of the orator C. Licinius Calvus as too attenuated (*attenuata*) to appeal to any other than the most attentive of audiences. Calvus was also one of the most prominent of the neoterics (cf. Ch. 3, pp. 65–8) who set out to bring a new stylistic refinement to Latin poetry and who paraded their rejection of a mass audience in favour of the select few who could appreciate their work. The protestation of slenderness becomes a watchword amongst their heirs, the elegists. The audience of the *Phormio* is lured with the chance to be part of the coterie, to belong to that refined grouping who truly appreciate the new literature.

A comparable principle underlies Terence's refusal in the *Brothers* to grow indignant at the accusation of the same 'malevolent old poet' that he has had a hand in writing his comedies from unnamed aristocratic friends. Terence just notes that he considers it a mark of distinction to please those who 'please the people and all of you'. If the poet embraces the implication that he is a friend of the most powerful his language reminds the audience that they share his esteem for the people who esteem him. They are not so detached from the circle which sustains the poet; they can choose to be part of the group.

The advantages of noble friends

There is a wonderful paradox in the idea that Terence, a 25-year-old Carthaginian former slave, was able to produce Latin of such purity and excellence that it became a school text for the rest of antiquity and the Renaissance. He is even claimed to have met his early death in a storm at sea as he sailed back to Italy from Athens with fresh texts of Menander to adapt for the Roman stage, a martyr to the cultural transformation of his adopted land. Perhaps the very strangeness of his achievement provoked the gossip and calumny to which he offers his insouciant response. For a certainty that gossip was not wholly unwelcome. The claim that Terence did not work alone inevitably rebounds on the detractors because it is a mark of his distinction that men so great should be willing to risk association with his work. Terence, meanwhile, enjoys the reflected glory of collaboration with the best public men that Rome could produce.

It will be noted that Terence does not identify his noble friends. Ancient writers are not slow to supply us with names. Around the end of the second or start of the first centuries BCE, the scurrilous poet Porcius Licinus identifies these men as the great P. Scipio Aemilianus, C. Laelius, and Furius Philus; he also alleges that the relationship was as sexual as it was literary, and implies that poor Terence was taken advantage of, tricked, and abandoned. Fifty or so years later, Cicero and Nepos also report the claim that Terence associated with Scipio and Laelius though they add none of the venomous allegations. Other authorities contest the association with Scipio, Laelius, and Philus on the grounds that they were too young at the time that the comedies were composed, and propose a rather older generation of friends. It is more than likely that none of our sources does more than offer a plausible supplement to Terence's deliberately unspecific references and that the identity of the noble friends will never be known. Yet the significance of the issue is not exhausted in this.

Half a century before Terence, the poet Naevius was put in prison. His offence was to have insulted the leading men of the day in his comedies. One line of verse attributed to him assaults a family closely allied with the Scipios, the Metelli, while another takes as its target the great victor of the Second Punic War, Scipio Africanus himself. A law of the archaic Twelve Tables banning malicious incantation was twisted to fit the offence and the first known libel trial at Rome begun. Plautus in the *Boastful Soldier* alludes darkly to the fate of his fellow poet. About a generation after Terence, two further libel trials took place. Both resulted from things said from the public stage in comic mimes. Accius the tragedian launched a successful suit for defamation, Lucilius the father of Roman satire failed. It is worth considering the implications of this pattern.

All six of the 'noble friends' who are alleged to have given Terence a hand in the composition of his comedies had held or were destined to hold the consulship, the highest magistracy at Rome. This is not accidental. What it represents correlates perfectly with the peculiar fact that the only libels recorded as having led to prosecution were those delivered in the theatre. The senatorial rhetoric of the late Republic is often magnificently free with its insults and abuse—the *Against Piso* of Cicero is the most obvious case—and it is unlikely that the orators of the second century were much different. Yet a slander delivered in the Senate, by one of equal status and before one's peers, can be absorbed and poses no threat to class solidarity. A slander from the stage and before the massed ranks of the festival audience is a far more threatening matter. It is evident that the senatorial class were only too aware of the threat to public order posed by the theatre. It is probably for this reason that no permanent stone theatre was permitted in Rome until 55 BCE. Many proposals were made for its construction, one was even set up in 154 BCE and then taken down stone by stone. The principle of the annual erection and then removal of a wooden structure is underscored by the sense that the theatre must be policed and cannot expect unconditional indulgence.

The account of the suits launched by Accius and Lucilius specifies their objection to being mocked by name; when Aulus Gellius states that the jokes against the great of Naevius followed the Greek manner he refers to the tendency of the comedian Aristophanes to make fun of named contemporaries. The link between the prosecutions is evident. Strange therefore to read in Horace and others that the true heir of Aristophanic comedy and Archilochean iambus at Rome was none other than one of our plaintiffs: Lucilius (148–103 BCE). There is indeed scarcely a description of the poetry of Lucilius in antiquity which does not emphasize the pile of insults under which he buried the likes of L. Cornelius Lentulus Lupus, the venomous mockery which he directed at the hapless Q. Caecilius Metellus Macedonicus. To anyone who feels that a satirist should be able to take what he himself dishes out, it will surely come as a relief to note that Lucilius failed in his own prosecution. Yet what truly requires investigation here is not why Lucilius was frustrated in his attempt to protect his own name, but rather how he was able for so long to get away with besmirching that of others.

The origins of satire are obscure. Livy and Valerius Maximus refer to the performance of dramatic *satura* on the stage but it is entirely unclear what form this took. Ennius composed literary *Satires* but only thirty-one lines of these remain. The different fragments touch on food and parasitism, wine-drinking, and a figure very like the comic running-slave; they also display some virtuoso word-play and deploy an Aesopic fable. The affinities to comedy in terms of content and style are therefore apparent, but it is hard to conceive how a complete Ennian satire might have looked. For later Roman satirists the true father is, in any case, Lucilius. For it is Lucilius who, after much experiment, fixes on the dactylic hexameter as the metre for satire and it is he who associates the form with the laceration of contemporary mores and of representative debased individuals. Even when Horace, Persius, and Juvenal confess the impossible hazards of emulating the outspokenness of Lucilius, he is still acknowledged as the authentic model for the satiric mode.

How then did Lucilius achieve the freedom to speak out as he did? In part, the answer must lie in his social status, which was considerably closer to the senatorial class than to that of a Naevius: a member of the equestrian order, a landowner of some significance, the uncle of the future Pompey the Great.

When Horace sizes himself up against Lucilius, he confesses that he is below him in rank as well as innate gifts. Even more significant perhaps is the emphasis of later writers on his close friendship with the very same men whom Porcius accuses of writing the comedies of Terence: Scipio Aemilianus and C. Laelius. The only difference is that Lucilius enjoyed their friendship, not in their early youth, but in their days of power, when they were truly the leading men of the state. There is a famous anecdote which tells of Laelius stumbling on Lucilius as he chases Scipio around the couches with a knotted napkin; it reveals a great deal about the position of safety from which Lucilius could fire off his attacks. Most important of all, however, must be the evidence supplied by Lucilius in what became confusingly listed as book 26 of his *Satires* but was in fact the very first which he published. In a significant passage, Lucilius disavows the desire to appeal to a very high-brow audience and chooses instead men of the middling sort like Decumus Laelius and Iunius Congus who are neither highly educated nor unlettered and untaught. What must be noted here is the phrase 'I care not that Persius should *read* me'. The works of Lucilius are book literature, not for performance from the public stage. They may insult the powerful but they are in no danger of reaching so wide an audience as to threaten the stability of the senatorial class.

The earliest writers of Latin literature engage with an ever-changing audience. The same work may pass through the hands of aristocratic admirers, satisfy both the watchful magistrate who buys it and the mass audience of the festival, then end up canonized for the purity of its diction and learned by heart in all the city's classrooms. In the examination of the *Little Carthaginian* and the *Annales* with which this chapter began, it was my aim to demonstrate that we can learn (or rather unlearn) a huge amount about the nature of the audience simply by remaining alert to the peculiarities of the work. If the *Little Carthaginian* remains an extremely eccentric cultural production for the years straight after the Second Punic War, then we should reconsider our assumptions about the Roman audience with which it was presumably such a success. With the closing investigation of the law of libel, the importance of powerful friends and the difference between festive performance and limited edition publication, I have endeavoured to show how the political, economic, and social conditions of reception can fundamentally alter the significance of a literary work. Naevius and Lucilius both bring the traditions of Aristophanes and Archilochos to Rome; but the same insult thrown out on the public stage can mean far more than when it is written down in a book by one who can always summon a Scipio to his aid.

2 | Forging a national identity: Prose literature down to the time of Augustus

CHRISTINA S. KRAUS

Greece and the beginnings of Latin prose

Cato was an old man when Karneades the Academic and Diogenes the Stoic philosopher came to Rome. . . . Karneades was highly charismatic, no less impressive in reality than in reputation, and it was he in particular who won large and sympathetic audiences. Like a wind, his presence filled the city with noise, as the word spread about a Greek with an extraordinary ability to amaze his audiences. People said that he had instilled in the young men of the city a fierce passion which caused them to banish all their other pleasures and pastimes, and succumb to love of knowledge. . . . Right from the start Cato . . . worried that the young men of the city might find a reputation for eloquence more desirable than one gained for practical and military achievements. . . . In the course of trying to turn his son against Greek ways, he predicts, in an almost oracular fashion, that Rome will be destroyed when it has become affected by Greek learning. But now we can see that this slander of his is hollow, since we live at a time when Rome is at a pinnacle of political success and has appropriated Greek learning and culture. (Plutarch, *Life of Cato the Elder* 22–3, trans. R. Waterfield)

Writing about the influential political and literary figure Marcus Porcius Cato (234–149 BCE), the first century CE biographer Plutarch here shows clearly how from an early point in its development Rome wrestled with the twin problems of foreign influence and imperial expansion (see pp. 8–9). The city's foundation myths, codified in the first century BCE but existing long before that, described a mingling of cultures: Trojan and native Italian; Etruscan, Sabine, and Roman; Greek and Roman. In the middle of Romulus' new city, founded, according to one ancient calculation, in 753 BCE, was a place called the 'asylum', designed to attract new citizens: 'some free, some slaves, and all of them wanting nothing but a fresh start', in the words of the Augustan historian Livy.

As the city grew by virtue of its exceptional military skill and boundless appetite for territory, it assimilated lands and peoples at first immediately adjacent—the Sabines and the Etruscans—and then further and further afield, until by the time of the birth of Christ Rome dominated the Mediterranean, Europe as far as the Rhine, Turkey, the Middle East, North Africa, and more. Each act of conquest was also an act of negotiation. The roads that the Roman armies marched down from the capital into the provinces carried Roman customs, laws, demands for taxes, and other instruments of imperialism. They also, however, famously led back to Rome: and on them, from the beginning, travelled foreigners bringing with them their own customs, ideas, and literature. Strikingly, almost no important Latin literary figure whose work has survived from the Republic and the Empire was born in Rome (see pp. 9–10): Ennius came from the heel of Italy, Cato the Elder from Tusculum, Cicero from Arpinum, Sallust from Amiternum, Livy from Padua (all small Italian municipalities); Catullus, Virgil, Horace, and Ovid from similar Italian towns; Tacitus and Frontinus from southern France, the Plinys from northern Italy; the Senecas, Martial, Quintilian, and Columella from Spain; Terence and Aulus Gellius (probably) from North Africa.

The process of assimilation, adaptation, and incorporation of Greek, native Italian, and other foreign ideas into Roman literature is one that is hard to document before the third century BCE, largely owing to our lack of evidence—and for all periods our best evidence is for the assimilation of Greek culture. We know that Greek cults were accepted into Roman religious practice beginning back in the fifth century; that Roman aristocrats took Greek nicknames in the late fourth and early third centuries; and that in 282 BCE a Roman ambassador to Taras, in southern Italy, tried to conduct his negotiations in Greek. His Greek was so flawed, so the story goes, and the Tarentines' insulting reaction was so humiliating, that the Romans ended up at war with Taras. True or not, the story is revealing. The Romans would eventually settle on Latin as the language of state, diplomacy, and formal occasions; but Greek increasingly became the cultural language of the literate élite, whose teachers and companions were Greek, and whose education often took place partly in Greece. These Romans, members of the governing aristocracy, wanted to show that, as they had mastered Greek territory, so they could master the language of Homer and Plato; but they also wanted to acquire some of that ancient intellectual and cultural heritage. Their intellectual project was fuelled by geopolitical reality: in the early second century Rome won distinguished victories over the royal successors to Alexander the Great. After each war, booty flowed back to the city: hundreds of statues, paintings, *objets d'art*, and at least one royal library. In 133 the last king of Pergamon, one of the two premier centres for scholarship and literature in the Hellenistic world, bequeathed to Rome his kingdom—including his library. And in 86, as the crowning touch, Sulla sacked Athens and brought Aristotle's library to Rome.

Along with the physical objects, during these years there also came to Rome Greek intellectuals, either as hostages (like the historian Polybios, who arrived in 167), as slaves or as voluntary exiles (the Stoic philosopher Panaetios, in the 140s), or as ambassadors, like Krates of Mallos in the 160s or Karneades the Sceptic, head of the Platonic Academy in Athens, in 155. The quotation from Plutarch's life of Cato the Elder which formed the epigraph above shows some of the excitement, and some of the ambivalence, that these Greeks aroused in Roman audiences. Karneades' speeches were show-piece orations, delivered on successive days, arguing for and against the idea of justice. These 'eristic' declamations, which demonstrated the priority of argument over substance, may have pleased the Roman youth, but they profoundly shocked the more conservative senators. Yet however much these men inclined towards Cato the Elder's (perhaps apocryphal) advice, 'grasp the content and the words will follow', they also recognized that governing a growing Empire increasingly demanded competence not only in military but also in political skills, first and foremost among them the ability to argue persuasively in favour of one's policies, both at home and abroad.

Political oratory—persuasive speeches delivered to a senatorial or a (primarily) citizen audience—existed at Rome before Karneades. When Lucius Postumius Megellus spoke at Taras, he spoke in prose, perhaps delivering a full-scale oration. Oratory is imagined as going back to the very beginnings of the Roman Republic: Livy has Brutus, one of the men who drove the kings from Rome, address the people in 509 BCE, and Cicero attributes a speech of popular appeal to Valerius Poplicola, consul in the first year of the Republic. The earliest speech for which there is more reliable historical evidence is one given by the patrician senator Appius Claudius the Blind in 280, advising the Senate against making a treaty with King Pyrrhos of Epeiros, who was leading the Tarentines against Rome. From that point until the first speech of the great orator Cicero *(For Quinctius,* 81 BCE), we have only fragments of Roman oratory. The largest number come from Cato the Elder, whose senatorial career, stemming from humble, non-aristocratic beginnings, spanned the period of geopolitical expansion mentioned above, and whose more than 100 published speeches marked the beginning of Roman oratory as a literary genre. He is a key example of someone whose ambivalent reaction to the Hellenization of Rome demonstrates both the appeal and the threat of Greek literature to its new, Roman audience. The considerable, though fragmentary, remains of his speeches show the unmistakable influence of Greek rhetorical training, and yet are throughout concerned with moulding his Roman audiences ethically and morally in ways consistent with Roman tradition. In one of the longest extracts, he persuades the senate not to take extreme vengeance on the island of Rhodes, which had failed to oppose Rome's enemy King Perseus of Macedon:

> As for me, I think that the Rhodians did not want us to win as complete a victory as we did. . . . They were frightened that, if we had no one to fear and could do what we liked, they might fall under our sole sway and be subservient to us. It is their concern for their liberty, in my view, that prompted them to follow this policy. Yet the Rhodians never aided Perseus officially. Consider how much more cautiously we behave between ourselves in private. For each one of us, if he thinks that his interests are threatened, strives his utmost to prevent this—and this is what has happened to them. . . . Shall we today abandon in one fell swoop such an exchange of services on both sides, so great a friendship? Are we going to be the first to set about doing what we accuse them of wanting to do? . . . If it is not right to receive a badge of honour if one has said that one wished to do good but has not done so, shall the Rhodians suffer prejudice not because they have done wrong but because they are said to have wanted to do so? (Cato, *Origins* fr. 5. 3, trans. M. R. Comber)

Cato here appeals to the traditional building-blocks of Roman self-image and imperial values: liberty, self-interest, advantageous alliances, and the importance of deeds over words. Speaking to an audience of equals, in power if not in prestige (this speech dates from the height of Cato's long and distinguished career as a senior senator), he also insists that they put themselves in the Rhodians' shoes. He interweaves his own opinion with that of the Romans, speaking for his audience, encouraging them to see things through his eyes. And yet he asks them to imagine that they are someone else as well, Greeks who have nothing in common with Roman traditions. Cato's audience can thus feel both superior to, and empathetic with, the people of Rhodes. This bold, persuasive strategy at once associates the Romans with their enemy and invites the Senate to practice mercy, in effect to treat the Rhodians as the Romans would like to be treated if the circumstances were reversed. It is a small but important example of the power of political oratory, specifically of its ability to manipulate audiences in more than one direction at once, and subtly to question, while at the same time to reinforce, cultural stereotypes.

Cato, followed in short order by Tiberius Gracchus and Gaius Gracchus, famous popular leaders of the 130s and 120s, used Greek technical virtuosity to make political oratory into an effective weapon. The ability to control persuasive discourse is the first step towards controlling opinion: hence Rome, as a growing imperial power, prized rhetorical skills. In the years between Cato's

The ability to control persuasive discourse is the first step in maintaining power.

death in 149 BCE and the start of the careers of the conservative statesman Cicero and the radical aristocrat Julius Caesar, around 80 BCE, Greek learning and literature steadily established itself as both a model and a challenge for Roman writers. And as the City (*urbs*) gradually overlapped with the world (*orbis*), so the Romans added a literary/cultural empire to their political one, developing the prose genres of oratory, history, philosophy, and technical prose with characteristic speed.

'The light of day, the Forum, the faces of my fellow citizens'

When Marcus Tullius Cicero returned to Rome in 74 BCE after a year as assistant governor of Sicily, he learned a valuable lesson:

> I thought at the time that no one at Rome was talking about anything but my quaestorship. . . . The Sicilians had dreamed up unprecedented honours for me. So I left Sicily expecting that the Roman people would rush to lay everything before me. But by chance on my trip I happened to call in at Puteoli [a sea-side resort near Naples] when it was crowded (as usual) with all the best people. Gentlemen, I nearly fell over with surprise when someone asked me what day I had left Rome and if there was any news. . . . That incident, judges, may have done me more good than if everyone had come up and congratulated me. Once I realized that the Roman people have slightly deaf ears, but that their eyes are keen and sharp, I stopped thinking about what people might hear about me and saw to it that they should see me in the flesh every day. I lived in their sight, I besieged the Forum. (Cicero, *For Plancius* 64–6)

The only place that mattered was Rome, and specifically the Forum, where trials, open-air speeches in the *comitium* (public gathering-place), and other business took place. During the last years of the Roman Republic, the three decades or so preceding the assassination of Julius Caesar in 44 BCE, Cicero and other advocates developed political oratory into what was later regarded as its finest, freest form. Cicero's are the only speeches which survive in their entirety; for that reason, as well as for the high quality of his work, he has long been known as 'eloquence personified', as the scholar Quintilian called him 150 years later. Though he spent a year in exile in Greece and another year as governor of the eastern province of Cilicia, and though he regularly travelled to his country villas in Italy, for most of his life he followed his own advice, making Rome his base of operations, building and then securing his reputation as the wittiest, the most patriotic, and (at times) the most respected, statesman in town.

Such a reputation depends on an audience. Cicero spoke both in the Senate House, to his peers, and outside, to juries and—in addresses to the people (*contiones*)—to anyone who wanted to listen. Despite the deep-seated Roman suspicion of any kind of intellectual activity for its own sake, the urban populace, both aristocratic and plebeian, was eager to listen to oratory. And Cicero—who himself, like Cato the Elder, was the first member of his provincial family to rise to the Roman Senate—knew how to manipulate a variety of audiences. He begins one of his most successful speeches with an apology for taking up a festal day with business:

> If, members of the jury, there should happen to be present among us here today anyone who is unfamiliar with our laws, courts and way of doing things, I am sure he would wonder what terrible enormity this case involves, since on a day of festivities and public days, when all other legal business is suspended, this court alone remains in session—and he would have no doubt at all that the defendant must be guilty of a crime so terrible that, unless action were taken, the state could not possibly survive!

Having raised his audience's expectations that they will be trying a spectacularly vicious crime, well worth missing the games, Cicero suddenly changes tack and as good as promises that his case will be just as entertaining as those missed theatrical shows (which themselves might well have featured young men at the mercy of prostitutes):

> If he were then to be told that no crime, no enormity, and no act of violence had been brought before the court, but that a brilliantly able, hard-working, and popular young man is being accused by the son of someone he has prosecuted . . . and that this attack on him is being financed by a prostitute, he would find no fault with the prosecutor's sense of filial duty, he would consider that a woman's passions should be kept under control, and he would conclude that you yourselves are overworked, since even on a public holiday you are not allowed the day off! (Cicero, *For Caelius* 1, trans. D. H. Berry)

Throughout the speech Cicero exploits the closeness of oratorical to theatrical performance, delivering a *tour de force* of comic argument that must have provided more than adequate compensation for the jurors' forgone holiday. The analogy between the two kinds of performance is an essential one. Roman literature had always been performative, both in the technical sense of the dramas of Plautus, Terence, and others (see pp. 14–23), and in the more general sense that it was more often heard than read silently. By the end of the 30s BCE, public recitations of literature were being given on a regular basis to small groups, usually friends of the author. But it is oratory which had always had particular affinities with stage performance. The three aims of a speak Cicero—who wrote handbooks of rhetorical instruction as well as pre examples of speeches—are 'to charm, to teach, and to move'. All are focuse the audience; the success of each depends on the orator's creation of a succes. ful bond between himself and his listeners, be that a group of his peers, a preselected jury, or a randomly assembled crowd in the Forum. And each audience required a slightly different technique: different levels of intimacy, different means of arousing sympathy or indignation, different applications of humour.

But acting was also dangerous, not least because it was the province of the lower classes and of Greek professionals. Aristocratic horror at the Emperor Nero's public performances in the first century CE arose primarily from his violation of class boundaries: aristocrats didn't act. But there was more to this fear of theatrical technique than class prejudice. Just as Karneades had demonstrated that words can be manipulated to argue both sides of any question, so acting exposed the inherent slip between appearance and reality. Cicero's most successful speeches are those in which he exploits his relationship with his audience, creating a persuasive persona which can carry his listeners along with him: the outraged, deeply traditional consul in the *Against Piso*; the sophisticated man-about-town and gentle but firm father-figure in the speech for Caelius; the ideal Roman politician, friend of the people and upholder of tradition in the *For Sestius*; the philhellenic Roman devotee of literature in the *For Archias*. But in every case he had to make sure that the mask was not perceptible as a mask, that the dramatic illusion was not broken—or, if it was, as in the *Caelius*, whose humour depends partly on the audience's complicity with Cicero's fun, that it was broken with the listeners' full awareness and acceptance. Nor were these easy audiences to fool, being both connoisseurs and experienced hecklers:

> I laughed at someone in court lately
> Who, when my Calvus gave a splendid
> Account of all Vatinius' crimes,
> With hands raised in surprise announced
> 'Great Gods, the squirt's articulate!'
>
> (Catullus 53, trans. G. Lee)

The crowd, or *corona*, was as important to an orator as any judge or jury, and Cicero was an expert at playing to it. So in his third speech against the revolutionary Catiline, for instance, Cicero uses the topography of the Capitoline hill and the Forum, and particularly a freshly erected statue of Jupiter Optimus Maximus (the Best and Greatest, the city's presiding deity), to sway the crowd:

'member that when Cotta and Torquatus were consuls
he Capitol were struck by lightning: the images of the
'e moved, statues of many ancient men were thrown
'e tablets of the laws melted. Even the statue of Romu-
...s city, was struck. . . . And the soothsayers said that
, ⎧ne end of the law, civil war, and the fall of the entire city and
..e were at hand unless we appeased the immortal gods. . . . They
ordered us to make a large statue of Jupiter, and to fix it in a high location
. . . saying that if that statue which you now see looked on the rising of the
sun and the Forum and the Senate House, those secret conspiracies directed against the safety of the city and of the empire would be brought to
light so as to be clearly visible to the Senate and the Roman people. And
the consuls ordered the statue to be so placed; but it was not set up . . .
before this very day. (Cicero, *Against Catiline* 3. 19–20)

Here the orator mixes appeals to fear, hope, and the power of the state persuasively to reassure the audience: at last the danger threatening Rome from
the rebel Catiline is under control, and Cicero lets us know that it is *his* control.

But what happens when the crowd is not friendly? In 52 Cicero spoke in
defence of his friend Annius Milo, who was tried on the charge of having
murdered a popular, and violent, fellow politician. The court was ringed with
the soldiers of the powerful general Pompey the Great, then sole consul, whose
rule was law. Cicero lost the case. Later, however, he published a new version of
the *For Milo*, a version which was never delivered orally but which shows how
he would have manipulated the audience if he had not been intimidated by the
fierce *corona* of soldiers:

I realize, members of the jury, that it is disgraceful, when beginning a
speech in defence of a man of great courage, to show fear oneself, and that
it is highly unbecoming, when Titus Annius is less concerned for his own
survival than for that of his country, not to show equal strength of character in pleading his case. But even so, the unfamiliar look of this
unfamiliar court alarms my very eyes. . . . You the jury are not hemmed in
by a ring of spectators as you used to be, nor are we surrounded by the
usual packed crowd. Those guards which you can see in front of all the
temples cannot fail to cause a speaker a twinge of alarm. . . . As for the rest
of the crowd gathered here, it is, inasmuch as it consists of Roman citizens,
entirely on our side. You can see the people looking on from every direction, from wherever any part of the Forum happens to be visible. They are
eagerly awaiting the outcome of this trial; and there is not a man among
them who does not support Milo's courage and believe that himself, his
children, his country, and his fortunes are this very day at stake. (Cicero,
For Milo 1–3, trans. D. H. Berry)

[handwritten: Cicero created a persuasive persona with the audience that carried himself along with them. Cicero had to make sure his]

As in the *Caelius*, Cicero asks his audience to identify with him, alarming them with the importance and novelty of their position. Also as in the earlier speech, he then lets them off the hook: the new situation is not as alarming as it seems; we are in fact being protected by these soldiers. He then turns to emotional appeal: it is not only the defendant whose life and family and country is at stake, but every one present. And as in the speech for Plancius (above), Cicero appeals not to sound but to sight: the spectacle of this trial, the sight of the Forum, is all-important. The emotional argument expands, therefore, to take in not only the speaker but also the man on trial, as the audience is moved to identify both with the orator guiding them and with the defendant whose fate they are to decide. It is a brilliant introduction to a brilliant speech. Milo, in exile in southern France (partly owing to the failure of Cicero's original effort), is said to have replied that he was glad Cicero had not delivered the rewritten version: otherwise, he would never have had the chance to taste the excellent Marseilles fish. The failure of the first speech did not stop Cicero from rewriting, and publishing, his second version. Though Roman oratory was a public phenomenon, fully integrated into the experience of citizens, who in turn had an important role in regulating the political and social prestige of the speakers, there was more than one venue for the distribution of political speeches—and, indeed, for the publication of other kinds of prose literature.

[handwritten: audience could not see the mask he wore, he published his speeches for everyone to read.]

Select audiences

It is not certain what proportion of Romans could read. Though the city was covered with inscriptions recording the texts of laws, treaties, dedications to the gods, epitaphs, and the achievements of statesmen and generals, it seems clear that a high proportion, at least, of this ubiquitous writing functioned simply as display, as reinforcement of status, a declaration and affirmation of Romanness. The market for books (as opposed to performances of drama or oratory) was restricted to a small, educated, and therefore largely affluent group, mostly comprising men who were also involved in government or in high-level business of some kind, such as Cicero's friend Atticus. The circumstances of book production had a great deal to do with keeping the market small: books had to be copied one by one, and the ancient format of a papyrus roll was easy neither to read nor to store. There may have been something of a more general market for technical manuals such as Vitruvius' *On Architecture* (from the Augustan period) or Columella's Neronian treatise on farming, and we know that in the late first century CE the professor Quintilian complained that notes from his lectures on oratory were being circulated without his

[handwritten: The market for books was a small group of elite men]

SCHOOLWORK. *On this sarcophagus from the second century* CE *a father (or teacher) is shown instructing a boy as is symbolized by the papyrus rolls they hold in their hands. Rhetoric would have been the fundamental element of all such education at this period.*

approval. But the tendency of Roman society to encourage a highly competitive governing élite, which judged its leisure (*otium*) as much as its work (*negotium*) by how it was perceived from the outside, reinforced the tendency even for literature to remain within a small, select circle (see pp. 336–8, 492–518). This élite took up new developments in so far as they reinforced traditional ways: hence the popularity of rhetoric, which could enhance traditional values via persuasive oratory. In other disciplines, too, the areas in which Roman intellectual growth is most marked in the late Republic are those which match aristocratic vested interests: agriculture, history, ethical philosophy, practical science such as engineering, grammar (a branch of rhetoric), law, and the history of religion, whose practice was also in the control of the political élite.

The producers of much of this prose literature as well as its consumers were members of the governing class. It is not until the Ciceronian period, or perhaps just slightly before, that any professional writers of history appear on the scene, and they are only isolated cases; other fields, especially mathematics, astronomy, music, and medicine were reserved for Greeks. But the period is rich in prose written by and circulated among the educated classes: political tracts such as the *For Milo* (and, indeed, Cicero's first major court success, the

Against Verres of 70); farming manuals (including an influential early one by Cato the Elder); grammatical treatises; histories of Rome and its conquests; and collections of 'antiquarian' information on ancient customs, religious ritual, and the like. The Sabine Marcus Terentius Varro (116–27 BCE) had a writing career which was itself a microcosm of this intellectual activity by and for the élite: a senator and general, he wrote over 600 books, including 150 of satirical verse; the core, however, was a series of wide-ranging studies in almost every branch of scholarly activity, the most influential concerned with Roman customs, language, and religious tradition.

The setting of many of these works brings their select audience home, as for instance the beginning of Varro's treatise in dialogue form on farming (37 BCE):

> On the festival of the Sementivae ['Sowing'] I had gone to the temple of Earth . . . where I found my father-in-law Gaius Fundanius, Gaius Agrius, a Roman knight and a Socratic philosopher, and the tax collector Publius Agrasius, all looking at a map of Italy painted on the wall. . . . When we had sat down, Agrasius said: 'You have travelled through many lands— have you seen one more cultivated than Italy?' (Varro, *On Rural Matters* 1. 2. 1, 3)

The inner circle here is not only close and familial, but each of the men with whom Varro will converse about farming has a name derived either from *fundus* ('estate') or *ager* ('field'): an inside joke for the educated reader. Varro's contemporary Cicero likewise begins several of his philosophical and political treatises with a group of close friends: so the *On Friendship*, *On the Laws*, *On the Nature of the Gods*, the *Brutus* (a history of oratory), etc. The ultimate models for these conversations are Greek dialogues, but the Roman writers cast them into distinctly Roman form, by devices such as Varro's punning names. What is more, these treatises are regularly dedicated to a single person—Varro's, for instance, to his wife *Fund*ania—enhancing the impression of a personal communication. The relationship between writer and dedicatee is often envisaged as that between one who requests and one who grants that request, as at the beginning of Cicero's *Orator* (46 BCE):

> I have long been in great doubt, Brutus, whether it is worse to refuse you . . . or to do what you have often asked. On the one hand, it seems very hard to refuse someone of whom I am particularly fond and who I feel returns my affection, especially since his request is reasonable and he longs for something ennobling; but I thought that to undertake so great a task . . . was scarcely appropriate for one who fears the criticism of learned and judicious men.

For what has Brutus (allegedly) asked? Only that Cicero, the fount of authority on the subject, write a treatise on the best kind of orator and the best method of public speaking. Cicero's introduction tellingly interweaves his own (under-played) qualifications, the importance and closeness of his addressee, and the larger, but select, audience of readers whose judgement he fears.

The enormous number of letters written by and to Cicero during the middle decades of the last century BCE provides both a glimpse into and an example of this close coterie of aristocrats. Several collections survive: sixteen books of letters to Titus Pomponius Atticus, Cicero's closest friend and a lifelong sounding-board for the orator's political ideas, personal feelings, and academic interests; letters to his brother Quintus, a smaller set which show the orator's familial, often protective persona, but which also give us an insight into the troubles of a family on its way up the social ladder; those to Marcus Brutus, one of Julius Caesar's assassins; and the letters to his 'circle', or *familiares* (often translated 'friends'), which range from personal communications to mini-essays on the good life and other topics, to official state missives. This last group in particular lets us hear the voice not only of Cicero but of his peers, as he kept copies of many of the letters he received as well as those he sent. Even the most personal of these missives shows a concern with self-image, as Cicero and his contemporaries strive to create personas that will show them to their best, or most persuasive, advantage. One example, from a famous letter consoling Cicero on his adult daughter's death, makes this clear:

> As I was on my way back from Asia ... I began to gaze at the landscape around me. There behind me was Aegina, in front of me Megara, to the right Piraeus, to the left Corinth; once flourishing towns, now lying low in ruins before one's eyes. I began to think to myself: 'Ah! how can we man-nikins wax indignant if one of us dies ... when the corpses of so many towns lie abandoned in a single spot?' ... You too must dwell instead on recollections worthy of the character you are. Tell yourself that Tullia lived as long as was well for her to live and that she and freedom existed together. She saw you, her father, Praetor, Consul, and Augur. ... Almost all that life can give, she enjoyed; and she left life when freedom died. ... And then do not forget that you are Cicero. ... We have seen more than once how nobly you sustain prosperity, and how great the glory you gain thereby. Let us recognize at last that you are no less able to bear adversity.
> (Cicero, *To his Friends* 4. 5, trans. D. R. Shackleton Bailey)

The writer, Servius Sulpicius Rufus, a prominent solicitor, shows a concern both for his own image and—especially—for Cicero's: even in the most personal grief, he exhorts the orator not to let his private feelings destroy his public image, and above all, to consider the impact of his actions on the state, and on posterity. The cosmopolitan setting, the Roman values, and the intimate yet

The wrote in fear of the judgment of their audience. Acero portrays an image that

formal communication are all typical of one strand of Cicero's correspondence.

The Roman model of intimate, mingled political and intellectual discussion fits well with the story which the Romans themselves told about the beginnings of scholarship in Rome. According to this story, Krates of Mallos, an eminent Homeric scholar and the head of the school of rhetoric at Pergamon, came to Rome (probably in 168 BCE) on a political embassy. While there he fell and broke his leg in the *cloaca maxima*, Rome's greatest sewer and a source of tremendous local pride (in engineering); during his recovery he gave lectures on rhetoric and grammar to aristocrats and intellectuals. The combination of the inner circle, the Greek teacher, and the concentration on the power of rhetorical knowledge would permeate all subsequent Roman philosophy, rhetoric, and political thought. *Persona that behef to his station*

The craze for rhetoric is understandable, given the Romans' desire for power and for controlling the knowledge that brings power. The question remains, however: what do farming, religious rites, dialectical logic, legal history, or technical grammatical questions (such as the proper way to spell words) have to do with social prestige, or indeed with politics? And why would men like Julius Caesar, who was busy conquering first Gaul, then Rome itself, interrupt his French campaign (in the mid-50s BCE) to compose a work *On Grammatical Analogy*? The answer lies at least partly in the political pressures of the late Republic and in the capacity of literature to generate and respond to the values shared by a community of readers.

During the last century BCE Rome was under extraordinary pressure from without and, particularly, from within. The Empire was now large enough to be difficult to control, and even the sensible Roman practice of letting the provinces run themselves (providing they paid taxes) was putting a strain on central administration. Military commanders were given increasing autonomy in the field, with correspondingly large and loyal armies; fierce competition between them meant that a few strong men—the most famous being Pompey the Great and his adversary Julius Caesar—eventually grew powerful enough to threaten the stability of the state and its traditional republican organization. Rome was on the brink of returning to the form, if not the name, of a monarchy. From the outside, pressures came in the form of foreigners and freed slaves thronging to Rome; as the provinces were gradually allowed more and more political rights, and as classes that were traditionally excluded from government became wealthy and powerful enough to participate in the administration of Empire, familiar systems broke down, some of them irreparably. Much of the technical prose literature of the last years of the Republic reflects an attempt, in various ways, to stabilize this decline.

So in his political and philosophical treatises, for example, especially his

This prose was intended to stabilize decline.

Republic, Cicero attempts to forge a stable language to bolster an increasingly unstable reality. Here he re-creates the nostalgic world of Scipio Aemilianus, the great general and statesman who died in 129 BCE just as popular political agitation was changing Roman politics for good. It is a world in which ancestral values and respect for authority hold sway, in which novelty is distrusted, and in which language follows orderly rules and mirrors a calm, predictable world. Cato the Elder provides the anchor of stability, as shown here in Scipio's introduction to his brief history of Rome:

> As you know, I was especially fond of old Cato and admired him greatly. . . . I devoted myself to him, heart and soul, from my early days. I could never hear enough of his talk—so rich was the man's political experience, which he had acquired during his long and distinguished career in peace and war. Equally impressive were his temperate way of speaking, his combination of seriousness and humour, his tremendous zest for obtaining and providing information, and the closest correspondence between his preaching and his practice. (Cicero, *Republic* 2. 1, trans. N. Rudd)

The key here is the harmony between Cato's life and his words: no gap between appearance and reality, between rhetoric and fact. This nostalgic picture was, by the time Cicero was writing the *Republic* (*c*.51 BCE), already lost; but this and other such treatises were powerful appeals against the inevitable changes that were in progress.

Similarly, works like Marcus Terentius Varro's on the Latin language or on Roman religious history—or even on the history of Roman theatre and the plays of Plautus—strove to reinforce a traditional way of life and an idealized morality. The collection of facts about the past and the establishment (as by Varro and Atticus) of a firm historical chronology offered one defence against frightening political and social change. Biographies of famous men, written by Varro and by Cornelius Nepos (the dedicatee of Catullus' poetry), provided a portrait gallery of exemplary lives to imitate and to avoid; Varro's was accompanied by a volume of 700 pictures with verse epigrams (the *Images*).

In philosophy too, an area up till now dominated by the Greeks, the writers of the late Republic successfully created a distinctively Roman genre, moulding Greek theories and ideas with Roman sensibilities and Roman ideology. Cicero, who is again our chief surviving example, was a leading figure, tackling topics not only of political philosophy (in works such as *The Republic* and *The Laws*, modelled primarily on the Platonic dialogues of the same name), but also of ethics (especially in *On the Limits of Good and Evil, On Duties,* and the *Tusculan Disputations,* on what makes the happy life), epistemology (the *Academica*), and theology (*On the Nature of the Gods, On Fate*). Cicero had been trained both in

Romans wanted to learn the knowledge they needed to gain control, power?

Greece and in Rome by eminent philosophers, while his rhetorical training allowed him to argue more than one side of any question. Though he was himself a moderate adherent of Scepticism, he shows special skill in putting arguments from different philosophical schools into the mouths of his characters—for many of his works are in dialogue form, imagined conversations among the learned, aristocratic Romans of the days, set during their leisure time. Writing with incredible speed (many of his philosophical works were produced between February 45 and November 44 BCE) and while pursuing his political career, Cicero created nothing less than a whole language and literature of Latin philosophy, from the most technical academic treatises (the *Paradoxes of the Stoics*) to the most relaxed and elegant of essays (such as *On Old Age*, centring on the character of Cato the Elder, and *On Friendship*).

Finally, to return to the opening of Varro's *On Agriculture*, the scene is set by the participants looking at a map (literally, a 'painted Italy') on the temple wall. Obviously appropriate to the subject of their conversation, this may have been a sort of agricultural survey map—or something more sophisticated. For a growing interest in maps, geography, and ethnography (the study of nations), present already in the Hellenistic scholars in Rome but fuelled by new Roman conquests, led writers like Julius Caesar, Nepos, and others to investigate and record the nature of the lands and peoples whom the Roman armies were conquering. In the midst of all this sat Rome, at the ideal centre of its geographical universe:

> How then could Romulus have achieved with more inspired success the advantages of a coastal city, while avoiding its faults, than by founding Rome on the bank of a river which flowed with its broad stream, smooth and unfailing into the sea? Thus the city could import whatever it needed, and export its surplus; and thanks to the same river it could . . . draw in by sea the commodities most necessary to its life and culture. . . . And so Romulus, in my view, already foresaw that this city would eventually form the site and centre of a world empire. (Cicero, *Republic* 2. 10, trans. N. Rudd)

Rome's position, as these writers made clear to their public, both justified and was justified by its Empire. Foreign tribes became not only a fascinating object of contemplation, but also a means of reinforcing national identity, as they demonstrated what Rome was not. The readers of Nepos' (now lost) *Geography*, for example, must have felt as proud about Rome as they were intrigued by the descriptions of the peoples on its frontiers.

Against this backdrop of imperial expansion and cultural anxiety, one can perhaps begin to see how scholarship itself became a political weapon. How

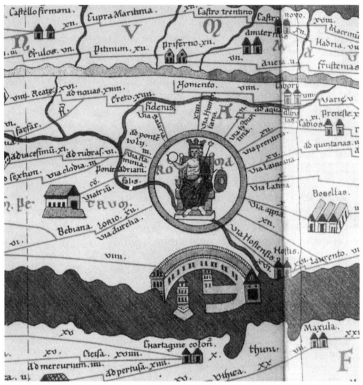

A PAINTED ROMAN WORLD. The map known as the Peutinger Table was made in c.1200 CE, but based on an itinerary map from the Roman imperial period. Some 7 m. long but only 34 cm. high, it gives a highly distorted version of the Mediterranean world and beyond. This segment is dominated by the city of Rome and its harbour Ostia.

people spoke, even what words they used and what style they favoured, was seen as a reflection of character, illustrating the doctrine that 'the style is the man' (or, in Latin, *qualis oratio, talis homo*). Correct Latinity, and especially *appropriate* Latinity, was a mark of breeding, judgement, and status. Anthropologists today speak of how a dialect or a local accent functions as cultural currency; Romans like Cicero spoke of those who were 'best' (the *Optimates*) and 'good' (the *boni*), setting up a scale of moral/ethical goodness matching a scale of intellectual and physical decorum. The equation of physical grace with mental dexterity and ethical fitness goes back to the *Iliad*, to the low character Thersites (who had neither); it is alive and well in the late Roman Republic. *Urbanitas*, a word which can mean everything from 'city-smarts' to 'elegance', meant at heart the quality of being Roman: properly Roman, that is, deeply and seriously committed to the city's traditions and to preserving them, as well as being able, in season, to be lighthearted and sophisticated.

What side one took in the debates on proper speech and spelling, what style of oratory one chose to use, what style of physical delivery one affected—all of these declared one's allegiance on the sliding scale of Romanness. Caesar scratched his head with one finger, and was immediately suspect (an effeminate gesture, it also suggested an unhealthy degree of self-absorption—did he perhaps also shave his body?); to wave one's arm too vigorously while orating might indicate a louche character; a toga worn unbelted signified loose morals. So, too, a fondness for Greek epigram or raunchy mimes could indicate an immoral disposition; and over-flowery oratory (tellingly called 'Asiatic'), which revelled in figures of speech, simile, metaphor, and extravagant verbal combinations, might be considered beneath proper Roman dignity. Clarity of expression, however, had to be matched with dignity of style: ordinary language could not become too ordinary, or its distinctively noble character would be lost. The language of comedy, for instance, so appropriate for public performance, was out of the question in a speech on political matters, or in a learned treatise addressed to educated readers. The grammatical, philological, and stylistic debates that occupied the attention of Caesar, Cicero, Brutus, Varro, and others were far from trivial: in them, these men were negotiating their own future and the future of the Republic.

Negotiating the past

They say that when someone asked the great Themistokles, the greatest man in Athens . . . whose voice he took the greatest delight in hearing, he answered that it was the voice of him who best celebrated his own merit. . . . And so the famous Marius particularly esteemed Lucius Plotius, whose talent, he thought, could best celebrate his achievements. . . . And the poets whose genius celebrates our generals' deeds celebrate at the same time the glory of the Roman people. . . . So we ought to wish that our glory and our fame extend as far as our weapons have reached. . . . How many historians of his deeds is Alexander the Great said to have had with him! And yet, when he stood at the grave of Achilles on Cape Sigeion, he said, 'What a lucky young man you are, to have had Homer as the herald of your glory!' He spoke the truth: for if the *Iliad* had not existed, the same tomb which covered Achilles' body would have also buried his renown. (Cicero, *For Archias* 20–4)

History. The word can denote many different kinds of writing: full-scale history, which in ancient Rome meant for the most part the history of the Roman Empire under the command of its successful and charismatic generals; biography, which can in some ways be seen as a slice of military history, concentrating on the deeds of single leaders; and *commentarii*, or 'commentaries', relatively unelaborated accounts of a period. Full-scale history could take one of three forms: (1) history 'from Remus and Romulus', as it was known, i.e. beginning with the founding of the city and continuing on, sometimes to the writer's own day; (2) monographs focusing on a particular slice of that long time period (usually a war); (3) 'universal' history, which covered the known world, including but not restricted to Rome. Examples of each type survive, though from the period before 35 BCE the monographs of Sallust on the *Conspiracy of Catiline* and the *War with Jugurtha* (both written in the 40s) and the *Commentaries* of Julius Caesar (and others) on the *Gallic, Civil,* and related *Wars* (from the late 50s and 40s), are all that have come down to us in their entirety.

Roman history was written in Greek before it was written in Latin; history in Latin, like oratory, began with Cato the Elder. He adopted a Greek genre, *ktisis* or 'foundation' literature, to his own purposes, producing seven books of *Origins* on the founding and early history of Rome and various Italian towns, a work which modulated (we are not sure how) into a chronological account of the growth of Rome to Cato's own time. At the end it became semi-autobiographical, as the writer included some of his own deeds and speeches (including the one on behalf of the Rhodians, quoted above). Even in the fragmentary remains, we can see that Cato's history testified to the greatness of Rome and Roman leaders—though, curiously, it is said not to have named the generals, but to have depicted them simply as representatives of the Roman people.

It also bore witness, as does the extract from Cicero just quoted, to the power of the written word. Here is Cato's story of a military tribune who during the first Punic War (mid-third century BCE) allowed the bulk of the army to escape by drawing enemy fire on his own small band. He fell together with the 400 men whom he commanded, but:

> The immortal gods accorded the military tribune good fortune to match his courage. This is what happened: although he was wounded many times, his head remained unharmed ... they picked him up and he recovered. Often thereafter he gave brave and energetic service to the state;

History would be written in a simple, memorable style. History was written for

and by his act of leading off those soldiers, he saved the rest of the army. Yet the same service is considered very differently according to the way in which it is viewed. The Spartan Leonidas did the same thing at Thermopylai and the whole of Greece adorned the glory and extraordinary popularity that his virtues had deserved by the most conspicuously magnificent monuments: portraits, statues, inscriptions, stories among other things showed the very high value placed upon his exploit. But the military tribune received only scant praise for his deeds, although he had done the same thing and saved the state. (Cato the Elder, *Origins* fr. 83, trans. M. R. Comber)

the governing class.

There is a determined rivalry here with Greek memorialization: Cato's history will do for the tribune what all of Greece did for Leonidas—and yet he will do it in a Roman way, without extravagance, in a Latin which avoids excessive ornamentation, in a simple, memorable style. The same tendency towards giving a moral lesson that we saw in Cato's oratory is visible here as well: it is not just the tribune's courage that earns his immortality in this text, but the fact that he saved, and continued to save, the state. He thus becomes an *exemplum*, a model for readers to imitate.

The political and military bias of most Roman history is hardly accidental. Cato's tribune would have been imitable not only in theory but in practice by many of his readers, as history was, above all, written by and for the governing class. Not until over half a century after Cato began writing were there any historians who were not also senators (i.e. politicians or commanders); and then only a handful of professional Roman historians came to any prominence. Of their works only that of the Augustan writer Livy has survived in any quantity.

As texts written by and for the men who ran the state, history at Rome occupied a peculiarly privileged position. It was a means of creating and preserving memory. What happened? When? What will be forgotten, what preserved? Which actors of the past will be remembered, and how? It is remarkable, for example, that as far as we know only one overtly pro-plebeian history existed—written by Licinius Macer, who held the office of tribune of the plebs in 73 BCE. The techniques of rhetoric, in which all educated Romans were steeped, offered a powerful tool for rewriting the past: for ancient history, even more than contemporary history, reflected the ideological aims and desires of its authors and its audiences. Being primarily moral and didactic, designed to teach while informing, history was envisaged as a communal effort, in which readers and writers alike participate.

It is easy to see how the writer could influence the reader; but it worked the other way as well, since the history that lasted would be the history that created an image of the Roman past that the Roman present wanted to use. This need

History was intended to be both moral & didactic.

History should preserve a inspiring social critique of the past.

not be purely panegyrical, like the military histories that Cicero praises in his *Archias*: Gaius Sallustius Crispus (Sallust), a politician and writer active in the 40s BCE, sees history and the memory of the past both as an inspiration and as a means of social critique:

> I have often heard that Quintus Maximus, Publius Scipio, and other eminent men of our country used to say that when they looked at the portrait masks of their ancestors, their spirits were enthusiastically fired with a desire for virtue. Obviously, the wax of the masks does not itself have such power in it, but because of the memory of their deeds this flame grows in the breasts of outstanding men, and does not die down until their virtue has equalled the reputation and glory of their ancestors. (Sallust, *War with Jugurtha* 4)

> One may become famous either in peace or in war. Both actors and those who describe actions are often praised. And though the narrator earns much less renown than the doer of deeds, the writing of history is, in my opinion, a peculiarly difficult task. . . . My inclinations led me, like many other young men, to throw myself into politics. There many things were against me. Instead of self-restraint, integrity, and virtue, unscrupulous conduct, bribery, and profiteering held sway. . . . So, after suffering many troubles . . . I decided that I must spend the rest of my life away from politics . . . and write the history of the Roman people, choosing portions that seemed particularly worth recording. (Sallust, *Conspiracy of Catiline* 3–4)

There is a close connection in the second extract between Sallust's own political career, which was derailed after he was tempted into 'unscrupulous conduct' (he does not tell us, but he was in fact expelled from the Senate), and the history he chooses to write about. For he does not, like Cato, go back to the beginnings of Rome, except in brief flashbacks; instead he picks relatively recent history, topics chosen to illustrate the decline of Roman society and to reveal the origins of the corruption in which he himself was caught.

Sallust has a preference for villainous heroes, flawed men like the rebel aristocrat Catiline or the African guerrilla fighter Jugurtha, figures whom he can use partly to mirror, and partly to contrast with, decent Romans. Catiline is a particularly apt illustration of the dangers of aristocratic competitiveness overwhelmed by luxury and greed. His conspiracy is especially close to Sallust's own times, coming as it did in 63 BCE, the year of Cicero's consulate, four years before Julius Caesar took command in Gaul, and the year of the future Emperor Augustus' birth. In Sallust's hands Catiline becomes a model for and reflection of an entire civilization, an object lesson in what Rome should avoid:

[handwritten: A history was a means of creating; preserving memory. Rhetoric was a powerful tool for writing (Rep...)]

> Lucius Catiline, a man of noble birth, had great power both of mind and of body but an evil and twisted nature. From his youth he had revelled in civil war, slaughter, robbery, and political strife, and among these he spent his early manhood. His body could endure incredible degrees of hunger, cold, and sleeplessness; his mind was reckless, crafty, and versatile, capable of any pretence or concealment. . . . His monstrous spirit constantly craved things extravagant, incredible, out of reach. . . . He was spurred on by a corrupt society plagued by two opposite and disastrous vices: extravagance and avarice. (Sallust, *Conspiracy of Catiline* 5)

In counterpoint to this figure, who incarnates the grim backdrop of contemporary corruption, Sallust places an impossibly rosy picture of what Rome was once like:

> Good morals were cultivated in peace and in war. The closest harmony prevailed, and avarice was almost unknown. Justice and goodness were strong not so much by law as by nature. Quarrels, strife, and enmity they directed towards their enemies; between themselves they contended only for virtue. In their offerings to the gods they were lavish; at home they lived frugally; to their friends they were loyal. With these two arts, boldness in war and justice when peace came, they took care of themselves and the state. (Sallust, *Conspiracy of Catiline* 9)

Sallust also wrote an extended *History*, covering the period from 78 BCE to (at least) 67, but its fragmentary state does not allow us to see much of its original effect. His monographs, however, show a fairly conventional thinker formulating ideas of the good old days and contemporary moral decline. He does so, however, in startlingly modern language. Though he may not really have been as stylistically innovative as he now seems (the lost history of Cornelius Sisenna, in particular, who wrote in the generation before Sallust, seems to have been similarly experimental), in our current state of knowledge his Latin stands out as a remarkable illustration of how language can reflect thought. Sallust's world is corrupt, broken, deceptive, unexpected: men act contrary to tradition, contrary to Roman values, pursuing only their own self-interest. So too Sallust's Latin. In the words of the later critic Seneca, his sentences are 'amputated, his words end before you expect it, and he considers an obscure brevity to be refinement'. His unbalanced syntax uses connectives where they are not wanted and omits them where they are, links non-parallel expressions by means of parallel structures, upsetting our expectations, and reverses the order of common expressions, especially those familiar from political or state language ('peace and war' rather than 'war and peace', for example). In choice of words as well, he defeats his audience's expectations, selecting diction now from the archaic language of Cato the Elder, now from the repertoire of high poetry such

[handwritten: Sallust defines the causes of the decline of the Republic]

as epic; he invents new words and extends Latin's syntactical range; and he shows up the clichés of contemporary oratorical and political rhetoric by putting them in a new context which reveals their essential emptiness. He thus created (or codified) a new language for history, distinctly different from the academic prose that Cicero was inventing for philosophy, and from Varro's clear but unadorned technical prose, and above all from the smooth, punchy, followable, aurally attractive style of the orators. It is a style that depends on its readers' surprise and hard-won understanding for its effects, thus demonstrating particularly well the close, almost collaborative relationship between history and its audience.

With the emergence of the powerful military leaders whose rivalry led to the bloody civil wars that ended the Republic, the history of Rome became the history of individuals—individuals whose often illegal actions needed justification, even fictionalization. The importance of the audience to history can be seen further in the development of the genre of autobiography and memoir, 'histories' designed even more than most to persuade their readers of the rightness of the author's position. The two Sallustian monographs fit, to some extent, into this pattern, but they lack the partisan slant: despite his service under Caesar, Sallust writes as the 'unbiased' historian, partisan only to a lost, moral Rome. In choosing to write short works based on the lives of individuals he is, in fact, drawing on an already existing trend. Starting in the second century BCE leaders such as Rutilius Rufus, Aemilius Scaurus, and the charismatic and dangerous patrician general Cornelius Sulla all wrote apologetic military memoirs. None of these survives; but from the very late Republic we have what must have been the most successful of all, the *Gallic War* and the *Civil War* of Gaius Julius Caesar, written during his French campaigns (59–49 BCE) and in the first years of his final war against the armies of his fellow senator Gaius Pompeius Magnus (Pompey the Great).

As commentaries, these are ostensibly 'camp notes', designed to be 'written up' by a later historian. But as Cicero remarked of these *Commentaries*, 'I think they are much to be commended. For they are naked, upright, and charming, stripped of all stylistic ornament. . . . Caesar aimed to give others a source from which those who wanted to could write history, and in this he may have done a favour to incompetents: men with sense, however, he has deterred from writing. For there is nothing sweeter in history than pure, shining brevity' (Cicero, *Brutus* 262). This, the reaction of a contemporary reader—albeit carefully and flatteringly worded—is telling. Caesar's Latin was famous for its purity—one word for one thing, nothing fancy, nothing out of the ordinary—following his own well-known advice, to 'avoid an unfamiliar word as you would a submerged rock'. The point, presumably, is to avoid jolting your reader—none of

Sallust creates a new language for history. There is a collaboration between the historian & the audience.

Sallust is a partisan to the lost Republic,

ROMAN SOLDIERS. The Column of Trajan was dedicated over Trajan's tomb in 113 CE. In a spiral of 155 scenes stretching more than 200 m. it narrates Trajan's successful campaigns against the Dacians (modern Romania). As well as battles it shows all the background to a campaign such as marches, constructing forts, sacrifices, diplomatic activities, etc.

Histories were designed to explain the rightness of a person,

Sallust's amputated thoughts here. But an unjolted reader can also be an unthinking reader. Caesar's prose is designed to produce exactly that: readers who trust; who are moved and thrilled and disgusted by the things Caesar shows them, and in the way Caesar wants them to be; and above all readers who accept Caesar's version of the motivations and the ethical stance of his characters.

He achieves all this partly through the deployment of a simple, clear, exciting military style; and partly through the brilliant choice of narrative voice. The man who speaks to us from his pages has no name; only on rare occasions is he 'I' or 'we', and then almost exclusively when speaking as the scholar-author, in discussing the habits of the Gauls, for example, or in posing as a commander evaluating strategy from a theoretical point of view. The actor 'Caesar' is always referred to in the third person. The effect is that of letting the story tell itself; the impression that of a competent historian, one with access to vivid first-person accounts (though, as often in ancient history, such vividness can be wholly an imaginary creation), and yet one detached from the action. Here is an example:

> The enemy formed up in battle order within the woods . . . then suddenly rushed out in full force and launched an attack on our cavalry. . . . They then ran at astonishing speed down to the river, and so seemed—almost at one and the same moment—to be near the woods, then in the river, and now already upon us. With similar speed they made their way up the hill to our camp and attacked the men who were working on the fortifications. Caesar had to see to everything at once. The flag had to be unfurled . . . the trumpet sounded, the soldiers recalled from working on the defences. . . . He must draw up his battle line, encourage the men, give the signal. There was too little time, the enemy pressed on so fast, to complete these arrangements.
>
> Two factors counterbalanced these difficulties. The first was the knowledge and experience of Caesar's men. . . . Secondly, Caesar had forbidden any of his officers to abandon either the defence-works or their individual legions before the fortification was complete. . . . Once he had given all the appropriate orders Caesar ran down where luck would take him to encourage the men—and ended up among the Tenth legion. His speech was long enough only to urge them to remember their long-established record for bravery, and not to lose their nerve but to resist the enemy assault courageously. . . . Then he gave the signal for battle. (Caesar, *Gallic War* 2. 19–21, trans. C. Hammond)

Classical scholars debate whether these *Commentaries* on the Gallic Wars were directed towards the Roman people as a whole—a possible, though difficult, audience to reach, given the way books were distributed, copy by copy—or towards the Senate, Caesar's peers. In either case, the prose is carefully tailored to produce a simultaneous impression of excitement and order. The enemy's attack is not trivial, the result turns on a knife-edge (and Caesar *did* lose engagements against these tribes): but the combination of the general's forethought and his troops' experience makes victory here inevitable. Caesar matches the enemy's speed with his own, and is carried along by luck as well as skill; the reader is drawn in not only by the hyperbolic prose ('astonishing speed', 'too little time', 'so fast') but also by words like 'our cavalry' (appealing to patriotism), and by the unexplained significance of the Tenth legion (Caesar's favourites and his best soldiers), designed to speak to an audience that already knows the players in this tense scene. All reinforce the sense of 'our brave lads' versus the frightening, but doomed, barbarian hordes.

Caesar's famous authorial detachment shows still more clearly in accounts of political action. Here, he presides over some elections: 'In his capacity as dictator [i.e. sole head of State, traditionally a position created only during a dire emergency] Caesar held the elections, at which Gaius Julius [i.e. Caesar] and Publius Servilius were elected consuls' (Caesar, *Civil War* 3. 1. 1). How many Caesars are there? Three, from all appearances: the dictator, the consul, and the author. And in explaining his position *vis-à-vis* his great rival Pompey, he stresses his own adherence to constitutional procedure:

> By means of legislation brought before the people by praetors and tribunes Caesar restored their property in full to some people who had been condemned under Pompey's law on electoral corruption . . . at a time when Pompey had legionary forces in the city [during the trial of Milo, 52 BCE]. . . . He acted like this because he had decided that these persons ought to receive restitution by decision of the Roman people before being seen as restored by his own favour, so that he would not seem to be either churlish in repaying a kindness or arrogant in pre-empting the right of the people to confer a favour. (Caesar, *Civil War* 3. 1. 4–5, trans. J. Carter)

'Legislation', 'the Roman people', 'repaying a kindness': Caesar, who in fact holds an irregular office of dictator, who is fighting a civil war against his fellow citizens, and who has himself held the city by force in the not too distant past, seduces his audience into seeing him as the upholder of law and fairness. Interestingly, he borrows a trick from the orators, widening the perspective at the end of this extract to include a hypothetical audience looking at him ('being seen', 'seen to be': one can compare Cicero's use of the foreign onlooker in the *Caelius* or the anonymous patriotic Roman in the *Milo*): reputation is what matters, and Caesar plays here both to an imagined crowd within the text and to the reader.

Both Caesar and Sallust look backward in many ways: Sallust from the vantage point of an irremediably corrupt present to a bygone ideal Rome; Caesar to the immediate past which has put him where he is today. In the next generation, a history will emerge that takes up the challenge of making the Roman past into something useful for the future. Livy's *From the Founding of the City* (see pp. 177–9) will confront the problem of change by engaging its audience in a process of comparison and imitation.

Historians seduce audiences into seeing the past from their perspective.

3 | Escapes from orthodoxy: Poetry of the late Republic

LLEWELYN MORGAN

Captivated Roman élite

In late 46 BCE Julius Caesar made a journey from Rome to southern Spain. To while away the time on the road he composed a poem entitled *Iter* ('Journey'), describing the trek as he made it. The upshot of this rather civilized-sounding journey was the final, most brutal act of the civil wars which had raged between Caesar and the supporters of Pompey the Great since early 49. In March 45 Caesar won a crushing victory at Munda, leaving 30,000 Pompeians dead on the battlefield.

Twenty years later, a Roman officer on active service at Primis in the very south of Egypt (ancient Egyptian Nubia) left behind the book he was reading, love poems by Gaius Cornelius Gallus (70/69–27/6 BCE). That officer's careless-ness provided us with the only sizeable chunk of Gallus' poetry we possess, but it also, along with Caesar's *Iter*, provides a vivid illustration of how central a place literature occupied in Roman culture. Here we see two Romans doing a characteristically Roman thing—fighting—and writing and reading poetry at the same time. It is a little paradoxical to picture that soldier, in a military encampment beyond the furthest reaches of the Empire, cumbersomely unwinding his 'book' (a long roll of papyrus), and reading out loud (as Roman poetry was designed to be) Gallus' trials and tribulations with his girlfriend in Rome.

Rome was ruled by a small aristocratic and militaristic élite. A Roman aristo-crat was first and foremost a soldier, trained from childhood to pursue success in the military and political arenas (for Romans these were two sides of the same coin), and it was this martial ethos which had won for Rome its enormous Empire. By the time of Caesar, however, this remarkable military entity had added to its accomplishments. The Roman aristocrat was now highly educated, sophisticated, and artistic. For example, Caesar was a brilliant and ruthless

EARLIEST ROMAN MANUSCRIPT. The frontier post of Primis far up the River Nile was occupied by the Romans only briefly in the 20s BCE. This scrap of papyrus excavated there in 1978 proved to contain some lines in elegiac couplets by the poet C. Cornelius Gallus. Gallus had been left as governor of Egypt by Augustus after the defeat of Kleopatra, but had been forced to commit suicide in 26 BCE. The name of Gallus' mistress Lycoris can be read in the first line.

general; but he was also the second-best orator in Rome (after Cicero), and wrote the *Iter* on the road and in only twenty-four days. Gallus, too, besides being a love poet, also enjoyed a very successful military career, before ambition got the better of him and he found himself on the wrong side of the Emperor Augustus.

This (to us) peculiar state of affairs was in fact a direct consequence of Rome's military success. In the course of the previous 250 years Rome had gradually conquered the sophisticated Greek communities first of southern Italy, and then of the eastern Mediterranean, and this contact with the Greek world had profoundly altered Roman culture, turning warriors into aesthetes. The Romans recognized the irony: a race they had conquered had come to dominate them culturally. As the poet Horace put it, 'captive Greece made a captive of her rough invader, and brought the arts to rustic Latium' (Latium is the area around Rome, modern Lazio). Rome's attitude to Greece was in consequence complex. A strong vein of anti-Greek prejudice persisted even amongst the most educated Roman aristocrats. Respect for their artistic achievements vied with contempt for their (perceived) lack of the 'Roman' qualities of military ability and administrative efficiency. So we shall find Lucretius bemoaning 'the poverty of our native language', as compared with Greek, but also Catullus managing to outrage Roman sensibilities by the ostentatious 'Greekness' of some aspects of his way of life.

One more anecdote will encapsulate this contradictory attitude. In the 70s and 60s BCE Rome was involved in a long-running series of campaigns against the Greek King Mithridates of Pontos. In the course of them the Greek poet Parthenios was taken prisoner, enslaved, and brought to Rome. The man who brought him to Rome may well have been the poet Cinna, most famous now for being lynched in Shakespeare's *Julius Caesar* (cf. Ch. 4, p. 75), but before his death a leading light of the so-called New Poets who dominated the Roman literary scene in the mid-first century BCE. Parthenios arrived in Rome as a slave, but was subsequently released in recognition of his learning, and went on to exercise a profound influence over two generations of some of the leading exponents of Roman poetry, including Cinna, Gallus, and Virgil. Rome was captive to a captive Greek.

Caesar and Gallus were thus writing for, and at the same time members of, a sophisticated audience of literature, but also a fairly small one. Familiarity with Greek culture did not filter very far down the rigidly stratified society of Rome. The readership of poetry was limited to the upper-class élite, and in the main (we have to assume) to the male members of that élite. The small scale of the audience, and the high level of education it possessed, explain the remarkable complexity and sophistication of the poetry composed at this time, but also the preoccupation with Roman public life which all the poets to some degree display. Poetry was rarely so immediately politically relevant as oratory or historiography—Caesar's *Iter* may have had no political rationale beyond wanting to give the impression that Caesar was an aesthete, not a butcher. But nevertheless the writers and readers of Roman poetry were still to a considerable degree coextensive with the men who wielded political power in Rome, and Rome in the first century BCE was a country in political crisis. Centuries of rapid expansion, fuelled by the aristocratic ethos, had given way to violent internal competition for power and status. A series of civil wars, punctuated by periods of serious civil unrest, eventually brought a bloody end to the aristocratic system of government, and ushered in a monarchical system of government under a single, all-powerful emperor. The terrible events of this period led some Roman aristocrats to question those cherished values which had underpinned their rise to power in the Mediterranean world. Both of the two main poets we shall meet in this section, Lucretius and Catullus, are directing their work at an audience traumatized by recent events and susceptible, potentially at least, to some very radical reassessments of how a Roman aristocrat should lead his life. The culture they were addressing had lost its centre, and the alternative ways of life promoted in contemporary literature are correspondingly diverse. What the authors share, however, is a profound disenchantment with orthodox Roman culture, given expression—paradoxically—in ambitious literary forms which bespeak considerable confidence about the potential of literature in Latin.

Revolution through familiarization

The poem *De rerum natura*, 'On the Nature of the Universe', of Titus Lucretius Carus (?97–?55 BCE) is sometimes claimed as the greatest poem ever written in the Latin language. It is certainly one of the most ambitious. Its aim, simply put, was to convert whoever read it to the philosophical school of which Lucretius was a passionate devotee, Epicureanism. We can gain something of a sense of the enormity of the task Lucretius set himself if we consider the main points of Epicurean doctrine, and ask ourselves how attractive it was likely to appear to the kind of aristocratic reader of Roman literature sketched in the previous section.

Epicureanism was named after Epicurus (Greek: Epikouros), its founder (341–270 BCE). Epicurus was a Greek thinker who formulated a startling solution to what he saw as the evils bedevilling human existence. Epicurus' *ethical* theory (i.e. his view of how humans should live their lives) was built upon an elaborate *scientific* theory about the structure of the universe. Lucretius follows Epicurus' theory very closely, and this explains why a poem with the stated aim of teaching its reader a new and better way of living spends most of its time in abstruse scientific arguments. It also explains the title of Lucretius' poem, which owes something to the title of Epicurus' most important philosophical work, 'On Nature', as well as to another 'On Nature' written by the Greek poet-scientist Empedokles. In addition, it accounts for the scale of the poem. The *De rerum natura* is written in the epic metre, dactylic hexameters, and on an epic scale (about 7,400 lines). This vehicle is appropriate to the poet's lofty aspirations: not only to convert his readership to a totally new pattern of life, but also in the process to present an account of nothing less than the entire universe.

Epicurus believed that human life was miserable, needlessly so. What made it

miserable were irrational anxieties, the most serious of which, in his view, were the fear of the gods and the fear of death. These anxieties caused pain to those who experienced them, and a central tenet of Epicurus' philosophy was that happiness was only possible if such pain was removed. Pleasure, the absence of pain, was the ultimate object of Epicureanism. This doctrine has often been misinterpreted. Epicureanism, we should appreciate (though many contemporaries did not), was an extremely rigorous and difficult creed, and the 'pleasure' which Epicurus had in mind was more of the nature of an unruffled psychological serenity than abandonment to sensual excess. In fact the *ataraxia* (Greek), *securitas* (Latin), or 'freedom from anxiety' to which Epicureans aspired often involved avoiding precisely such sensual abandonment. Epicureans were *not* hedonists.

To secure *securitas*, Epicureans believed, the first and most important step was to develop a rational, clear-sighted understanding of the way the physical world worked. In particular, Epicurus adopted a scientific theory developed by the fifth-century BCE Greek thinker Demokritos, Atomism, the theory that everything in the universe is ultimately constructed of tiny, indestructible particles. Epicurus made this theory the basis of his own radically materialistic account of the universe. If absolutely everything consists of atoms moving in a void, and nothing else; and if everything in the universe is created when these atoms, falling through the void, happen to combine, and destroyed when the atoms that compose it disperse and go on to form other things, then some important consequences follow. First, there is no room for the gods, not at any rate in their traditional role as powers which created the world and interfered in it at will. The gods did exist, according to Epicurus, but were utterly irrelevant to human life: they lived far away in a state of Epicurean *securitas*. Terrifying events commonly attributed to the action of the gods, like earthquakes or thunderbolts, had a perfectly rational explanation, and the gods were thus nothing to be afraid of.

The second consequence of the Atomic Theory was that death was nothing more dramatic than a dispersal of atoms, just as birth was simply a combination of them. In fact death was a prerequisite of life: only through death could the atoms become available which were necessary to create something new. Death and life were thus interdependent. As Lucretius beautifully expresses it,

> With the sound of funerals mingles the howl
> that children raise when first they see the shores of light.
> And no night has ever followed day, or dawn night,
> which has not heard, mingled with these feeble howls,
> the wailing that attends death and black funerals.
>
> (2. 576–80)

Human souls are made up of atoms in the same way as anything else, and there is consequently nothing that can survive after death to suffer punishment in the underworld, a major cause, according to Epicureans, of the fear of death. Hence the *ethical* implications of Epicurus' *scientific* theory: a proper understanding of the physics of the universe proves the irrationality of the anxieties which on his view prevent us from attaining to happiness.

Lucretius stuck very closely to Epicurus' theories, but he also invested the doctrine with a strong contemporary relevance for Romans of the first century

BCE: his poem was probably completed in the late 50s BCE. We know next to nothing about his life, but he gives the impression of being himself a member of the Roman upper classes, attempting to convert men who are his equals to the liberating truth of Epicureanism. But a lot stood in his way. The Epicurean credo conflicted point after point with some of the most cherished values of the aristocratic society at which the poem was directed.

All anxiety, according to Epicurus, is inimical to true pleasure. Lucretius gives particular emphasis to two sources of anxiety (besides the fear of death and the gods), love affairs (4. 1037–287) and political ambition. Lucretius actually sees these 'subsidiary' anxieties as direct consequences of the underlying fear of death. Desperate to affirm their existence in the face of annihilation humans hunt out tangible symbols of life :

> Moreover the greed and blind lust for distinctions
> which drive unhappy men to overstep the bounds
> of law and at times make them accomplices and instruments of crime,
> straining night and day with extreme effort
> to rise to the top in power—these wounds of life
> are fed in no small part by the fear of death.
> For shameful ignominy and bitter poverty
> seem far removed from sweet and secure life,
> and like lingering already before the gates of death.
> From there, driven by groundless terror,
> men wish to escape and remove themselves far, far away,
> and amass a fortune in civil bloodshed, double
> their riches in their greed, piling slaughter on slaughter.
> Heartlessly they rejoice at the tragic death of their brother;
> and they hate and fear the hospitality of their own kin.

(3. 59–73)

The Epicurean will withdraw from all the tensions and distractions of public life and nurture a serene philosophical calm in private. But for a traditionally minded Roman aristocrat this was a revolutionary doctrine. The Roman male was trained from the cradle to value, and struggle for, military and political success and the status that went with them. Status meant being *recognized* for one's achievements: success without visibility was worthless. But Epicurus' central ethical tenet was *lathe biôsas*, 'Live unnoticed' or 'Pass unremarked'. How could Lucretius possibly persuade his readership to abandon what was arguably the very essence of their culture?

For these reasons in particular Epicureanism did not exert a natural attraction for Romans. They tended to find Stoicism, a philosophy which encouraged participation in public life, much more agreeable. But as we have seen, the upheavals which Rome experienced in the first century BCE had created a fertile environment for the questioning of traditional values, and Lucretius' poem is explicitly a response to these upheavals. This is clear from the passage I have just quoted, with its reference to civil warfare, and clear, in fact, from the very beginning of his poem, where Lucretius prays to the goddess Venus and begs her to put a stop to the violence in which Rome is involved. In the very first words of the poem Lucretius identifies Venus as 'mother of the race of Aeneas', 'mother of Rome' in other words.

In addition, Lucretius addresses his poem to 'Memmius'. This was Gaius Memmius, a senior politician of the period. Lucretius thus takes pains to adapt the doctrine he is expounding to his Roman readership in the mid-first century BCE—we shall return to the question of whether a Memmius could possibly have felt sympathy for statements like the following on the political career to which he, as a typical Roman aristocrat, had devoted himself. The ambitious Roman politician is compared to Sisyphus, an over-ingenious mortal punished for eternity in the underworld, according to myth, by having to roll a boulder to the top of a hill, only for it to roll back down again :

> Sisyphus also is here in this life before our eyes,
> thirsty to win power from the people,
> and always retiring defeated and depressed.
> For to seek power, a vacuous thing which is never given,
> and always to endure hard toil in pursuit of it—
> this is to push a boulder laboriously up a steep mountain,
> only to see it, once the top is reached,
> roll back down in a rush to the flat levels of the plain.
> (3. 995–1002)

'The plain' here is a loaded term. The *Campus* or 'plain' in Rome was where political elections took place.

The *De rerum natura* is a 'didactic' poem, that is, it teaches a lesson, and the stance that Lucretius adopts is very much that of a teacher, albeit a rather strict, 'Victorian' teacher, dunning knowledge into wayward children. One of the greatest strengths of the poem is Lucretius' mastery of teaching technique. For example, a good teacher will explain the unfamiliar by analogy with the familiar: if the earth is a grain of sand, and the sun a cherry stone three feet away, the nearest other star in 140 miles away, and so on. 'Familiarization' of this kind is one of Lucretius' basic strategies. He has an astonishing gift for evoking the everyday, and using it to clarify the often very difficult scientific theories he is attempting to explain. Since his illustrations have to be familiar to his reader-pupil it is natural that he selects images from contemporary Roman life. At

4. 973–83 he is explaining why we tend to dream about events we have recently witnessed, and he chooses for his illustration the games, which might include exotic theatrical performances, at which his male readers enjoyed relaxation from their busy lives :

> And whenever men have given their unremitting attention
> to the games for many days on end, we usually see that,
> when they have now ceased to perceive them with their senses,
> nevertheless there are paths in the mind left open
> where the same images of things can enter.
> And so for many days those same things hover
> before their eyes, so that even while awake they seem
> to perceive figures dancing and swaying supple limbs,
> and to hear in their ears the fluid tune of the lyre and its speaking strings,
> and to perceive the same crowd and along with it
> the brilliant, multicoloured decorations of the stage.
>
> (4. 973–83)

Elsewhere Lucretius brings vividly before our eyes the ceaseless movement of atoms in the void, the cause (according to his theory) of all phenomena in the world :

> Of this phenomenon there is, now I think of it, an illustration and image
> constantly hovering and present before our eyes.
> Do but pay attention whenever the beams of the sun
> are admitted into a house and pour their light through its dark places:
> you will see many tiny particles mingling in many ways
> throughout the void in the light of the beams,
> and, as if in everlasting conflict, battling, fighting,
> struggling in hosts without a pause,
> agitated in constant meetings and partings.
> From this you may picture what it is for the first elements of things
> to be tossed about perpetually in the great void.
>
> (2. 112–22)

This is a particularly significant sight, Lucretius goes on to say, because the movements of the particles in the sunbeam are actually a *consequence* of the unending movements of the atoms which are hidden from our sight. It is the motion of the atoms which sets off the movements of the visible particles. Here Lucretius renders abstruse science immediately familiar: the poet shows us the atoms, mainspring of the entire universe, in our own front rooms.

As I have suggested, this is good teaching technique. But that doesn't convey what great poetry it also makes. At the same time as Lucretius 'familiarizes' these mysterious elemental processes, he also invests everyday phenomena like motes of dust with all the momentousness and grandeur of the universe: that dust exemplifies the nature of the entire cosmos. This is an important point, since many readers have been put off the *De rerum natura* by what they see as its unpoetic material. And it has to be admitted that Lucretius' poem is an acquired taste. Its often austere scientific content makes it 'difficult', as the later author Quintilian called it (and as the poet himself admits more than once). John Ruskin, the influential Victorian art critic and reformer, asserted that he 'held it the most hopeless sign of a man's mind being made of flint-shingle if he liked Lucretius', but many others have appreciated the power of his vision. Some of these have been atheists and materialists like Karl Marx, who regarded Epicurus as a forerunner of many of his own beliefs, and in the conclusion of his doctoral dissertation, *The Difference between the Democritean and Epicurean philosophy of Nature* (1841), quoted Lucretius' praise of Epicurus as the conqueror of religion at 1. 62–79. But the twentieth-century philosopher George Santayana recognized that the philosophical vision of the totality of things which Lucretius presents to the reader makes for a powerful poetic experience: 'But the vision of philosophy is sublime. The order it reveals in the world is something beautiful, tragic, sympathetic to the mind, and just what every poet, on a small or on a large scale, is always trying to catch.' There is a tremendous intellectual excitement in the idea that dust in the sunlight reflects the fundamental creative principle of the universe.

Redirecting the reader's mind

Lucretius' core strategy of *making familiar* pervades every level of the poem. Epicureanism was a revolutionary doctrine, and it is a truism that the most successful revolutions are those that bear as close a resemblance as possible to the state of affairs that preceded them. In this way they are less unsettling, more acceptable, and more likely to succeed. Lucretius' appreciation of this fact explains many aspects of his poem, but in particular the striking way he introduces it.

A contemporary, non-Epicurean reader of the *De rerum natura* would feel quite at home in the first few lines of the poem. It begins in a very conventional way with a hymn to a god, Venus, requesting her help with the composition of his poem: a standard poetic approach. But this opening has bothered critics greatly, for the simple reason that a central tenet of Epicureanism, and a central argument of the *De rerum natura*, was that gods did not interfere in the world: they did not do things like cause earthquakes, hurl thunderbolts—or inspire poets. The only conclusion seemed to be that Lucretius was being plain inconsistent. But this is to misunderstand the purpose of the poem, by interpreting the *De rerum natura* as a testament of Lucretius' beliefs rather than what it really is: a course of teaching. Like the good teacher that he was Lucretius meets his pupils on their own ground, starts with what is familiar to them, and leads them gently from this starting-point to the (very different) truth. This is precisely how the hymn to Venus works. In the course of the poem the powers attributed to the goddess Venus in the hymn are piece by piece reattributed to the rationalistic Epicurean guiding principle of *natura*, 'the laws of nature'. Gradually, imperceptibly, the non-Epicurean belief in the gods with which we started is replaced by orthodox Epicureanism. As we read the poem, in other words, we are being delicately *converted*.

As will be clear, Lucretius, though a hard taskmaster, tried very hard not to startle his readers. He wants the truth (as he sees it) to seem obvious to us. Consequently, he does not simply reject out of hand the beliefs his readers started with, but redefines them. He even does this with the notions of the gods and the afterlife which he regards as the great bane of human existence. In one passage (partially quoted on p. 59) he dismisses a set of myths concerned with the underworld. There is no such thing as life after death, no Sisyphus suffering eternal punishment in the underworld. Or at any rate there are no such figures *in the underworld*, because the underworld does not exist. There *are* such figures, but they are here, in the real world: they are the poor benighted creatures who have not heard, and acted upon, the wisdom of Epicurus. Their lives are truly a 'Hell on earth' (line 1023). The same applies with the gods. The gods have no involvement in human affairs, and as far as human life is concerned they might as well not exist. But there *are* people here, on earth, who fulfil the role of the traditional gods, Epicurus above all, of whom Lucretius declares, 'he was a god, a god, noble Memmius' (5. 8); but also anyone who internalizes the precepts of Epicureanism and lives a life of unruffled calm: 'He therefore who has vanquished all these anxieties and banished them from his mind, by words not by weapons, will he not surely be worthy of a place among the gods?' (5. 49–51).

Again, this is a subtle revolution. Our cherished beliefs are, as far as possible, adapted rather than abandoned. We shall 'worship' Epicurus, not Venus, 'fear' the fear of death, not death. The conversion is made as easy as it can be, although the revelation of the Epicurean 'truth' of the nature of the universe is none the less compelling for that. Another way of describing Lucretius' overall strategy is as *demystification*. His world-view, like Epicurus', is a thoroughgoing form of materialism. Everything that matters is here, now, and tangible. Repeatedly Lucretius insists that we should never give way to *wonder*. Everything (no matter how bizarre) has a rational explanation: there is nothing mysterious, or disturbing, about death, for example—it is merely a dispersal of atoms, and those figures from myth—like Sisyphus are here, now, visible all around us. As for the gods, *you* can be a god. Just read this poem . . .

But as with the hymn to Venus at the start of the poem, the religious emotions Lucretius criticizes are not so much to be rejected as *redirected*. Lucretius *does* feel wonder, but this is wonder before the marvellous doctrines which will heal his readers' lives; and for a philosopher committed to a strictly rationalistic approach to life he is perhaps strangely passionate. The following passage, from his argument to prove that 'Death is nothing to us' (3. 830), nothing worth concerning ourselves with, is representative. Lucretius demands his reader to think why he should be anxious about death when so many great men have undergone the same experience in the past :

> Epicurus himself died when his life's light had run its course,
> he whose intellect surpassed humanity and made them all
> look dim, as the rising of the heavenly sun does the stars.
> And will *you* hesitate and complain about dying?
> You whose life is almost death while you still live and have sight,
> who waste the greater part of your life in sleep,
> and snore while awake and never stop dreaming,
> and bear a mind harried by empty fears . . .

(3. 1042–52)

The criticism of the non-Epicurean life is aggressive and passionate, but the result of a characteristic empathy on Lucretius' part for his fellow humans. The poet fully recognizes the power for ill of the human fear of death, and consequently reserves some of his most powerful arguments and rhetoric to counter it. There is also a remarkable intimacy and humanity about the relationship Lucretius maintains with his readers, even at his most hectoring. Addressing his arguments in the first instance to Memmius, for example, makes a critical difference to the effect of the poem. Reading is an essentially solitary activity, and Epicureanism a doctrine which is all about withdrawing in on oneself and abandoning wider society. Consequently a poem on Epicureanism could easily become quite a bleak and lonely experience. Memmius is one of the strategies Lucretius employs to create the illusion that we are engaging in a form of social interaction, when in fact we are reading to ourselves. As the poem goes on, in fact, the references to Memmius become fewer and fewer, to be replaced by the intimate *tu*, 'you' (in the singular). Vitruvius, a writer on architecture, aptly described the experience of reading the poem as 'like arguing face to face with Lucretius about the nature of the universe'. So Lucretius is capable of powerful and passionate rhetoric, but it always takes as its starting-point an acute understanding of the state of mind of the readership he is trying to convert, and of how best to mould it.

The psychological sophistication of passages like this makes our only contemporary response to Lucretius' poem all the more disappointing. In a letter to his younger brother in 54 BCE (our best evidence for the date of the poem) Cicero writes that 'Lucretius' poetry is as you say, sparkling with natural talent, but with plenty of technical skill. But we'll discuss it when you come.' It would certainly have disappointed a poet who stated that his poetry was merely an attractive vehicle for a life-changing revelation (cf. 1. 926–50, 4. 1–25) to see his poem assessed in such formal, literary-critical terms. Cicero and his brother enjoyed the poem as a poem, but were they converted? No. When Cicero's Epicurean friend Atticus tried to persuade him to withdraw from the perilous political scene after the assassination of Julius Caesar in 44 BCE he received a blunt response: 'You mention Epicurus and *dare* to say "keep out of politics"?' For most Roman aristocrats politics was in the blood.

It is the same story with Memmius, the addressee of the poem, but in his case dramatically so. In two letters Cicero refers to a dispute in the city of Athens in 51 BCE between a leading Epicurean named Patron, and Memmius. Memmius had had an unfortunate few years. A candidate for the consulship in 54 BCE, he had lost the election, been convicted of electoral bribery, and gone into exile. The dispute centred around the ruins of Epicurus' house. Memmius seems to have intended to build on the site, a plan to which Patron (naturally) objected. The situation suggests in Memmius a man far from sympathetic to Epicureanism, in fact violently antagonistic towards it. Certainly his no-holds-barred pursuit of the consulship was, in Lucretius' terms, the behaviour of a classic Sisyphus. Even after decades of violent political upheaval there were few Roman aristocrats ready to retire from the fray.

Lucretius' poem attempts to persuade and control his reader to an unusually intense degree. As we have seen, it even maps, in its course, the psychological development of its ideal reader. But for all his pedagogical genius there was no guarantee he would have any more success than teachers generally do. Ovid, a generation later, warmly praises the *De rerum natura*: 'The poems of lofty Lucretius will perish only when one day gives over the world to ruin.' The *De rerum natura* had become a literary classic. But for Lucretius the work of art was just a means to an end, to be left behind when that end—enlightenment—was attained. Lucretius insistently tells us to *visualize* the universe he describes, to understand his philosophy in our own minds, internalize it, and leave the text behind. The *De rerum natura* will have served its purpose when we have learnt to live the good life. But the prevailing literary climate tended to value art for its own sake, not for its message. Then again, Lucretius, who died in the late 50s, would not (on his own principles) have been in a position to worry :

> When we no longer exist, when the parting has happened
> of body and soul, from which we are made a single being,
> then (have no doubt about it) nothing at all will be able to happen to us,
> who will then no longer exist, or to stir our feelings,
> not if earth be mingled with sea and sea with sky.

(3. 838–42)

We do not find in Lucretius the kind of aspiration to poetic immortality so common in other poets. The dead Lucretius is blissfully unconcerned about his audience.

The erudition of the 'new poets'

Lucretius and Gaius Valerius Catullus were contemporaries. Catullus' dates (perhaps 84–54 BCE) are no less uncertain, but his poetic output seems to date, like Lucretius's, from the 50s BCE. Nevertheless, at least at first sight, they could hardly seem more dissimilar. Where Lucretius warns against the dangers of involvement in day-to-day life, Catullus engages passionately with the urban culture of contemporary Rome. And whereas Lucretius reserved his special disapproval for men who abandoned themselves to the pursuit of love, Catullus is above all a love poet: a large proportion of his poems concern an ill-starred love-affair with a married woman he calls 'Lesbia'. But these sharp dissimilarities between the two poets are themselves symptomatic of the splintering of Roman culture at this juncture. Despite their differences, the poets have at least one thing in common: each offers an aggressive critique of traditional Roman values; and each offers alternative, and (as they see it) more satisfactory, ways of life.

Lucretius' revolution was as much literary as cultural. He took the format of the hexameter epic, conventionally the vehicle for panegyric of Rome, or of successful Roman generals, and used it instead to promote a man (Greek, at that), and a way of life, which constituted an outright rejection of Roman military and public values. Catullus' poetry also constitutes a literary rebellion which entails simultaneously a rebellion against the whole traditional Roman way of life. Catullus prides himself on being part of a literary movement which rejects Roman models of poetry in favour of Greek, and one Greek poet in particular, Kallimachos. Poem 66, Catullus' version of a poem in honour of an Egyptian queen from Kallimachos' most influential work, the *Causes*, emphatically advertises the Roman poet's literary affiliations. These poets claimed to be breaking with the past, to be modernizers: Cicero calls them 'new poets', probably reflecting the way they talked about themselves.

There was in fact nothing especially new about a lot of what the New Poets were doing: Roman poets had been imitating Kallimachos for quite some time. But as the manufacturers of washing powder, and political spindoctors, know so well, claiming one's formula to be new, whether it is or not, is always an effective marketing device. The literary ideals which *these* New Poets found and admired in Kallimachos were careful craftsmanship, intellectualism (the ethos of the 'scholar poet'), and above all *brevity*: Catullus, like Lucretius, rejects the option of writing the traditional, long epic in praise of Roman national achievement. He dismisses an example of that kind of poetry, the *Annals* of Volusius, as 'paper crap' (poem 36). Poem 64 is written in the epic metre, dactylic hexameters, but deliberately avoids both the kind of material and the predictable narrative style a reader would normally expect in that metre. The exotic and erotic material of poem 64—Peleus' marriage to Thetis and the abandonment of Ariadne by Theseus—could not be further removed from the nationalistic themes of poems like Volusius' *Annals*. A major model for this poem was Kallimachos' *Hekale*, another hexameter poem which sets out to defeat the expectations which readers had of that metre. Crucially, too, poem 64 is highly polished, learned, and (comparatively) *short*: only 400 lines long.

C. Helvius Cinna was a friend of Catullus and a fellow New Poet. What ancient poetry did or did not survive through the Middle Ages to the Renaissance was always largely a matter of chance; though it does seem true that contemporaries of the two late-Republican poets who did survive, Catullus and Lucretius, regarded them as the best of their time. Nevertheless, Catullus only just made it, rediscovered on a single, very corrupt manuscript in the fourteenth century. The other New Poets (including the poet-orator Gaius Licinius Calvus) were not so lucky, and very little survives of their work, but we do have an epigram which Cinna wrote about a copy he had brought to Rome of Aratos' *Phainomena*, a poem which enjoyed great popularity in first-century BCE Rome:

> This poem, which informs us of the fires of the sky,
> the product of long vigil by the lamps of Aratos,
> written on the dry bark of the smooth mallow plant,
> I have brought to you as a gift, in a little Prusiac ship.

This poem was evidently typical of Cinna's style of poetry. It was deliberately recondite, or, put another way, 'allusive': whereas Lucretius aimed at clarity—he dismisses Herakleitos as 'renowned for his opaque sayings | among the more empty-headed of the Greeks' (1. 639–40)—with a view to persuading the reader of his argument, Cinna offered hints to his audience which only the very well-informed reader was in a position to follow up. As compared with Lucretius, then, the reader is given much more work to do. In this little poem, for example, Cinna expects his readers firstly to understand that he is talking about Aratos' *Phainomena*, then to pick up an allusion to a poem by Kallimachos in praise of Aratos (which has the effect of associating Cinna with Callimachean literary ideals), recognize that the ship comes from Bithynia, a country which had once had a king called Prusias, and also recognize a pun in the word which I have translated 'on the . . . bark': it can also mean 'in a little book'—the odd material that the book is written on, not paper but bark, is designed to match the recondite nature of the poetry written on it. The enjoyment of the wit and brilliance—the *exquisiteness*—of the poetry is what Cinna is trying to encourage in his readership, and also the intellectual pleasure the readers derive from their involvement in the interpretation of the poem: reading Cinna is a bit like doing a cryptic crossword. Only a generation later readers needed a commentary to interpret Cinna's most important poem, *Zmyrna*. The author of the commentary, Crassicius Pansa, was praised in a humorous poem:

> The lady Zmyrna has agreed to give herself to one man—Crassicius:
> leave off trying to win her in marriage, you ignorant men.
> She has said that she is only willing to marry Crassicius,
> since only he knows her intimate secrets.

In Cinna's poem Zmyrna was a young woman who had an incestuous relationship with her father Cinyras. This poem amusingly suggests that Crassicius, her interpreter, has replaced Cinyras in her affections. It is an interesting insight into the intellectual complexity of this poetry that readers soon needed commentaries, but also an indication of the type of reader it was written for—and created—that Crassicius' commentary on Cinna's brilliant poem elicited a witty and allusive poem in response. The New Poets made poets of their readers.

Perhaps the major difference from Lucretius here is that the artistry of the poet, rather than information he is conveying, is the primary focus of interest. This was the case with Aratos too. Like the *De rerum natura*, the *Phainomena* was also, theoretically, a 'didactic' poem, an explanation of celestial phenomena. But it did not *really* aim to teach anybody anything. The greater part of the *Phainomena* was a versification of a scientific treatise by the astronomer

Eudoxos, and if you wanted to learn something about astronomy *that* was the only sensible place to look, not in Aratos' poem. What readers like Cinna enjoyed in Aratos was the skilful and witty way he converted prosaic or scientific material like astronomy or the croaking of frogs when it is about to rain (lines 947–8) into poetry, rather than the intrinsic interest of the material itself. Again, this was a very *formal* achievement, art for art's sake, and this, we recall, was pretty much how Cicero responded to Lucretius' poem. Cicero liked Aratos too (he had translated the poem in his youth), so it is perhaps understandable that he responded to Lucretius' didactic poem as if it was a didactic poem like Aratos'.

Catullus also wrote a poem to welcome the arrival of Cinna's *Zmyrna* :

> The *Zmyrna* of my Cinna, at length nine harvests
> and nine winters after it was begun, is published!
> Hortensius, meanwhile, every single year
> has spawned fifty thousand verses.
> *Zmyrna* will travel far, to the deep-channelled waves of the Satrachus;
> long will the white-haired centuries read *Zmyrna*.
> But the *Annals* of Volusius will die before they cross the Padua
> and often make loose-fitting jackets for mackerel.
> Dear to my heart is the small-scale monument of my comrade . . .
> But let the mob enjoy long-winded Antimachus.

(Poem 95)

The same 'allusive' approach to poetry is evident as we saw in Cinna's epigram about Aratos. Future generations are 'white-haired centuries'; the Satrachus is a river in Cyprus associated with Adonis (son of Zmyrna and Cinyras) which Cinna will have mentioned in his poem; Antimachus was the author of a poem criticized by Kallimachos for its excessive length. Cinna's poem—and by implication Catullus' poem—thus encapsulates the ideals of the New Poets: poems must be short, highly polished (Cinna spent no less than nine years over his), un-Roman (Volusius' *Annals* were probably a Roman epic in the tradition of Ennius), and erudite. We must never forget that even the most passionate, and apparently spontaneous, of Catullus' poems were composed with the same degree of effort and artistry.

A cultivated 'madness'

Catullus and the New Poets claimed that their poetry was for a small and sophisticated audience of friends: everybody else ('the mob') will have to be satisfied with 'long-winded Antimachus'. There will have been some truth in this, but it isn't the whole story. On the one hand, the knowledge required to appreciate this style of poetry was such that only a relatively few readers would be up to it: Kallimachos' poetic ideals had been developed in the context of the highly educated audience of the court of the Ptolemaic kings of Egypt. But in Catullus' mouth this is also a stance. By claiming that his poetry is only suitable for a select few he is implying how *special* his poetry is, and at the same time forging a bond with his readers: read Catullus and you too become one of his special friends. This is Catullus' way of doing what every writer must—gaining the loyalty and interest (and readiness to read on . . .) of his audience.

Although the Roman reading audience was never very large, Catullus' audience was certainly larger than he suggests. For example, Catullus waged an extended campaign of abuse against Julius Caesar, partly through direct attacks on the general and partly through attacks on Caesar's lieutenant Mamurra, to whom Catullus often refers simply as 'Prick'. According to the biographer Suetonius, Caesar believed that this series of attacks did lasting damage to his reputation. This would hardly have been the case if Catullus' poetry was only being read by his friends. Nevertheless, whether Catullus is addressing one of his close friends or some of the most powerful figures in the state, his poetry always maintains an air of intimacy and informality. Affectionate or abusive, the poems sound like first-hand exchanges between close associates, exchanges to which the reader is given privileged access. This makes a twentieth-century reader's experience of Catullus particularly exciting: we often feel as if we have been admitted into the charmed circle of the Roman aristocracy. Of course, a lot of work has gone into producing this impression of spontaneity and immediacy.

But what response did he expect to receive from this audience to his poetry? A difficult question. The reaction to the poetry in the young Roman 'smart set' of which Catullus was a part is liable to have been very different from that of the wider ruling class. Catullus' poetry offers an oblique insight into this area of contemporary Roman life: oblique, because even at his most passionate Catullus is first and foremost a consummate artist, who does not so much pour his soul into his poetry as re-create his experiences in art. Poem 41, an attack on Mamurra's girlfriend, is a case in point, blunt and obscene, but skilfully crafted, with a succinct but vivid portrait of the girl and a perfectly timed punchline:

> Ameana, a well-fucked girl,
> has asked me for a cool ten thousand sesterces,
> that girl with the rather ugly nose,
> girlfriend of the bankrupt from Formiae.

> You relatives who are responsible for the girl,
> summon friends and doctors.
> The girl's unwell, and is not in the habit of asking
> the image-filled bronze what she looks like.

Even obliquely, though, Catullus' poetry presents a fascinating picture of his social world, profoundly influenced by Greek culture, and also strikingly feminine. In contrast to Lucretius' almost exclusively male world, Catullus' poetry is populated by comparatively powerful and assertive women like Lesbia and Ameana. Ameana is defamed, but she is not ignored, which was the more traditional fate of Roman women. One of the unconventional aspects of Cinna's *Zmyrna* and Catullus' poem 64 was the prominence they gave to female characters, a departure from the generally military and male preoccupations of traditional epic. It is risky to infer from this that women also formed a significant part of Catullus' readership, but poem 35 humorously describes the effect on a girl of reading a similar short epic by another New Poet, Caecilius.

Furthermore, Catullus had a particular attachment to the work of the female poet Sappho, an important model for the passion, eroticism, and intensely personal quality of his shorter poems. Poem 51 is a version of one of Sappho's poems, an example (incidentally) of Catullus' great metrical proficiency: Catullus makes Sappho's rhythmical scheme a natural vehicle for the Latin language, a harder task than he makes it look. But there is a further implication to the rhythm. This poem describes the beginning of Catullus' affair with 'Lesbia', and poem 11 the devastating end of it, and both are in Sappho's characterisic metre. The affair thus began,

> That man is seen by me as a God's equal
> Or (if it may be said) the Gods' superior,
> Who sitting opposite again and again
> Watches and hears *you*
> Sweetly laughing—which dispossesses poor me
> Of all my senses, for no sooner, Lesbia,
> Do I look at you than there's no power left me . . .
>> (51. 1–7, trans. Guy Lee)

and ended ,

> Simply deliver to my girl a brief dis-
> courteous message:
> Farewell and long life with her adulterers,
> Three hundred together, whom hugging she holds,
> Loving none truly but again and again
> Rupturing all's groins;

> And let her not as before expect my love,
> Which by her fault has fallen like a flower
> On the meadow's margin after a passing
> Ploughshare has touched it.
>
> (11. 15–24, trans. Guy Lee)

The metre is appropriate, because the pseudonym Catullus chose for his girl-friend, 'Lesbia', 'woman of Lesbos', equates her with Sappho. The girl of poem 35, also, is complimented as 'more learned than the Muse of Sappho'. The Catullan ideal was apparently a woman as educated, sophisticated, and self-sufficient as himself; and for the time this was a very unorthodox attitude indeed.

In wider society, though, the typical response to Catullus must have been shock. In poems like the fragmentary 14b ('If by any chance there are any of you who will read my idiocies and not shudder to lay your hands on us . . .') Catullus seems to anticipate (with relish) this kind of reaction. For a reader possessed of more traditional moral values much of what Catullus wrote would have been highly provocative. The provocation consisted in the extremely unconventional lifestyle he documented in his poems. Catullus invested his aristocratic energy not in the pursuit of the conventional Roman targets of wealth and status, but in the pursuit of boys and women. In a famous poem addressed to Lesbia (poem 5) Catullus extols the life of love and rejects out of hand traditional modes of behaviour:

> Let us live, my Lesbia, and love,
> and as for the mutterings of over-critical old men
> let us value them at a single farthing!

'Old-fashioned' moral values are thus dismissed as emphatically as 'old-fashioned' literary values. From a conventional Roman point of view the kind of obsessive love-affairs Catullus involved himself in were, as Cicero puts it, 'no different, or not far different, from madness'.

The same can be said of Catullus' more overtly political poetry. Poem 93 is a devastatingly simple, two-line attack on Julius Caesar which dramatically asserts Catullus' distance from Roman convention:

> I am not overly keen, Caesar, to wish to be liked by you,
> nor to know whether you are a white or a black man.

Quintilian uses the same word of Catullus' feigned ignorance of Caesar—'madness': *everyone* had heard of Caesar, and it was precisely in pursuit of this recognition and status that Caesar (in this respect a typical Roman aristocrat) had embarked on his remarkable career. Roman aristocrats lived to achieve, and to be seen to have achieved by their peers. This is what makes Catullus' apparently innocuous statement so striking. For Catullus to tell Caesar, conqueror of Gaul, that he couldn't care two hoots about him strikes at the very essence of Roman aristocratic self-motivation.

Similar in implication are a couple of poems (10 and 28) where Catullus, with a characteristic frankness, abuses Gaius Memmius, the addressee of Lucretius' poem. In 57–56 BCE Catullus and Cinna served on Memmius' staff when he was governor of Bithynia (this may also have been the date of Cinna's poem about Aratos). In poem 28, addressed to two friends also on service abroad, Catullus brutally attacks the traditional system of public service abroad:

> O Memmius, well and truly did you get me on my back,
> and mouthfuck me at your leisure with the full length of your beam.
> You, my friends, as far as I can see, have fared the same—
> stuffed by no less a prick.
> Find influential friends, they say!
> May heaven send you [i.e. the two governors] plagues aplenty,
> you slurs on the name of Romulus and Remus.

Memmius, that representative of traditional Roman values, is under assault from all sides, the Epicurean on the one and the thoroughly disenchanted *enfant terrible* on the other. By calling the governors 'slurs on the name of Romulus and Remus', the founders of Rome, Catullus is actually suggesting that he and his friends have more right to be called Romans than traditional aristocrats like Memmius: Catullus is radically redefining aristocratic norms of behaviour. The extent to which Catullus' readers sympathized with this radical stance is as hard to assess as it is with Lucretius. Who did read this poetry? Just the radical youth of Rome, or the Ciceros too? If the latter—and poem 49 is addressed to Cicero—we may suspect that most found it as hard to accept as Epicureanism.

But for an audience with a taste for style over content like that of contemporary Rome, there was much to be enjoyed in the sheer creative virtuosity of Catullus. There is an astonishing variety to his poetry, which ranges from short personal poems to the mythological content of poem 64, and right across the spectrum of metres and genres. One poem in particular, 68, stands out even in Catullus' eclectic collection, a remarkable blend of the autobiographical—Catullus refers to his affair with Lesbia and the death of his brother at Troy—and the myth of Laodamia and her husband Protesilaus, who was the first Greek to be killed at the siege of Troy. Not all critics regard poem 68 as an unquestioned success, but there is no doubting the boldness of the piece; and the same can be said for poem 63, the exotic story of a devotee of the eastern goddess Kybele who castrates himself (and then regrets it), which is composed in an correspondingly outlandish metre, the fast and frenzied galliambic. This latter poem, in particular, seems to have a purely literary rationale, as if Catullus encountered the galliambic metre (probably in a poem by Kallimachos), recognized its potential, and only then found a theme adequate to it, rather than the other way around. It is a *tour de force* of literary and metrical technique, without any obvious further justification.

We have already seen that the readers of the New Poetry were themselves potentially poets, equipped with the capacity to interpret this allusive verse. Whereas Lucretius' poem sought to control his audience like a firm teacher, this type of poetry gives its readers much more autonomy: *we* are left to do much of the work of interpretation. But this can cause interesting problems of interpretation, both in the New Poets and in the generation of poets which followed, who were greatly influenced by them. This style of poetry is a very delicate mechanism. In the context of its immediate reception—the readership of the 50s BCE—it made for a complex, stimulating literary experience, ultimately quite as controlling and manipulative of the audience as Lucretius, but in a very different way: the readers of Catullus were drawn into the game the poet had set for them, and motivated by the intellectual pleasure of that game to pursue the poet's design. But once the original context of a poem has gone, the allusiveness of the poetry—the insistence that subtle, inexplicit allusions be followed up if a poem is to be understood—is liable to have the effect of suggesting readings which the author did not intend, and leaving us little grounds to judge one reading against another. Put another way, we today are often in the position of not knowing how far we should read inexplicit meaning into poems.

In the Renaissance it became a question of almost international significance whether the 'sparrow' referred to in poems 2 and 3, 'my girl's pet, with which she likes to play and which she likes to hold in her lap' (2. 1–2) was in fact an allegory for Catullus' penis. Politian, a scholar from Florence, forcibly promoted this interpretation of the poems; only to be violently contradicted by scholars from Verona, Catullus' home town, enraged at the aspersion on their national poet. The debate continues, but is, arguably, incapable of resolution: the Callimachean style of poetry leaves much of the creation of poetic meaning to its audience. In the next generation we find poets equally influenced by Kallimachos, but now under an obligation to write politically directed poetry, poetry where it becomes very important what a poem does or does not mean. The problem of containing and controlling the various interpretations to which the poetry is open will become acute.

Poem 49 poses similar problems of interpretation. Superficially it is a gushing poem of thanks to Cicero for some unspecified service. It could be translated

> Most eloquent of all the descendants of Romulus
> that are and have been, Marcus Tullius,
> and ever will be in other years,
> Catullus, the worst poet of all,
> gives you his greatest thanks,
> as much the worst poet of all
> as you are the best advocate of all.

But the entire poem *could* in fact be bitterly ironic. The Latin I have translated as 'the best advocate of all' may be translated quite differently. Catullus may be calling Cicero 'the best advocate-of-all', i.e. a man without principles prepared to defend absolutely anybody.

If the latter interpretation is more compelling, that is because it seems more in tune with the lack of respect for conventional notions of public achievement and success which Catullus generally evinces. The Lucretius that Cicero and his brother read and enjoyed (but were not in any way persuaded by), and the Catullus who either eulogized or traduced the orator (probably the latter), seem *prima facie* to share little more than the period and the language in which they both happened to be writing. But the time of writing is a significant common factor. Each of these poets, whether in the fleshpots frequented by Rome's gilded youth or in the limitless tracts of the Epicurean universe, offers a vision of escape from the catastrophe which the orthodox values men such as Cicero embodied had visited upon Rome.

4 | Creativity out of chaos: Poetry between the death of Caesar and the death of Virgil

LLEWELYN MORGAN

Early Virgil: Pastoral and patronage

The last survivor of the New Poets, Cinna, died in the violent aftermath of Julius Caesar's funeral. His cries of 'I am Cinna the poet, I am Cinna the poet' (according to Shakespeare's version) were of no avail, and his death is emblematic. Julius Caesar's assassination in 44 ushered in the most murderous period of the Roman civil wars, and neither poets nor poetry were exempt. But despite the general chaos—or more accurately in direct response to it, and in an attempt to make sense of it—this period also witnessed a creative efflorescence in Roman literature such as had never been seen before. Some of the greatest poets in the Latin language began their careers in this, the darkest period of Roman history. In particular, the years immediately after the death of Caesar formed the context for the first major work by Publius Vergilius Maro (70–19 BCE: styled 'Virgil' by Christian commentators by association with the word 'virgin'), the greatest of all Roman poets. This was a collection of ten poems known as the *Eclogues* or *Bucolics*: *Bucolics* (originally *Bucolica*), meaning 'Herdsmen's songs', was apparently the original name, whilst *Eclogues* (*Eclogae*), meaning 'short poems' and referring to the ten independent poems which make up the collection, has become the name standardly used of the collection today. These poems gave powerful, albeit oblique, expression to a yearning for release from the ghastly circumstances under which its author and readers were labouring. They have justifiably won a reputation as one of the most mysterious and beautiful collections of poetry ever composed. And in more than one respect they exemplify the characteristics of Roman poetry after Caesar.

The *Eclogues* are an example of one of the strangest genres of literature, a genre which has become known as Pastoral (or Bucolic) Poetry. Pastoral depicts a utopian world of simple, carefree herdsmen relaxing in an idealized rural landscape (the so-called *locus amoenus*) and whiling away their time singing songs to the accompaniment of a rustic pipe. Virgil's main model for this style of poetry was Theokritos, a Sicilian poet who shared Kallimachos' literary ideals of brevity, polish, and allusiveness, and who (in a typically Hellenistic way) enjoyed the paradox of applying his sophisticated poetic style to 'low-life' material, including the interactions of herdsmen. This is poetry of the countryside, then, and although the countryside of the *Eclogues*—as we would expect from a writer influenced by the Hellenistic poets—is a very artificial, literary construction, Virgil is careful to relate this pastoral world to the contemporary realities of the real Italian countryside.

There, the situation was very grim indeed. In the aftermath of Caesar's assassination the Roman Empire found itself divided between two competing factions. On one side stood Marcus Antonius ('Mark Antony') and C. Iulius Caesar Octavianus ('Octavian', later to become 'Augustus' cf. p. 438), the political heirs of Caesar. On the other were the assassins of Caesar, led by M. Iunius Brutus and C. Cassius Longinus (Brutus and Cassius). In 42 BCE Antony and Octavian crushed Brutus and Cassius at the Battle of Philippi in northern Greece, a massacre in which perhaps as many as 50,000 men fell. Antony and Octavian were victorious, and secure (until they starting fighting between themselves). But they found themselves with vast numbers of soldiers awaiting demobilization who had nowhere to go. Their solution was of a callousness typical of the times. Land across Italy was abruptly confiscated from its rightful owners and given to the ex-soldiers. The effect on rural life in Italy was predictably shattering, and finds recurrent echoes in the *Eclogues*.

The allusive, 'Hellenistic' tone of the collection is established from its very first lines. At 1. 1–2 Virgil sketches a *locus amoenus* in which the pastoral musician Tityrus blissfully reclines:

> You, Tityrus, reclining beneath the spreading beech tree's cover
> practise the woodland Muse on a slender reed.

A simple rustic scene, apparently: but the simplicity is only superficial. To concentrate on just one element of the scene: the word for beech-tree here, *fagus*, recurs frequently in the collection, and in fact comes to epitomize the idyllic landscape Virgil constructs in the poems: the *fagus* provides the shade under which his rustics sing and pipe. The precise variety of tree is carefully chosen, and fraught with significance. The *fagus* is a native Italian beech-tree, but will have reminded Virgil's more alert readers of a tree which featured in the pastoral *Idylls* of Theokritos, the *phagos*. By using an Italian tree which looks (on paper) so much like one of Theokritos' trees Virgil is advertising—with great subtlety—the kind of poetry of which the following collection will consist: pastoral in a tradition inaugurated by Theokritos. But there is a further implication. Theokritos' *phagos* is in fact a completely different tree from Virgil's beech-tree. It is a species of oak, and Virgil's replacement of the Greek *phagos* with the pointedly Italian *fagus* symbolizes that, whilst he is indebted to Theokritos, he is also in another respect being highly original, remaking the Greek genre of pastoral in the Latin language.

So it goes without saying that reading the *Eclogues* is very different from experiencing the real countryside. And yet, for all their artificiality, the *Eclogues* nevertheless managed to be powerfully relevant to the ugly realities of contemporary Italy. Pastoral is an intensely nostalgic genre. It speaks to the fantasy of a carefree existence in the country shared by every city-dweller, and it was this escapist quality that Virgil exploited to give a contemporary relevance to his poems. The poet represents himself in the collection as a pastoral singer like Tityrus, and invests the poems with a musicality in style and sound which corroborates the impression that they are themselves pastoral song, the products of the pastoral idyll. We can imagine what impact this beautiful poetry, redolent of the peaceful, carefree existence of Theokritos' herdsmen, will have had on an audience mired in the most brutal spell of the civil wars. Its evocation of this seductive rural paradise must have been, in the circumstances, impossibly nostalgic.

The perfection of the pastoral life contrasted implicitly with the far from idyllic conditions of contemporary Italy, ruined by war and dispossession. But repeatedly and explicitly Virgil allows the unhappy contemporary realities of the Italian countryside to intrude, jarringly, into the pastoral idyll, sharpening the sense of its desirability (and impossibility). For example, the first *Eclogue* is a dialogue between Tityrus, a conventional pastoral character enjoying the bucolic life reclining at ease beneath his beech-tree, and Meliboeus, a victim of the real-life land confiscations which followed the Battle of Philippi. The poem begins with Meliboeus:

> You, Tityrus, reclining beneath the spreading beech tree's cover,
> practise the woodland Muse on a slender reed.
> I am leaving the bounds of my fatherland and its sweet fields.
> I am fleeing my fatherland. You, Tityrus, easy in the shade,
> teach the woods to echo 'Amaryllis is beautiful'.

The pastoral experience offers the possibility of release from the grim reality of contemporary life, the utopian hope of transcending the troubles of the everyday world, and the desperate need for salvation from the prevailing troubles is a recurrent theme of this collection. Tityrus describes a visit to Rome and an audience with a divine young man, who will most likely have suggested Octavian to Virgil's contemporary readers (but Virgil's failure to name him explicitly is a sign of the insecurities of the times), who exempts his land from confiscation and thus allows him to continue his happy pastoral existence.

Eclogue 4 also offers the hope of salvation. Drawing on a complex web of mystical imagery, Virgil welcomes the birth of a divine child who will inaugurate a golden age of innocence and peace:

> The final age of the Cumaean song has now come:
> the great order of the ages is born anew.
> Now also returns the Virgin, now returns the kingdom of Saturn,
> now a new people is let down from the lofty sky.
> Bless the newborn boy who will first put an end
> to the iron race and give rise to the golden, throughout the world,
> chaste Lucina: your brother Apollo is now king.
> In your consulship, yours, this glorious age will begin,
> Pollio, and the great months start to move;
> under your leadership, whatever traces of crime remain,
> nullified, will free the earth of its endless fear.
> He will receive the life of the gods, and will see
> heroes mingled with gods, and will himself be seen by them,
> and will rule a world pacified by his father's virtues.

(ll. 4–17)

Yet despite these intimations of redemption the dominant impression of the collection is of a yearning, inevitably unfulfilled, for an impossible dream. In *Eclogue* 9 two herdsmen attempt (unsuccessfully) to remember pastoral songs, once again in the context of the land confiscations. The *locus amoenus* which formed the backdrop for the monologue by the rustic Corydon in *Eclogue* 2, 'the shady tops of the dense beech-trees' (2. 4), has decayed into 'the now shattered tops of old beech-trees' (9. 9): trees which can provide no shade. One of the herdsmen pessimistically asserts that 'our songs have as much power, Lycidas, amid the weapons of war as they say Chaonian doves have before the onset of the eagle'. Pastoral song is powerless in the prevailing conditions, and song is the main component of the pastoral idyll. *Eclogue* 9 exposes the dream of escape into this dreamlike utopia as no more than a pious hope.

In broader terms, though, the 'young man' of *Eclogue* 1 is a significant departure. A characteristic element of Roman literary culture which starts to gain particular significance with this collection is *patronage*. In this respect the poetry which followed the death of Julius Caesar differs significantly from the poetry of the previous generation. Lucretius and Catullus had addressed poetry to specific, named individuals, and these figures—Memmius, Lesbia, Caesar, and so on—constitute, ostensibly at least, the primary audience of the poetry, the people to whom a poem was especially pertinent, although we may often suspect that the poet had a much larger audience in mind when he was writing. Crucially, though, both Lucretius and Catullus write as the social equals of their addressees: deference is a very rare commodity in either author.

With the following generation the situation is rather different, and much closer to the state of affairs earlier in the Republic (cf. pp. 23–4). A strong note of deference has made an entrance. The named individuals in this poetry are often *patrons* rather than simple addressees, the distinction being that these are men who are in a position to help a poet in return for the honour he pays them by making them, for all to see, the privileged readers of his poetry. The patronage system was an old Roman institution, which applied as much outside the artistic world as in it: a system of duties and obligations between the powerful and less powerful in society which provided protection for the weaker, and respect and status for the stronger. Nevertheless it is hard not to see its return to prominence in the literature of this period as a sign of the limitations being placed on freedom of speech, and the concomitant dangers attendant upon literary creativity. We cannot imagine Catullus saying, 'From you is my beginning, with you shall I end: receive poems undertaken at your bidding', as Virgil does at *Eclogue* 8. 10–11, *apparently* to C. Asinius Pollio. Only 'apparently', because the object of Virgil's praise at the start of *Eclogue* 8 is left intriguingly anonymous. Pollio was an important facilitator of literature at this time, and made a number of contributions to the literary scene, both in the form of his own writings and more generally (as we shall see), but his role as a patron of poetry was apparently short-lived, and for significant reasons. Although he seems originally to have fulfilled the role of Virgil's patron during his composition of the *Eclogues*, he seems by the time the collection reached its final form to have lost out somewhat to Octavian and his circle: the 'young man' of *Eclogue* 1, respectfully placed at the very centre of the poem, effectively dedicates the collection to Octavian, albeit obliquely. And the same, subtle movement away from Pollio may perhaps explain Virgil's failure to name him in *Eclogue* 8.

Literary patronage could take very blatant forms. The *Thyestes* of Varius Rufus, a play performed in 29 BCE at games celebrating Octavian's victory at Actium, was awarded one million sesterces (enough to make him instantly super-rich) by him. In general, though, patronage was more discreet. Precisely what benefits Virgil gained from Maecenas for the honour the poet paid him in the *Georgics* (see below), for example, is less clear. It is often easier to see how the system benefited the patron. Being a patron of poets could bring a Roman aristocrat some of the status that was so important in Roman culture. As Virgil says to Alfenus Varus, a man who apparently had designs to be seen as Virgil's patron, whoever reads *Eclogue* 6 will associate it with his name (6. 9–12). And a poem did not need actually to be *about* Varus, or in praise of him, to bring this kind of credit to the patron. It is important to appreciate, however, that patronage was a free association on both sides. The patron did not tell the poet what to write: what held the relation together was a sense of mutual obligation rather than any influence being brought to bear by the patron.

Patronage could confer prestige on aristocrats who in the new political circumstances had a shrinking number of contexts in which they could assert themselves. The free politics which had been the main source of aristocratic status in the past was now limited, and power centralized in the hands of Octavian and Antony. In time their power came to be felt in the literary arena as well. Aristocratic patrons like M. Valerius Messalla Corvinus (the patron of Tibullus) or Asinius Pollio were gradually overshadowed by these superpowers dominating the state. The most important literary impresario of the generation after Caesar was not Pollio or Messalla but C. Maecenas, one of Augustus' right-hand men. In fact, of the four poets we shall discuss in this section—Virgil, Horace, Propertius, and Tibullus—all but Tibullus had Maecenas as their patron at some stage or other. A 'drift towards the centre' is discernible in a number of these collections. Virgil, Horace, and Propertius all apparently only started to enjoy Maecenas' patronage when their literary careers were well under way. Power at Rome was gradually becoming concentrated in a single pair of hands, and the effects of this process were felt in literature as well as in the wider world.

Pollio, Virgil's one-time patron, is credited with other important contributions to Roman literary life at this time. Besides establishing the first public library at Rome, he was also the first to organize, on a formal basis, the recitation by an author of his work to an invited audience. In the first instance this was Pollio's own work, but the practice was picked up by others and became a central institution of Roman aristocratic life in the imperial period. It is likely that every author we shall meet here performed at some point in such select gatherings. These 'live' performances could be memorable. The poet Julius Montanus used to say that he would happily steal material from Virgil if only he could steal his voice and face and delivery as well, so compelling were Virgil's recitations: 'the same verses sounded beautiful when he recited them, but banal and inexpressive without him.' Recitation was also, as compared with private reading, an interestingly unstable medium of communication. An audience, unlike a reader, can get rowdy. We are told that once when Virgil was reciting his *Georgics*, and reached 1. 299, 'Strip to plough and strip to sow; winter is a farmer's free time' (a poetic way of saying 'only farm in warm weather'), a listener interposed after 'Strip to plough and strip to sow' the rhythmically perfect supplement, 'and you'll have a 'flu in winter'.

Anecdotes like this are interesting, and incidentally alert us to the high sophistication of the literary public to whom our poets addressed themselves. But we should not overestimate the role of the recitation at this juncture. It is true that the poetry of this period was written to be read aloud by the private reader, and true that occasionally the poet himself would do the reading, in (relatively) public contexts or more privately, to friends. It is also the case that certain texts, the *Eclogues* in particular, found an avid audience in the theatre. But the Rome upper classes who were the core audience of this poetry—it is impossible to put a number to the immediate readership of texts like the *Eclogues*, but it is unlikely to have exceeded a couple of thousand (when the population of Rome was one million)—still had an essentially bookish culture rather than a performative culture. We are told that Virgil was an unenthusiastic reciter who as a rule presented his work in public only when he wanted a second opinion about passages with which he was unhappy, and in this he may well have been typical. It will be clear again and again that the poetry we are going to encounter catered first and foremost to readers, not an audience.

Nevertheless, the musical quality of the *Eclogues* helps to explain the intriguing fact that soon after its publication parts of the collection were performed on stage. The theatre, by its very nature, caters for a much larger audience than we would expect for poetry as complex and allusive as this; and we know that it continued to be an important—and much more 'democratic'—context for the performance of literature, and in particular Virgil, for some time. In the late fourth or early fifth century CE St Augustine distinguished between the few members of his congregation who knew Virgil's poetry from books and the much greater number who knew it from performances in the theatre. The only permanent theatre in existence in Rome at the time of the publication of the *Eclogues*, the Theatre of Pompey, could hold as many as 11,000 people, a much larger number than the *readership* of poetry of this degree of sophistication.

But how much of the complex experience of the *Eclogues* was accessible to a theatre audience? Theatrical performance was bound to alter profoundly the way the poetry was interpreted. *Eclogue* 2 is a monologue by the herdsman Corydon bewailing his unrequited love for a boy from the city, Alexis; and Virgil manages to imply that Corydon is way out of his league. But the appearance of passages from *Eclogue* 2 on the walls of Pompeii, presumably inscribed at some date close to the eruption of Vesuvius in 79 CE, suggests that, as far as this wider audience was concerned, the poem had lost that original element of amused condescension of the rustic Corydon, and was now treated as straightforward, unironic love poetry. The authors of this graffiti presumably knew the

Eclogues from the theatre. This ironing out of the complexities of poetry as its audience expands is a pattern we will see repeated.

In the longer term, however, it was (paradoxically) precisely the difficulty and allusiveness of the collection, as well as the name that Virgil went on to gain with his epic *Aeneid*, which ensured the survival of the collection beyond antiquity. In the Renaissance, and later, the *Eclogues* inspired a flourishing tradition of pastoral poetry in Italian, French, and English, poetry which shared the *Eclogues'* studied simplicity and a tendency to comment on contemporary events: Milton's *Lycidas* is the best-known English example.

But by far the most influential poem in the collection is *Eclogue* 4, ironically the least 'pastoral' of them all. This poem is tied very specifically to a date and time: 40 BCE, the year of Asinius Pollio's consulship and date of the Pact of Brundisium which temporarily patched up the differences between Antony and Octavian. The miraculous child whose birth is celebrated in the poem is most likely to have suggested to contemporaries the son expected of the marriage of Antony and Octavia, Octavian's sister, the alliance which had cemented the agreement. But the poem is deliberately enigmatic and unspecific, and sensibly so: no son ever came of the marriage (Antony was too busy having children by Kleopatra, queen of Egypt), and the marriage itself rapidly disintegrated as relations between Antony and Octavian deteriorated. The golden child was mysterious enough for Pollio's son, Asinius Gallus, to be able to claim to be him a generation later. But the dominant interpretation of the poem throughout the Middle Ages and beyond was that it prophesied the birth of Christ, and the Kingdom of God that would ensue. One line of the poem in particular, *iam redit et Virgo, redeunt Saturnia regna*, 'Now also returns the Virgin, now returns the kingdom of Saturn' (line 6), became the most quoted line of classical literature. In its original context 'the Virgin' is Justice, who will return to dwell amongst men when the Golden Age, or Age of Saturn, is restored. But Christians found it easy to interpret her as the Virgin Mary, returning to earth in the company of her son. Virgil consequently gained the status of a prophet of the coming of Christ, which is how he appears (for example) in Dante's *Divine Comedy*.

The poem thus developed a wealth of meaning and associations unimaginable to its author. Perhaps nobody exploited it more fully than Elizabeth I. With the new-found classical knowledge of the Renaissance the Virgin could again be identified as Justice, and Elizabeth could combine the Christian associations of the poem, the classical motifs of Justice and the return of the Golden Age, and her own mystical image as the pure virgin married to the welfare of her subjects, into a potent political manifesto.

Agriculture as a metaphor for Rome

The *Eclogues* probably appeared as a collection in 39 or 38 BCE. Virgil's second collection, the four-book poem *Georgics* (originally *Georgica*), was apparently published in 29. In between these dates Virgil had joined the circle of Maecenas, whose name appears at the very outset of the poem;

> What makes the cornfields happy, under which constellation
> it is best to turn the earth, Maecenas, and train the vine on the elm;
> the care of cattle, the method for keeping
> a flock, the skill you need for frugal bees:
> this is where I shall begin to sing.
>
> (1. 1–5, trans. C. Day-Lewis)

Maecenas proceeds to reappear with an uncanny regularity at the beginning of the remaining three books: at line 41, precisely, in books 2 and 3, and back at line 2 in book 4. Octavian also features prominently: extravagant eulogies begin (1. 24–42) and end the poem (4. 559–66), and also mark its middle (3. 1–48). Virgil clearly indicates his proximity at this time to Octavian's party: he describes the poem as the *haud mollia iussa*, 'far from easy bidding' of Maecenas (3. 41). We are told in an ancient biography of Virgil that the poem was recited to Octavian after his return to Italy from the Actium campaign in 29, when he was recovering from a throat complaint in Atella, near Naples. Virgil read it to Octavian over a period of four days, Maecenas taking over the task whenever Virgil's voice gave out.

The strict truth of this anecdote is less important than the light it sheds on Virgil's relation to his patrons. As we have seen, great works of literature bring status not only to the author but also to the author's patrons. It was put about in anecdotes like this that the *Georgics* was written, in the first instance, for Octavian. The poem itself is a farming manual (*Georgica* means 'Farming Matters'), or rather the highly literary and artificial version of a farming manual we would expect of the author of the *Eclogues*. Anyone seeking advice on agriculture would be far better advised to consult Varro's prose *On Rural Matters* (cf. p. 37), published in 37 BCE and a clear inspiration for Virgil's work, though Varro's work was itself more of a pleasant diversion for the landed gentry than a scientific treatise. One of the major sources of enjoyment for a contemporary reader was Virgil's achievement in making poetry out of something as intrinsically unpromising as the mud and ordure of farming. Seneca wrote of the poem that Virgil 'saw not what it was most truthful to say, but what would be most agreeable, and wanted not to teach farmers, but please readers'. To prove his point Seneca quotes from Virgil's instructions as to when different crops should be sown:

> It is our task, again, to observe the star of Arcturus,
> The days of the Kid, and the shining Serpent, as carefully
> As sailors who homeward bound on windy waters are daring
> The Black Sea and the straits by the oyster-beds of Abydos.
> When the Scales make the hours for daytime and sleeptime balance,
> Dividing the globe into equal hemispheres—light and darkness,
> Then set your bulls to work, farmers, and sow your barley
> Up to the last showers on the frost-bound limits of winter:
> The flax-plant and corn-poppy
> You should cover now in earth, and keep on hard at the ploughing
> While a bone-dry soil allows it and the weather has not yet broken.
> In spring you sow your beans: then too the softening furrows
> Will take lucerne, and millet requires its annual care;
> When the milk-white Bull with gilded horn begins the year
> And the Dog Star drops away.

(1. 204–18, trans. C. Day-Lewis)

Seneca helpfully points out that millet is actually sown in June, not spring. But we do not need information like that to see that Virgil's emphasis is more on poetic expression than textbook accuracy.

The landscape of the *Georgics* is thus a very literary landscape, owing no less to Hesiod and Aratos than to contemporary agricultural reality. The kind of detailed advice about farming practice that Virgil offers in the poem can have been of no interest *per se* for the privileged élite who read his poem: they had slaves to deal with that kind of thing. And conversely, the demands made of the reader by this extremely complex poem required vastly better education than the average farmer would have enjoyed. One fairly extreme example: sharp-eyed scholars have noticed that whenever the river Euphrates is mentioned in Virgil's works its name is placed six lines from the end of the book: *Georgics* 1. 509, *Georgics* 4. 561, and *Aeneid* 8. 726. The explanation for this strange coincidence lies in Kallimachos' *Hymn to Apollo*, one of the most important statements of Kallimachos' literary principles, which contains a reference to the Euphrates—six lines from the end. Virgil is subtly communicating to his readership (and this device says astonishing things *about* that readership) his allegiance to Kallimachos' poetics. It goes without saying that the device also presupposes *written* texts which can be numbered, and compared.

Like Lucretius' poem, to which Virgil owes a lot, the *Georgics* is a didactic poem, a poem which teaches a lesson. But in the case of the *Georgics* this function is more apparent than real. A comparison of the roles of the addressees of each poem, Memmius and Maecenas, will clarify the differences. We saw in the previous chapter how Lucretius sought to guide his readers' response to his poem by means of an 'internal audience', Memmius, who 'stood for' the broader aristocratic audience at which Lucretius was aiming, and Lucretius' choice of him as the target of his argument *personalizes* the argument of the poem. In other words, Memmius is a teaching tool, an integral element of Lucretius' strategy for persuading and converting his readership. Can we say the same about Maecenas in the *Georgics*? No. Lucretius' poem is explicitly a course of tuition, with a pupil: Maecenas never fulfils any such role. After 1. 2 he is not mentioned again until the beginning of the next book, and the advice about farming which Virgil proceeds to give is directed at a very vaguely defined farmer figure. There are none of the teaching techniques here which Lucretius so brilliantly employed, and if the *Georgics* were really aiming to teach it would be supremely ineffective. But if Maecenas is not in the poem to be taught, his presence is nonetheless significant. First, his name at the beginning of every book informs the reader that the author of the most admired poem of recent years, the *Eclogues*, has deep respect for Maecenas, and the status that would accrue to Maecenas (and Octavian) from such a gesture should not be underestimated. Secondly, it would have been well known to Virgil's readers that Maecenas had minimal interest in farming, but did have an enthusiasm for the higher things in life. He had carefully fostered an image of decadent sophistication which concealed the political power he actually wielded. Amongst other things, then, the mention of Maecenas at the start of the *Georgics* would have alerted a contemporary reader that the *Georgics* was closer in function to Aratos' didactic than to Lucretius'.

Finally, however, it is hard not to think that the repetition of Maecenas' name, alongside the generous compliments paid to Octavian, encourages us to seek in the work some favourable commentary on Octavian's activities in the 30s. The Battle of Philippi in 42 had been followed by the Treaty of Brundisium in 40 between Antony and Octavian, the terms of which divided the Empire between Octavian and Antony. Antony went east to Alexandria (and to Kleopatra), and Octavian took control in Italy and the West. The 30s saw continued violent upheaval, in particular an extended and bloody sea war between Octavian and Sextus Pompeius, the son of Pompey the Great. The arrangement between Antony and Octavian, meanwhile, was fragile. After many false alarms it broke down decisively, and they came to blows. At Actium in 31 Octavian's forces defeated Antony and Kleopatra. Octavian now found himself with absolute control of Rome, but it was in a devastated and demoralized state. The period when the poem was composed (36–29) corresponds to the latter period of these upheavals, a time which also saw sustained propagandistic self-promotion on the part of Octavian as he sought to bolster his precarious position.

But whilst contemporary events certainly do impinge upon the poem, Virgil's attitude to them in the *Georgics* remains a source of enormous controversy. This poem is perhaps of all Roman poems the most fiercely debated by scholars. What we *can* say is that the agricultural world described in the poem is often not to be taken literally, but as a metaphor for the contemporary Roman world. In the *Georgics* Virgil exploits a powerful symbolism which the agricultural life exerted on the Roman upper classes, who for all their high urban sophistication liked to consider themselves at root farmers made good (hence the success of books like Varro's *On rural matters*). It was from their rustic origins, Romans felt, that all that was best about their culture—discipline, levelheadedness, a capacity for hard work—derived; and this myth of the rustic origins of Rome appears more than once in the poem. In the so-called 'Praise of Italy' (2. 136–76), for example, the success of Rome is attributed to the genius of the Italian countryside:

> Active her breed of men—the Marsians and Sabellians,
> Ligurians used to hardship, Volscian javelin-throwers;
> Mother she is of the Decii, Marii, great Camilli,
> The Scipios relentless in war; and of you, most royal Caesar,
> Who now triumphant along the furthest Asian frontiers
> Keep the war-worthless Indians away from the towers of Rome.
> Hail, great mother of harvests! O land of Saturn, hail!
> Mother of men!

> (ll. 167–74, trans. C. Day-Lewis)

But if as a consequence Virgil's countryside is always likely to symbolize contemporary Rome, it is an uncompromising picture of Rome that the poet offers. Repeatedly the advice offered to the farmer by the poet is shown to be quite unequal to the elemental forces with which the farmer has to contend. The world of the *Georgics*, whether that be the agricultural world or the world of Rome it represents, is frequently out of control:

> So, when racing chariots have rushed from the starting-gate,
> They gather speed on the course, and the driver tugs at the curb-reign
> —His horses runaway, car out of control, quite helpless.

> (1. 512–14, trans. C. Day-Lewis)

These are the last words of book 1. Book 3, concerned with the raising of flocks, punctuates its advice with two disturbing accounts of natural processes which are quite beyond the farmer's control, sex and disease. The book ends with a harrowing account of a plague among farm animals:

> And now they died by whole companies, and the corpses
> Rotting with vile decay lay piled in the very sheep-folds,
> Till men had learnt to put them in pits, covered with earth.
> The hide was no good, and no man
> Could cleanse the carcass in water or burn it up with fire:
> You could not even shear the fleece, it was so corroded
> With the foul pus, or work the rotten wool in the loom:
> But if you were so foolhardy as to wear the hideous garment,
> Inflamed pustules and a noxious-swelling sweat appeared
> All over your limbs: not long then
> Before the fiery curse ate up your tettered frame.
>
> (ll. 556–66, trans. C. Day-Lewis)

In book 4, which is devoted to apiculture (bee-keeping), the establishment of a bee colony and the needs and habits of bees are carefully described—but the account ends, as in the previous book, with a plague, which wipes out the hive. Again, certain elements of Virgil's account of bee civilization serve to establish parallels between the beehive and Rome; it is not hard to see in these destructive plagues a reflection of the civil wars which had had such a devastating effect on the Roman state.

Yet the poem does seem to promise some kind of solution to this catastrophe. It concludes with an extended mythological account of the hero Aristaeus, the loss of his beehive to disease, but then his recovery of his bee swarm under the direction of his mother Cyrene. The figure of Aristaeus cannot but have reminded contemporary readers of Octavian, who at the time was claiming to have restored the Roman state to life in a manner analogous to Aristaeus' regeneration of his bees. But few readers of the end of the *Georgics* have found the resolution very satisfactory. The cost of Aristaeus' success is the death of Orpheus, whose failed attempt to lead his dead wife back from the underworld is described at some length:

> And now he's avoided every pitfall of the homeward path,
> And Eurydice, regained, is nearing the upper air
> Close behind him (for this condition has Proserpine made),
> When a moment's madness catches her lover off his guard—
> Pardonable, you'd say, but Death can never pardon.
> He halts. Eurydice, his own, is now on the lip of
> Daylight. Alas! he forgot. His purpose broke. He looked back.
> His labour was lost, the pact he had made with the merciless king
> Annulled. Three times did thunder peal over the pools of Avernus.
> 'Who,' she cried, 'has doomed me to misery, who has doomed us?
> What madness beyond measure? Once more a cruel fate
> Drags me away, and my swimming eyes are drowned in darkness.

> Goodbye. I am borne away. A limitless night is about me
> And over the strengthless hands I stretch to you, yours no longer.'
> Thus she spoke: and at once from his sight, like a wisp of smoke,
> Thinned into air, was gone.

(4. 485–500, trans. C. Day-Lewis)

This is the passage which has captured the imagination of most readers, and it was Virgil's Orpheus, not his Aristaeus, who became a favourite theme of all artistic media—not least in *L'Orfeo* of Claudio Monteverdi, the first great achievement of the operatic tradition.

As Seneca's remarks in the mid-first century testify, the poem continued to be read by the upper classes—though judging by the absence of any graffiti of the *Georgics* at Pompeii it never developed the broader popularity of the *Eclogues* (and later the *Aeneid*). It is noticeable that Seneca omits any reference to the contemporary, political content of the poem. By his time the *Georgics* was apparently just a charming poetic evocation of the country life, and it was as such that it enjoyed a revival among those eighteenth-century English gentlemen who liked to consider themselves farmers but were happier with books than billhooks. It was, of course, an extremely good thing for the Agricultural Revolution that these readers did not attempt to apply any of Virgil's 'teachings'.

Early Horace: Us blaming them

The 'triumviral period' between the death of Julius Caesar and Octavian's final victory also saw the first works of Quintus Horatius Flaccus, or Horace (65 BCE– 8 BCE). One was the two books of verse *Sermones* (a term which covers the ground from 'chats' to 'sermons' or 'homilies') or *Satires* (a name which captures their mildly critical nature), following in the tradition of the second-century BCE Roman poet and social critic Gaius Lucilius (cf. pp. 25–6). The other book, modelled on the abusive 'iambic' poetry of the Archaic Greek poets Archilochos and Hipponax, was probably originally named *Iambi*, but is now known as the *Epodes*, a technical term derived from their metrical scheme.

As with the *Georgics*, the very first words of the *Satires* immediately betray Horace's allegiances:

> How is it, Maecenas, that no one lives content with the lot
> which either choice has given him or chance thrown in his way,
> but praises those who follow different paths?

(1. 1–3)

Both books of *Satires*, the first probably published in 35 BCE and the second in 30, were written under the patronage of Maecenas; in fact the first book describes Horace's admission into Maecenas' circle in some detail. But the situation with the *Epodes* is rather different. Although the beginning of the *Epodes* advertises Horace's proximity to Maecenas (his name appears in the fourth line of the first *Epode* and the whole poem is about him), many of the poems which make up the collection give the impression that they pre-date his adoption by Maecenas in about 38.

Poems like *Epodes* 1 and 9 glorify Maecenas' participation in the Battle of Actium in 31. This is the beginning of *Epode* 9:

> When shall I celebrate great Caesar's victory and drink
>   the Caecuban laid down for sacred feasts
> with you, heaven-blest Maecenas, in the lofty home
>   the gods have given you,
> to mingled music of the lyre and pipe,
>   Dorian the one, the other barbarous?
> Just so not long ago we drank when Neptune's admiral
>   was routed and his galleys fired,
> although he once had threatened Rome with chains
>   struck off his friends, our treacherous slaves.
> Now Romans are a woman's slaves—O hear you this
>   you generations yet to come—
> carrying arms and stakes for her, and at the beck and call
>   of wrinkled eunuchs,
> and there the sun among our eagles sees
>   —the shame of it—mosquito nets!
>
> (trans. David West)

What particularly appalled Romans about the civil wars was that they involved not the conquest of foreigners, which Romans bore with an easy conscience, but of other Romans. This is why in this poem Horace celebrates some of Octavian's activities in the civil wars—both Actium and earlier actions against Sextus Pompeius—as the conquest of Romans, yes, but treacherous Romans, Romans who have abandoned Roman values. Pompeius has thrown his lot in with slaves, and Antony himself is a love slave to Kleopatra. They are as good as foreigners, deserving defeat and death in return for their eastern effeminacy (mosquito nets, indeed!). There was a strong vein of racism and sexual and class prejudice in the Roman upper classes for poems like this to exploit.

But other poems in the *Epodes* collection sit awkwardly with such propaganda. In poems 7 and 16, in particular, civil war is a far less glorious business. Poem 16 despairs of an end to it all. Rome will destroy itself, and all the Romans can do is sail off to the Elysian Fields beyond the Ocean. Poem 7 presents the poet demanding of the Roman people an explanation of their compulsion for civil war:

> Why this mad rush to join a wicked war? Your swords
>   were sheathed. Why do you draw them now?
> Perhaps too little Latin blood has poured upon the plains
>   and into Neptune's sea,
> not so that Rome could burn the lofty citadels
>   of Carthage, her great enemy,
> or that the Briton, still beyond our reach, should walk
>   the Sacred Way in chains,
> but so that Rome might fall by Roman hands
>   and answer all the prayers of Parthia.
>
> (trans. David West)

Receiving no reply he supplies his own explanation:

> It is harsh fate that drives
>   the Romans, and the crime of fratricide
> since Remus' blameless lifeblood poured upon the ground—
>   a curse to generations yet unborn.
>
> (ll. 17–20)

Romulus killed his own twin brother in the course of founding the city, and Rome, according to Horace, is cursed to repeat the crime unendingly. *Epode* 1, it could be argued, aims to 'neutralize' the *Epodes*, frame the collection as a whole as loyal to Maecenas, despite the disconcerting sentiments of poems like 7. But where readers place the emphasis of the collection is (arguably) ultimately up to them, in the privacy of their own reading.

Horace wrote the *Epodes* and the *Satires* simultaneously, and this was a natural choice. Though very different styles of poetry they have a lot in common. Archilochos and Hipponax wrote 'blame poetry', poetry which chastised the moral failings which the poets perceived in the people around them. Similarly, Roman satire, although different from modern satire in being a literary genre, shares with its modern counterpart the basic function of criticism. Lucilius' satires had already substantially conflated the two genres (cf. pp. 25–6). Horace's choice of two very different genres with the shared element of *blame* has an obvious contemporary rationale: Rome was not an exemplary society at this juncture.

But Horace had certain more subtle aspects of the genres in mind as well. Blame poetry, by its very nature, distances the poet and the reader from the vices it attacks. But by the same token it unites poet and audience in their moral outrage, and it reminds them of their shared moral values. Paradoxically, then, blame poetry makes *friends* of its audience, as it makes enemies of its targets. Friendship is a preoccupation of both the *Epodes* and the *Satires*, and it was one shared by Horace's contemporaries. *Amicitia*, friendship, was the value that bound Roman society together. But civil war had ripped it apart, pitting close associates and even family members against each other (hence the equation with fratricide). To Romans this felt like the breakdown of *amicitia*.

In poems like *Epode* 7 Horace addresses his target, here the Roman people, and attempts to 'blame' them into changing their terrible behaviour. But more subtly, whilst a contemporary Roman reader shared the blame being meted out to the Roman people he is also constructed by the poem as a counterpart of the outraged, blaming authorial voice: we also ask, in the process of reading, 'Why this mad rush to join a wicked war?' We read, and become part of Horace's group of right-thinking friends, berating the fratricidal madness of the Romans. So the *Epodes* restore friendship.

The *Satires* or *Sermones* offer a milder form of criticism, but in this respect their effect is somewhat similar. The poems have a very informal style, and aim to give the impression of immediacy, as if Horace is conducting a conversation with us. They thus dramatize an act of friendship, a conversation between friends, and like the *Epodes* offer an alternative to the social breakdown of civil war. But what makes Horace's strategy more pointed is that the friendships which Horace idealistically depicts in the *Satires* are largely those between the members of Maecenas' 'set'. In other words, the group being set up by Horace as the representative of decent values, which Rome needs in order to escape from civil war, just happens to be one of the parties vying (violently) for control of Rome. The reader witnesses an exemplary group of Romans, and is drawn into that group himself by the process of reading: Horace's friendly immediacy makes us feel we too are part of the group.

The underlying political rationale is exemplified by 1. 5. This poem describes a journey undertaken by Maecenas and his literary 'friends' from Rome to Brundisium, during which the group experiences various amusing misfortunes: stomach upsets, travel delays, wet dreams, fire, mud, and so on. It is an attractive picture of an ordinary group of male friends. In passing the poem also mentions the purpose of the journey:

> To Anxur excellent Maecenas was to come, with
>   Cocceius, both despatched on important business,
> as ambassadors, well used to reconciling estranged friends.
>   Here I smear black ointment on my eyes

for my conjunctivitis. Meanwhile Maecenas arrived with
Cocceius and Fonteius Capito, an exemplary
individual, Antony's closest friend.

(ll. 27–33)

The friends are going to attend a meeting, probably in 37 BCE, to patch up differences (again!) between Octavian and Antony. It is a mission of great seriousness, the failure of which would mean renewed civil war. But there is no hint of this in Horace's poem. Normality reigns. Even the split between Antony and Octavian is depicted as a temporary, and easily remedied, difference between friends. The reader witnesses, and enjoys, a scene far removed from the trauma of civil war—and we associate its harmony and good sense with Maecenas.

Horace, no less than Virgil, was profoundly influenced by the Callimachean ideals of the New Poets. Part of the reason Horace chose to wrote iambic poetry modelled after Archilochos and Hipponax was that Kallimachos had done so. The very first word of the *Epodes*, *ibis*, 'you will go', probably alludes to the title of a piece of invective by Kallimachos, the *Ibis*, and this degree of Callimachean complexity and allusiveness is maintained throughout the collection. The same, more surprisingly, goes for the *Satires*. Surprisingly, because the intricacy and polish demanded by Kallimachos was profoundly alien to the genre invented by Lucilius, which took pride in breaking the literary rules. Its concerns were humble and un-poetic, everyday life and (bad) behaviour, and the language of satire was the colloquial speech of the ordinary Roman. Yet the metre of satirical poetry was the dactylic hexameter, the rhythmical scheme associated with epic verse. Horace's readers would have felt about the colloquial language of the opening hexameter line in Horace's *Satires*, 'How is it, Maecenas, that . . .', the same as we would about a Shakespearian actor reciting a newspaper: the sublime perfection of the hexameter is being abused.

Horace's claim that his satire obeyed the tenets of Kallimachos pushes the Lucilian paradox of poetic satire a step further. Callimachean satire was a contradiction in terms. Horace's audience knew it, and enjoyed the literary joke. *Satire* 1. 10 is a statement of Horace's literary ideals in which he criticizes Lucilius for his verbosity and lack of polish:

If his life had been postponed by fate until our present age,
he would file off a lot from his work, and cut back everything which
trailed beyond what was ideal, and in composing his verse
he would often scratch his head and gnaw his nails to the quick.

(ll. 68–71)

But the end of the poem amusingly undermines Horace's claim to be a follower of Kallimachos. He concludes his literary criticism, and adds (line 92),

> Away, boy, and quickly append this to my book

as if his poetry is not the product of laborious care at all, but something dictated off the top of his head.

So the *Satires* were, as we would expect, sophisticated poetry for a sophisticated audience, in which play with the conventions of literature provides much of the diversion. But the wit and artistry concealed a deadly serious political intent. The Rome of the *Satires* is one of absolute normality: friends act like friends, civil upheaval is scarcely to be seen, and Horace chats in a homely style which it is hard to square with the grim reality of the 30s BCE. The unanswerable question, however, is whether the collection had the effect Horace intended. Were readers of Horace's *Satires* lulled into a contented acceptance of Octavian's leadership, or did the strenuous efforts which Horace put into *not mentioning the war* simply draw attention to the anxieties which were motivating him, and the grim realities he was trying to disguise? We cannot say, but we can recognize the various interpretative possibilities, and we know that Horace was dealing with an audience quite capable of second-guessing him. But whatever their immediate reception, the *Satires* join the list of Maecenas' success stories, reinventing the genre in a form which would be imitated and developed by Persius in the first century CE, Juvenal in the second (see pp. 217–18, 220–2), and the English satirists, especially the master of 'Horatian Satire', Alexander Pope, in the eighteenth—none of them, apparently, suspecting the disguise of genial social critic which Horace had assumed.

The elegists: All for love?

In comparison to Virgil and Horace our next poet, Sextus Propertius (*c*.50–*c*.5 BCE), has seemed to some readers a breath of fresh air, a writer determined to assert his independence from the regime of Octavian or Augustus. This is the Propertius of Ezra Pound, for example, whose paraphrase of Propertius' love elegies, *Homage to Sextus Propertius* (1917), makes of the poet a passionate, independent-minded lover of poetry for its own sake rather too obviously reminiscent of Ezra Pound. His version of Propertius' anticipation of Virgil's epic *Aeneid* is typical, importing as it does an explicit tone of condemnation quite absent from the original:

> Upon the Actian marshes Virgil is Phoebus' chief of police,
> He can tabulate Caesar's great ships.

He thrills to Ilian arms,
    He shakes the Trojan weapons of Aeneas,
And casts stores on Lavinian beaches.
Make way, ye Roman authors,
    clear the street O ye Greeks,
For a much larger Iliad is in the course of construction
    (and to Imperial order)
Clear the streets O ye Greeks!

(2. 34. 61–6)

Pound saw in Propertius' poems a reaction against 'the infinite and ineffable imbecility of the Roman Empire', and a vehicle he could use at the height of the First World War to express his disgust at 'the infinite and ineffable imbecility of the British Empire'.

A contemporary assessment of the poet would have been more qualified. Propertius was an exponent of one of the most characteristically Roman genres, Love Elegy, so called because it was love poetry composed in the metre known as the elegiac couplet. Love Elegy had originated with Cornelius Gallus (cf. pp. 52–3), whose poetry (despite the influence it exerted on Virgil as well as the elegists) has almost completely disappeared. But we know enough about it to see that, young as the genre was, Propertius was already working within a set of rules and conventions. Gallus was a man of action who wrote poetry in which he represented himself as a very different kind of person, a man in thrall to a dominating mistress called Lycoris. We can assume that the persona he adopted in his poetry had little to do with real life, and that his readers did not expect it to. In other words, the poetry of the love elegists did not come 'straight from the heart', by any means.

The first book of Propertius' elegies was published in 30 or 29 BCE. There were probably five books in all, produced between 30 and about 16 BCE, although modern texts are divided into four (the text of Propertius rivals Catullus for the corrupt state in which it emerged from the Middle Ages). Most of his poetry is devoted to an account of an unequal relationship with a girlfriend, Cynthia, who dominates the poet's life. The first verses of book 1 set the scene:

Cynthia first, with her eyes, caught wretched me
    Smitten before by no desires;
Then, lowering my stare of steady arrogance,
    With feet imposed Love pressed my head,
Until he taught me hatred of chaste girls—
    The villain—and living aimlessly.
And now for a whole year this mania has not left me,
    Though I am forced to suffer adverse Gods.

> Milanion by facing every hardship, Tullus,
>   Conquered the cruelty of Atalanta.
> Sometimes, distraught, he roamed the glens of Parthenius
>   And was gone to watch the long-haired beasts.
> Stunned by that blow from Hylaeus' club he even
>   Groaned in anguish to Arcadian crags.
> So he was able to master his fleet-footed girl;
>   Such power in love have prayers and kindnesses.
> For me, though, Love is slow, can think of no devices,
>   And forgets to go his legendary way.
>
> (1. 1. 1–18, trans. Guy Lee)

An author has to catch the reader's attention, preferably at the beginning of a collection. The strategy of the love elegist is to be outrageous. The lifestyle described here breaks every rule of Roman aristocratic morality. By allowing himself to be dominated by a woman Propertius is abrogating his position as a dominant Roman male; and by a woman, what is more, of dubious social status, in a society where status was everything. And whilst the Roman male was trained to aspire to success and honour in the public arenas of politics and war, Propertius describes his pursuit of Cynthia, an unworthy aspiration in itself, as his sole occupation. The slave-like devotion to a low-status woman which Propertius describes is thus an outrageous reversal of conventional ethics. And Propertius knows how to rub it in:

> Had I not better be the slave of some harsh tyrant
>   And moan in cruel Perillus' bull?
> Not better be turned to stone by the Gorgon's glare
>   Or even devoured by Prometheus' vultures?
> No, I'll stand firm. Steel blades are worn away
>   By rust, and flint by dripping water,
> But love's not worn away by an accusing mistress;
>   Love stays and puts up with her unjust threats.
> When scorned he asks again. Though wronged he takes the blame,
>   And back he comes, if on reluctant feet.
>
> (2. 25. 11–20, trans. Guy Lee)

But this poetry is very aware how shocking it is. Notice how at the opening to book 1 Propertius condemns his own behaviour, guiding his readers to do the same (if they are not so minded already). Propertius is *self-consciously* immoral, and this helps to suggest to us the nature of his relationship with his audience: it is an audience which, as with all the poetry of this period, enjoys a literary game, and which recognizes (and takes pleasure in the fact) that what poets say about themselves need only bear a very oblique relation to reality. Propertius recounts his feckless, out-of-control lifestyle in elegant and witty verse and carefully constructed poems and collections, and illustrates his humiliating condition with erudite allusions to myth. For example the myth of Milanion he cites in his first poem has more significance than meets the eye. Milanion finally managed to endear himself to the unwilling object of his affection, the huntress Atalanta, by sharing her outdoor lifestyle; but he was also a figure with whom Gallus had identified himself in his efforts to gain the goodwill of *his* beloved, Lycoris. A contemporary reader would appreciate that Propertius' use of the myth says as much about his place in the history of the elegiac genre as his actual love life: in an allusive way Propertius informs his readership that he is working in the same tradition as Cornelius Gallus, but that his poetry is a new departure in the genre. The stratagems of Milanion, i.e. Gallus, do not work for Propertius. He will have to try others, which will be recounted in this (brand new) collection of love elegies . . .

We have already seen plenty of evidence that the sophisticated readership of Roman poetry could tell the difference (and enjoy the difference) between art and life. We don't know much about the historical figure Propertius, but what we do know suggests—not very surprisingly—that he was a respectable married man: at the turn of the first and second centuries CE there is an elegist who claims to be his descendant. Similarly, Cynthia, his girlfriend, is moulded as much by literary convention as by whatever real woman underlay her (*if* any in fact did). Her name gestures at a cult title of Apollo, god of poetry, 'Cynthius', and she operates in the collection as the source and inspiration of Propertius' poetry as much as the object of Propertius' love. As he says at the beginning of book 2:

> You ask me how it is I write so often of love
>   And how my verses come soft on the tongue.
> These no Apollo, no Calliope sings to me;
>   My only inspiration is a girl.
>   (1. 1–4, trans. Guy Lee)

It is the poetry that shapes the love-affair, not the love-affair that shapes the poetry.

The audience Propertius pretends to write for is the ardent lover. In poem 3. 3 Apollo berates him for attempting to write epic poetry when his talent lies elsewhere:

> Idiot, what right have you to such a stream? And who
>   Told you to turn your hand to epic?
> There's not a hope of fame, Propertius, for you here;
>   Your little wheels must groove soft meadows.

> Let your slim volume be displayed on bedside table
> And read by lonely girls waiting for their lovers.
> (ll. 15–20, trans. Guy Lee)

But Propertius' verse is more than simple love poetry, and his audience correspondingly wider, potentially as wide as for any poetic text at this time. In this particular instance we should be suspicious of the suggestion that Propertius' audience might be female. There may well have been women amongst his readership, but men predominated, and there is a strong voyeuristic element, aimed at his male readers, in this image of a girl reading love poetry in bed in preparation for her male lover's arrival.

There were, though, as with other writers, certain privileged readers. Propertius' first book is dedicated to Tullus, a young man from an eminent aristocratic family. The publication of book 1 clearly brought Propertius to the attention of important men, since in the first poem of book 2 it is Maecenas' name which appears. Propertius has followed Virgil and Horace into Maecenas' circle of patronage, and his poetic success would henceforth bring credit, by association, to the ruling regime.

Love elegy is in some respects an unusual style of poetry for Maecenas to associate himself with. But with a sophisticated readership alive to the highly artificial nature of love elegy, Propertius could represent his poetic persona as hopelessly immoral without necessarily implicating his real self. It is nevertheless a delicate balance. In a remarkable poem (3. 11) the poet exploits his immoral persona for propaganda, comparing his own condition as a slave to a woman with Kleopatra's domination of Antony—and condemning both. The effect of this poem depends on the capacity of the audience to distinguish the poet who condemns this lifestyle from the poet's lover persona, who lives it. But this is asking a lot, particularly since love elegy is a very 'realistic' genre. The relentlessly autobiographical nature of the poetry strongly encourages the reader to believe in, and identify with, the lover figure. The bruised lover who scribbled a couplet from Propertius on a wall in Pompeii was probably not alive to the irony:

> Now anger is fresh, now is the time to part:
> once the pain has gone, believe me, love will return.
> (2. 5. 9–10)

Here it may be a question of education. Once Propertius' poetry had penetrated beyond the circle of sophisticates its author originally had in mind its reception was, as we have seen, liable to change. Ezra Pound was much more sensitive to the irony and playfulness of Propertius than his Edwardian and Victorian predecessors, but even he underestimated the remarkable artifice of the poetry.

If the same fate has not befallen another love elegist, Albius Tibullus (*c*.50–*c*.19 BCE), it is mainly because he has been too seriously neglected, despite having had a generally higher reputation than Propertius amongst ancient critics. His first book of poetry came out in 27 or 26 BCE, and in broad terms his love elegy resembles that of Propertius. Tibullus too is subservient to a mistress, Delia in his first book (another 'literary' name, based on 'Delius', a cult title of Apollo), and the ominously named Nemesis in the second:

> So, I see, slavery and a mistress await me:
>   farewell, freedom that was my birthright.
> And a harsh slavery is my lot—I am held in chains,
>   and never, alas, does Love loosen my fetters.
> Whether I have deserved it or am guiltless, he burns me.
>   I am burning: ow! cruel girl, remove the torch.
>
> (2. 4. 1–6)

The slave motif, so offensive to Roman sensibilities, is shared with Propertius. But Tibullus gives his own twist to the elegiac rejection of traditional Roman values. His aspiration is the simple life of a small farmer in the company of his loved one:

> Not for me the riches of my fathers, and profits
>   which the gathered harvest brought my grandfather of old:
> A small crop is enough, it is enough if I may sleep on my bed
>   and ease my limbs on my accustomed couch.
> How pleasant to hear the harsh winds as I lie
>   and hold my mistress in my gentle embrace!
> Or when the wintry South Wind pours down freezing showers
>   to pursue sleep in safety, helped by a fire.
> Let this be my lot: let him by right be rich
>   who can endure the rage of the sea and grim rain.
> O sooner let all the gold and all the emeralds in the world perish
>   than any girl weep because of my travels.
> It is right for you, Messalla, to campaign by land and sea
>   to adorn your house with the enemy's spoils:
> but I am held fast by the chains of a beautiful girl,
>   and I sit as a gatekeeper before her cruel doors.
>
> (1. 1. 41–56)

Messalla is M. Valerius Messalla Corvinus, Tibullus' patron, a successful politician and general. It is noticeable how Tibullus distances Messalla from the elegiac lifestyle; Propertius had similarly been careful not to implicate Tullus or Maecenas in his immorality. But with Tibullus even more clearly than with Propertius we are dealing with a literary fantasy. The little information we have about Tibullus' real life shows us a conventional Roman aristocrat who, despite the anti-war sentiments in his poetry, was decorated for bravery on campaign with Messalla.

Messalla is regularly mentioned, and honoured, in Tibullus' poetry. His 1. 7 is a poem in honour of his birthday which praises his military achievements in Gaul and the Eastern Empire, as well as the repairs he had carried out on a stretch of the Via Latina, an important road, using some of the wealth he had won in his campaigns in Gaul. These are classic instances of Roman patronage, a poet giving his patron the benefit of honour in his poetry in return for the more tangible benefits the more powerful man could provide to him. Messalla in fact surrounded himself with quite an extended literary circle. Ovid was given his start in the literary world by Messalla (he calls him 'the encourager, cause and guiding light' of his poetry).

In 'Tibullus'' 'third book', which is in fact a collection of poems not by Tibullus at all but by poets associated with Messalla, we find a *Panegyric of Messalla* by an unknown poet and a short sequence of love poems by that rare phenomenon in the ancient world, a female poet, Sulpicia, who also addresses herself to Messalla and was probably his niece. This 'salon' is as close as any Roman aristocrat came in the Augustan period to the prominence in the literary world of Maecenas and his circle.

The benefits for Messalla were the status which association with good literature could bestow. It follows that although Messalla is given the role in this poetry of the 'first reader', and one of the charms of the poetry of his circle is the impression it gives of a small and intimate group (they have a particular fondness for birthday poems, for example), it clearly sought a much wider readership. Messalla would only gain the credit due him if people outside his circle read the poetry he had patronized and facilitated, and the occasional poems which directly praise him. Ovid in fact repaid him after his death with a poem in his honour which was recited in the Forum.

The case of Sulpicia is intriguing, though. She was another love elegist, and wrote (like Propertius and Tibullus) in the first person. If male love elegy already trod a thin line, it is hard to imagine the first-person account of respectable woman's extra-marital liaison finding a Roman readership outside her immediate circle:

> Venus has kept her promise. My joys can be the talk
> of all who are said to have none of their own.
> I would not wish to send a message under seal
> so no one could read it before my man.
> But I'm glad to sin, and bored of wearing reputation's
> mask. The world will know I am matched with an equal.

We can readily imagine the kind of voyeuristic male audience these superficially artless sexual confessions by Sulpicia might have appealed to. But if her poetry had anything like a wide circulation it cannot have helped but be extremely controversial.

Tibullus' poetry makes an interesting test case for the degree of influence that the patron exerted over a writer. As compared with Propertius, Tibullus' style is plain, almost austere. There is much less in his poetry of the learned allusion and self-conscious literary play which we associate with Propertius and the other Callimachean poets, and it has been suggested that Tibullus' style betrays the influence of Messalla, since he had the reputation of being a literary purist. But this is a mistake. The Roman literary patron gave his writers great autonomy, and did not impose his tastes upon them, a fact for which we can be heartily grateful if we read the surviving fragments of the poetry that Maecenas produced, which was notoriously bizarre: Maecenas' words, according to Seneca, 'constructed so faultily, thrown out so carelessly, arranged so eccentrically, show that the man's character was equally strange, depraved and outlandish': it could hardly be more different from the poetry of Maecenas' circle. Tibullus' simplicity of style is quite adequately explained as the perfect vehicle for expressing his simple ideal of life: the countryside, an absence of unnecessary luxury, and the company of an appropriately unadorned girlfriend (1. 3. 91–2): 'Then, just as you are, your long hair tousled, | run to meet me, Delia, in your bare feet.' This is poetry *au naturel*, which of course betrays itself as the creation of a highly educated author. Tibullus' 'refined and elegant' love elegy, as the later critic Quintilian described it, was appreciated by an audience who enjoyed the fantasy of escape to an innocent rural life (cf. Virgil's *Eclogues*), but were alive to the artificiality of the message (they knew that Tibullus had no real intention of decamping to the country . . .) and the artificiality of the vehicle (. . . and that it takes a lot of effort to write so effortlessly).

Horace's *Odes*: The full range of lyric poetry

Horace's three books of *Odes* or *Carmina* (both words mean 'songs') came out as a collection in 23 BCE. A fourth book would be added later, in about 13 BCE. They were a fairly natural step on from the *Epodes*. Whereas the *Epodes* had been modelled on the Greek iambic poets, the *Odes* imitated the 'lyric' poets of the same period, and in particular Alkaios. The term 'lyric' is derived from 'lyre', and Greek lyric poetry such as Alkaios composed was *sung*, to the accompaniment of this lyre, and only subsequently written down. Quite how the audience of Horace's lyric 'songs' compares to these archaic audiences is a complicated issue we can best approach through Ovid's recollection of the poetic scene of his youth:

> Macer, much older, read to me his poem
>   On birds and snakes and herbs that bring relief.
> Propertius would recite his fiery lyrics,
>   So close a comradeship linked him and me,
> And epic Ponticus, iambic Bassus,
>   Were pleasant members of my coterie.
> Horace too, master-metrist, charmed me, singing
>   His polished stanzas to the Latin lyre.
> Virgil I only saw . . .
>   (*Tristia* 4. 10. 43–51, trans. A. D. Melville)

Ovid describes the members of his poetic circle: Aemilius Macer (a writer of didactic poetry), Propertius, Ponticus (epic), and Bassus (a writer of *iambi* like Horace in the *Epodes*). At first sight it seems that Horace was a member of the same circle; what Ovid appears to be describing is a *performance* by Horace, singing his poems to a lyre. But Horace's poems were not designed to be performed at all. Unlike the lyric poetry he was imitating, the *Odes* were the product of an essentially *literary* culture, a culture where poetry was written down and read, not performed. Everything about the poetry we have been considering—its complexity, its allusiveness—tell us that it was designed to be appreciated by a reader rather than an audience member. And the *Odes* are no different.

But authors of works designed to be read rather than heard always aspire to create a richer experience than the mere process of reading—good literature 'leaps off the page', as the saying goes. Furthermore, in accordance with the ancient rules of literary imitation Horace was obliged to mimic the originators of the lyric genre closely enough to be able to claim membership of the same genre. How could he, when the conditions of performance in sixth-century Lesbos and first-century Rome were so different? Horace's solution was to *build* everything that a live performance had contributed to Alkaios' poetry—a lyre, an audience, spontaneity, and immediacy—into his unperformed poems.

The first thing Horace added into his poetry was personality. The 'monodic' (solo) lyric of Alkaios was an essentially autobiographical genre, a genre in which poets (ostensibly, at any rate) talked in the first person from the standpoint of their own life and circumstances. The first person is the dominant mode of speech in the *Odes* too, but this 'I' should not simply be equated with Quintus Horatius Flaccus. It is an artificial persona, lifelike and credible, but largely moulded by the traditions of the genre rather than by the reality of the author. The canon of lyric poets allowed Horace a lot of scope here. From

Alkaios Horace constructed the persona of a mature individual who had seen some life and learnt from it, but knew how to enjoy his leisure time. The more elevated stance of the priest-poet which he occasionally adopts, particularly at the beginning of book 3, is reminiscent of choral lyric, as associated particularly with the name of Pindar, performed by choruses and in general of much higher aspirations than the monodic variety. Clearly the very flexibility of Horace's lyric persona reveals the *Odes* for what they are: a highly artificial lyric which is even less close than archaic lyric to being the expression of an individual's subjectivity.

If the 'I' of the performer had to be invented, so did the 'live' audience to which the Archaic lyric 'I' had addressed himself. Archaic monodic lyric began as a performance before an audience of friends, typically in the context of a drinking party or 'symposium'. Again, Horace's written text has no such delimited audience: its readership is potentially as wide as the educated public of Rome. But the impression of intimacy was an essential component of the lyric experience. Horace's problem was to create it *on the page*. He overcomes the problem by addressing most of the poems to a single named 'friend', and thereby creating the illusion that the audience of the poem is smaller and more intimate—but also more vividly *present*—than it really is. Horace has thus created for himself an 'I' which was reasonably credible whilst not departing from the traditions of the genre, an audience—even a lyre, even though he doesn't really have one:

> We pray, if ever we have relaxed with you in the shade
> and played a melody that may live a year
> or more, come, my Greek lyre,
>   and sound a Latin song.
>
> (1. 32. 1–4, trans. David West)

In short, Horace has constructed a lyric performance on the written page. The *Odes* achieve the remarkable effect of giving the impression of performance in reading. So, to return to Ovid, in 'Horace too, master-metrist, charmed me, singing | His polished stanzas to the Latin lyre' he is not describing a performance at all, but evoking Horace's allusions to the way lyric was originally performed.

Nothing in Latin poetry, as we are now aware, is that straightforward. The fact that Horace addresses his poems to named individuals does not, of course, preclude a wider audience, or limit the poetry's relevance. *Odes* 1. 7 ends with an admonition to L. Munatius Plancus to put his troubles behind him:

> The bright south wind will often wipe the clouds from the dark sky.
>   It is not always pregnant with rain.

So you too, Plancus, would be wise to remember to put a stop
    to sadness and the labours of life
with mellow, undiluted wine, whether you are in camp among
    the gleaming standards or whether you will be
in the deep shade of your beloved Tibur. When Teucer was on the run
    from Salamis and his father, they say that nevertheless,
awash with wine, he bound his brow with a crown of poplar leaves
    and spoke these words to his grieving friends:
'Allies and comrades, Fortune is kinder than a father.
    Wherever she takes us, there shall we go. Do not despair
while Teucer takes the auspices and Teucer is your leader.
    Apollo does not err and he has promised
that in a new land we shall find a second Salamis.
    You are brave men and have often suffered worse
with me. Drive away your cares with wine. Tomorrow
    we shall set out again upon the broad sea.'

                                (ll. 15–32, trans. David West)

The sentiment is conventional enough, but gains both piquancy and a wider
application from the person to whom Horace has chosen to address it. Plancus
was a native of Tibur who had benefited from the upheavals which followed the
assassination of Julius Caesar, becoming consul in 42 BCE. But his brother had
been killed in the proscriptions of 43, and Plancus apparently suffered much ill
will on the grounds that he had acquiesced in the killing of his brother. The
myth of Teucer subtly alludes to Plancus' circumstances. Teucer had to flee
Salamis because of his father's (unjust) anger at Teucer's failure to prevent the
death of his brother Ajax. Teucer's circumstances match Plancus' closely, but
the uplifting optimism and hope for the future of Teucer's speech—'Tomorrow
we shall set out again upon the broad sea'—will have had force for all of
Horace's readership, still less than a decade after the end of the civil wars, when
many wounds remained unhealed. The imperative to *move on* from the civil
wars is a recurrent theme in the *Odes*.

The *Odes* were dedicated to Maecenas again, and in both narrower and
broader terms they collaborate in the reorganization of Rome which Augustus
undertook after his victory at Actium. Poems like 3. 6, one of a series of poems
at the start of book 3 on moral themes, known as the 'Roman Odes', delivered
in the loftier priestly persona of choral lyric, give expression to the highly
reactionary social policies with which Augustus concealed the revolutionary
political changes through which he was putting the Roman state:

        Though innocent, Roman, you will pay for the sins
        of your fathers until you restore

> the crumbling temples and shrines of the gods
> and their smoke-blackened images.
> You rule because you hold yourself inferior to the gods.
> Make this the beginning and the end of all things.
> Neglect of the gods has brought many ills
> to the sorrowing land of Hesperia.
>
> (3. 6. 1–8, trans. David West)

Horace's encouragement to his readership to restore the religious buildings of Rome corresponds to an Augustan policy. Besides the building undertaken by himself and his family, Augustus encouraged other senior aristocrats to construct, restore, or embellish public buildings—Plancus, for example, restored the temple of Saturn. In Augustus' building policy we have a good illustration of his strategy as ruler. In order not to alienate the aristocrats on whom his administration depended Augustus needed to give them as much freedom as possible to lead the traditional status-seeking life aristocratic culture demanded, whilst not threatening the unity of the state. The *Odes* project an analogous image of aristocratic Rome. Horace's equivalent to Alkaios' circle of aristocratic friends is a cross-section of contemporary Rome—Pollio, Messalla, Plancus, Tibullus, Maecenas—each given that much-desired prestige by his appearance in a collection of such brilliance, but a collection unified under the overarching carapace of Augustus.

But in broader terms, if Augustus' cultural policies were about restoring confidence to Rome, the very fact of the writing of the *Odes* conveyed to its readers the sense of a new and confident age. Here was a Roman author equalling the achievement of the Greek lyricists, in fact encapsulating in his collection the achievement of all nine canonical lyricists, a remarkably ambitious undertaking. With the *Odes* and Virgil's *Aeneid*, in particular, Rome developed a literature which they could claim was the equal of the literature of Greece, a culture to which Rome had traditionally felt an oppressive inferiority.

But whatever the broader implications conveyed by the three books of *Odes*, it is poetry which works in intricate detail. Ovid called Horace *numerosus*, 'master-metrist'. It was an astonishing achievement on Horace's part to match the complex, strict, and highly diverse metres of Greek lyric with the Latin language, and so skilfully that the match seems easy. Some of the metres which Horace employs in the *Odes* had already been introduced to Latin—the characteristic metre of Sappho had been used by Catullus, for example (cf. pp. 70–1)—but the astonishing range of lyric metres was unprecedented, and when Horace begins the first book of *Odes* with nine poems all in different metres, he is impressing on the reader his absolute control of the lyric tradition.

IMPERIAL PIETY. *The Altar of Piety in Rome dedicated by the Emperor Claudius in 43 CE shows a sacrifice in front of a precise rendering of the architecture of the Temple of the Great Mother.*

An even more astonishing achievement was that, as well as mastering the metres, Horace created a Latin lyric style, concise and meticulous, of great expressive power. His greatest talent is in using his metres to place and arrange the words of his poetry to optimum effect: a later author talks of his *curiosa felicitas*, 'painstaking felicity'. Many of his *mots justes* are still familiar to us: *carpe diem* ('pluck the day'), 'golden mean' (*aurea mediocritas*), *dulce et decorum est pro patria mori* ('sweet it is and honourable to die for one's native land'), *exegi monumentum aere perennius* ('I have wrought a monument more lasting than bronze'). Thought is as intricate as word placement, and the expertise and pleasure in the game we have come to expect of contemporary readers was fully exercised. The relevance of the Teucer myth to Plancus in 1. 7 is never explicitly stated by the poet, but left to us to decipher for ourselves. The reader of the *Odes* begins from this aesthetic delight; the sense of belonging to the new Augustan dispensation comes later.

Horace sets out to transfer the essence of the whole (enormous) extent of Greek lyric poetry to the Latin language, and to this end he covers the full range of Greek lyrical themes, from wine and women to hymns to the gods and moral statements of high seriousness. The richness of metres is paralleled by a wealth of lyrical models: all nine canonical Greek lyricists have their place at some point or other in this Latin lyric. At all stages, though, the Archaic ethos of his models is filtered through the Hellenistic sensibility common to all Roman poets of this period. *Odes* 1. 33, addressed to Tibullus, will give a final sense of the richness and complexity of the collection:

> Do not grieve, Albius, remembering too well
> your bitter-sweet Glycera and do not keep chanting
> piteous elegies wondering why she has broken faith
>   and a younger man now outshines you.
> Love for Cyrus scorches the beautiful,
> narrow-browed Lycoris; Cyrus leans lovingly
> over hard-hearted Pholoe, but sooner will roe-deer
>   mate with Apulian wolves
> than Pholoe soil herself with a foul adulterer.
> Such is the decree of Venus, who decides in cruel jest
> to join unequal minds and bodies
>   under her yoke of bronze.
> I myself once, when a better love was offered me,
> was shackled in the delicious fetters of Myrtale,
> a freedwoman wilder than the Adriatic sea
>   scooping out the bays of Calabria.
>
>   (trans. David West)

Superficially this is an intimate tête-à-tête between the older Horace, with his mature, hard-earned worldly wisdom, and the young (though not so young as he was) Tibullus. Tibullus, Horace suggests, should gain perspective on the nature of love, and plump for comfort (Myrtale) over passion (Glycera). The poem manages vividly to characterize both the younger and the maturer man in just four short stanzas. But a contemporary reader would recognize another level to the poem again. What they would appreciate is that behind the naturalism of the encounter between the two men lies a statement of literary affiliations. Horace here expresses the characteristic world-view of Alkaios' lyric (love is a trivial diversion, nothing more), and Tibullus embodies the contrasting elegiac view of love as an all-consuming passion. Horace's readers, besides anything else, would enjoy the literary game of the lyric persona and the elegiac persona being thrown together. In other words, Horace has grafted on to the archaic atmosphere of lyric a Callimachean compulsion to play with his readers' knowledge and expectations of literary genre.

In the final poem of book 3 Horace predicts the eternal fame of his poetry:

> I shall not wholly die. A great part of me
> will escape Libitina. My fame will grow,
> ever-renewed in time to come, as long as
> the priest climbs the Capitol with the silent Virgin.
> I shall be spoken of where fierce Aufidus thunders
> and where Daunus, poor in water,
> rules the country people. From humble beginnings
> I was able to be the first to bring the Aeolian song
> to Italian measures.
>
> (3. 30. 6–14, trans. David West)

There is some evidence that the *Odes* were initially not quite the success Horace had hoped, but in the long term their success has been astonishing, far outlasting the collapse of the Roman Empire. Horace's persona in the *Odes* has shown a remarkable capacity to appeal to readers of all periods and nationalities as one of their own. In Victorian Britain this combination of archaic Greek and first-century Roman was felt to be a prototype English gentleman. As a consequence the most famous modern reader of Horace was a hostile one. We have already seen Latin poetry informing and enriching responses to the First World War in Pound's *Homage to Sextus Propertius*. When Wilfred Owen attacked the romantic imperialism fed to schoolboys it was the English gentleman Horace he had read at school (and learnt so much from poetically) who came to mind. He is describing the victim of a gas attack:

> If you could hear, at every jolt, the blood
> Come gargling from the froth-corrupted lungs,
> Obscene as cancer, bitter as the cud
> of vile, incurable sores on innocent tongues,—
> My friend, you would not tell with such high zest
> To children ardent for some desperate glory,
> The old Lie: Dulce et decorum est
> Pro patria mori.

The Roman classic

With Virgil's twelve-book epic, the *Aeneid*, the literary efflorescence which coincided with the establishment of the Augustan regime, and both shaped and was shaped by these new political circumstances, reached its climax. It is a staggeringly ambitious work. Its first words are so familiar that it is hard to appreciate how audacious they would have seemed to a contemporary reader. *Arma virumque cano*, 'Arms and the man I sing', encapsulates in three words the two poems which were simultaneously Virgil's models and rivals in his writing of the *Aeneid*: the martial *Iliad* ('Arms') and the *Odyssey*, which began, 'Tell me of the *man*, Muse . . .'. The brevity of Virgil's evocation of his great epic predecessor dramatizes his absolute, confident control of the highest genre it was possible to aspire to, and implies an astonishing lack of anxiety about the task of rivalling Homer which he had set himself. Homer was much more than a poet. Greek culture rated him as the greatest poet there had ever been and could ever be, but, more, Homer was where all the wealth of Greek culture started, the source of all subsequent literary and intellectual culture—as a Hellenistic poet calls him, 'the ageless mouthpiece of the entire universe'.

Virgil never completed the *Aeneid*. He died in 19 BCE, before he had carried out the final revision: tradition relates that on his death-bed he demanded to be given the manuscript so that he could burn it, but no one would give it to him. Even before its release this was a work which generated a palpable excitement in the public. Propertius' remark that 'something greater than the *Iliad* is coming to birth' (2. 34. 66) has been interpreted by some as not entirely unequivocal. But there is no doubting Augustus' excitement, recorded in an ancient biography of Virgil: 'When Augustus was away on his Spanish campaign, he used to write insisting with pleas and even jocular threats that he be sent—to use his own words—"just the preliminary sketch or just a chunk of the *Aeneid*".' The enormity of the task was such that Virgil despaired of being able to achieve it; but the same impulse which prompted Virgil to burn it made Augustus desperate to see it, and the whole of Rome agog to read it. The *Aeneid* turned heads.

The *Aeneid* is the story of Aeneas (in Greek, Aineias), the son of the goddess Venus and ancestor of the Roman race who fled from Troy at its sacking by the Greeks and travelled with his followers to Italy, encountering great hardship on the way, and fighting a brutal war once they had arrived to secure their settlement. It is both a national epic and a poem honouring Augustus. Augustus is not directly referred to in the *Aeneid* particularly often, but he is a constant presence in it. Contemporary events are addressed *obliquely*, and this approach brings some advantages for Virgil. On the one hand tackling contemporary events through ancient myth softens the impact of the contemporary message: for all its political content, the *Aeneid* is always a compelling story, a 'self-sufficient' narrative which tells a coherent story. In addition the figure of Aeneas introduces a useful ambiguity as to the focus of the poem. Aeneas was the national ancestor of Rome: Lucretius' opening invocation of Venus, 'Mother of the sons of Aeneas' (cf. pp. 61–2), refers to the citizens of Rome in their entirety. But he was also, more specifically, the ancestor of the family of the Julii to which, through his adoption by Julius Caesar, Augustus had been

VIRGILIAN VIRTUE. This mid-first-century wall-painting from Pompeii is closely inspired by a passage towards the end of the Aeneid *(12. 383–416). While the doctor attempts to heal Aeneas' wound his mother Venus descends with a healing herb.*

admitted. We are never quite clear in this poem whether Aeneas is a proto-Roman or a proto-Augustus, and this tends to blur the distinction between 'Roman' and 'Augustan'. Augustus of course wanted the two categories to be indistinguishable, and wanted his personal success to be identified with the interests of Rome.

But if the *Aeneid* is a nationalistic poem, it is never a simple national anthem. Though it certainly did aim to celebrate the city of Rome and, more narrowly, to bolster the political position of its patron, Augustus—an aim it shares with more straightforwardly eulogistic works such as the *Panegyric of Messalla* (cf. pp. 98–100)—the *Aeneid* is in every respect a more subtle piece of work. Virgil recognized as well as Horace the devastating effect recent history had had upon the educated upper classes of Rome, his core audience. This was a section of society demoralized by decades of civil war. The twenty years between 49, when Julius Caesar crossed the Rubicon, and 29, when Augustus returned to Rome after his defeat of Mark Antony, seemed to represent to the Roman aristocracy the breakdown of their entire moral and cultural order. The later historian Tacitus talks of 'twenty years of unrelenting discord, no morality, no law'. Instances like Plancus' 'murder' of his brother became emblematic of a conflict which tore the tight Roman ruling class apart and set it against itself, friend against friend, father against son, brother against brother. No one was free of responsibility, but Augustus was particularly guilty, at the forefront of some of the most callous actions of the period.

The remarkable thing about this poem, a product of the patronage of the Augustan regime, is that it engages without embarrassment with the intense anxieties its audience felt about the civil wars and the regime which had emerged from it. Repeatedly the reader is confronted with, and emotionally drawn into, conflicts deeply reminiscent of the Roman civil wars. To a contemporary reader it will have been a deeply gruelling experience.

This *controversial* quality is evident right from the start. In an eleven-line introduction Virgil summarizes the plot of the poem and, in a conventional epic device, asks the Muse to explain the sufferings which the gods had inflicted upon Aeneas:

> I sing of arms and the man who first from the land of Troy,
> an exile by destiny, came to Italy and the Lavinian
> shores, a man much tossed on land and deep
> by the powers above, because of the unforgetting anger of fierce Juno.
> Great too was his suffering in war until he could found a city
> and carry his gods into Latium, whence rose the Latin race,
> the Alban fathers and the high walls of Rome.
> Tell me, Muse, the reasons, how he abused her divinity,

from what resentment the queen of heaven drove
a man renowned for piety to suffer so much calamity
and experience such toils. Are the gods capable of such anger?

The Muse replies to this question:

There was an ancient city . . .

In the light of the first eleven lines there will have been little doubt in the minds of Virgil's readers as to the city to which the Muse is referring. The *Aeneid* is about the destruction of one city, Troy, and Aeneas' escape from it to found another city which will replace it, Rome. The *only* place this 'ancient city' can be is Troy. But the Muse continues:

. . . occupied by colonists from Tyre,
Carthage, opposite Italy and the Tiber's distant
mouths

Carthage. If only we could be the first readers of this text, in 19 BCE, the intrusion of this name, of all names, into a poem which has just advertised itself as the national poem of Rome would have astonished us. Carthage was 'opposite Italy' in more than just the geographical sense. It was Rome's great enemy in the fight to dominate the Mediterranean basin, a fight quite literally to the death (cf. pp. 6–7). Neither city had felt secure whilst the other stood. The moment in 211 BCE when the great Carthaginian general Hannibal rode right up to the walls of Rome and, according to tradition, cast a spear into the city itself loomed large in Roman folklore. A striking moment in book 9 of the *Aeneid* has Turnus, Aeneas' great enemy in the second half of the poem, mimic that action of Hannibal, riding up to the camp which the Trojans have established and hurling a spear over its walls. To Roman thinking the conflict with Carthage had been a matter of 'kill or be killed'. In 146 BCE Carthage was utterly destroyed by Scipio Aemilianus, and a curse laid on anybody who should attempt to rebuild it.

The rest of book 1 is set in Carthage, and it is not until the end of book 4 that we leave it. Aeneas is shipwrecked on the coast near Carthage, and takes refuge with the queen of the city, Dido, an exemplary ruler engaged in founding a city, exactly as Aeneas wanted to do (and exactly as Augustus was claiming to have done, by bringing the civil wars to an end, an achievement he styled as the refoundation of Rome). Naturally they fall in love. The first view of Carthage which Aeneas sees, a bustle of constructive activity, will have reminded Virgil's first readers of nothing more than Rome in the grip of the building programme instituted by Augustus, which 'found Rome brick and left it marble', in Augustus' own words. This Carthage *looks like* Rome:

Aeneas marvels at great buildings, where once were shanties,
Marvels at city gates and the din of the paved streets.
The Tyrians are busy at work there, some extending the walls,
Manhandling blocks of stone and building the citadel,
Others choosing a site for a house and trenching foundations:
Laws are being made, magistrates and a parliament elected:
Here they dig out a harbour basin; here they are laying
Foundations deep for a theatre, and hewing from stone immense
Columns to grace one day a tall proscenium.

(ll. 421–9, trans. C. Day-Lewis)

Yet ultimately Dido will die. Book 4 recounts the love-affair between Dido and Aeneas, which is abruptly terminated when Aeneas is ordered by the gods to stop neglecting his destiny—which is to found Rome—and leave. His departure provokes Dido's suicide, which she carries out with Aeneas' own sword.

What is most striking in all this is the *sympathy* which Virgil elicits for Dido and the city she represents, despite the status of Carthage as Rome's ultimate *bête noire*. Carthage in the *Aeneid* is not the demonized 'other' of Roman folklore, but a fully humanized and attractive community. There will be many more victims of Aeneas' mission after Dido, right up to the brutal slaying of Turnus which concludes the poem. But the same always applies: we are never allowed to disregard these victims.

In fact Virgil insists that we identify with them. In books 2 and 3 Virgil constructs an 'internal audience' within the poem. Dido and her court listen to Aeneas' account of the fall of Troy and his travels as far as Carthage. Virgil repeatedly plays on the fact that in the course of two long books we are bound to forget who is narrating: Aeneas' narrative to the Carthaginians inevitably becomes confused with Virgil's narrative (the overarching 'voice' of the whole poem) to us. It is with some shock that at the end of book 3 we are reminded that we have been reading Aeneas' account to Dido, not Virgil's account to us, and have, in a sense, been occupying Dido's space, listening along with her and her courtiers to Aeneas' narration. An anecdote about the pre-performance of the *Aeneid* can focus this idea. Shortly before his death Virgil is said to have recited three books to Augustus and his close family, 2, 4, and 6. (The story goes that Augustus' sister Octavia was so moved by the lament for her son Marcellus towards the end of book 6 that 'she fainted and was revived with difficulty'.) Augustus, emperor of Rome, seated, listening to book 2 (recited by Virgil) corresponds to Dido, queen of Carthage, seated, listening to book 2 (recited by Aeneas).

But, for all this, Aeneas' mission to found Rome will bring about Dido's death. And when Virgil compares the aftermath of her suicide to the sacking of a city it is clear that Dido's death prefigures the historical destruction of Carthage by Rome in 146:

> She had spoken; and with these words, her attendants saw her falling
> Upon the sword, they could see the blood spouting up over
> The blade, and her hands spattered. Their screams rang to the roofs of
> The palace; then rumour ran amok through the shocked city.
> All was weeping and wailing, the streets were filled with a keening
> Of women, the air resounded with terrible lamentations.
> It was as if Carthage or ancient Tyre should be falling,
> With enemy troops breaking into the town and a conflagration
> Furiously sweeping over the abodes of men and of gods.
>
> (4. 663–71, trans. C. Day-Lewis)

Now as we have seen, the defeat of Carthaginians, and the destruction of their city, was in general to Roman thinking an unquestionably good thing, a prerequisite of their own survival: *delenda est Carthago*, 'Carthage must be destroyed', was the mantra of one of the most respected figures of the Roman past, Cato the Censor (cf. pp. 44–6). When Virgil makes us *sympathize* with the arch enemy, recognize her humanity, he is making of the Rome/Carthage conflict something in which his readers would recognize the experience of the recent civil wars, wars where demonization of the enemy was impossible because the enemy was known to you, even *related* to you. The destruction of Carthage was *callous*, Virgil is suggesting, but it was also *necessary* if Rome was to survive and prosper, and *the same goes for the civil war*. Virgil is thus not shy of confronting the civil wars. On the contrary, his poignant portrayal of Dido *replicates* the traumatic emotions of civil war. The contemporary Roman reader of the *Aeneid* was being trained, emotionally as well as intellectually, to accept the brutality and loss of civil war as a prerequisite of future success.

Or at any rate that is one way of reading the poem, one likely (I think) to have been a dominant reading in Virgil's core audience. But the *Aeneid* is a controversial text. What makes it so, above all, is the intricacy of its poetry. In undertaking the *Aeneid* Virgil had abandoned the imperative not to write Grand Epic (which was how Roman poets interpreted the precepts of Kallimachos, whether or not this was actually what he meant), but in his stylistics he remains loyal to the allusiveness and refinement of his New Poet mentors. Octavia's swoon, for example, is more explicable when we appreciate that the lament for Marcellus spoken by Aeneas' father Anchises in the underworld impersonates, with great subtlety, the address delivered by Augustus at Marcellus' real funeral in 23 BCE:

Fate shall allow the earth one glimpse of this young man—
One glimpse, no more. Too puissant had been Rome's stock, ye gods,
In your sight, had such gifts been granted it to keep.

(6. 869–71, trans. C. Day-Lewis)

The *Aeneid* is meticulous in detail, but huge in scope. Epic is the grandest of all genres, both in style and theme. This epic manages to encompass the whole of Roman history, from the fall of Troy to the rise of Augustus—not only the life of Aeneas, but all that followed. In book 8, for example, we visit the site of Rome before Rome was built, a village of simple cottages, but then at the end of the book enjoy a vision of contemporary Rome, engraved on a great shield made for Aeneas by the god Vulcan. Similarly, the war between Trojans and Italians which occupies the second half of the poem in a sense prefigures every war the Romans ever fought, but in particular the Punic Wars against Carthage and the recent civil wars—the war, between two peoples who will subsequently make up the population of Rome, is a civil war *avant la lettre*. The poem is also 'huge' in spatial terms. In its course we travel from the east of the Empire all the way to the vicinity of Rome (via Carthage), and are witness at all times to the responses of the great powers of Virgil's world, the gods, to the events going on on earth. In book 6 we even follow Aeneas down to the underworld to visit his father and hear, with Aeneas, about Rome's great future. The whole world, Virgil implies, is implicated in the struggle to found the Roman Empire, an event which (in turn) will shape the whole of history.

At the same time Virgil sets out to fulfil the expectation that epic, the first genre of them all, should encompass all other forms of literature. In Dido alone we hear echoes of Apollonios' Medea, the heroes and heroines of tragedy, Berenike, the queen of Egypt complimented by Kallimachos (and later Catullus), the Kleopatra of Augustan propaganda, and Carthaginians from Roman folklore and historiography. This impression of literary scope and ambition matches and reinforces the geographical and historical nationalisms which the poem communicates. Virgil's 'conquest' of the universal epic voice of Homer— the origin and essence of Greek literary culture—is closely analogous to Roman military dominion over the world. The Roman readers of the *Aeneid* experienced, besides everything else, an entire world of literary possibilities in Roman dress. It is with the *Aeneid* that Latin literature seemed to Romans once and for all to have come into its own.

Like Lucretius' *De rerum natura*, then, the *Aeneid* provides its readers with a vision of a totality, not the Epicurean universe of atoms and void but a world dominated now and forever by Rome. Emblematic of the Romanness of this text is the scene which unfolds at the poem's conclusion. All the conflict of the poem comes down to a duel to the death between Aeneas and Turnus for the hand of the princess Lavinia and the sovereignty of Latium. As the two mighty warriors battle it out, no longer mere mortals but massive heroes who seem to embody the powers of the universe, Romans would have recognized a cosmic struggle for global control, but one being fought out in a characteristically Roman context. The struggle between the two champions would have reminded contemporaries strongly of the gladiatorial combats which Romans held to celebrate ceremonial occasions. The Roman readership was at this point the audience in a Roman amphitheatre watching Roman destiny unfold (12. 919–29). (Note once again that the 'internal' audience whose viewpoint the reader is asked to share are the Italian supporters of Turnus . . .)

> So Turnus faltered: the other brandished his fateful spear,
> And watching out for an opening, hurled it with all his might
> From a distance. The noise it made was louder than that of any
> Great stone projected by siege artillery, louder than
> A meteorite's explosion. The spear flew on its sinister
> Mission of death like a black tornado, and piercing the edge of
> The seven-fold shield, laid open the corselet of Turnus, low down.
> Right through his thigh it ripped, with a hideous sound. The impact
> Brought giant Turnus down on bent knee to the earth.
> The Italians sprang to their feet, crying out: the hills all round
> Bayed back their howl of dismay, far and wide the deep woods echoed it.
> (12. 919–29, trans. C. Day-Lewis)

Virgil himself compared his laborious and painstaking technique of composition to a mother-bear slowly licking her cubs into shape. Every one of the 10,000 lines is crafted with meticulous care. But we have seen before that the Callimachean style *emancipates* the readership, gives it the freedom to pursue an allusion as far as they choose. A generation later Ovid was able to exploit meanings of *arma virumque* which Virgil certainly did not have in mind in order to make a subversive joke at Virgil's (and Augustus') expense. At *Tristia* 2. 533–6, addressing Augustus and ostensibly attempting to justify the erotic content of his poetry, Ovid points to its presence even in Virgil's poem:

> Yet the blessed author of your great *Aeneid*
> Landed 'Arms and the man' in Dido's bed,
> Love linked in bonds illicit; in the whole long
> Poem there's really nothing that's more read.
> (trans. A. D. Melville)

The joke is that both the word for 'arms', *arma*, and 'man', *vir*, could carry a sexual meaning. A contemporary would be liable to translate the second line as 'brought his tackle and his manhood to Dido's bed'. Could anybody who had read the *Tristia* subsequently read the opening of the *Aeneid* without a snigger? The paradox of the *Aeneid* is that it is a text which appears to have a very specific message to convey, but a style that militates against unequivocal communication.

The history of the reception of the *Aeneid* by its readers after its *post-mortem* publication is the history of Western artistic culture, which, along with Ovid's *Metamorphoses*, it dominates. But the text which aspired to survive as long as 'the house of Aeneas dwells by the immovable rock of the Capitol and the father of the Romans keeps his Empire' (9. 448–9), and yet was also so closely tied to its contemporary context, had to cope with dramatic changes in the ways its readers interpreted it in the subsequent two thousand years. Ovid informs us, for example, that at the end of Augustus' reign 'in the whole long | Poem there's really nothing that's more read' than the story of Dido and Aeneas. Book 4 has continued to be far the most popular portion of the poem, often read, and imitated (in all artistic media) in isolation from the rest of the whole. But such segmentation undermines the carefully constructed argument of the poem. Taken on its own, without the explanatory framework of the rest of the *Aeneid*, book 4 can be treated as a simple love story, and a love story, what's more, in which Aeneas can be dismissed as a cad for abandoning Dido, as in Henry Purcell's opera *Dido and Aeneas* (1689).

The *Aeneid* was an instant classic, and from its publication onwards suffered the classic's fate of an audience largely consisting of students at school, for many centuries and throughout the Empire (and for many centuries after the fall of that Empire). This expanded its audience beyond the relatively narrow circle of sophisticates for whom it was primarily designed, but it also radically altered its reception. In school the poem was studied for the exercise it could provide in grammar rather than its literary qualities: at Pompeii disaffected youth often proceeded to scribble what they had learnt on the walls.

As an example of how its role in education affected its reception we need only to consider the fate of Ennius (cf. pp. 10–13). Virgil's *Aeneid* replaced Ennius' *Annals* as the national epic of Rome—*and* as the dominant school text. The adoption of the *Aeneid* by schools largely explains the failure of Ennius' epic to survive antiquity intact. But of course Virgil's original audience *did* have Ennius. For them, after all, it was still the national epic. Naturally enough, Virgil regularly alludes to the *Annals*. Some allusions we can still recognize. At 2. 268–97, for example, the dead Hector appears to Aeneas and urges him to leave Troy and found a new city elsewhere. We are still able to see that Virgil is alluding to a passage near the beginning of the *Annals* where Ennius described how Homer had appeared to him in a dream and told him that he, Homer, had been reincarnated in Ennius. Hector is a Homeric character. When Hector

THE AENEID IN SOMERSET. *Virgil's* Aeneid *is the one work of Latin literature which is found reflected in art throughout the Roman Empire. This is even evidenced by several mosaics from remote Britain. This one, found at Low Ham in Somerset, shows scenes from the story of Dido and Aeneas in book 4.*

hands the future of the Trojans to Aeneas we can recognize, with the help of Virgil's allusion to Ennius, a further suggestion of Virgil's relationship with his epic predecessors: Hector handing the future to Aeneas is Homer handing on the epic tradition to Virgil. We can recognize it *because* we happen to have some knowledge about this point of Ennius' poem. But most allusions to Ennius we are just missing, and the paradox of this is that it is a direct consequence of Virgil's unparalleled success in finding an audience.

But if the *Aeneid* inevitably suffered 'dumbing down' as its audience expanded, this was a circumstance which the poet had arguably catered for.

The poem can be read on a number of levels. *Paradise Lost* is one of the greatest poems in the English language largely because John Milton was one of the most acute readers of the *Aeneid* there has ever been. But just a few years after the publication of Milton's epic it was the sheer visual exuberance of Virgil's narrative which inspired Claude Lorrain to paint *Aeneas Hunting in Libya*. He had been reading an Italian translation of the *Aeneid*. We know this because a preliminary drawing of the scene is marked 'Libro di Virgilio folio 10', 'Virgil's book page 10'.

5 | Coming to terms with the Empire: Poetry of the later Augustan and Tiberian period

PHILIP HARDIE

Authorities poetical and political

'Virgil I only saw' (Ovid, *Tristia* 4. 10. 51, quoted on p. 101). Ovid's rueful comment in his verse autobiography, largely an account of his own place in the literary circles of Augustan Rome, is emblematic of a wider rupture between the works of what might be called the heroic age of Augustan literature and the poetry produced from the second decade onwards of Augustus' rule. We are not of course dealing with any absolute divide: many of the poets active in the 40s to 20s BCE continued to produce after the death of Virgil in 19 BCE, chief among them Propertius and Horace; and Ovid himself was very probably reciting his earliest love elegies in the mid-20s. Nevertheless both poets and public were quick to recognize that after the output of the 30s and 20s Rome could now boast of a canon of poetry, in the fields above all of epic, didactic, lyric, pastoral, and elegy, that need not fear comparison with the classics of Greek literature; and in the case of satire, Horace had brought to classical perfection a genre that Quintilian, the academic rhetorician of the late first century CE, could claim was all Roman. Already by the mid-20s Propertius proclaimed, perhaps not entirely respectfully, that with the slow gestation of the *Aeneid* 'something greater than the *Iliad* is coming to birth' (2. 34. 66). After 19 BCE the Roman public felt confident that they could point to a native work that was the equal of Homer, and to have equalled Homer was to have equalled the best and greatest that Greece had produced.

The consequence is a shift in the relationship of later Augustan poetic texts to their models. Latin poets continue to engage at all levels with Greek models, but they now come to measure themselves in the first instance against the Latin classics, and above all the *Aeneid*—and in so doing start a habit that will last for the rest of ancient Latin poetry, and indeed for much of post-antique poetry in the classical tradition (see pp. 115–16). Virgil in the *Aeneid* is deeply

SACRIFICIOQVE · PERFECTO · PVER) (VII · QVIBVS · DENVNTIATVM · ERAT · PATRIMI · ET · MATRIMI · ET · PVELLAE · TOTIDEM
CARMEN · CECINERVNT · EO) (QVE·MODO·IN·CAPITOLIO
CARMEN · COMPOSVIT · Q · HOR) (IVS · FLACCVS ·
XV · VIR · ADFVERVNT · IMP · CA\ \AR · M · AGRIPPA · Q · LEPIDVS · POTITVS · MESSALLA · C · STOLO · C · SCAEVOLA · C · SOSIVS ·
C · NORBANVS · M · COCCEIVS · M · LOLLIVS · C · SENTIVS · M · STRIGO · L · ARRVNTIVS · C · ASINIVS · M · MARCELLVS · D · LAELIVS
Q · TVBERO · C · REBILVS · M\ \ALLA · MESSALLINVS
LVDIS·SCAENICIS·DIMISSIS·H\ \IVXTA·EVM·LOCVM·VBI · SACRIFICIVM·ERAT·FACTVM · SVPERIORIBVS · NOCTIBVS · ET
THEATRVM·POSITVM·ET·SC\ \NA·METAE·POSITAE·QVADRIGAEQ · SVNT · MISSAE · ET · DESVLTORES · MISIT · POTITVS · MESSALLA
EDICTVMQVE·PROPOSITVM \EST·IN·HAEC·VERBA   XV · VIR · S · F · D I C
LVDOS · QVOS · HONORARIOS) (HERVM · VII · ADIECIMVS·LVDIS·SOLLEMNIBVS·COMMITTIMVS·NONIS IVN LATINOS·IN · THEATRO
LIGNEO·QVOD·EST·AD·TIBERI) (·II·GRAECOS·THYMELICOS·IN THEATRO POMPEI·II·III·GRAECOS·ASTI   N · THEA
IN · CIRCO · FLAMINIO · H · I \

HORACE AS POET LAUREATE. Augustus set up an inscription recording all the activities at the great games he organized in 17 BCE to mark the end of an alleged cycle of 110 years. In the third line of this passage can be seen CARMEN.COMPOSVIT.Q.HOR[AT]IVS.FLACCVS *'Q. Horatius Flaccus composed the hymn' (now known as the* Carmen Saeculare—see p. 410).

concerned, it is true, to define his relationship to his *Latin* epic predecessor, Ennius, but the chief object of his imitative emulation is always Homer. Ovid, by contrast, for all that he is in many respects a continuator of the graecizing, neoteric, 'Alexandrian' school of poets (see pp. 65–8), is obsessed above all with the presence of Virgil. Not surprisingly his *Metamorphoses*, a long hexameter narrative poem, is a sustained challenge to Virgil's epic; but the first word of Ovid's first and least epic work, the *Amores*, is the same as the first word of the *Aeneid*, *arma* ('arms', 'warfare'); this is elegy that sets out by serving notice to the reader that it is love poetry *after Virgil*. The 'anxiety of influence' is displaced from the great Greek models to the Latin poems that imitate and successfully rival those models. The poetry of this period is marked by a sense of coming later than, of being a supplement to, the works of the early Augustan period (in the cases of some poets, notably Horace, of supplementing their *own* earlier poetry); the poets address themselves to a public that they know will measure them against these earlier achievements.

The poetry of this time is characterized also by its relationship to that other kind of authority, the political authority of the emperor. The poetry of the triumviral and early Augustan periods rarely loses sight of the momentous political and military developments of the 40s, 30s, and 20s, and is itself a vital part of the turbulent and experimental process out of which emerged the fully fledged principate. By the late 20s, when the dust had settled and the clear outlines of the new system had emerged, poets and their publics turn from an interest in the processes of constructing and defining a post-civil war order to the issues of how to live with the finished product. This period sees the emergence of a 'court poetry', particularly in the fourth book of Horace's *Odes* and in various of Ovid's works, that merges Roman ways of praising great men with

Alexandrian models for addressing the Hellenistic king. Horace's *Epistles* explore the etiquette of approaching and talking to the ruler; Ovid in his later works forges ways of coping with the less pleasurable consequences of an absolute autocracy and with a growing censorship, and in so doing helps to create the language used by later first-century CE analysts and critics of the imperial regime.

The poet confronts his audiences: Horace *Epistles* 1

> My Muse's first and final theme, Maecenas,
> I've been on show enough, obtained my discharge,
> yet you try to squeeze me back into those old games.
> I'm not the same age or the same man. The fighter [Veianius]
> has hung up his arms and is lying low in the country:
> no more begging the public for his life.
> A voice keeps ringing now in my unclogged ears:
> 'Be sensible: quick, loose the ageing horse,
> or they'll laugh when his flanks heave and he falls at the finish.'
> So now I lay down verse and all those games;
> my whole concern is to ask what is right and fitting.
>
> (*Epistles* 1. 1. 1–11, trans. Colin Macleod)

Horace's first book of *Epistles* was probably presented to the public in 20 or 19 BCE, and self-consciously defines itself by reference to the publication in 23 BCE of *Odes* 1–3, in terms both of Horace's previous role as author of lyric poetry, and of the public's reception of the *Odes*. Claiming at the age of 44 that his youth is now behind him, the poet now turns to the serious business of philosophical self-improvement, and claims (in hexameters, ironically) that he is no longer even writing poetry.

In the penultimate epistle (1. 19), also addressed to Maecenas, Horace lets slip that the reason for turning from lyric to philosophical verse may be not so much a self-generated desire for wisdom as disgust at the response to the publication of the *Odes*:

> If you want to know why ungrateful readers love
> my things at home, but disparage them elsewhere:
> I do not chase the fickle public's votes
> with costly dinners and presents of old clothing.
> I do not care to hear 'distinguished writers'
> (and get my own back) at the critics' hustings.
> There's the rub. I say, 'Light verse recited
> in close-packed theatres would gain too much weight,'

and one replies, 'Joker! You keep your stuff
for the highest ears; you dote on your image,
sure you're the sole source of poetic honey.'
(*Epistles* 1. 19. 35–45, trans. Colin Macleod)

The public's hostility is presented as the hypocritical expression of envy, conventionally the enemy of the poet's fame, and the poet's reaction is framed as yet another instance of the Callimachean scornful rejection of the undiscriminating crowd. But some readers have sensed here a genuine disappointment on Horace's part to a less than enthusiastic welcome to the *Odes*, poems that may genuinely have proved too difficult, too new, for the Roman reading public at large—an ancient example of the unrecognized genius, perhaps?

Be that as it may, in *Epistles* 1 the solipsistic Horace, who in the allusion at 1. 1. 7–9 (quoted above) to the inner voice of Socrates envisages the extreme case of a philosophical dialogue with *himself*, betrays a sustained concern with audiences and with the reception of his writings. In particular he screws up to breaking point a tension, long present in ancient literature, between poetry addressed to a select individual or group of individuals personally known to the author, and poetry intended for a generalized readership both during and after the poet's lifetime (cf. pp. 68–70, 102). Horace achieves this by choosing for his new book the form of the verse epistle. For this he had precedent in isolated letters in verse by Lucilius and Catullus, but Horace seems first to have put together a whole collection of verse epistles, to be followed by Ovid in the *Heroides* (see pp. 139–40 below). Each epistle presents itself as a written communication typically addressed to a more or less close friend, to whom Horace can bare his inmost concerns; and the *Epistles* are an important document in the history of autobiographical writing as well as of epistolary fictions. Some of the poems purport to have an immediate and ephemeral purpose, for example to invite a noble friend to dinner, or to recommend a younger acquaintance to Tiberius; but whether or not these texts ever really had this immediate communicative function at discrete moments in the poet's life, the reader who picks up this scroll of twenty carefully arranged epistles is never in doubt that they aim at a readership beyond the named addressees.

In the first instance they are all intended for the eyes of Maecenas, who is effectively established as dedicatee of the whole book by the addresses to him in the first and penultimate epistles, significantly those with least pretence to epistolary form. That pretence is completely unmasked in the last poem, an address by the author not to a human friend, but to the book of epistles itself, personified as a vain slave-boy eager to run away from his master and prostitute himself to the world at large:

I see, book, you're eager for change, for openings
in town—to sell your charms, all smooth and glossy.
You loathe a chaste reserve; 'I'm not displayed
enough!,' you moan, and clamour for publicity.
With *your* upbringing!—but follow your urge to a come-down.
Once out, you can never return. 'What made me do it?'
you'll say when you're rejected; yet you know
you're put on the shelf when your sated lover flags.
Well, if disgust does not impair my forecast,
you will be prized at Rome till your freshness leaves you;
but when everyone has pawed at you and soiled you,
you'll end up dumbly feeding mindless vermin,
or packed off to an exile in the colonies.
And there's worse to come: your old age lisping sentences
with a classful of beginners at street-corners.

(*Epistles* 1. 20. 1–18, trans. Colin Macleod)

A heavy dose of Horatian irony barely conceals the poet's own desire for an international and posthumous audience, for a return in fact to the amphitheatre from which the retired gladiator Veianius escapes in the opening lines of the book (quoted above). The reference to booksellers in the second line of the passage acknowledges the importance for the poet of circulation through a by now well-established book trade, a form of textual distribution diametrically opposed to the delivery of a letter to a friend by personal courier. The transient occasionality of the letter is superseded by the canonization of the book in the syllabus of the grammar-school teacher, fulfilling the basic educational function of literary texts in antiquity, but one far removed from the more advanced philosophical pedagogy that Horace proposes as the purpose of the book in the first epistle.

No doubt part of the attraction of *Epistles* 1 for a Roman audience was its poise between a social and intellectual exclusivity and a wider accessibility: eavesdropping, particularly on those close to the centre of power, is irresistible. This balancing act is manifested in other ways. Despite the opening rejection of poetry, *Epistles* 1 mounts a sustained exploration of the philosophical uses of poetry, and is itself an example of the poetic popularization of ethical-philosophical themes. Philosophical didactic, with its individualized addressee, is one of the models, but the second epistle draws on the prevalent ancient belief that other poetry, in particular the great Homer, could yield philosophical lessons through moralizing or allegorizing readings. These connections between poetry and philosophy are largely alien for a modern audience, but were still very much alive in the eighteenth century, for example in the poetry of Alexander Pope, whose adaptations of selected Horatian epistles are among his most complex poetry.

Philosophical ethics in antiquity extended to the discussion of friendship and of social intercourse, topics also of ancient poetry, which in many of its manifestations was a medium for personal relationships. *Epistles* 1 may be read almost as a handbook of social etiquette, a verse parallel to Cicero's *On Duties*, another favourite text of the eighteenth-century gentleman (cf. Ch. 10), in which Horace displays his tact and discrimination in adapting his manner to the different statuses and ages of his addressees. Two of the epistles give advice to younger men on how to behave towards great men within the client-patron system at Rome. The greatest man at Rome of course was Augustus, whose presence radically transformed the whole nature of the power structures that determined social interaction among the upper classes. None of *Epistles* 1 are in fact addressed directly to the emperor; the closest that Horace comes to the imperial presence is in a 'letter' (1. 13) addressed to the doltish courier entrusted with the task of bearing to Augustus some poems of Horace (usually supposed to be *Odes* 1–3), and advising him on how best to make an entrance. This is typical of the displacements and evasions that only serve to reveal Horace's interest in establishing viable relationships with the great, and his corresponding desire to preserve a space of personal freedom, one of the book's obsessive themes, all with Augustus as their invisible or partly visible centre. Although the book is dedicated to Maecenas, that great patron of the triumviral and early Augustan period was in fact in eclipse by the time that Horace wrote *Epistles* 1 (and is not the dedicatee of any later Augustan poetry book). In *Epistles* 1. 19 Horace says that his opponents sneer at him that 'you keep your writings for the ears of Jupiter', i.e. of Augustus. By telling a story against himself Horace deflects envy from what he no doubt hoped for, that Augustus would be one of his readers, his ideal reader perhaps.

The attention of the emperor might not be an unmixed blessing. In the *Satires* Horace snobbishly describes the nuisance of being buttonholed by outsiders curious about life in the circle of Maecenas and Augustus. But Augustus might also be perceived as an inquisitive busybody, a Big Brother, by poets with their own lives to lead and their own poetic axes to grind. The presence of the emperor as at least a potential reader of every text written in Rome, the all-seeing eavesdropper, changed the way in which writers thought about their audiences. For understandable reasons this concern will come to be an obsession with Ovid.

Horace's second book of *Epistles* consists of just two very long poems, primarily on literary matters, thus extending what had emerged as a major theme in book one, despite its opening gesture of rejecting poetry. The first, now addressed to Augustus himself, is a complex account of the cultural and literary history of Rome, and of the poet's relationship to his community and to the ruler; beneath the courtly surface we catch Horace measuring his own authority with that of the emperor. The conversational tone and indirection of these works are continued in the *Ars poetica*, in form another letter in hexameters, to the Pisones. As the one surviving Latin treatise on poetics, it has had an immense influence on the later European tradition, and is the source of some well-known tags, such as *ut pictura poesis* ('as a painting, so is a poem'), on which great critical edifices have been built, despite the fact that as a didactic poem it consciously strives against systematic clarity of the kind that Lucretius had set as his goal.

Public and private audiences: Horace *Odes* 4 and *Carmen Saeculare,* Propertius 4, Tibullus 2

> Offspring of the good gods and best guardian
> of the race of Romulus, too long have you been absent.
> You promised the sacred council of the Fathers
>   a swift return, so return.
>
> Give back your radiance, good leader, to your homeland.
> When your face shines like springtime
> on your people, the day passes more joyfully
>   and the sun is brighter.
>
> As a mother calls with vows and prayers and the taking
> of omens, upon her young son detained across
> the Carpathian sea by the jealous blasts of the South wind,
>   as he waits till the sailing year is over,
>
> far from the home he loves, and she never
> takes her eyes from the curve of the shore,
> so does your faithful homeland, stricken with longing,
>   look for its Caesar.

(*Odes* 4. 5. 1–16, trans. David West)

According to the ancient biographical tradition Augustus himself commanded Horace to write the fourth book of *Odes*. At best this will be an over-simplification of the more subtle relationship between the imperial patron and the poet, who after the death of Virgil had no rival, but it is true that the last book of odes contains a high proportion of poems praising the emperor and his stepsons, Tiberius and Drusus, the princes who represented the future of the imperial house. These poems are anything but crude and perfunctory command performances, but, in comparison with the more experimental essays in imperial panegyric in *Odes* 1–3, they conform more straightforwardly to the rhetorical schemata for praising a king or emperor as we know them from what remains of Hellenistic ruler panegyric and from the rhetorical handbooks of later antiquity (and would no doubt find them in the now lost prose panegyrics of the Augustan period). Poet and public have now become familiar with the vocabulary of praising the emperor.

If Horace had been disappointed by the reception of *Odes* 1–3, the fourth book both commemorates and may in part have been prompted by the glory that he had won as composer and impresario of a unique lyric performance, the *Secular Hymn* (*Carmen Saeculare*) that was sung by twin choruses of boys and girls at the Secular Games of 17 BCE, a long-planned ceremony by which Augustus sought to mark the beginning of a new age (in Latin *saeculum*; according to religious tradition such an age was supposed to begin every hundred, or hundred and ten, years), and in so doing to incorporate his own new regime within a divine historical rhythm. The *Secular Hymn* is unique in Horace's *œuvre* not least because here at last the Roman *uates*, 'bard', was able to actualize a direct link between written composition in the poet's study and ritual public performance in a way that seems to restore the original conditions of Greek choral lyric as written by an Alkman or a Pindar for ceremonial performance. Generically the *Secular Hymn* is a 'paean', a hymn to Apollo and Artemis, a Greek form used in the context of a Roman ritual. The Secular Games as a whole were an exercise on Augustus' part in the invention of tradition, in which Roman and Greek religious elements were inextricably intertwined. From this point of view the gap between Roman social and political 'reality' and the artifice of the Hellenizing poetry of Horace (and other Augustan poets) becomes insignificant: Augustus' combination of Greek and Roman in the ritual of the Secular Games is analogous to Horace's use of Pindaric, Greek, panegyrical forms to celebrate the victories of the Roman general in poems such as *Odes* 3. 4 or 4. 4.

As composer of the *Secular Hymn* Horace becomes a part of public Roman religion; in that role his name may still be read in the public inscription of the Acts of the Games, discovered in 1890 and now in the Museo Nazionale in Rome (*carmen composuit Q. Horatius Flaccus* 'the hymn was composed by Quintus Horatius Flaccus'—see illus. on p. 120). Horace 'inscribes' his own name (the only time that he declares his name in the odes) in his proud assertion of the future commemoration of the occasion of the *Secular Hymn* on the lips of a member of the choir of girls, a very direct example of the impact on an audience (in this case also a performer) of the poet as teacher:

In time to come when you are a Roman wife, you will say,
  'When the Secular Festival brought back its lights,
I performed the hymn which so pleased the gods,
  and was taught the music of the poet Horatius'.
                                        (*Odes* 4. 6. 41–4, trans. David West)

By its nature (composed for passing occasions, originally to be sung to the measures of the lyre) lyric is a genre bound up with time and an awareness of the passage of time, an awareness given added urgency in *Odes* 4 by Horace's complaints about his own ageing. In order to immobilize the effects of time he adopts two, contradictory, strategies that nevertheless both seek to ground the poet and his works in a context guaranteed durability by the Roman community at large under the leadership of Augustus. By the first strategy, continued from *Odes* 3. 30 ('I have completed a work more long-lasting than bronze . . . '), Horace attempts to convert his fleeting words into a fixed inscription or public monument, but of a kind superior to the perishable materials of real inscriptions or monuments. In *Odes* 4. 3 he hints at his transformation into a kind of living statue, pointed at by the fingers of passers-by. Poetry becomes a part of the new monumental landscape of Rome that Augustus was creating at the time. Virgil had already made brilliant use of the favourite Hellenistic device of ecphrasis (the verbal evocation of a visual work of art (cf. pp. 108–10)) in order to develop analogies between poetry and the visual iconography of Augustan Rome; the task of constructing a 'virtual Rome' in words was to be continued by Propertius and Ovid.

By the second strategy Horace ensures the survival of his poetry in its repeated oral performance and commemoration by successive generations of Romans, whose future continuity is guaranteed by the peace and prosperity brought by Augustus. In *Odes* 4. 6 the girl in the choir will speak of her role in the *Secular Hymn* when she is grown up and married, telling stories about her childhood to her own children, one imagines. At the very end of the book Horace goes so far as to merge his individual lyric voice in the recurrent communal celebration by nuclear Roman families of Roman history and of the Julian family, in a romantic fantasy of the recovery, through the benefits of Augustan rule, of a primitive *Gemeinschaft*:

and on ordinary days as on holy day,
among the gifts of cheerful Bacchus, let us first
  with our children and our wives
    offer due prayers to the gods

and sing a song to the Lydian pipe in praise
of leaders who have shown the virtues

of their fathers, in praise of Troy, Anchises,
and the offspring of life-giving Venus.
(*Odes* 4. 15. 25–32, trans. David West)

Horace alludes to the tradition that in early Rome the great deeds of the ancestors were sung at banquets (a kind of original folk-poetry that Macaulay tried to reconstruct in *The Lays of Ancient Rome*). In this kind of community the learned individual poet, always anxious about his relationship to society at large, becomes superfluous, withering away like political hierarchies in the perfected communist society.

In answer to the question of what prompted Horace to return to lyric poetry in *Odes* 4, the poet himself gives quite a different answer: not a nod from the emperor, not pride at becoming the poet laureate, but the renewed onslaught of the goddess of love:

> Back to war, Venus, after all
> these years? Spare, spare me, I beg you.
>   I'm not the man I was
> in good Cinara's reign. Cruel mother
>
>   of the sweet Cupids, stop
> driving a long-since hardened fifty-year-old
>   with your soft commands. Away with you!
> Go and answer the charming prayers of young men.
>   (*Odes* 4. 1. 1–8, trans. David West)

Like the earlier books, *Odes* 4 contains a mixture of personal (erotic and sympotic) and public (political and panegyrical) poems, a combination that may puzzle modern audiences. One may appeal to generic considerations: Horace is merely being faithful to his archaic Greek lyric models, which include the same range of personal and public subject-matters. But generic origin should not unthinkingly be identified with the meaning of poetic forms in a different historical context; for one thing the nature of political power and the relationship between the public and private spheres hardly remained constant between the sixth-century Greek world and Augustan Rome. Furthermore, while *Odes* 4 introduces itself as a continuation, after an intermission, of Horace's previous lyric output, it is not simply business as usual. One difference from the earlier books is indeed a heightening of the contrast between the personal and the public components. The first ode focuses on the poet's slavery to desire for the boy Ligurinus, while the second explores different poetic and non-poetic ways of praising the triumphant Augustus. In the first ode the treatment of Horace's homosexual obsession frames an instruction to Venus to divert her attack to the young nobleman Paullus Maximus who will offer her some kind of semi-public worship, possibly an allusion to the forthcoming marriage of Paullus to Augustus' cousin Marcia. This may suggest a possibility of containing the irresponsible force of personal desire within the institutional structures of imperial Roman society, but we are not bound to find in it a way to an integrated reading of the several poems that make up book four of the *Odes*.

How to read the juxtaposition of self-centred erotic poems with poems about Rome and Augustus has become one of the most contentious issues in the criticism of Augustan poetry. Any answer must include some attempt to reconstruct the horizons of the Augustan reader. The problem seems to become particularly acute in later Augustan poetry. The fourth book of Propertius' *Elegies*, whose composition overlapped with that of Horace *Odes* 4, also stages the drama of a return to erotic subjects after the decisive and formal renunciation of Cynthia with which the third book ends. In the first poem of book four Propertius addresses an unnamed visitor to Rome and contrasts the present-day splendours of the city with the simple buildings and customs that would have been visible in Rome's primitive past; the poet then turns to a statement of his own poetic ambitions and a syllabus for the book on which he is embarking:

> Be gracious, Rome. For you the work proceeds. Grant happy
> > Omens, citizens. Sing, bird, favouring the attempt.
> I'll say 'Troy, you shall fall and rise again as Rome';
> > I'll sing of distant graves on land and sea.
> I'll sing of rites and days and the ancient names of places.
> > This is the goal towards which my steed must sweat.
> > > (Propertius, 4. 1. 67–8, 87–8, 69–70, trans. Guy Lee)

Propertius is then rudely interrupted by the astrologer and fortune-teller Horus, of Greek and Oriental extraction, who warns him away from his historical and antiquarian Roman project and orders him instead to stick to his erotic elegiac matter:

> 'Unstable Propertius, why this ignorant rush to turn prophet?
> > Your thread was not spun from a dexterous distaff.
> Your cantillations will end in tears. Apollo's against them
> > You'll rue the words you force from a reluctant lyre.
> > > .   .   .   .
> Well, make up elegies. Tricky work! This is your field.
> > Let crowds of others write with you as model.
> You'll face campaigning under Venus' deceptive arms
> > And make a useful target for her Cupids.
> Whatever palms of victory your hardships gain
> > One girl will mock them and your grasp.

> Though you shake off the hook imbedded in your chin
>> It's no good—the gaff's prong will spike you.
> At her dictation you will see darkness and light
>> And shed a tear but when she orders it.
> To seal her door and post a thousand guards won't help you;
>> A chink's enough if she's resolved to cheat.
>
> (Propertius, 4. 1. 71–4, 135–46, trans. Guy Lee)

Propertius here gives a new spin to the conventional elegiac *recusatio* (the 'refusal' to write a grander kind of poetry than humble love elegy): the rest of book four turns out to be neither one thing nor the other, but a mixture, as aetiological poems on Roman institutions alternate with erotic elegies. Further, this juxtaposition of the antiquarian and the erotic is instantiated within single poems, as in the account (4. 4) of the origin of the name of the Tarpeian Rock, in which Tarpeia's motive for betraying the Capitol to the enemy general is, unusually, love rather than greed. At the centre of the book (4. 6) is a kind of hymn celebrating Augustus' Palatine Temple of Apollo and including an extended and mannered narrative of the battle of Actium, turned in Octavian's favour by Apollo. The book concludes (4. 11) with a speech to the judges of the dead in the mouth of the deceased Cornelia, stepdaughter of Augustus, in which she gives an account of herself as the very type of the old-fashioned matronly virtues actively encouraged by Augustus' moral and legislative programme (in particular the marriage laws of 18 BCE and 9 CE), and the polar opposite of the irregular lifestyle of the elegiac girlfriend.

Formal literary considerations may take us so far. The Alexandrian privileging of novelty took on new urgency after the first wave of Augustan literary production; one way to tickle the public's jaded palates was to present old material in new combinations. Propertius reinvents himself as an elegist by forcing together elements familiar from earlier elegy with historical and nationalist matter hitherto considered alien to love elegy. This craving for the new is one (but only one) of the roots of the love of paradox that is so striking a feature of later Augustan and first-century CE literature. In the case of Propertius' fourth book a further twist is given by this new kind of self-legitimation by elegy as a faithful reproduction of a Greek model. Propertius boasts that he is a 'Roman Callimachus' (4. 1. 64). The Callimachean rejection of poetry on heroes and kings had been used by Roman poets writing in the 'Alexandrian' manner as a way of declining grand Roman themes since at least the time of Virgil's sixth *Eclogue*. But to be truly faithful to Callimachean elegy (the *Aitia*) a Roman elegist should write aetiological elegy, and to write Roman aetiology is inevitably to peddle national legend and history, particularly as elaborated in Virgil's *Aeneid*. The piquancy of Propertius' fourth book would be keenly savoured by a Roman public fresh from a reading of the new national epic. The versatility of this new Propertian poetics is embodied in the speaking statue of Vertumnus in the second elegy of book four, the god who can turn (*uertere*) himself to any number of disguises. Like Propertius, Vertumnus is of Etruscan origin, but he now stands in the Roman Forum in full view of the Roman crowd as it passes about its business.

But at what point does generic 'contamination' cease to be a purely formal play with literary kinds and turn into ideological challenge? Many modern critics read subversive intent into the incongruous combination of the erotic and the Roman in a work such as Propertius' fourth book. Fewer would make the same claim for Tibullus, whose second book of elegies, probably written shortly before his death in 19 BCE, juxtaposes poems on his love for the girl Nemesis with a hymnic account of the religious festival of the Ambarvalia (2. 1), largely drawing on Virgil's *Georgics*, and with a poem celebrating the inauguration of Messalla's son as one of the priests in charge of the Sibylline Oracles (2. 5), including accounts of early Rome and of the mission of Aeneas that substantially overlap with material in Propertius 4. 1. In Tibullus' case this does not mark a decisive break with the practice of his first book, which includes a full-blown celebration of the triumph of Messalla in 27 BCE (1. 7) in the midst of poems about his loves for Delia and the boy Marathus.

Tibullus frames panegyric of one of the leading Roman noble families within his love elegy, but Propertius deals with the ruler of Rome himself and his family. The compartmentalization of personal and public interests within a poetry book becomes problematic in an age when state supervision and regulation extend further into the private sphere than they had ever done under the Republic. It is difficult to feel that Ovid, for example, is not being at least provocative when near the beginning of his how-to-do-it manual for would-be lovers, the *Art of Love* (*Ars Amatoria*), in a list of good places to pick up a girl he includes the prospective triumph of the adopted sons of Augustus, Gaius and Lucius, where it will be easy to impress one of the girls in the crowd of spectators:

> Then one great day our darling we'll behold,
> Drawn by four snowy steeds and clad in gold.
> In front shall walk the chieftains fettered tight,
> Lest they take refuge in their wonted flight;
> While youths and maids look on in blithe array,
> And every heart is gladdened by the day.
> And if a damsel ask what chiefs are those,
> What towns or hills or streams the pageant shows,
> Tell everything she asks and more than that,
> And though you know not, give your answers pat.

That's the Euphrates with his crown of reeds,
And that the Tigris with the long grey weeds;
Yonder are generals; add a name or two,
Names that are fitting, though they mayn't be true.
(*Art of Love* 1. 213–28, trans. A. D. Melville)

Suetonius' *Life of Augustus* shows us an emperor not without his lighter side, a keen gambler, with a well-developed sense of humour, but also with strong ideas about the right place and time. On one occasion when he saw Romans wearing informal dress in a public assembly he indignantly quoted a Virgilian line (*Aeneid* 1. 282), 'Romans, masters of the world, the people of the toga', and thereafter forbade anybody to appear in or near the Forum except in a toga (the Roman formal dress) (Suetonius, *Life of Augustus* 40). It is legitimate at least to ask what he would have thought of using a triumph to cruise for pick-ups.

Ovid and the cultured reader

Ovid (Publius Ovidius Naso, 43 BCE–17 CE) is the dominating literary presence of the later years of Augustus' reign, and (from exile) forms a bridge into the first few years of Tiberius' reign. The influence of Ovid on the Western tradition over the last two millennia has arguably been greater than that of any other Greek or Latin writer (including Virgil). To take an example from English literature, there is much to reflect on in Francis Meres's judgement of 1598 that 'the sweete wittie soule of Ovid lives in mellifluous and hony-tongued Shakespeare'. It is only in the last century or so that, as a result of particular views about the seriousness and sincerity expected of 'great' literature, the mellifluous wit of Ovid has turned to his disadvantage, his sophistication denigrated as the mark of a superficial fluency. On the other hand, part of the appeal of Ovid for both ancient and later audiences has been the effortless fluency of his language and metre, cloaking a content that is also, at least on some levels, immediately accessible. After over a century and a half of refinement of the Greek models, Latin dactylic poetry finally attains with Ovid a seemingly natural ease and regularity. All of Ovid's extant poetry is in elegiac couplets or hexameters (had his tragedy *Medea* survived we would probably see a similar confidence in the handling of tragic metres, foreshadowing the pointed facility of Seneca's tragedies, cf. pp. 164–6). A leading authority on Ovid, referring to a tradition of classical education only recently defunct, remarks that 'The Ovidian manner, as generations of clever English schoolboys have discovered, is imitable; Virgil's is not.' One might compare the difference between Virgil and Ovid in this respect to that between the blank verse of Milton, sovereign in its control but heroically laboured, and the ready versatility of Dryden, himself an important translator and adaptor of Ovid.

Over the past couple of decades Ovid has undergone a remarkable rehabilitation, both inside and outside the academic world. Professional classicists have responded to the more 'difficult' aspects of Ovidian sophistication, exploring his self-reflexive and narratological games and that constant engagement with fictionality and textuality that makes of Ovid an ideal subject for the concerns of post-modernism. Modern poets and novelists have returned to what has always been one of Ovid's main attractions, the seductiveness of his storytelling, and also found a specifically late twentieth-century interest in Ovidian anticipations of the mode of magical realism. Ovid's later career has come to hold a fascination for an artistic intelligentsia attracted by the figurative image of exile for its own condition.

Like Cicero, that other great Roman exile, whose own complaints from exile, together with the legendary sufferings of the exile who founded the Roman race, Aeneas, are an important model for Ovid's construction of his own exilic image, Ovid found exile particularly hard to cope with because he identified himself so thoroughly with the city of Rome itself. For Cicero Rome meant above all the city of the ancestors, the site of the traditional constitution and values that as consul he had preserved against the threat of Catiline. Ovid's urban values are rather different, as may be seen from a well-known passage in the third book of the *Art of Love*:

> I start with care of body [*cultus*]: glebe and vine
> Well-cared for yield rich crops and bounteous wine.
> Beauty's a gift of God. How few can boast
> Of beauty? It's a gift denied to most.
> Looks come by art: looks vanish with neglect,
> Yes, though the charms of Venus they reflect.
> Women of old ne'er groomed themselves, it's true,
> But in those days the men were ungroomed too.
>
> .   .   .   .
> Once life was rude and plain; now golden-paved,
> Rome holds the treasures of a world enslaved.
> The old and modern Capitols compare;
> Built for two different Jupiters, you'd swear.
> The Senate-house, fit home of high debate,
> Was wattle-built when Tatius ruled the state,
> And ploughmen's oxen grazed on Palatine
> Where glitter now the palace and the shrine.

> The good old days indeed! I am, thanks be,
> This age's child: it's just the age for me;
> Not because pliant gold from earth is wrought,
> Not because pearls from distant coasts are brought,
> Not that from hills their marble hearts we hew,
> While piles encroach upon the ocean's blue:
> It's that we've learnt refinement [*cultus*], and our days
> Inherit not our grandsires' boorish ways.
>> (*Ars* 3. 101–8, 113–28, trans. A. D. Melville)

Ovid the urban poet is Ovid the urbane poet. In Latin the terms denoting city-dweller (*urbanus*) and country-dweller (*rusticus*) had long been used in an evaluative sense to distinguish the civilized, urbane, and stylish in both life and literature from the boorish, rustic, and gauche (cf. pp. 42–3). The key-word in this passage is *cultus*, immediately the 'adornment' or *toilette* that the female addressee of the didactic poet must cultivate in order to attract a lover. But it is widened to embrace the senses of 'elegance', 'refinement', 'sophistication', that is to say, a particular aspect of our still wider term 'culture'. This is the value that the neoteric poets had established as the distinguishing mark of members of their exclusive smart set; Ovid extends membership of the cultivated circle to all modern Romans, who by implication will (all) be the ideal readers of Ovid's cultivated poetry on female adornment and other cultivated subjects. This redefinition of the audience for cultured poetry may mark a watershed in the Roman poet's awareness of his reading public, and of that public's awareness of itself. Mario Citroni claims that 'Ovid's work marks a crucial moment, a true turning-point in the development of the relationship between author and public in European literature. In Ovid for the first time on the poetic page there is an open dialogue between the author and the general reader.'

Another point of difference from the neoteric poets' definition of their 'fit audience, though few' is that Ovid makes no attempt to cordon off the interests of a cultured readership as something apart from the more practical pursuits of traditional-minded Romans. Instead Augustan city-building and empire-building themselves are the material precondition and manifestation of Roman culture. The wealth of Rome's world-empire, achieved by Roman armies, creates this new 'golden age' of civilization, whose products include the Temple of Apollo, built on the Palatine by Augustus to celebrate the Battle of Actium, as well as an advanced technology of cosmetics. Ovid sees Rome as the successor to the Greek world-city, Alexandria, whose immense wealth and cosmopolitanism fostered the artistic and intellectual sophistication of the Museum and of poets like Callimachus. The sole exclusion—and an important one given the Romans' habit of defining themselves in terms of their past—is the rustic audience of ancestors, who would certainly not understand or appreciate Ovid's poetry. Ovid sees himself as perfectly in tune with his age; but this 'Ovidian age' is at best a partial definition of the 'Augustan age', which for Augustus himself would include the strong continuing presence of the values of the ancestors, as embodied for example in the emperor's marriage legislation or, in physical form, in the statue galleries of Roman ancestors in the Forum of Augustus (dedicated in 2 BCE). In this passage from the *Art of Love* Ovid in fact acutely identifies an irresolvable tension at the heart of Augustan ideology: Augustus is both the representative of modernity, the emperor who boasted that he found Rome a city of brick and left it a city of marble, and the increasingly austere upholder of what were held to be traditional values.

Ovid's games of love: Women reading and writing

Ovid's first work, the *Amores*, is pitched at the general reader, and is already a consummate display of literary *cultus*. In an opening epigram in which the three books present themselves as a slimmed-down version of an original five-book edition, Ovid's love poetry announces itself not as an instrument to win a girl's favours but as a text that may (or may not) afford pleasure to the reader at large. Corinna herself is not addressed until the third poem in the first book, and then in a manner that teasingly suggests that Ovid's real-life lover may have as much or as little reality as famous literary heroines such as Io and Europa.

In the first elegy the personification of love, Cupid, steals a 'foot' from a poet who pretends to be embarking on a grandiose military epic in hexameters, and thus condemns him to the limping metre of elegiac couplets (alternating the six feet of the hexameter with the five feet of the pentameter). This reveals its full significance only to a reader familiar with the texts, Propertius' elegies above all, to which it alludes (although, as usual, the Ovidian text makes a perfectly lucid sense even to a reader who does not come armed with literary learning). Latin love elegy had always been written to conventions, but Ovid foregrounds the conventionality of the genre in order to comment and ring the changes on it to a still greater degree than his predecessors. The term 'parody' is often used, but this is to suppose a seriousness of personal commitment to their elegiac life and art by Gallus, Propertius, and Tibullus that may be the result of wishful thinking on the part of the modern reader. It has been argued that the Latin elegist *always* invites the reader to laugh at the pitiful figure cut by himself as the slave of love (cf. pp. 95–6).

But the disempowerment of the elegiac poet debarred from writing hexameter epic may be more apparent than real. The first word of Ovid's first elegy is *arma* 'weapons', not coincidentally the first word of the *Aeneid*. Warfare turns out, in fact, to be an integral part of the elegist's world. It is not just that the god of love and virtual personification of love elegy, Cupid, uses his bow to shoot his victim, but the enamoured poet himself boasts of the military-style endurance and violence that carry him through to success in his campaign against a resistant girl, a theme explored at length in *Amores* 1. 9, beginning 'Every lover is a soldier'. Ancient works were often referred to by the first word or words of the text: 'weapons' is not a totally misleading title for the *Amores*.

A reading of the *Amores* is not exhausted at the level of literary playfulness. The cultured Augustan reader will have enjoyed the sensation of intermittently abandoning him- or herself to the 'reality effect', of following the sequence of elegies almost as a soap-opera serialization of the ups and downs of the poet's love-life. Ovid already shows a mastery, abundantly displayed in the *Metamorphoses*, of the manipulation of the reader's suspension of disbelief. In an exquisite moment he projects this equivocation between pretence and reality onto an unnamed female reader of the *Amores*:

> There's one I know who broadcasts she's Corinna;
> What would she not have given to really be!
> (*Amores* 2. 17. 29–30, trans. A. D. Melville)

Realism is a literary mode, but the realist *Amores* are also anchored in the personal and social realities of the author and his readership. An example of the fine balance between the real and the literary is the elegy on the death of Ovid's fellow elegist Tibullus (*Amores* 3. 9), which was undoubtedly written on the real occasion of his friend's death and, almost as undoubtedly, expresses the real grief of Ovid. Yet at the same time it uses sustained allusion to Tibullus' own love elegy to give a fictionalized picture of the death and the grief. Now for two examples of how the eternal experience of love is set within the political and historical context of Augustan Rome. First, at the end of *Amores* 1. 2 a highly artificial description of the Triumph of Cupid is directly related to the triumphs celebrated by the emperor when the god of love is asked to show as much clemency as his 'relative' Augustus, a cousin many times removed of Cupid through their shared descent from Venus. Beyond the immediate joke this passage reminds us that the Roman audience for Augustan ideology routinely exercised a sophisticated suspension of disbelief in responding to imperial fictions such as the legend of Aeneas. Secondly, in *Amores* 2. 14 the poet reproaches Corinna for having endangered her life through procuring an abortion; and he mimics the moralizing arguments attested for Augustus' own oratory in support of his marriage legislation, partly designed to bolster a falling birthrate among the upper classes:

> If in times past that practice had found favour,
>   The crime would have destroyed the race of men,
> The empty world would need someone for throwing
>   The stones of our creation once again.
>   (*Amores* 2. 14. 9–12, trans. A. D. Melville)

The elegist's appropriation of the conservative and imperial rhetoric of 'the customs of our ancestors' is breathtaking.

In the *Art of Love* Ovid takes to its logical conclusion the relevance for the audience's own experience of the elegiac poet's lifestyle, by writing a didactic poem on how to succeed in love (followed later by the shorter *Remedies for Love*, giving instruction in how to fall out of love).

> Who in this town knows not the lover's art
> Should read this book, and play an expert's part.
> It's art that speeds the boat with oars and sails,
> Art drives the chariot, art in love prevails.
> Automedon was skilled with car and rein,
> And Tiphys steered the Argo o'er the main:
> For young Love's guide has Venus chosen me.
> Love's pilot and Love's charioteer I'll be.
>   (*Art of Love* 1. 1–8, trans. A. D. Melville)

This is a deliberately paradoxical project in a number of ways. Traditionally the elegiac lover is at the mercy of an overwhelming force that sweeps away the conventions of society and civilization, but Ovid proudly presents himself as the Master of Love (a role in which he became very influential in the Middle Ages), with a body of rational precepts to convey, an art or science. Furthermore, while the traditional elegist portrays himself as an outcast from society, excluded from the normal pursuits of the male Roman citizen by his enslavement to his girl, in the *Art of Love* the second-person singular addressee conventional in the genre of didactic becomes the Roman everyman: this is written for you, any and every one of this people who is not an expert in the art of love. There is another paradox in the idea that love and sex should be a science like astronomy, philosophical ethics, farming, or hunting (the subjects of other surviving Latin didactic poems). By choosing this particular topic it might be thought that Ovid finally debunks any lingering idea that in this late age the real function of didactic poetry is still that of instruction. On the other hand, the *Art of Love* was perhaps the one Latin didactic poem that *was* eagerly unrolled by young, and not so young, sweaty palms looking for tips on how to make a catch, and what to do in bed once you had made the catch.

The readership for the *Art of Love* is not envisaged as exclusively male; at the beginning of the poem Ovid is careful to warn off (and thereby of course also to tempt) just one class of potential female reader, the *matrona*, the married woman viewed as the bearer of the Augustan family values to which the elegiac lifestyle is constructed as a self-conscious alternative. Already in *Amores* 2. 1. 5–6 Ovid had defined his ideal readers as *both* the passionate girl *and* the inexperienced boy. The *Art of Love* methodically addresses both sexes: the first two books instruct the male lover, and the third is addressed to women:

> Greeks have I armed 'gainst Amazons to stand,
> Remains to arm Penthesilea's band.
> Fair be the field, and to the cause success
> That Venus and her world-wide flyer bless.
> For men-at-arms are unarmed maids no match,
> A sorry triumph that for men to snatch.
> (*Art of Love* 3. 1–6, trans. A. D. Melville)

The image of the Amazons is an uneasy one: Ovid extends the elegiac cliché of the warfare of love (on which see p. 136 above) and puts his male and female readers on an equal footing by casting the latter in a mythological role that in Greco-Roman culture both symbolized the diametrical opposite of the sexual and social roles expected of women, and expressed male anxieties about maintaining their dominance within home and city. The image of the bare-breasted female warrior had also by this time become a highly eroticized one.

This passage raises difficult questions about the role of women in Ovid's poetry and as readers of Ovid's poetry. There is no doubt that at this time in Rome there was a significant readership of educated upper-class women; of all (male) Latin writers Ovid appears to invest most heavily in writing for a female audience and from a woman's point of view (on Catullus' female readers, cf. p. 70 above). But it would be too simple to claim him as a proto-feminist. At every point we must ask how far Ovid caters to a male voyeurism, whether he is more interested in woman as subject or as object. In the case of the third book of the *Art of Love* the illusion of an equality on the battlefield of love is quickly broken when we come to the instruction proper addressed to the would-be female lover. Ovid begins from *cultus*, female adornment, which places the woman in the passive role of a lure for the actively questing male. By contrast in the first book the male reader is told to go about his business like a hunter marking out the ground for his nets and traps, and is thus figuratively cast in the role of the reader of the established species of didactic poems on hunting (of which an example in Latin, the *Cynegetica*, survives by a contemporary of Ovid, one Grattius). Ovid elsewhere establishes his credentials within the didactic tradition by a heavy use of georgic (farming) imagery, in obvious allusion to the most important Latin didactic text, Virgil's *Georgics*. The use of both cynegetic and georgic imagery establishes an asymmetrical relationship between the male as the agent of culture, the hunter or farmer, operating on the female as a natural object, an animal wild or domestic, or a piece of land to be cultivated. In defence of the poet one might point to the endings of the second and third books where Ovid recommends simultaneous orgasm as the climax of the art of love, although even this advocacy of an equality of sexual enjoyment is qualified by the appended advice to the girl to fake it if she cannot manage the real thing.

The *Amores* are 'autobiographical' elegies written from a male point of view but about an experience that inverts the expected dominance in antiquity of male over female. Ovid next turned to a work that places elegiac complaints on the lips, or rather flowing from the pens, of powerless women, famous mythological heroines who have been abandoned or betrayed by their husbands or lovers. The *Heroides* ('Heroines') consist of fifteen letters written by separate characters; it may have been the popular success of this collection that prompted Ovid to follow it up with three pairs of double *Heroides* in each of which a letter from a male character is followed by the reply from the woman. Like the *Amores*, the *Heroides* combine psychological with more literary kinds of interest: these epistolary effusions forced out of women by acute emotional stress are cunningly inserted in undocumented 'gaps' in their histories as recorded in earlier literary texts, to which the writers of the epistles are made anachronistically, and in some sense unknowingly, to allude.

A major strategy of the love elegist had been to lend a romantic glamour to his affair by viewing it in the light of the great passions of the mythological past; this is reversed in the *Heroides* where mythological characters behave in the manner of a first-century BCE Roman lover. In the first poem, for example, Penelope, the great epic example of wifely fidelity, unburdens herself of the self-pitying complaints of the elegist. These arch games with anachronism and the modernization of myth have precedents in Hellenistic poetry, and the formula presumably worked for a Roman audience, as Ovid was repeatedly to use it for effect in the *Metamorphoses*. The verse epistle itself was a new form (see p. 406 above), and Ovid makes the written letter into a bearer of modernity: not only are the main models for the heroines' written complaints the predominantly oral performances of characters in Greek epic and tragedy, but Ovid's writers display a self-consciousness about the act of writing itself, that mirrors at another level the author Ovid's own self-consciousness about his interventions in a textual tradition. Dido ends her letter to Aeneas (*Heroides* 7) by appealing to him to visualize the image of herself as she writes:

> If only you could see the picture of me as I write!
>   I write, with the Trojan sword in my lap,
> the tears glide down my cheeks on to the drawn sword,
>   which will soon be stained with blood, not tears.
> How well your gift-offering matches my fate! —
>   your funeral arrangement for me comes cheap.
> Not for the first time is my breast now struck with a weapon;
>   that place already bears the wound of cruel love.
> Anna my sister, sister Anna, all too much party to my guilt,
>   soon you will make the last offerings to my ashes.
> After the pyre my inscription will not be 'Elissa, wife of Sychaeus';
>   this will be the only epitaph on my marble tomb:
> AENEAS PROVIDED THE CAUSE OF DEATH AND SWORD;
>   DIDO'S OWN HAND IT WAS BY WHICH SHE FELL.
>
>   (*Heroides* 7. 183–96)

Of course the sword of Aeneas, and the use to which Dido will shortly put it, are well known to the reader from another written text, the *Aeneid*.

Ovid's Dido concludes with reference to another form of writing, the inscription of her name and of a brief outline of her story on her tomb. This is at once a more permanent kind of writing than the flimsy and (as we all know) totally ineffectual letter that she is writing at this moment. It is also a written monument that challenges the version of the story of Dido and Aeneas inscribed in the great written monument that is the *Aeneid*, placing the blame for what happened fairly and squarely on the shoulders of Aeneas. *Heroides* 7 is the first of a long line of rewritings of the Virgilian story from Dido's point of view, of which Chaucer's *House of Fame* and Purcell's *Dido and Aeneas* are examples. Here perhaps a feminist critic might find an Ovid ventriloquizing a female voice in true sympathy with the victim of the male hero of the Roman epic, that most masculine of genres. Or is the male reader of the *Heroides* in the position of a voyeur, enjoying the spectacle of a defenceless female victim? As in the case of Horace's very personal *Epistles*, there is the added *frisson* of eavesdropping on a private communication: the Medea of the tragic stage addresses her impassioned monologues to the world at large, whereas the Medea of *Heroides* 12 writes a letter not intended for our eyes.

Similar questions about how to read Ovidian women are prompted by the mythological narratives of the *Metamorphoses*, which include a number of examples of the Euripidean type of tragic monologue delivered by a woman in an impossible erotic dilemma. One of the most typical narrative motifs in the *Metamorphoses* is that of the female rape victim 'saved' from her pursuer's attentions through transformation out of her human shape. Ovid certainly does often explore the point of view of the rape victim, but there is also an undoubted pleasure for the male viewer/reader of the female victim's plight. Metamorphosis itself can function not just as an escape route from sexual penetration, but as the narrative realization of the transformation of the female body into an object under the male gaze.

In the archetypal example of this motif Daphne eludes Apollo's embrace in her flesh-and-blood existence, but hardens into a beautiful tree, the laurel, an object which will for ever be 'possessed' by Apollo as one of his attributes. The *Metamorphoses* also provides the classic image of the female body eroticized and objectified under the male gaze in the figure of Andromeda chained to the rock and waiting to be devoured by the sea-monster, viewed through the eyes of her rescuer and lover Perseus, who is almost induced by her petrified motionlessness to think that what he sees is a statue, a work of art.

> Andromeda was pinioned to a rock.
> When Perseus saw her, had a wafting breeze
> Not stirred her hair, her eyes not overflowed
> With trembling tears, he had imagined her
> A marble statue. Love, before he knew,
> Kindled; he gazed entranced; and overcome
> By loveliness so exquisite, so rare,
> Almost forgot to hover in the air.
> He glided down. 'Shame on those chains!' he cried;
> 'The chains that you deserve link lovers' hearts.
> Reveal, I beg, your name and this land's name
> And why you wear these shackles.' She at first
> Was silent, too abashed to face a man,
> So shy she would have held her hands to hide
> Her blushing cheeks had not her hands been chained.
> But weep she might and filled her eyes with tears.
> (*Metamorphoses* 4. 672–84, trans. A. D. Melville)

This 'image of beauty' was to be replicated many times in later art and literature, from Ariosto's Angelica to sadomasochistic bondage magazines.

The *Metamorphoses*: Ovid's Roman poem

The *Metamorphoses*, Ovid's hexameter narrative poem in fifteen books, is a kaleidoscopic and constantly shifting text that has appealed to many different kinds of audience, who have read it at different times through the centuries as an encyclopaedia of Greco-Roman myth, a Scheherezade-like treasury of

ANDROMEDA EXPOSED. A large villa at Boscotrecase near Pompeii was lavishly painted in about 40 BCE and then buried in the eruption of Vesuvius. This painting shows the myth of Andromeda exposed to be consumed by a sea monster before being rescued by Perseus.

seductive story-telling, a store of philosophical and ethical profundity (often accessed through allegorical modes of interpretation), the subversive expression of a counter-culture in defiance of the Augustan norm, or a celebration of the cultural and political achievement of the principate.

The sheer reach and variety of the poem will have appealed to a contemporary audience's awareness of the power and riches of Augustan Rome. The temporal scope of the *Metamorphoses* extends from the creation of the universe down to the poet's own day, and the last major narrative episode is the transformation of the murdered Julius Caesar into a god (and the prospective apotheosis of Augustus). The work is thus a version of the popular prose genre of universal history (cf. p. 44), which by leading up to the narrative of Roman success flattered the Romans' sense that their empire was the natural culmination of the history of the world. The poem also traces a trajectory from the world of Greek myth and literature to Italy and the stories that fashion the

Roman identity. Taken as a whole the *Metamorphoses* is the supreme monument to the Roman appropriation of Greek culture, which from another point of view is the story of the Hellenization of Rome.

The *Metamorphoses* embodies another kind of literary 'imperialism' in its inclusion within its hexameter narrative (the form of epic) of a multiplicity of other genres, hymn, tragedy, pastoral, elegy, and so on. This inclusiveness makes it very difficult to define the poem, and twentieth-century critics have argued endlessly whether it should be described as an epic or as a loose con-catenation of recherché mythical narratives in the manner of the Alexandrian 'epyllion' (short, mannered, narrative poem). The recent trend has been to see the question of definition as a theme of the poem itself, the answer to which is always teasingly deferred. But this too had an extra-literary resonance for the contemporary audience, confronted with the need to define the new order at Rome, for example with reference to ancestral traditions on the one hand and Greek monarchical structures on the other. Modern historians' accounts of the nature of Augustus and his power are as various as attempts to circumscribe the essence of the *Metamorphoses*.

The pluralism of the poem is also paralleled in the diversity and eclecticism of Augustan art and architecture, in which the formal and solemn classicism sometimes associated with the period is in fact but one register among many. Here we touch on the thorny issue of the ideological 'correctness' or otherwise of the *Metamorphoses*: some would claim that piquant juxtapositions such as the two appearances of Jupiter in book one, firstly as the king of the gods presiding over a celestial Senate and punishing mortal sinfulness, and secondly as the philandering rapist of the defenceless girl Io, whom he transforms into a cow in an attempt to deceive his shrewish wife Juno, would have caused no more offence than the co-presence in Augustan art of archaizing images of the gods alongside rococo decorative fantasies. Against this one might point to the importance in Roman culture of a hierarchy of decorum. What Augustus might think of as appropriate for the decoration of his recently excavated private study on the Palatine is very different from what was required in the major iconographical features of the Forum of Augustus. Ovid is as aware of the con-straints of decorum as is any ancient poet, and a sustained testing of those constraints is characteristic of all of his works; ultimately it is for the reader to decide whether he oversteps the limits or not.

These features—the universal pretensions of the *Metamorphoses*, its 'literary imperialism', its investment in issues of national and literary definition—can all be predicated of Virgil's *Aeneid*. Ovid's fifteen-book hexameter poem demands to be read as a continuous engagement with and overbidding of Virgil's twelve-book epic. Ovid's relationship to Virgil is that of a respectful but unabashed epigone; as in the case of his reworking of earlier love elegy, 'parody' may be a misleading term. As he works through universal time, Ovid naturally catches up with the timespan of the *Aeneid;* and books 13 and 14 contain an elliptical and oblique retelling of the story of Aeneas (sometimes referrred to as Ovid's 'Little Aeneid'). But the structures, themes, and detailed verbal matter of the *Aeneid* are spread over the whole poem in displacements and recombinations—metamorphoses, if you will.

For example book nine opens with the river-god Achelous' narration, at a banquet, of his own defeat by Hercules in a fight for a woman:

> Why the god groaned and how his brow was maimed
> Theseus enquired, and Calydon's great river,
> His tangled tresses bound with reeds, began:
> 'Sad is the task you set. For who would wish
> To chronicle the battles that he lost?
> Yet the whole tale I'll tell. It was less shame
> To lose than glory to have fought the fight:
> Much comfort comes from such a conqueror.
> You may perhaps have heard of Deianira,
> Once a most lovely girl, the envied hope
> Of many a suitor. I was one of them.'
> (*Metamorphoses* 9. 1–10, trans. A. D. Melville)

This combines elements from the beginning and end of the story of Aeneas in the *Aeneid*: the agreement to narrate a personal sorrow despite the grief it causes echoes Aeneas' introduction of his narration of the Sack of Troy to Dido at the beginning of the second book of the *Aeneid*, also at a banquet; but Achelous' misadventure is modelled on the final duel in *Aeneid* 12 between Aeneas and Turnus, and in this perspective it is Hercules, rather than Achelous, who takes the part of the victorious Aeneas. This is only to begin an exploration of the intertextual links: for example Ovid's allusive identification of Hercules and Aeneas is true to Virgil's own use of Hercules as a model for the character and exploits of Aeneas. Also the occasion for the fight between Achelous and Hercules reminds the reader that the climactic duel between Aeneas and Turnus, a foundational moment in Roman history, also concludes a quarrel over a woman, the Latin princess Lavinia. Ovid never tires of drawing attention to the fact that all the great epic plots can be reduced to contests or quests for a woman.

The *Metamorphoses* also shows itself to be a text of the moment in its address to a sophisticated audience accustomed to kinds of performance and spectacle both old and new. One of the big gaps in our knowledge of Augustan literature is the history of stage performance. We have lost the two tragedies of the period that won a lasting reputation, Varius' *Thyestes* of 29 BCE, and Ovid's own *Medea*. Under Augustus the performance of tragedies became marginalized, although there is evidence of an intense interest in the condition and possible revival of Roman theatre. Horace's two major exercises in literary history and criticism, the *Art of Poetry* and the *Letter to Augustus*, are both largely concerned with the theatre (rather than with the kinds of poetry that Horace himself wrote, to the frustration of some modern students). As regards tragedy, there may already have been a move towards performance in the recitation hall rather than on the public stage. In the *Metamorphoses* Ovid follows Virgil's lead (above all in the Dido story) in the wholesale importation into a narrative poem of tragic material, with long dramatic monologues that would lend themselves well to recitation, for example in the episodes of Medea and Althea, the mother of Meleager; the Hecuba episode in book thirteen is modelled closely on an extant play of Euripides, and was particularly appreciated in the Renaissance for its horror and pathos (and correspondingly deprecated by more recent taste).

The stage performance of tragedy, however, was edged out after 22 BCE by the 'pantomime', in which a solo dancer performed scenes often taken from tragic subjects, with instrumental music and a chorus. The emphasis on individual episodes, often of a sensational kind, and the versatility and skill required of the dancer, catered to a taste that might also be satisfied by certain aspects of the *Metamorphoses*. The earlier literary mime also flourished under Augustus, and its popular subject-matter of escaping tricksters, the concealment of adulterous lovers, and the like, influenced more elevated forms. Elements of mime may be detected in some of Ovid's *Amores* and in some episodes of the *Fasti*. More generally one might point to an Ovidian interest in widening the scope of literary imitation to include more popular forms within traditionally 'high' literature. There are intriguing similarities between some episodes in the *Metamorphoses* and the surviving prose novels from later antiquity that suggest that Ovid was drawing on the prose fiction of his own time. Such a combination of high literary forms with popular and (real or supposed) 'folk' forms has precedents in Alexandrian literary practice; and within the narrative fiction of the poem Ovid likes to include a number of low-class or naïve narrators.

The links between the *Metamorphoses* and stage performances and dramatic texts are part of a wider tendency to evoke the spectacular and the visual, that makes of the poem an important stage in the development of what in first-century CE literature becomes a dominant aesthetic of theatricality and spectacularity. Once again the aesthetic is closely linked to the political: the emperor expresses his power and communicates with the audience of the Roman people through elaborate displays of pageantry, triumphal and otherwise, through performances in the theatre and amphitheatre, and through great works of architecture, sculpture, and painting. Roman readers cannot have kept their response to literary scenes of physical violence separate from their experience of the real violence staged in the arena. The fascinated gaze directed at the grotesque deaths and wounds suffered in the Battle of Lapiths and Centaurs in book twelve—an episode substituted by Ovid for the narrative of the Trojan War that is expected at this point in the poem—has a strong feel of the amphitheatrical; the half-man, half-beast Centaurs may be read as a phantasmagoric image of the confusion of man and beast in the arena.

The poem works hard to evoke the visual through the verbal, both in descriptions of works of art (ecphrases), such as the Palace of the Sun at the beginning of the second book, or the tapestries of Arachne and Minerva at the beginning of the sixth book, in descriptions of landscape; and, in the ultimate test of the poet's ecphrastic power, in a series of major personifications, detailed visualizations of an abstract idea such as Hunger:

> She found Hunger in a stubborn stony field,
> Grubbing with nails and teeth the scanty weeds,
> Her hair was coarse, her face sallow, her eyes
> Sunken; her lips crusted and white; her throat
> Scaly with scurf. Her parchment skin revealed
> The bowels within; beneath her hollow loins
> Jutted her withered hips; her sagging breasts
> Seemed hardly fastened to her ribs; her stomach
> Only a void; her joints wasted and huge,
> Her knees like balls, her ankles grossly swollen.
> (*Metamorphoses* 8. 799–808, trans. A. D. Melville)

The poem's opening account of cosmogony is modelled in part on Homer's famous description of the Shield of Achilles, depicting the several divisions of the universe. Ovid's demiurge is a figure for the poet himself, the creator of a poetic world of words that is offered to us programmatically as a version of the oldest and most famous ecphrasis of a visual artefact in the Greco-Roman literary tradition.

Ecphrasis more often than not describes something that does not exist; the trick is to create the persuasive illusion of a visual presence. Ovidian narratives of metamorphosis function in the same way. In many instances the process is strongly visualized, often through the eyes of an internal spectator whose surprised experience of the reality of the supernatural event is the model for the effect that the narrator aims at on the external reader. One of the pleasures of the text is its power to convince us of the actuality of events that we know to be impossible. Ovid writes for a sophisticated reader well able to savour the paradoxes involved in the suspension of disbelief on the part of both viewers and readers. Ancient art and literature had long explored the problems of visual illusion and verbal fictionality, but Ovid's extended thematization of these issues is distinctive.

The theme of the illusion of reality in the visual arts comes to a climax in the story of Pygmalion (and it should not be forgotten that the tale is narrated by Orpheus, the archetypal wonder-working poet whose words have a magically direct effect on the world outside):

> Pygmalion, his offering given, prayed
> Before the altar, half afraid, 'Vouchsafe,
> O Gods, if all things you can grant, my bride
> Shall be'—he dared not say my ivory girl –
> 'The living likeness of my ivory girl.'
> And golden Venus (for her presence graced
> Her feast) knew well the purpose of his prayer;
> And, as an omen of her favouring power,
> Thrice did the flame burn bright and leap up high.
> And he went home, home to his heart's delight,
> And kissed her as she lay, and she seemed warm;
> Again he kissed her and with marvelling touch
> Caressed her breast; beneath his touch the flesh
> Grew soft, its ivory hardness vanishing
> And yielded to his hands . . .
>   .   .   .   .
> His heart was torn with wonder and misgiving,
> Delight and terror that it was not true!
> Again and yet again he tried his hopes —
> She was alive! The pulse beat in her veins!
>   (*Metamorphoses* 10. 273–89, trans. A. D. Melville)

The lifelikeness that the ancients valued so highly in their art is narrativized and transformed into life itself. The challenge taken up by the poet in turn is to persuade the reader of the plausibility of this miracle, to rival the power of a painter like Zeuxis whose painted grapes were said to be so realistic that the birds flew down to peck at them.

In a similar way Ovid's ongoing fascination with the nature and power of textual fictions is inscribed into the fictional narrative of the poem itself. There are many occasions when the reader is delightfully brought to an awareness of the paradoxical simultaneity of assent and disbelief that is involved in reading a text like the *Metamorphoses*. But few are as intense as the moment, significantly at the very heart of the poem, when two internal mythological narrators argue about the truth-value of the stories that they themselves narrate. The river-god Achelous has just told (a *river* telling a story?) a tale of metamorphosis in which he was personally involved:

> The river finished and fell silent. All
> Were moved and marvelled at the miracle.
> Ixion's son, a daredevil who scorned
> The gods, laughed at their gullibility.
> 'Fables!' he said, 'You make the gods too great,
> Good Achelous, if they chop and change
> The shapes of things.' All were aghast; such talk
> They all condemned, Lelex especially,
> Mature in years and mind, and he spoke up.
> 'The power of heaven is great and has no bounds;
> Whatever the gods determine is fulfilled.
> I give you proof. Among the Phrygian hills
> An oak tree and a lime grow side by side. [trees into which the pious
>   Baucis and Philemon have been transformed]
> > (*Metamorphoses* 8. 611–23, trans. A. D. Melville)

The implications even of this passage cannot be confined to an autonomous world of art, for the question of what the gods can or cannot do, and whether indeed they exist, is one that bears on the contemporary reader's experience of the state religion of Rome. As we have seen, the poem's final tale of divinely engineered change is the transformation of the real Roman ruler himself into one of those same gods. Just a poetic fiction? Or is it we moderns who misread Ovid if we assume that ancient religion can be discussed in terms of a simple belief or disbelief in the gods?

The delights of antiquarianism

The murder and apotheosis of Julius Caesar are also briefly narrated in the *Fasti* ('calendar'), a poem in elegiac couplets on the Roman religious calendar, planned in twelve books to cover the twelve months, but of which only the first six survive (or were ever written). The *Fasti* and the *Metamorphoses* were composed during the same period, and are best read as being in constant dialogue with each other, in some sense two parts of the same project, one way of understanding which is as a two-pronged response to the *Aeneid*. But the history of the reception of the *Fasti* has been very different from that of the *Metamorphoses*. The latter has become an almost timeless centrepiece of the Western literary canon, while the *Fasti*, which is indeed a poem about Roman ways of thinking about time, came to seem irrelevant as a work of literature, useful only as a quarry for the historian of Roman religion. Just recently the work's critical fortune has undergone a revolution and the *Fasti* has been restored to a central place in Ovid's poetic output. But this has been achieved only through the careful location of the poem within its contemporary historical and cultural contexts, and it may be true that its readership will be largely confined to a circle of classical scholars or those prepared to acquire a certain baggage of historical background.

Scholarship of a kind is in fact what the Roman reader would have looked for in the *Fasti*. One of the main features shared by the *Fasti* with the *Metamorphoses* is an interest in origins, in aetiology. The *Metamorphoses* narrates the origins of the world itself, of Rome, of Augustus. Metamorphosis is an aetiological device, offering a fantastic account of the origin of a species of animal, a plant, a geographical feature. The *Fasti* deals in antiquarian origins, the historical causes of the various rituals and festivals in the Roman religious calendar. Given the centrality of religion in the Roman view of its past, the poem comes to be a fragmented and partial history of Rome, arranged not according to an annalistic chronology but in the accidental order within the calendar year of the days that commemorate historical events. The appeal of such a poem for an educated Augustan readership is twofold. First, it caters for connoisseurs of Alexandrian poetry; specifically, the *Fasti* is the Roman version of Callimachus' *Aitia*. Secondly, the late Republic had developed a keen antiquarian interest in the recovery of the remote Roman past, both the history of the Roman state and of individual Roman families (obsession with genealogies is not a modern phenomenon), an interest that Augustus had diverted to the legitimization of the new principate through the claim to be restoring the institutions and the values of the Roman past. Ovid draws heavily on the learning of scholars such as Varro and Verrius Flaccus; as in Hellenistic Alexandria there was no sense that scholarship and poetry were quite separate pursuits.

The *Fasti* develop aspects of the *Aeneid*, which might be defined as an aetiological epic, and had been anticipated more closely still in the fourth book of Propertius, whose claim to be the Roman Callimachus, as we have seen, rests on his project of writing a Roman *Aitia*, proclaimed in the first poem and in part realized in the rest of the book. Aetiological poetry is closely related to didactic poetry. A poem on the calendar inevitably deals with the heavenly bodies whose movements define the course of the year, and Ovid at various points signals his dependence on the Hellenistic astronomical didactic poem by Aratos, the *Phainomena*. For reasons that are not entirely easy to explain, Aratos' poem enjoyed a long-lasting popularity in Rome, and was frequently translated and adapted in Latin, by among others the young Cicero, Ovid himself in a lost

Aratea, and by an imperial prince, the nephew and adoptive son of Tiberius, Germanicus. Ovid naturally hoped to find in him a most receptive audience when, after the death of Augustus, the exiled poet rededicated the *Fasti* to Germanicus in the proem to the first book.

This taste is also exemplified in the astronomical and astrological didactic poem, the *Astronomica*, of Marcus Manilius, written in the last years of Augustus and the early years of Tiberius, and today perhaps the least read of all the major surviving Latin poems of antiquity. Like Aratos, Manilius propounds a Stoic view of the divine order of the universe, and polemicizes against the Epicureanism of Lucretius. The *Astronomica* will have appealed to those educated Romans who found in Stoic physics and theology an outlet for a religious sense, and also to the many Romans (including Augustus and Tiberius) who took astrology seriously.

Like Ovid's other poems, the *Fasti* has become a battleground between those who claim that a Roman audience would have read it as straightforwardly supportive of Augustus' religious and antiquarian programme, and those for whom it would have provoked subversive thoughts, above all through the constant irruption of themes and attitudes associated with Ovid's earlier elegiac works, all of them erotic.

> . 'Kindly mother of love, requited or slighted, indulge me.
>> She turned her face in this poet's direction.
> 'What do you want with me? Surely you were singing a grander song.
>> Have you got that old wound in your sensitive heart?'
> 'You know, goddess,' I replied, 'about the wound.' She smiled,
>> and at once that region of the sky was cloudless.
> 'In sickness or in health, have I ever deserted your service?
>> You were my only subject, my only work.
> In my early years, as was proper, I dallied innocently;
>> now my horses are running on a bigger track.
> The dates—and their origins—dug up in ancient chronicles,
>> stars rising and setting—of that I sing.
> I have come to the fourth month, full of honour for you;
>> Venus, you know both the poet and the month are yours.'
> Stirred by this, she gently touched my temples with her myrtle
>> from Cythera, and said, 'Complete the work you've begun.'
> I felt it, and suddenly the origin of the days was revealed.
>> (*Fasti* 4. 1–17, trans. B. R. Nagle)

The generic play between different kinds of subject, public and personal, weighty antiquarianism and light eroticism, is clear (complicated here by allusion to the Venus of the proem to Lucretius' didactic poem. Once again the reader has to judge whether the elegiac Venus is safely contained within the religious project, or whether love's empire swallows up the world of state religion.

Exile poetry—in search of an audience

'I've come, an exile's book, sent to this city,
    Frightened and tired; kind reader offer me
A calming hand. Don't fear that I may shame you:
    In these sheets no line teaching love you'll see.
My master's fate's not such that he could rightly
    Cloak it, poor soul, in any levity.
That work too, once his green youth's wrong amusement,
    He's learnt too late to censure and to hate.
See what I bring: there's nothing here but sadness,
    Poems that suit their sorry time and state.
If in alternate lines the couplets hobble,
    Blame the long journey or the limping metre.
If I'm not pumice-smooth or cedar-yellow,
    My master's drab; I'd blush if I were neater.
If there are any letters blurred and blotted,
    The *poet's* tears have done the harm you've scanned;
And if some phrase seem perhaps not Latin,
    The place he wrote in was a barbarous land.
Readers, if it's no trouble, tell me where I,
    A book strange to the city, ought to stay
And where to go.'

                (*Tristia* 3. 1. 1–20, trans. A. D. Melville)

In 8 CE Ovid was exiled by Augustus to Tomis on the Black Sea coast; he tells us that the charges were a poem, the *Art of Love*, and an 'error'. What the precise nature of the latter was he never says, prompting endless speculation ever since, but it was probably connected with a scandal in the palace, open discussion of which would only have compounded the offence. It is dangerous to use the exile as evidence that Ovid's poetry had been widely perceived as subversive at an earlier date. The *Art of Love*, the work which purports most directly to urge the reader to an elegiac life of 'naughtiness', may have been a convenient pretext to divert attention from an offence which the emperor himself did not wish to air too publicly. Furthermore in his later years Augustus became more suspicious and censorious, so creating a very different climate for the reception of Ovid's way of writing about public and private matters.

In his elegiac epistles from Tomis, the five books of *Tristia* ('sad, gloomy poems') followed by the four books of *Ex Ponto* ('from the Black Sea'), Ovid presents his exile as a complete break with his previous life and literary career. Exile is felt as a kind of death; the post-exilic writings are a communication from the tomb. He complains repeatedly of a loss of poetic power; among the barbarians of the frozen north he is in danger even of forgetting Latin. All too often Ovid has been taken at his word, and the exile poetry written off as the pathetic and tedious whining of a poet starved of the metropolitan oxygen that fuelled his wit. But this is to commit the fallacy of taking too simply at its word the poet's account of his own experience, a mistake that no reader today would make in the case of the supposedly confessional works of the Latin love elegists—and that no skilled reader in the early first century CE is likely to have made in the case of Ovid's exile poetry either. The continuities with the earlier works are as carefully cultivated as the protest at discontinuity, to the point where the reader might be forgiven for feeling that had Ovid never suffered exile it would have been necessary for him to invent it.

The genre of elegy had long been associated with complaint: the complaints of the lover are now replaced by the more urgent complaints of the exile, for whom Rome and Augustus become the objects of desire for the excluded lover. In exile Ovid is condemned to become a further instalment in his own catalogue of tales of metamorphosis, his fortune so utterly transformed that he experiences the loss of identity and even of humanity that is a recurrent focus of psychological interest in the *Metamorphoses*. As always Ovid confuses the boundary between life and literature: the picture of his (real-life) location on the Black Sea is processed through ethnographical conventions for describing barbarian peoples at the end of the world. In the exile poetry the not intolerable climate of the region is turned into the extreme cold of the Scythian north.

Ovid is as powerless as the heroines for whom he had written the *Heroides*, desperate letters doomed to fail in their attempt to persuade their addressees. In the exile poetry Ovid develops to the limit the potential of the epistolary form for exploring both the spatial and temporal gap between writer and addressee, and the uncertainty as to whether the written words will have their intended effect on the reader. As with Horace's *Epistles*, one of Ovid's models, Ovid exploits the tension involved in penning letters to individual addressees that are at the same time intended to be 'public songs' (*Ex Ponto* 5. 1. 23). It is indeed only in these last works Ovid returns to the older practice of addressing poems to individual addressees, and the personalized system of literary patronage takes on an immediacy of purpose for the client-poet that it can rarely ever have had. For there can be little doubt that Ovid did hope that his circle of well-connected friends at Rome might intervene with Augustus, and later Tiberius, to secure his recall.

Under an authoritarian emperor, however, the smooth working of the patron-client system is impaired. The addressees of the *Tristia* (unlike those of the later *Ex Ponto*) are left pointedly unnamed, lest an approach from the disgraced Ovid may involve them too in danger. For the general reader this is of course an additional titillation, for not only is he or she privy to a private correspondence, but has to guess who the addressee is. For the ultimate reader, the emperor himself, there is an implied rebuke: what kind of a society is it where friends dare not address each other by name?

Anonymity is also a potent device in another Ovidian exile poem, the bizarre *Ibis*, a stream of violent but extremely learned abuse, modelled on a lost curse poem by Callimachus, directed at an unnamed enemy of the poet, whose identity inevitably provokes the same kind of curiosity as the unnamed error which led to exile. The *Ibis* is at once Ovid's most outspoken and his least forthcoming poem.

In *Tristia* 3. 1 (quoted above) and in other poems Ovid dramatizes the hesitant approach of his books of exile letters to the general reader in Rome: will his books find any audience, will they be turned away from the public libraries in Rome? Even more anxious is his approach to the emperor himself, the 'god' who has struck him down with a thunderbolt and who alone has the power to restore him to life. Horace's humorous treatment in *Epistles* 1. 13 of how to gain an audience with the emperor has now become a far more serious business altogether. Ovid's exile poems are a suitable point at which to end this chapter; their self-conscious rhetoric of obsession, dissimulation, and suspicion will become a dominant strain in certain types of literature of the first century CE.

6 | The path between truculence and servility: Prose literature from Augustus to Hadrian

CHRISTINA S. KRAUS

The power—and danger—of books

The Augustan period is variously dated from 44 BCE—the year of Julius Caesar's assassination and the appearance on the scene of his heir, the 19-year-old Gaius Julius Caesar Octavianus (Octavian), later Augustus—or from 31 BCE, the year in which Octavian defeated Mark Antony and the Egyptian Queen Kleopatra at the Battle of Actium, and after which his rule received no serious challenge (see pp. 75–6). A third possible date is 27 BCE, when Octavian 'restored the Republic' and took the title 'Augustus', with its connotations of *augury* and *authority*. The flexible starting-point appropriately indicates the uncertain, shifting perceptions of the times. It was not clear then, or indeed later, what role Augustus would play: he called himself *princeps*, 'first man', an *ad hoc* title with republican precedent (as in the 'first man of the Senate', the senator with dominant authority) which would, ultimately, become a proper imperial title: 'Prince'. His dominance in Rome lasted until 14 CE, when he died at the age of 76; in that half-century he gradually encroached on many of the powers of the Senate, and devised some new powers of his own. Through a process today often characterized as 'trial and error', or experimentation, Augustus invented a kind of sole rule that was, by and large, acceptable to the majority of Roman citizens, despite their traditional hatred of kings. It preserved the names and forms of most Republican offices and privileges, though replacing their content by revolutionary measures; and, most important, it ended the protracted and bloody struggles that marked the decades of civil war between the late-republican 'strong men'. By the time he died, Augustus' rule was definitively established as a hereditary monarchy (though the emperors were never called *Rex*, 'King'), passed on to his adopted son Tiberius without debate—though not without private objection on the part of those aristocrats who wished a return, however unrealistic, to their republican power. On his deathbed, the former Octavian is said to have asked if he had played his part in the 'mime of life' well, an apt metaphor for one whose life was spent creating and coping with paradox, making radical change look like the preservation of sanctified tradition.

The Empire would survive, in various forms, until the fall of Constantinople in the fifteenth century—though Augustus' own dynasty lasted only until 68 CE, ending with the suicide of his great-great-grandson Nero. This chapter will chart some of the developments in Latin prose literature between (roughly) Actium and the end of the reign of Hadrian (138 CE). Some of the same issues that we saw in republican prose will reappear here, together with some new ones, and some new kinds of literature. Throughout, we can trace a consciousness of decline, a model that until recently was used by literary scholars and historians alike to describe the imperial period: it is silver, not golden, debased, not classical. The trouble with all such schemata, however, be they chemical or biological, is that they oversimplify; in this case, moreover, the schema locates the 'golden' apogee of Latin literature in the principate of Augustus—the very place where ancient literary theorists also located the beginnings of decline. For this is an ancient model as well as a modern one, applied particularly to oratory, as the genre that most fully represented the intersection between literary and public life, between theory and practice. It is also a model that reflects the essential conservatism of Roman audiences: in a culture in which the phrase 'new things' (*res novae*) denoted 'revolution', the past always exerted a powerful pull. In imperial Latin prose, much as in Hellenistic literature, the two poles of tradition and originality vibrate in constant tension. Imperial literature is some of the most inventive, experimental, exciting literature in the ancient Mediterranean world—and yet it is permeated with the sense of its own belatedness (see also pp. 119–20).

Between September 44 and April 43 BCE Cicero delivered a series of fourteen orations against Mark Antony, whom he accused of trying to seize despotic power after Caesar's murder; he called them the *Philippics*, a deliberate reference to the orations with which Demosthenes tried to rally the Athenians against their future conqueror, Philip of Macedon. The speeches were landmarks, in more ways than one. First, they led directly to Cicero's execution on Antony's orders, on 7 December 43:

> Marcus Cicero had left the city at the approach of the triumvirs [Antony, Octavian, and Lepidus], rightly regarding it as certain that he could no more be rescued from Antony than Cassius and Brutus from Caesar. . . . He put out to sea several times, but sometimes the winds were against him and forced him back, sometimes he himself could not endure the tossing of the vessel. . . . Finally he grew weary of flight and of life, and returning to the inland villa . . . said, 'I shall die in the country I so often saved.' There is no

authors' books were burned.

doubt that his slaves bravely and loyally showed readiness to make a fight of it; and that it was Cicero himself who ordered them to put down the litter and suffer calmly the compulsions of a harsh fate. He leaned from where he sat and offered his neck without a tremor; his head was struck off. . . . The soldiers . . . cut off the hands, too, cursing them for having written attacks on Antony. The head was taken back to Antony, and, on his orders, placed between the two hands on the rostra [the speakers' platform in the Forum] where as consul, and often as ex-consul, and in that very year attacking Antony he had been heard amid such admiration for his eloquence as had rewarded no other human voice. The Romans could scarcely bear to lift eyes wet with tears to look on his mutilated body. (Livy, fragment from book 120 = Seneca the Elder, *Suasoria* 6. 17, trans. M. Winterbottom)

There is a layering of audiences in this extraordinary account: an unspecified one—posterity?—to whom Cicero directs his (alleged) last words; the slaves; the soldiers; the Roman audience in the Forum, whose opinion of Cicero is quoted as defining his importance; and the reader, both contemporary (who might well remember Cicero) and modern. Most importantly, however, there is Mark Antony. This is an early example of something that would soon become more common, that is, a political execution resulting from the publication (in Latin, *editio*, 'giving forth', either orally or in writing) of a work of literature. No more direct connection between author and audience can be imagined; no more eloquent testimony to the power, and danger, of books.

From this point on, even if authors remained unmolested, their books could be burned, a punishment that was particularly Roman. Cicero, at least, lived on through his books. Not so everyone, even under the comparatively tolerant Augustus:

It was for Labienus that there was first devised a new punishment: his enemies saw to it that all his books were burnt. It was an unheard of novelty that punishment should be exacted from literature. Certainly it was to everyone's advantage that this cruelty that turns on genius was devised later than the time of Cicero: for what would have happened if the triumvirs had been pleased to proscribe Cicero's talent as well as Cicero? . . . How great is the savagery that puts a match to literature, and wreaks its vengeance on monuments of learning; how unsatisfied with its other victims! Thank god that these punishments for genius began in an age when genius had come to an end! (Seneca the Elder, *Controversies* 10 Preface 5–7, trans. M. Winterbottom)

(Paradoxically, it was the mad tyrant Caligula who saw to it that copies of Labienus' works were returned to the libraries.) This excerpt from Seneca's

Political executions continued as a consequence of literary works.

memoirs of the Augustan practitioners of declamation shows many typical features of the Latin of imperial Rome: a desire to shock the audience; the use of emotive devices like rhetorical questions and exclamations to draw readers in. Then there is the striving for novelty of expression and content, both pernicious and perniciously attractive; and above all, a love of paradox: genius is punished only after genius has perished. In that is summed up the feeling of the post-Augustan age: 'after the Battle of Actium,' Tacitus would write (of historians) some eighty years later, 'that literary genius fell idle.' Lucius Annaeus Seneca, known as Seneca the Elder, an orator and scholar of oratory, is here writing under the Emperor Tiberius, Augustus' immediate successor. For him, Cicero marked the end of oratorical genius. What is it about the Augustan period that so definitively spoke to Seneca of immediate and irretrievable decline?

The answer lies in the second respect in which Cicero's *Philippics* represent a landmark in the history of ancient oratory. They were the last time a political orator spoke so publicly, and so freely, on a matter of state importance: they are, in short, the last example of truly outspoken republican oratory. As the emperors arrogated more and more power and responsibility to themselves, so the Senate's sphere of influence contracted; increasingly, political matters and even trials were decided in the emperor's private council, with advocates and prosecutors speaking directly to him, not to an audience of their peers or to a large jury. Though senatorial debates continued, their content, according to Tacitus, was a sham: speakers would try to anticipate the emperor's wishes, even if he were not present, and all argument took on an extra dimension of self-consciousness. How would the emperor react? What motives would he attribute to the speaker? Should the senators indulge in flattery or freedom of speech—a specious demonstration, says Tacitus, since it was never really free:

> I would hardly mention this year's adjournment if it were not worth noting the differing opinions of Gaius Asinius Gallus and Gnaeus Calpurnius Piso regarding it. Although the emperor had said he would be away, Piso opined that this was an additional reason for business to continue, as it was in the public interest that the Senate and knights could undertake their proper duties in the *princeps*' absence. Gallus, since Piso had anticipated him in the display of freedom, said that nothing had enough distinction or was compatible with the national dignity unless it happened in the presence and under the eye of the emperor. . . . Tiberius listened in silence as the matter was hotly debated—but the adjournment was carried. (Tacitus, *Annals* 2. 35)

> So tainted were these times, so meanly obsequious, that not only did the leading men of the state have to protect their positions by subservience . . .

but all ex-consuls, most ex-praetors, even many ordinary senators vied to propose the most repulsive and excessive motions. There is a story that whenever he left the Senate House Tiberius used to exclaim in Greek, 'Men fit for slavery!' Even he, who opposed public freedom, clearly was tired of such grovelling endurance in his slaves. (*Annals* 3. 65)

There was still room for free senatorial action on matters less close to home, especially concerning embassies from the provinces bringing petitions for citizenship, or asking to be allowed to dedicate temples to members of the imperial family, or claiming possession of ancient religious sites. Tacitus in his *Annals* devotes what may seem an inordinate amount of space to these debates, partly because some of the emperors were themselves interested in such matters, but partly because in them at least the Senate had relatively free rein.

Some civil and criminal cases were still held in public, though no longer outside in the Forum. Pliny (see pp. 173–4 below) describes a particularly lurid one:

> Attia Viriola was a woman of high birth, the wife of a praetorian senator, disinherited by her eighty-year-old father ten days after he had fallen in love and brought home a stepmother for his daughter, and now suing for her patrimony. . . . One hundred and eighty judges were sitting . . . both parties were fully represented and had a large number of seats filled with their supporters, and a close-packed ring [*corona*] of onlookers, several rows deep, lined the walls of the courtroom. The bench was also crowded, and even the galleries were full of men and women leaning over in their eagerness to see and also to hear, though hearing was rather more difficult. Fathers, daughters and stepmothers all anxiously awaited the verdict. (Pliny, *Letters* 6. 33. 2–4, trans. B. Radice)

The audience's engagement here is personal: the outcome of this trial may have an impact on their own families. Often, however, the crowd of spectators consisted of hired claques, brought in to distract the speakers and cause a disturbance:

> Audiences follow who are no better than the speakers, being hired and bought for the occasion. They parley with the contractor, take the gifts offered on the floor of the court as openly as they would at a dinner-party, and move on from case to case for the same sort of pay. The Greek name for them means 'bravo-callers' and the Latin 'dinner-clappers'; wittily enough, but both names expose a scandal which increases daily. Yesterday two of my attendants . . . were induced to add their applause for three *denarii* each. That is all it costs you to have your eloquence acclaimed. (Pliny, *Letters* 2. 14. 4–6, trans. B. Radice)

Historians discussed the provinces because it was more acceptable.

A similar technique was occasionally used towards the end of the Republic, and simple intimidation—or so the story goes—worked effectively to silence Cicero in the trial of Milo. Also under the Republic, orators had to contend with interruptions from unexpected sources, such as the noise from a passing funeral procession. Under the Empire, however, there is a pervasive sense that affairs are being stage-managed. Oratory becomes a spectacle, indeed a spectator sport, choreographed long in advance, even to the point of providing cue cards for the audience: 'for this sum seats can be filled, any number of them, a huge crowd assembled, and endless cheering raised whenever the chorus-master gives the signal. (A signal there must be for people who neither understand nor even hear; most of them do not listen but cheer as loud as anyone.)' (Pliny, *Letters* 2. 14. 6–8, trans. Radice.)

Another way in which formal oratory diverged from republican forms was through its increasing transformation into panegyric (praise oratory). This certainly existed under the Republic (Cicero's speech of 66 BCE, *For the Manilian Law*, is a thinly disguised panegyric of Pompey the Great), but the genre became formalized under the Empire. Pliny the Younger delivered our only completely extant example from the early Empire, the *Panegyric to Trajan* of 100 CE; more examples exist from the fourth century onward (see pp. 539–41). The written text that Pliny published is an expanded version which he first delivered to a circle of friends in three sessions of about two hours each. The expansion may have been due to Pliny's desire to speak at greater length than the Senate session allowed; but the resulting double audience also reflects the same kind of self-consciousness that we have seen above in Tacitus' accounts of the Senate. Though Pliny retains the second-person singular address, Trajan will not have heard the longer piece; nevertheless, it shows the loyal Pliny to best advantage, as well as demonstrating his rhetorical skills:

> As for the lives and characters of the young—how you are forming them in true princely fashion! And the teachers of rhetoric and professors of philosophy—how you hold them in honour! Under you the liberal arts are restored, to breathe and live in their own country—the learning which the barbarity of the past punished with exile, when an emperor acquainted with all the vices sought to banish everything hostile to vice, motivated less by hatred of learning than by fear of its authority. But you embrace these very arts, opening arms, eyes and ears to them, a living example of their precepts, as much their lover as the subject of their regard. Every lover of culture must applaud all your actions, while reserving his highest praise for your readiness to give audiences. Your father had shown his magnanimity by giving the title of 'open house' to what . . . had been a stronghold of tyranny—yet this would have been an empty formula had he not

adopted a son capable of living in the public eye. (*Panegyric* 47. 1–5, trans. B. Radice)

A little of this does go a long way! It is worth noticing, however, the intimate connection that Pliny draws between the moral character of the young, the liberal arts, and the emperor's willingness to open his palace, indeed his own character, to inspection. Learning has authority, and particularly authority both to expose vice (hence the tyrant's fear of it) and to guide human actions. Underlying Trajan's openness is the same accord that Cicero perceived between Cato the Elder's words and his actions: a perfect match, fostered by a love of the precepts found in literature, between a man's inner thoughts and outer actions. Such a vision of the Empire contrasts sharply with the (contemporary) Tacitean picture of the flattering servility shown by the Senate to their emperor; instead, it offers a positive formulation made by a senator trying to live in a system that could turn randomly violent. Words *are* dangerous, and the emperor as audience is especially so. In praising Trajan, Pliny chooses to highlight an ideal situation, in which author and audience live in reciprocal harmony.

Pliny delivered the original, shorter version of this speech in the Senate during the two months that he was consul. Similarly, during his consular months in 97 CE Tacitus famously delivered an eloquent eulogy of a distinguished ex-consul, Verginius Rufus. For comparison, reckon that during his consular year Cicero delivered four orations against the revolutionary Catiline; a speech in defence of the consul-elect on a charge of electoral corruption; three speeches against an agrarian law designed to distribute land to the plebs; and several others, a collection of orations of which he claims to have published twelve and of which we still have nine. Though Cicero maintained that oratory truly flourishes under a peaceful state, it would seem that the diagnosis in the *Dialogue on Orators*—whether serious or not about the 'one wisest man'—comes closer to the truth:

> Great and famous oratory is the protégé of licence, which fools call freedom, an associate of revolution, a spur for an unbridled populace. It has no obedience, no self-restraint; it is defiant, thoughtless, overbearing; it does not arise in well-regulated communities. . . . So long as the state was unsettled, so long as it destroyed itself with factions and dissensions and discord, so long as there was no peace in the Forum, no concord in the Senate, no control in the courts, no respect for great men, no restraint in the magistrates, Rome certainly grew sturdier eloquence, just as untilled fields produce more luxuriant vegetation. . . . [But] what need is there for long arguments in the Senate when the best men agree so quickly? What is the use of many public harangues [*contiones*], when the ignorant multitude

does not decide political issues, but one man, and he the wisest? (Tacitus, *Dialogue on Orators* 40. 2–41)

Declamation and the layering of meaning

Where, then, did all the Roman oratorical/rhetorical energy go? One phenomenon of the Augustan period, due partly to an increased interest in all types of scholarship (see below), partly to the diminished use for practical oratory, was a development of rhetorical theory. As with many trends, this began earlier: the *Rhetoric to Herennius*, once ascribed to Cicero, is a treatise on speaking written in the 80s BCE; and Cicero himself wrote rhetorical handbooks, some very technical (e.g. *On Invention* or *The Divisions of a Speech*), some more wide-ranging (*Brutus*, a history of Roman oratory, or the *Orator* on the best kind of public speaker and oratorical style). Still, with the beginning of the Empire came a flowering of such theoretical studies, culminating around 96 CE in the great *Education of an Orator* by Quintilian (Marcus Fabius Quintilianus), which contains not only practical and theoretical precepts but also hundreds of anecdotes about and quotations from earlier oratory. One of the methods by which a young man could learn to be a good speaker was by imitating established orators, using them as living examples; another way was by practising himself, learning to speak on any side of any topic—in short, to do exercises like those delivered by Karneades to the shocked Senate over a century earlier (see p. 27). The technique derived from Greek education, and dates back at least to the Sophists in the fifth century BCE. In the Augustan period and for centuries after, well into the Byzantine Empire, it became a means not so much of training as of display, a literary amusement for the educated classes, and a way of thinking that permeated literature at all levels, prose and poetry, from tragedy to epic, history to letters.

There were two basic kinds of specimen speeches or declamations: the *controversia* and the *suasoria*. In the former, an orator spoke for one or the other side of an imaginary court case. The topics, which are preserved for us in the Elder Seneca's memoirs of the Augustan declaimers and in two later collections of declamations attributed to Quintilian, range from the melodramatic to the downright fabulous:

> A woman condemned for unchastity appealed to the goddess Vesta before being thrown from the Tarpeian rock. She was thrown down, and survived. She is sought to pay the penalty again.

> A man killed one of his brothers, a tyrant. The other brother he caught in adultery and killed despite the pleas of his father. Captured by pirates, he

PAYING FOR CONCORD. The great temple to 'Harmony' (Concordia) was dedicated by the future Emperor Tiberius in 10 CE. It is quite accurately reflected on this coin issued by Tiberius in 36 CE.

> wrote to his father about a ransom. The father wrote to the pirates, saying that he would give double if they cut off his hands. The pirates let him go. The father is in need; the son is not supporting him.
>
> While a certain city was at war, a hero lost his weapons in battle, and removed the arms from the tomb of a dead hero. He fought heroically, then put the weapons back. He got his reward, and is accused of violating the tomb. (Seneca the Elder, *Controversiae* 1. 3, 1. 7, 4. 4, trans. M. Winterbottom)

The *suasoriae*, or 'persuasions', are designed to develop skills at extended argument, typically inviting an orator to deliberate on a course of action. The topics, again, are somewhat removed from reality. Should Alexander the Great sail the Ocean? Imagine that Antony promised to spare Cicero's life if he agreed to burn his books—what should he do? Even mythical characters speak, as in this extract in which Agamemnon deliberates whether to sacrifice his daughter in order to calm the storm that is holding back the Trojan expedition:

> God poured forth the waters of the sea on the express understanding that not every day should go as we hope. And it is not only the sea that is thus limited: look at the sky—are not the stars subject to this same condition? Sometimes they deny their rain and burn up the soil, and when the wretched farmers collect up the seed, it is burnt. . . . Sometimes the clear skies are hidden, every day weighs down the firmament with cloud. . . . Perhaps this is the law of nature; perhaps, as the story goes, the regulating factor is the course of the moon. . . . Whatever the case, it was not on the orders of a god that the sea held no perils for the adulterer [Paris, who carried off Helen of Troy]. . . . I was pursuing him so as not to have to fear

for the virginity of my daughter [i.e. and now I have to fear for her life instead]. When Troy is conquered, I shall spare the daughters of the enemy. —*Priam's* maiden daughter as yet has nothing to fear. (Seneca the Elder, *Suasoria* 3. 1, trans. M. Winterbottom)

Seneca's excerpts stress the epigrammatic and the *outré*; moreover, he gives no complete text, only pieces of the argument. Still, it is possible to see the fundamental lack of emotion in this rhetoric, even when, as here, the speaker takes on the role of the anguished protagonist. And emotion, especially emotion projected by the orator's own (often simulated) feelings, was what Cicero had chiefly relied on as a persuasive force. If you can rouse the audience's indignation, anger, fear, or pity, you can make them believe what you want them to. Here, in the hands of the famous declaimer Arellius Fuscus (one of Ovid's teachers), Agamemnon makes a laboured point about the fact that the gods are not immediately responsible for the storm that failed to impede Paris and Helen, nor (presumably) for the one that is keeping the Greek ships from giving chase. He then moves to a paradox involving his own and the enemy's virgin daughters: his (Iphigenia) is due to be sacrificed to the angry gods, but he will spare (or so he claims) Priam's. Like the other declaimers, Fuscus speaks at one remove from 'genuine' emotion, and in so doing shows what one might call a postmodern approach to oratory, an exploration of form at the expense of content, or, in one critic's words, of 'the primacy of language over spectacle'.

Declamation was a phenomenally popular activity among poets, prose writers, senators, and the leisured class in general. Even the emperors declaimed, and listened to declamation. And it happened not only in Latin: glamorous Greek sophists and rhetors declaimed throughout the first and second centuries CE to packed audiences. It was a competitive genre, each speaker trying to outdo the next in novelty, paradox, and compression of language and argument. Despite its popularity, however, it is still essentially literature for the inner circle, for those educated men whose energies would, under the Republic, have been directed elsewhere. And as such, it could sometimes be used, albeit obliquely, for very relevant political purposes. Like other scholarship it could even be, the imperial scholar Suetonius tells us, a vehicle for topical debate, with its continued popularity guaranteed by its prestige and by the nobility of those who practised it:

Gradually, rhetoric itself also came to be regarded as useful and honourable, and many people cultivated it for the sake of both protection and prestige: Cicero continued the practice of Greek declamation all the way down to his praetorship, whereas in Latin he declaimed when already elderly . . . certain historians report that on the very eve of the civil war Gnaeus Pompeius resumed the habit of declamation, the better to rebut the very articulate young Gaius Curio, who was supporting Caesar's claims, and that even during the war at Mutina both Marcus Antonius and Augustus maintained the habit; Nero Caesar gave a declamation in public during his first year as emperor, and had done so twice before. Furthermore, a large number of orators also published declamations. Accordingly, when people had been filled with a great enthusiasm for the discipline, there also arose a great flood of professors and teachers, who enjoyed such favour that some were able to rise from the meanest circumstances to reach the senatorial order and the highest offices of state. (Suetonius, *On Teachers of Grammar and Rhetoric* 25. 3, trans. R. Kaster)

Later, when the freedom of debate enjoyed by Pompey and Curio was no more, declaimers might use topics such as the popular *controversiae* about tyrannicide covertly to advocate the elimination of the emperors and a return to the Republic (see p. 185). Such criticism could be risky, not least because its effect depended entirely on the sensitivity of the audience. Cicero's *Philippics* were directly and undeniably hostile to Antony, and the orator paid the penalty for his freedom. Speaking in figurative language against an emperor, however, was an especially dangerous game, in which one had to bet either that the emperor was a worse 'reader' than the rest of the audience or that he would be unwilling to show himself insulted by a piece of rhetorical display. Seneca has an early example of a risky declamatory argument, from a case which involved adopting the son of a prostitute:

Latro was declaiming . . . in the presence of Augustus and Marcus Agrippa, whose sons—the emperor's grandsons [by his daughter Julia, later exiled for adultery]—the emperor seemed to be proposing to adopt at that time. Agrippa was one of those who were made noble, not born noble. Taking the part of the prostitute's son . . . Latro said, 'Now he is by adoption being raised from the depths and grafted on to the nobility'—and more to this effect. Maecenas signed to Latro that the emperor was in a hurry and he should finish the declamation off now. . . . The blessed Augustus, I feel, deserves admiration if such licence was permitted in his reign; but I cannot feel any sympathy for those who think it worth losing their head rather than lose a jest. (Seneca the Elder, *Controversia* 2. 4. 12–13, trans. M. Winterbottom)

Roman audiences were used to reading one character 'through' another—seeing Hektor and Achilles in Virgil's Aeneas, for example—so such layered effects would not be lost on them. Drama was traditionally the place for such covert criticism (see pp. 15–17); during the late Republic, for instance, a line from a tragedy had to be repeatedly encored, as the crowd cheered the playwright's 'judgement' against Pompey: 'To our misery are you great [or 'the

Great']!' Such play continued under the Empire, as when an Augustan audience turned a line about a eunuch priest into a slur on the emperor by clapping loudly and pointedly: 'Do you see how that pervert controls the globe with a finger?' (Suetonius, *Life of the Deified Augustus* 68).

Such large-scale public misreading would be difficult to punish, given that the Roman people did not (much to Caligula's regret) have a single neck. But more pervasively pointed drama may have gone underground. Heavily rhetorical, owing both shape and content to the influence of declamation, are a series of tragedies on Greek mythological themes by Lucius Annaeus Seneca, called Seneca the Younger, son of the orator and declaimer. He was not only one of the richest men of his day, but a prominent Stoic philosopher and tutor to the young Emperor Nero. His plays, which date from the 40s and 50s CE, are meditations on anger, lust, greed, and other typically monarchical characteristics. Seneca's work shows the same fascination with shock value, epigrammatic paradox, and novelty as his father's collection of declamatory titbits. And like some declamations, Senecan tragedy often cut close to the bone, its legendary characters revelling in the same sort of bloody megalomania as the all-too-real Roman emperors. Here is the Greek tyrant Atreus, after murdering his brother's children and feeding them to their unhappy parent:

> I walk equal to the stars and above all men,
> Touching with my proud head heaven's height.
> Now I hold the glory of the kingdom,
> Now my father's throne. I release the gods:
> I have reached the utmost of my desires.
> Well done, and more than well—now it is enough even for me.
> But why should it be enough? I will go on,
> And fill this father with his dead children.
> Lest shame deter me, daylight has departed.
> Would that I could hold back the fleeing gods, drag them back by force
> So that they all might see my vengeful feast!
> But the father shall see it—that is enough.
>   .   .   .   .
> Crowds of slaves, open the doors, let the festal hall lie open.
> It pleases me to see his face change colour
> When he looks on his children's heads—
> To hear the words his pain first pours out,
> To see his body stiffening, stupefied,
> His breath gone. This is to be the reward
> For all my trouble—to see him not only miserable,
> But to watch the misery as it comes upon him.

[Seneca, *Thyestes* 885–95, 901–7]

We do not know if these Senecan plays were ever performed, even as recitations. But in the *Dialogue on Orators* Tacitus' fictional character Maternus is imagined as having just recited his own *Cato*—based on the life of Cato the Younger, Julius Caesar's most heroized opponent. Maternus' friends fear that his writing might be too easily 'misunderstood'—but the playwright knows exactly what he is risking, and plans to go on to a *Thyestes* which will say whatever the *Cato* left unsaid (see pp. 184–6).

The dramatic date of the *Dialogue* is 75 CE, during the reign of Vespasian, the only emperor who, according to Tacitus, changed for the better. But it was written by a man who had lived through the tyranny of Vespasian's son Domitian, whose reign—like Nero's—quickly degenerated into a terror of executions, paranoia, and covert opposition. That experience, generalized to all emperors, resonates in the apprehension felt by Maternus' friends. Despite the danger, however, both the fictional Maternus and the real Seneca show a certain glee in their work, a delight in manipulating declamatory themes, in using their audience's familiarity with the rules of literary genres to push the boundaries out a little further each time—in short, to use all their imagination and energy in the continued creation of a literature that in spite of its apparent aridity could be an exciting, intellectually challenging game.

The glamour of libraries and recital halls

One of the major changes from the Republic to the Empire was the increased visibility and prestige accorded to scholarship. Our impression of this is partly due to our concentration on the person of the emperors, who possessed not only power but star quality, and who, like the Sicilian and Hellenistic monarchs before them, well understood the importance of creating a climate in which literature and intellectual study could be seen to flourish, demonstrating the nurturing, sophisticated, and enriching atmosphere of the regime. Literature could also, not incidentally, directly celebrate the achievements of the ruler, while the study of and commentary on earlier poetry, together with research into historical or cultural topics, had potential political use as well: the way literature is interpreted, after all, can provide a powerful key to manipulating opinion. Many of the Roman emperors in the period under discussion had serious literary or scholarly interests of their own: Augustus wrote at least one tragedy (though not, according to him, a very good one) and was fond of culling literature for exemplary stories to send to his friends; Tiberius studied philosophy and rhetoric on Rhodes and maintained a lifelong passion for legal

The emperors took greater control over the dissemination of literature.

and grammatical study; Claudius wrote histories of Rome, Etruria, and Carthage, plus an autobiography, and added three letters to the Latin alphabet; Nero composed all kinds of poetry, sang, and patronized many different arts before turning tyrant; Hadrian was a practising architect, wrote poetry, and debated. And though the Flavians, Nerva, and Trajan were not themselves as artistically inclined, they recognized the importance of intellectual endeavour to the emperor's image. Though scholarship at Rome began long before Augustus, it is under his rule that the prestige of teachers and grammarians began to increase, and a whole imperial industry in antiquarian research grew up around his projects to restore the dilapidated temples and revive the traditional laws and festivals of republican Rome (see pp. 40–3).

The emperor tended to look out towards the larger populace, avoiding the close, inner focus of the aristocratic republican Senate. Hence, perhaps, the move, also beginning with Augustus, from private to public libraries, as emperors took more and more control over the public dissemination of literature. Books had always travelled, whether as booty or by special request (so Cicero, for instance, would order books from Athens from his friend Atticus). Private citizens certainly still owned books, and some of them had impressive collections; to house such collections the Augustan architect Vitruvius advises on the ideal orientation for a private library. But books could also be a symbol of prestige, as for the 'many ignorant men' who, according to Seneca the Younger, buy books 'not as instruments of learning but as decorations for their dining rooms'; or for the freedmen parodied by the Neronian novelist Petronius (see pp. 218–20), whose Trimalchio piques himself on his learning:

> Tell me, Agamemnon my dearest friend; have you any recollection of the twelve labours of Hercules, or the story of how Ulysses had his thumb twisted off by the Cyclops with his pincers? I used to read these stories in Homer when I was a boy. . . . But in case you think I am an ignoramus, I'm perfectly aware how Corinthian bronze originated. At the capture of Troy, that rascally slimy lizard Hannibal piled all the statues of bronze, gold, and silver on a pyre, and set fire to them; all the various elements merged into an alloy of bronze. . . . I have something like a hundred three-gallon bumpers . . . with the motif of Cassandra killing her sons . . . and a bowl which King Minos bequeathed to my patron; on it Daedalus is enclosing Niobe in the Trojan horse. (Petronius, *Satyricon* 48, 50, 52, trans. P. G. Walsh)

The imperial libraries, in particular, will have fostered this association of books and prestige, together with a rivalry between Greek and Latin that was itself fuelled by the literary critics' comparisons of authors in the two languages, the most famous being found in book 10 of Quintilian's *Education of an Orator*. So Cicero is the Roman Demosthenes, Sallust the Roman Thoukydides, Livy the Roman Herodotos. The first public library in Rome, sponsored by Julius Caesar, was to be assembled by the great scholar Varro, though he never completed the task. Gaius Asinius Pollio, the anti-Caesarian historian and tragedian, founded one in the 30s, pointedly located in the 'Hall of Liberty'. This was quickly overshadowed by Augustus' two libraries, one adjoining the temple of Palatine Apollo and presided over by the learned freedman Hyginus, the other near the Theatre of Marcellus; they were later joined by buildings by Tiberius, Vespasian, Trajan, Caracalla, and Diocletian. The aim of these collections was not only cultural equality with the Greeks, but also literary immortality: even as genres such as history and epic could ensure the immortality of their subjects (not least the Roman people), so any work of literature made its author live on. All you needed was a place in a library niche—though not all papyrus rolls were so lucky, as one of Ovid's banned books of exile poetry tells us:

> Here were the works of learned men, both ancient
>   And new, open to every reader's eye.
> I sought my brother books . . .
> I searched in vain; the library's custodian
>   Commanded me to leave his holy shrine.
> I sought another temple, near the Theatre;
>   This too might not be trod by feet of mine.
> And Liberty's halls, too, the first thrown open
>   To learned books, refused me access there.
> My author's fate redounds upon his offspring:
>   The exile he has borne, from birth we bear.
> Perhaps, one day, to us and him great Caesar,
>   By long years vanquished, will be less severe. . . .
> Meanwhile since I'm debarred a shelf in public,
>   Let me lie hidden in a private place.
> You too, the people, if you may, receive my
>   Rejected verse, dismayed by its disgrace.
>   (Ovid, *Tristia* 3. 1. 65–82, trans. A. D. Melville)

The picture of Apollo as stern librarian is a comic one, but the situation is far from humorous; it shows, moreover, how much control an emperor might be thought to have even over (theoretically) public collections. Ovid's poetry has to hope for private circulation among 'the people'—presumably his friends. The emperor's control could be absolute: when Caligula allowed Labienus'

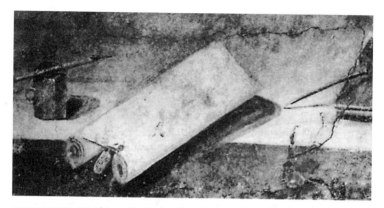

READING MATERIALS. *This wall-painting from Pompeii shows an ink-pot and pen, a half-unwound papyrus roll (with title-tag), and an open set of wax tablets with stylus for inscribing temporary contents on them*

vitriolic prose to circulate again, he did so for political point, despising as he did the classics of Greek and Latin literature:

> He allowed the writings of Titus Labienus, Cremutius Cordus, and Cassius Severus [Labienus' prosecutor] to be chased down, circulated, and read, though they had been suppressed by senatorial decrees, it being entirely in his own interest that all events be handed down to posterity. . . . He even considered suppressing the Homeric epics, asking why he should not have the same power as Plato, who expelled Homer from his ideal state. And he came close to removing the writings and the portraits of Virgil and Livy from all the libraries, railing at the one as having no talent and very little learning, and at the other as a wordy and careless historian. . . . He regarded smooth, well-groomed style with such disdain that he used to say that Seneca, who was very popular at the time, composed 'mere school exercises' and that he was 'sand without lime'. (Suetonius, *Life of Caligula*, 16, 34, 53)

Labienus, Cremutius, and Cassius had the merit of sophisticated rarity (and, of course, of having been banned by Caligula's imperial predecessors); the judgements on Virgil and Livy show Caligula exploiting the public library system to thumb his nose at the conservative reading public and the snobbish, literary élite.

With the decline of political oratory, when not declaiming (above), that élite had to find something else to do. Throughout the period under discussion, but especially in the second half of it, from the Emperor Claudius (reigned 41–54 CE) through to Hadrian (117–38), they practised scholarship and literary dalliance in almost equal parts. Some, like Julius Caesar before them—who could keep four secretaries busy at once and who is said to have written his *On Grammatical Analogy* 'while the javelins were flying about him'—lost no chance to pursue scholarship, reading, and taking notes at table, while riding, even at the baths.

Gaius Plinius Secundus, known as Pliny the Elder, who died in the eruption of Mount Vesuvius in 79 CE, is the most famous example of this type. He wrote many works, including a treatise on using a throwing-spear, a biography of his patron G. Pomponius Secundus, a history of the German wars, a collection of pointed remarks for use in declamation, a history of the Roman Empire under the Julio-Claudians, and—the only one to survive—a *Natural History* in thirty-seven books, containing (according to its preface) 20,000 facts from 2,000 written sources. It was, among other things, an 'inventory of the world', an attempt to preserve the wonders of nature and of human achievement: along with his readers, Pliny himself is an astonished spectator of this collection of marvels, biological facts, historical information, architectural details, recipes, charms, measurements, etc. He is conscious of the potential aridity of his subject; yet he advertises it to the future Emperor Titus, its dedicatee, as a service to mankind:

> My subject is a barren one: the nature of things, that is, life; and life in its least elevated aspect. . . . Moreover, my way lies not along a road well trodden by scholars, nor one in which the mind seeks eagerly to travel; no one among us has made the same attempt. . . . It is hard to give novelty to what is old, authority to what is new, shine to the dingy, light to the obscure, attraction to what is scorned, credibility to the dubious. . . . Even if I have not succeeded, it is fully honourable and glorious to have tried. And indeed I feel that there is a special place in scholarship for those who, having overcome their difficulties, prefer the useful service of helping others to the popularity of pleasing them. (Pliny the Elder, *Natural History*, Preface 13–16)

By showing his awareness of the desirability of novelty and polish in a work of literature Pliny uses the conventional ploy of authorial modesty, one familiar from oratory, as for instance from the beginning of the *Milo* (above, p. 34), in which Cicero plays down his own courage. Obviously, the reader is to understand that this book *will* be novel, polished, interesting—and on top of that, *useful*, a quintessential old-fashioned Roman virtue. For Pliny the Elder was nothing if not old-fashioned, at least in the persona he chose to present in the

Natural History. Like the Elder Cato, Sallust, and other moralists, he attacks luxury and conspicuous consumption, arguing for the force of traditional Roman values even in the face of the astounding diversity and threatening bulk of the Empire, which now encompassed the known world. As we saw of prose under the late Republic, such conservatism can be a weapon designed to bolster social and cultural structures that are perceived to be at risk. Unfortunately, Pliny's opening bluff has not succeeded in distracting modern readers from the ponderousness of his book, which since the Renaissance was little read or even consulted, until recently, when it is receiving some attention. Older audiences were less critical: until the fifteenth century the encyclopaedia was an extremely influential work.

Fifty years after Pliny, Gaius Suetonius Tranquillus, one of Hadrian's senior secretaries, exploited his access to the imperial archives to write biographies of a dozen Caesars and brief lives of literary figures, as well as treatises on Greek and Roman games and festivals, weather signs, the names of winds, the Roman calendar, and many others. The breadth of his learning and interests recalls that of Varro (see pp. 37, 38–41), though in some ways he was even more of a professional scholar than his republican precursor, probably gaining his imperial post as director of libraries (*a bibliothecis*) at least partly as a recognition for his literary achievements.

Other imperial officials who wrote technical treatises in the first century include Sextus Julius Frontinus, the Flavian overseer of the water supply who produced a treatise on how to do his job, perhaps directed at future curators of aqueducts. Some compiled manuals both in Greek and in Latin on military strategy and generalship, continuing the process of which Cicero had complained a century earlier, of teaching young men how to fight out of books. One of these, also by Frontinus, is a collection of famous stratagems employed by famous generals, culled from ancient histories and presented in list form as a source of examples to imitate. Similar is the collection of moral examples by Valerius Maximus, written during the reign of Tiberius and perhaps designed as a source book for declaimers, perhaps as a sort of reference book for would-be gentlemen, a rising class of entrepreneurs and *arrivistes* who needed quick exemplary history to provide a sort of 'instant ancestry'. Finally, Pliny's near-contemporaries Aulus Cornelius Celsus and the wealthy landowner Lucius Junius Moderatus Columella—authors respectively of an encyclopaedia of knowledge (of which only the book on medicine survives) and a twelve-book treatise on agriculture—wrote a stylish, up-to-date Latin. Columella even incorporated a book of verse on gardens in explicit imitation of Virgil's *Georgics* (see pp. 187–91).

Like the Elder Pliny, the Neronian philosopher and politician Seneca the Younger had an active public career, though interrupted by a period of exile and ended by one of voluntary retirement; unlike Pliny, however, he was anything but old-fashioned. He, too, wrote an encyclopaedia, three books of *Natural Questions*, a sort of Stoic philosophy of nature which in style was fully modern. He also wrote a bitingly funny satire of the Emperor Claudius—well after his death!—called the *Pumpkinification* (the Latin title, *Apocolocyntosis*, parodies the Greek *apotheosis*, or 'divinification'). Apart from his tragedies (discussed above), he is best known for his ethical philosophy, a collection of ten dialogues on themes such as *Anger*, *The Tranquil Spirit*, and *Providence*. Seneca has a fine sense of humour, a cutting wit, and a good eye for a self-deflating anecdote. Here is the scholar on the vanity of scholarship:

> This was particularly a Greek disease, to ask how many rowers Ulysses had and whether the *Iliad* or the *Odyssey* was written first, and besides, if they are by the same author, and other things of the same sort. If you keep them secret, they do your private knowledge no good; if you tell people about them, you appear not a scholar but a bore. And lo, now this empty enthusiasm for learning useless things has invaded the Romans as well. Recently I heard someone reporting which Roman leader did what first: Duilius was the first to win a naval battle, Curius Dentatus was the first to lead elephants in a triumph. (Seneca the Younger, *On the Shortness of Life* 13)

Seneca's 124 philosophical letters, addressed to his friend Gaius Lucilius, show a remarkable combination of modesty, humour, and gentle advice—the optimum combination, carefully learned in the schools of rhetoric, for delivering potentially unpalatable lessons. Here too he can be biting on the habits of contemporary scholarship and on what this learned audience misses in literature, being too caught up in matters of linguistic detail and literary history:

> A future grammarian [that is, an explicator of poetry], on looking at Virgil, does not read that famous line, 'time flies beyond catching,' in this spirit: 'we must pay attention; unless we hurry we will be left behind; swift time drives us and is driven; we are carried along, unknowing . . . ' but he reads it to observe that when Virgil speaks of the swiftness of time he uses this word 'flees'. . . . And the grammarian reading Cicero's *Republic* first notes that Cicero says 'the thingself' [*reapse*], that is, 'the thing itself' [*re ipsa*]. . . . Then he moves on to usages which have changed over time, such as the finishing line in the Circus which we now call '*creta*', the ancients used to call '*calx*'. Then he compares some Ennian verses . . . (Seneca, *Moral Letters* 108. 24, 32–3)

Seneca's technique is close to that of the didactic poet Lucretius (see pp. 55–65), whose famous simile of the honey on the cup of medicine would equally fit Seneca's approach to teaching Lucilius the rudiments of Stoic philosophy. And, through Lucilius, he teaches the wider world: for Seneca's ethical philosophy, like Cicero's, is designed to reach the literate reading public of Rome, not simply its private addressees.

Since Augustus, literature maintained at least the façade of reaching a wider audience. Asinius Pollio, in addition to founding his library, instituted the habit of fairly formal recitation, either in a private home or in a hired recital hall. These literary performances, which became increasingly fashionable, are most memorably parodied by the Neronian poet Persius (see the passage quoted on p. 222).

Recitations of prose works, though not targeted by the satirist, are well attested throughout the period, being best documented in the letters of Gaius Plinius Caecilius Secundus, called Pliny the Younger. These, modelled on the letters of Cicero, are carefully written for future publication by a man constructing his own image with one eye on the past and one on the opinion of posterity. They give us a remarkable picture of imperial society, with a special concentration on literary circles. The biographies of the emperors by Suetonius provide another rich source of information about recitation and its audiences.

As usual, the most prestigious auditor was the emperor himself (see p. 486, on Domitian as 'super-reader'). So, for example, besides listening to declamation, Augustus heard recitations of history, oratory, and philosophical dialogues; Claudius recited his own history and listened to that of Servilius Nonianus. The Younger Pliny recited speeches, including his *Panegyric*, and listened to history, invective, and eulogies of famous men; the Younger Seneca speaks of crowds of philosophers reciting their works. On a less elevated level, fabulous tales such as the ghost stories in one of Pliny's better-known letters, or the animal fables of Phaedrus, might be told for entertainment at dinner parties (see pp. 208–34). This flurry of recitation did more than simply fill the aristocrat's increasingly vacant leisure time, though there was certainly something of that about it. Except for those in business, public service no longer occupied as much senatorial attention when the emperor and his bureaucratic staff were in control, and so they put their talents to work elsewhere. But, just as during the Republic, competition and display were at the heart of this new public activity.

A select audience's reaction was particularly important as a form of critical feedback, as the younger Pliny explains (see pp. 211–12):

I am too diffident to feel confident that I have done everything I can to what has only my own approval. I have therefore two reasons for reading in public; the reader is made more keenly critical of his own work if he stands in some awe of his audience, and he has a kind of panel of experts to confirm his decision on any doubtful point. He receives suggestions from different members and, failing this, he can infer their various opinions from their expressions, glances, nods, applause, murmurs and silence, signs which make clear the distinction between their critical judgement and polite assent. . . . But now I am arguing this point as if I invited the general public to a lecture hall instead of having my friends in my own room—though if I have many friends to invite this has been a source of pride to many people and a reproach to none. (Pliny, *Letters* 5. 3. 8–10, trans. B. Radice)

Pliny's modest persona, which pervades his letters, is a deliberately assumed mask: diffident he may have been, but he was also intensely proud of his talent. And the process he describes here on a small scale may operate on a large one: audience tastes and expectations could determine the style of a whole generation, as happened with declamation. But the process could become a vicious circle, with audiences going on to imitate the bad habits they have themselves encouraged in their taste for novelty. Quintilian, in his discussion of Latin authors, has strong views on Senecan style (which the nineteenth-century English historian Macaulay memorably compared to a diet of anchovy sauce):

Seneca had many great virtues: a quick and abundant talent, with much learning and wide knowledge (in which, however, he was sometimes deceived by those to whom he entrusted his research). For he handled almost every area of scholarship: speeches and poems and letters and dialogues circulate under his name. He was not very critical in philosophy, though he was a remarkable denouncer of vice. His works contain many notable epigrammatic formulations and much that is worth reading to improve one's character—yet his style contains many corrupt things which are exceedingly dangerous because they abound in attractive faults. One could wish that he had spoken with his own intelligence, but with someone else's judgement. . . . If he had not been so enamoured of all his ideas, and if he had not fractured the dignity of his subject with epigrammatic brevity, he would be approved by a consensus of learned men rather than by infatuated boys. (Quintilian, *The Education of an Orator* 10. 1. 128–30)

We saw the same worries surfacing under the Republic; now, however, in a literary society in which a small coterie of experts engaged in an intimate process of improvising, competing, imitating, and striving always to outdo each other, the dangers of solipsism and unregulated display are much to the fore. Quintilian is worried about Seneca's style at least partly because he sees how popular it has become, and wants to warn the young against it. It is, in fact, from Seneca himself that we have the most explicit discussion of the dangerous effects of imitation, in his letters to Lucilius. Though acknowledging that imitation is not in itself the sign of a corrupt mind or of decadence, he nevertheless points out that a charismatic figure's faults can be those of an entire age:

> Maecenas [one of Augustus' friends] was clearly effeminate, not gentle. . . . His misleading word order, expressions that get in the way, and extraordinary thoughts—often great, yes, but emasculated in their expression—make it clear that his head was turned by excessive success. This fault is due sometimes to a man and sometimes to his times. When prosperity has poured out luxury far and wide, bodily culture starts to get too much attention. . . . When the mind has become used to scorning ordinary things and regarding customary things as shabby, it begins to look for novelties in speech also, sometimes recalling and displaying obsolete, old fashioned words, sometimes coining new words . . . sometimes bold and frequent metaphors are considered sophisticated. Some amputate their sentences hoping to make a good impression if the meaning is left in doubt and the listener suspects his own lack of wit; some dwell on their sentences and stretch them out; others, too, not only fall into stylistic fault (for someone aiming high must do this) but actually love the fault for its own sake. (Seneca, *Moral Letters* 114. 8–11)

Seneca's criticism of Maecenas modulates into a discussion of the interconnection between literary style and culture, and finally centres on the relationship between speaker and audience, for it is there that a literary character can most clearly be perceived and (more importantly) judged.

Styles change; literary fashions come and go. Just after our period, there was a revival of archaic Latin, with the orator Marcus Cornelius Fronto (tutor to the Emperor Marcus Aurelius) imitating Cato the Elder in preference to Cicero. The modernity of Senecan prose must have looked very dated indeed. And lastly there is Aulus Gellius, a scholar living in the second half of the second century CE, both in Athens and in Rome. He compiled a miscellany in twenty books, the *Attic Nights*, a collection of quotations, facts, and trivia concerning philosophy, law, and grammar, including literary and textual criticism. Though intended as a source of entertaining information for his children, it enjoyed a wide influence in late antiquity and beyond. Like much of imperial scholarship, especially the books of Frontinus, Valerius Maximus, and Pliny the

Elder, it was produced both for use and out of a delight in collection for its own sake. It gives us an interesting picture of one ancient scholar's reading—and an invaluable trove of fragments of Latin literature that would otherwise be lost to us.

The power of memory

History continued to be as popular as ever under the Empire, although, as the future Emperor Claudius' experience showed, choice of topic was as important as sturdy furniture in the recital hall:

> As a young man he began to write history with Livy's encouragement and the help of Sulpicius Flavus. But when he first recited to a large audience he barely got through it, since he more than once gave himself a 'chill'. For at the beginning of the reading a laugh arose when several benches broke under the weight of a fat man, and not even after the disturbance was quieted could Claudius help recalling the incident and chuckling all over again. . . . He started his history with the death of the dictator Caesar, but moved on to a later period, beginning at the 'civil peace' since he understood that he was not allowed to speak frankly or truly about the earlier time, having often been taken to task both by his mother and by his grandmother. (Suetonius, *Life of the Deified Claudius* 41)

Even a member of the imperial household could not afford to be too critical of the regime, or to reveal what the emperor's family preferred not to reveal. People outside the royal family who did risk complimenting the 'Liberators' Brutus and Cassius, for example, could pay with their lives, as did Cremutius Cordus, one of the historians whose works had been restored by Caligula after he was disgraced and his books burnt, under Tiberius. Curtius Rufus, who (probably) lived under Claudius, took an indirect way around this problem, choosing instead to write a history of Alexander the Great. His Alexander bears a remarkable resemblance to a Roman emperor, but he is a foreign, exotic figure, distant enough from the potentially dangerous present. Another route was ethnography, the history of distant peoples; our only complete ethnography from antiquity is Tacitus' monograph on Germany, the *Germania*. It, too, reflects obliquely on the Empire, especially in its portrait of a nation of noble savages untouched by the corrupting effects of civilization.

Finally, one could write an epitome, or short history, touching on only the high points of the Roman past. The conventional epitome-writer's excuse of being in a hurry could enable one to pass by a number of uncomfortable incidents—even if, like the Tiberian writer Velleius Paterculus, you were in fact loyal to the regime (Velleius had served in the army under Tiberius and so had first-hand knowledge of his considerable military abilities and virtues). Another epitome, by Lucius Annaeus Florus, may date from the second century CE: it is far more florid and panegyrical than Velleius' text, employing exclamation and exaggeration to enhance the author's enthusiasm for his often lurid subject:

> First luxury, then lack of money pushed Catiline into his unspeakable plan. . . . With what allies—oh, horrible!—did he undertake to run the senators through, butcher the consuls, rip the city apart with fire, ransack the treasury—in a word, to uproot the whole state from its foundations and do things that not even Hannibal seems to have desired! (Florus, *Epitome of Roman History* 2. 12)

Florus preserves the minimum of Sallust's social critique, but seeks more to thrill his reader with the horror of Catiline's plans than to offer any historical analysis; this really is history as entertainment, a far cry from Pliny the Elder's call for difficult but useful topics.

Florus is, however, an exception in imperial historiography. The genre begins 150 years earlier with Titus Livius (Livy), a private citizen from Padua in northern Italy, who spent most of his life in Rome, writing what would become itself a monument: 142 papyrus rolls of Roman history from the beginning through to Livy's own time, probably ending in 9 BCE. Three-quarters of it, including everything after 167 BCE, is lost, making it impossible to tell how Livy would have treated the problematic years of the early Empire. The earliest books, which cover the legendary and regal periods, are restrained by comparison with Livy's contemporary, the Greek-speaking historian Dionysios of Halikarnassos, who took eleven books to cover what Livy does in three. They show the scepticism, sometimes bordering on cynicism, that pervades the whole of the work as we have it:

> One day during a meeting to review his troops on the Campus Martius . . . a sudden storm with mighty thunder claps enveloped the king in such a dense cloud that the crowd lost sight of him. Nor was Romulus seen again on earth. . . . Although the soldiers readily believed the senators who had been standing closest that he had been snatched up in the air by a whirlwind, still . . . they were stricken with the fear of having been orphaned, so to speak, and for quite a time stood in mournful silence. Then, after a few proclaimed Romulus' divinity, the rest joined in, hailing him with one accord as a god, born to a god, king and parent of the city of Rome. . . . I

believe that even then there were some people who maintained privately that the king had been torn apart by the hands of the senators—for this version, though little known, has also been handed down. Still, admiration for the man and the alarm felt at the time gave the other version wider currency, and it was further strengthened by the testimony of a single individual. This man was Proculus Iulius, a highly respected citizen according to tradition . . . who stepped forth in a public assembly to affirm the truth of a most extraordinary event. . . . It is astonishing how absolute was the conviction that Proculus Iulius' words carried and how, once belief in Romulus' immortality had been confirmed, the grief felt by the army and people was mitigated. (Livy, *From the Founding of the City* 1. 16, trans. T. J. Luce)

Livy is particularly fond, as in this episode, of using internal audiences (as we saw also above, in his description of Cicero's death). Here, he plays with layers of audiences: the crowd at the time, later tradition—split in two by the distinctly anti-tyrannical story of Romulus' murder—and the contemporary reader, joined by Livy himself in trying to sort out some kind of truth about this legendary past. It is possible to read it either completely straight or with tongue-in-cheek. Proculus Julius, for instance, has a remarkably significant name in this story of the divination of a Roman emperor, and was probably invented by the Julian family in order to heighten their clan's importance. Livy could not possibly comment: 'it is astonishing,' he says simply, a comment which can be taken two ways, in Latin as in English.

Livy's construction of early Rome and the first centuries of the Republic is both sentimental and postmodern. He accepts that it is impossible to tell what really happened, about such matters ranging from the number of battles fought in third century BCE wars to the real story behind Scipio Africanus' charismatic appeal. It *is* possible to use good historical methods, including arguments from analogy and from probability, and he painstakingly teaches his reader how to deploy those sifting tools to reach a likely version of the past. But what he is most interested in is not what actually happened, but how the past is remembered, and how that memory functions in and can help change the present and the future.

Through a process of careful analysis, vivid reconstruction, rhetorical technique, and allusion to the topographical and literary monuments of Rome, he enlists his reader in a process of recovering what the Roman people saw as their past, and in using that past critically as an exemplary guide for the future. While his own persona is patient, diffident, and often misleadingly uncertain, his history is dynamic and demanding:

Whether in writing the history of the Roman people from the foundation of the city the result will be worth the effort invested, I do not really know (nor, if I did, would I presume to say so). . . . My wish is that each reader will pay the closest attention to the following: how men lived, what their moral principles were, under what leaders and by what measures at home and abroad our empire was won and extended: then let him follow in his mind how, as discipline broke down bit by bit, morality at first foundered; how it next subsided in ever greater collapse and then began to topple headlong in ruin—until the advent of our own age, in which we can endure neither our vices nor the remedies needed to cure them. The special and salutary benefit of the study of history is to behold evidence of every sort of behaviour set forth as on a splendid memorial; from it you may select for yourself and for your country what to emulate, from it what to avoid, whether basely begun or basely concluded. (Livy, *From the Founding of the City*, Preface 1, 9–10, trans. T. J. Luce)

Livy takes his Sallustian awareness of Rome's current debasement and turns it into a programme for socio-political improvement. His approach is almost clinical (and indeed in this passage uses medical language), and has much in common with Augustus' own plan to use ancient monuments and tradition to rebuild a radically new Rome. Owing to the loss of the later books, it is impossible to tell how radically new Livy's Rome would have been. We can tell, however, that his work is particularly important in being open-access history, written not by a senator but by a historian uninvolved in the government or the military, directed neither exclusively at the élite nor the non-élite, a mix of scholarship and popularizing, avoiding the polemics of the late-republican memoir and insider histories such as Sallust's or Asinius Pollio's.

Sallust and Livy together were formative influences on the greatest historian of the imperial period, Cornelius Tacitus. Like Livy, he came from the north (probably from southern France); unlike him, however, he was a senator, with a successful career even under the tyrant Domitian, ending up under Trajan as governor of the province of Asia (112–13 CE). His two works of narrative history, the *Histories* and the *Annals*, borrow the annalistic or year-by-year form from Livy's history, structuring the narrative around the annual rotation of consuls, the chief magistrates of the old republican government. Deliberately anachronistic, and jarring with the reality of imperial rule, this structure sets the tone for his bleak, overpoweringly cynical view of the first sixty-five years of the Empire, from the death of Augustus through to the accession of Vespasian in 70 (later books of the *Histories*, which continued through Domitian's rule, together with the reign of Caligula and parts of Claudius and Nero from the *Annals*, are lost).

Tacitus' world is populated with duplicitous, violent emperors, craven senators, unexpectedly brave freedwomen, charismatic but useless military

SETTING EXAMPLES. The background to trials in the Forum of Augustus was a curving portico with the statue of one of the great men of the past and an inscription recording his deeds in each niche.

leaders, gluttonous aristocrats, exaggeratedly stubborn philosophers, poisoners, spies, and innocent doomed youths. His style combines Sallustian unpredictability with consummate Livian structure and variety to produce a dazzling, challenging Latin that demands repeated readings. It is a Latin whose deceptive surface conceals a hidden meaning, like the world about which Tacitus is writing, in which only those survive who manage to steer a middle course between 'precipitous obstinacy and a wasteland of servility'. The only successful readers in Tacitus' text are those who can read the all-powerful emperor who, as the focus of aristocratic and plebeian attention alike, has himself become a dangerous new text which demands, yet frustrates, correct reading. Tiberian opacity we have seen above, in discussing oratory and the Senate. Nero, who delights in exploiting the range of theatrical effect, is even worse: misinterpreting such an emperor can easily be punished by death.

There is a dense concentration of such theatrical scenes in *Annals* 15, culminating in the great fire of Rome. First, the emperor himself takes to the stage, not at Rome but in a town of Greek foundation, the better to foster the illusion of performance in the country which invented literary festivals:

> Hitherto Nero had sung in private houses or gardens . . . but these he now scorned, as too little attended and too restricted for such a fine voice. Not daring, however, to start at Rome, he chose Neapolis [Naples] because it was a Greek city. From this starting-point he could cross to Achaia. . . . Accordingly, a crowd of townspeople was collected . . . and filled the theatre at Naples. There an incident took place which many thought unlucky, though Nero believed it due to the providence of the auspicious gods. For after the audience had left, the empty building collapsed without harm to anyone. (Tacitus, *Annals* 15. 33–4)

Lucky for the spectators—though perhaps not so, considering the lengths to which, it is alleged, Nero later went to keep his audiences captive: it is said that since he allowed no one to leave his performances, pregnant women gave birth in the theatres, while some men tried to leap from the walls, others even going so far as to feign death so that they could be carried out of the building.

Instead of continuing to Greece, however, and though wanting badly to go to the exotic province of Egypt, Nero stays in Rome, making himself popular with the people—though not, it goes without saying, with the conservative senators:

> To assure people that no place pleased him as much as Rome, Nero gave banquets in the public places, treating the whole city as his private house. Of these feasts the most famous . . . were those given by Tigellinus, which I will describe as an example. . . . He constructed a raft on Agrippa's lake, put the banquet on board and had it towed by other boats. These vessels were decorated with gold and ivory; the degenerate crews were arranged according to age and experience of vice. . . . On the quays stood brothels filled with noble women, and on the opposite bank were seen naked prostitutes. As darkness approached, nearby groves and surrounding buildings resounded with song and shone with lights. Nero, polluted by every lawful and lawless act, had omitted no abomination by which he could be further corrupted—except that a few days later, in a solemn wedding ceremony, he became the wife of one of that filthy herd, a slave named Pythagoras. The bridal veil was put on the emperor; witnesses, dowry, couch and nuptial torches were there—everything, in a word, was visible. (*Annals* 15. 37)

Constructing what is essentially a stage set covering a large portion of Rome (and one which, it has been argued, is deliberately intended to reproduce the

Egypt which Nero longed to see), Nero takes over public entertainment for his own obscene pantomime, even going so far as to play the part of a bride in a homosexual wedding. Tacitus singles out the most lurid elements, emphasizing that this was done to be seen—and, of course, is here laid out for you, the reader, to see. Both the emperor and his historian play to their respective audiences. But it is Nero who will have the best part:

> A disaster followed, one . . . more serious and dreadful than any which has ever happened to this city by the violence of fire. . . . The flames first swept through the level portions of the city, then rising to the hills . . . outstripped all preventive measures by their speed, and by the fact that the city was vulnerable owing to its narrow alleys winding here and there and its irregular blocks. . . . In addition the wailing of terror-stricken women, the feebleness of age and the inexperience of childhood, people looking after themselves and looking after others, dragging the weak along or waiting for them, some delaying, some fleeing, all got in the way. . . . Nero at this time was staying at Antium and did not return to Rome until the fire was nearing his house. . . . A rumour spread that at the very moment when the city was aflame, the emperor had gone on to his private stage and sung the destruction of Troy, comparing modern evils with ancient disasters. (*Annals* 15. 38–9)

The fire becomes a backdrop to the mad emperor's private performance, an opportunity for bringing life to ancient history: on Nero's stage, Rome becomes Troy, and the emperor is author, actor, and audience rolled into one.

It is Tacitus, however, who has the last word. Though his history is neither sentimental nor hopeful, it does share with Livy's an intense desire to be useful, to turn the past, however horrifying, into something from which one can learn. One of the new genres that sprang up under the Empire was the martyrology, or eulogy of political victims. Though none of these survives from before the Christian period (where they commemorate victims of religious persecution), we know the subjects of some of them. They are mainly Stoic philosophers, men whom Tacitus characterizes as uselessly indulging their opposition to the Empire, going to an ostentatious but ultimately pointless death. Yet he borrows from the genre in his first monograph, the *Agricola*, a historical biography of his father-in-law, a man who Tacitus says managed to follow that path between truculence and servility. It is a testament not only to the man, but to the power of the written word to reach out beyond its immediate circumstances to audiences unimaginably far away:

> If there is any place for the spirits of the just, if, as philosophers believe, great souls do not perish with the body, may you rest in peace. May you

call us . . . to contemplate your noble character, for which it is a sin either to mourn or to shed tears. May we rather honour you by our admiration and our undying praise and, if our powers permit, by following your example. . . . Images of the human face, like that face itself, are weak and perishable. The beauty of the soul lives for ever, and you can preserve and express that beauty, not by the material and artistry of another, but only in your own character. All that we have loved in Agricola, all that we have admired in him, abides and is destined to abide in human hearts through the endless procession of the ages, by the fame of his deeds. Many of the men of old will be buried in oblivion, inglorious and unknown. Agricola's story has been told for posterity and he will survive. (Tacitus, *Agricola* 46, trans. A. R. Birley)

Tacitus wants to turn his history into something from which Romans can learn.

7 | Oblique politics: Epic of the imperial period

MATTHEW LEIGH

Cultures of recitation

In his *Dialogue on Orators*, Tacitus depicts a small gathering of writers and orators at the house of one Curiatius Maternus (cf. p. 166). The dramatic date is 75 CE, the actual date of publication around a quarter of a century later. The initial context is intriguing. For this is the day after the recitation by Curiatius of his new tragedy *Cato* and all the town is buzzing with talk of the offence given to the powerful by the energy with which Curiatius threw himself into the part of the eponymous hero of his work. Now the tradition attaching to Cato the Younger (cf. p. 233) is of immense significance for the political and philosophical thought of this period and the impassioned impersonation of this figure must give out messages which are hard to misunderstand. To a Seneca, Cato's inflexible devotion to virtue and resolute dedication to the position he has once adopted make him the great Roman example of the Stoic wise man. To Cato's Neronian biographer, Thrasea Paetus, his Stoicism must be inseparable from his republicanism. For Cato had led the forces of the Senate in the civil wars of the early 40s BCE against Julius Caesar and the convictions to which he so rigorously adhered were those of the traditional political order. Finally defeated at the Battle of Utica, he committed suicide rather than accept the principle of autocracy, and in doing so set down a standard for other critics of imperial rule to emulate. To put words into the mouth of the dying Cato could be an indirect way of commenting on whichever tyrant currently held sway in Rome.

That politics is the most prominent concern of Curiatius' play is apparent from Tacitus' description of his initial exchanges with the first of his guests, Julius Secundus:

> Well, on entering Maternus' room we found him sitting with a book in front of him—the very same from which he had given his reading on the

previous day; whereupon Secundus said, 'Has the talk of your detractors no terrors for you, Maternus? Does it not make you feel less enamoured of that exasperating Cato of yours? Or is it with the idea of going carefully over it that you have taken your drama in hand, intending to cut out any passages that may have given a handle for misrepresentation, and then to publish your *Cato*, if not better than it was at least not so dangerous?'

To this he rejoined, 'The reading of it will show you what Maternus considered his duty to himself: you will find it just as you heard it read. Yes, and if *Cato* has left anything unsaid, at my next reading it shall be supplied in my *Thyestes*; for so I call the tragedy which I have already planned and of which I have the outline in my head. It is just because I want to get the first play off my hands and to throw myself whole-heartedly into my new theme that I am hurrying to get this work ready for publication.' (Tacitus, *Dialogue on Orators* 3. 1–3)

Those passages which risk misrepresentation and which may be considered dangerous acquire this status through their political content. Curiatius has retired from forensic rhetoric and later—however disingenuously—proclaims the blessings of the current peace; but he can put into the mouth of his Cato a commentary on tyranny and liberty which the audience will interpret as transcending the specific historical context of the play. That this mediated expression of dissent is what is at issue is apparent from the reference to the forthcoming *Thyestes*: how a play on the woes of ancient Mycenae can elucidate a previous work on the Roman civil wars is unclear until one notes the recurrent tendency of a succession of Roman writers from Ennius and Accius onwards to use this theme, and in particular the psychopathic rule of Atreus, to evoke the perils of autocracy.

It is unclear where exactly Curiatius has given his recitation, but he seems almost to have courted the attention of those at the imperial palace who might wish to denounce him. The same recklessness shows through in his attitude to the eventual published version of his work, which Secundus expects him to make more anodyne but which Maternus promises to deliver unchanged. Maybe these are hints at what has been inferred from other evidence: that the dialogue is set immediately before the death of the tragedian. Contrast Thrasea Paetus and his *Cato*. The Neronian books of the *Annals* close with Tacitus' description of the suicide of Thrasea. He has been denounced by the loathsome Cossutianus Capito and the principal accusation is that, for all his unrelenting withdrawal from the Senate, Thrasea has not abandoned political life but rather is engaged in a form of politics by other means. Central to this claim is the literary circle surrounding Thrasea, and it is no accident that Tacitus has him receive the news of his condemnation when gathered in his gardens with a number of prominent friends in order to listen to the Cynic philosopher Demetrios. It is as if the Roman politician's house is a miniature state in which he can rule virtuously over those who elect to follow him. In public the followers of Thrasea are damned and mocked in equal measure for their high-minded, contumacious air; in that small space apart formed by his house and gardens, Thrasea must give readings from his *Cato* and affirm his political tradition.

We have so far encountered Cato the Younger in tragedy, history, and philo-sophical dialogue. He is also prominent in at least one epic poem of the period: the *Pharsalia* or *Civil War* of Lucan. Yet there are other epics to be considered as well, poems on anything from the Second Punic War to the expedition of Jason and the Argonauts, the war between the sons of Oedipus for rule over Thebes, and the life of Achilles. What did it mean to recite and then to publish works on these themes? Does all literature fall into the pattern of mediated comment suggested above? A very different picture is supplied by the opening of the first satire of Juvenal (cf. pp. 186–7):

Must I always be a listener only, never hit back,
although so often assailed by the hoarse *Theseid* of Cordus?
Never obtain revenge when X has read me his comedies,
Y his elegies? No revenge when my day has been wasted
by mighty Telephus or by Orestes who, having covered
the final margin, extends to the back, and still isn't finished?
No citizen's private house is more familiar to *him*
than the grove of Mars and Vulcan's cave near Aeolus' rocks
are to *me*; what the winds are up to, what ghosts are being tormented
on Aeacus' rack, from what far land another has stolen
a bit of gold pelt, how huge are the ash-trunks Monychus hurls —
the unending cry goes up from Fronto's plane-trees, his marble
statues and columns, shaken and shattered by non-stop readings.
One gets the same from every poet, great and small.
I too have snatched my hand from under the cane; I too
have tendered advice to Sulla to retire from public life
and sleep the sleep of the just. No point, when you meet so many bards, in sparing
paper (it's already doomed to destruction).
But why, you may ask, should I decide to cover the ground
o'er which the mighty son of Aurunca [Lucilius] drove his team?
If you have time and are feeling receptive, here's my answer.

(Juvenal, *Satires* 1. 1–21)

Juvenal unleashes his scorn against epic, tragedy, comedy, and elegy alike but it is epic which is most prominent in this passage. The very title *Theseid* proclaims the poem of Cordus an epic; the standard motifs of the grove of Mars, the cave of the winds, the golden fleece, and the arms of the Centaurs are the stock-in-trade of mythological epic. All these epicists, to whose voices the villa of Fronto resounds, share with Juvenal the same training: anyone who has advised Sulla to retire from political life and sleep securely has studied the stock speech of persuasion known as the *suasoria* so central to the curriculum of the declamation schools (cf. pp. 161–4). In this educational system, no scene from history is too controversial to be trivialized by eager schoolboys in search of point and paradox, not even, as Persius shows, the death of Cato the Younger himself. What Juvenal therefore affects to damn are windy, empty poems on hackneyed themes, all pullulating with the same rhetorical figures and tricks. Satire, the path of Lucilius, must somehow be different. Wherein that difference lies is made explicit in the final lines of the poem:

> So take this man who administered poison to three of his uncles –
> is he to go by, looking down on us all from his aery cushions?
> 'Yes, when he comes to *you*, seal your lips with your finger.
> Simply to utter the words 'That's him!' will count as informing.
> Without a qualm you can pit Aeneas against the ferocious
> Rutulian; no one is placed at risk by the wounded Achilles,
> or Hylas, so long sought when he'd gone the way of his bucket.
> Whenever, as though with sword in hand, the hot Lucilius
> roars in wrath, the listener flushes; his mind is affrighted
> with a sense of sin, and his conscience sweats with secret guilt.
> *That's* what causes anger and tears. So turn it over
> in your mind before the bugle. Too late when you've donned your helmet,
> for second thoughts about combat.'
> 'I'll try what I may against those
> whose ashes are buried beneath the Flaminia and the Latina.'
>
> (Juvenal, *Satires* 1. 158–71, trans. N. Rudd)

The image of Lucilius in his chariot sums up the impression of the early satirist's remorseless aggression; now he brandishes his sword and rages while his imitator dons his helmet and waits for the trumpet to sound. In other words, to denounce one's contemporaries after the manner of Lucilius would be to act like the great warriors celebrated in epic verse. Those, meanwhile, who compose such verse can sleep easy at night because their poetry is so vacuous that it has no chance whatsoever of causing offence: the duel of Turnus and Aeneas, the death of Achilles and the loss of the Argonaut Hylas are shorthand for epic. That Juvenal actually closes by choosing the safer course of speaking ill only of the dead is scant comfort to the epicists whom he pillories. Do they really, he asks, have anything to say at all?

Recitation is central to the literary culture of the imperial period. The passages chosen from Tacitus and Juvenal illustrate the range of experience which can be accommodated under the heading. In what follows, we shall see poets who write for an audience as determined to interpret and find meaning as that of Curiatius Maternus, poets who write for an audience whose benevolence is acquired in the market-place of literary patronage, poets even whom we may secretly suspect were rather too like those whose inanity Juvenal lampoons.

It is no accident that Tacitus sets his *Dialogue on Orators* in 74 CE. No more than six years have passed since the fall of the Emperor Nero, the last representative of the Julio-Claudian dynasty, and only five since the civil wars which engulfed Rome in 69 CE, the famous Year of the Four Emperors. The reign of Vespasian is still new and scores are still being settled from the years of Nero. Malicious prosecutors have been targeted for retribution by the families of their victims; fresh efforts have been made to reassert the authority of the Senate. Yet Vespasian will give way to his son Titus and he to his brother Domitian. Nero is dead but the autocratic spirit lives on. The impact of these years is palpable in all the epic poets of the age.

The *Pharsalia* or *Civil War* is Lucan's account of the conflict between Caesar and Pompey and their climactic struggle in 48 BCE on the fields of Pharsalos in Thessaly. It is perhaps the most overtly political and, indeed, rebellious work of its age and is unsparing in its condemnation of the corruption of Rome in the age of the emperors. Its youthful author did not live to see the overthrow of Nero. Lucan's fall from grace with the emperor and eventual enforced suicide at the age of only 26 is testament to the potential hazards of composing verse on the same controversial themes as Curiatius employs for his tragedies.

M. Annaeus Lucanus was the nephew of the philosopher and tragedian L. Annaeus Seneca (cf. pp. 165–7). Born in Spain in 39 CE but educated in Rome and Athens, Lucan declaimed with distinction in both Greek and Latin, held the quaestorship at a prematurely early age, performed verse in honour of Nero and became a member of the emperor's cohort of friends. His swift advance must have owed as much to his uncle's role as tutor to the young emperor as it did to his prodigious abilities. All this before one most unfortunate event.

The worst misfortune which a reciter could endure was known as a *frigus* or a 'chill'. Where an enthusiastic audience would call out its approval through various familiar terms, those who were hostile to the poet could subject him to the silent disdain of the *frigus*. Suetonius records in his life of Lucan that the poet suffered just such a rebuff and from none other than the Emperor Nero himself. The motivation for Nero's behaviour is not stated by the biographer but we may perhaps infer from his decision to end the performance by calling a meeting of the Senate that this was the best way to break up an audience of some of the leading men of the day.

The exiguous remains of Nero's poetry bear witness to his artistic ambitions. The emperor was also enamoured of the tragic stage and is said to have acted the roles of Orestes the matricide or Canace in labour. Tacitus records the distaste at these transgressions which helped drive the loyal centurion Subrius Flavus to conspire against his ruler. Yet the man whom he sought to place on the throne in his stead, C. Calpurnius Piso, had himself performed in Greek at the theatre in Naples while that notorious sober-sides Thrasea Paetus had sung in tragic dress at the games of Antenor in his native Patavium. Among Lucan's own works are counted an unfinished tragedy entitled *Medea* and fourteen plays with dancing. There is no evidence of his having actually appeared on the stage.

The course of Lucan's early career in public life was meteoric but the feud with Nero soon put a stop to this. The displeasure which the emperor showed at Lucan's verses had far-reaching consequences. The 'chill' was extended to a ban on performance and on work as a lawyer—the public voice of Lucan was silenced. The poet responded by assaulting Nero and his friends in defamatory verses and never held back from abusing him. The image suggested by his biographers up to this point smacks less of steely republican conviction than of petulance and backbiting in a small and competitive group. Suetonius even describes Lucan in the latrines of the imperial palace: the poet lets rip a magnificent fart and caps his achievement with a snatch of Nero's own verse 'You might think that it had thundered beneath the earth'—all those sitting around him flee as fast as they can rather than associate themselves with this levity. When finally Lucan becomes involved in the conspiracy to replace Nero with C. Calpurnius Piso, Suetonius has him declaiming against tyrants and offering Caesar's head to his associates, while Tacitus and Vacca report his attempt to shift accusations of participation onto his mother Acilia. Is this the Lucan whom the auditoria heard recite his *Pharsalia*?

Immature, egotistical, treacherous—Lucan is not flattered by his biographers. Yet this is not the only story. When Tacitus in the *Annals* tells of the death of Annaeus Mela, he states that it is a great aid to his distinction that he was the father of the poet; in the *Dialogue on Orators*, M. Aper urges speakers to draw quotations from the sacred shrine of a Horace, a Virgil, or a Lucan. Both Statius in his birthday poem for Lucan and Martial in a series of epigrams testify to the efforts of Lucan's widow to celebrate his memory and both pay tribute to his work. Statius becomes the first writer to treat Lucan as a heroic enemy of tyranny and his *Pharsalia* as an underground work surviving the best efforts of Nero to suppress it. One might compare the story in Seneca the Elder of the incorrigible Pompeian Labienus who broke off a recitation of some of his histories, skipped some passages, and announced that they would be read after his death. Tacitus, similarly, tells of Cremutius Cordus, the historian driven to his death by Tiberius but whose works lived after him and only grew in reputation as a result (cf. pp. 168–70).

The ancient evidence for the life of Lucan is of huge significance for any account of his *Pharsalia*. It is difficult, however, to know how to handle it. To refuse to imagine a Lucan who is any better than the worst of what we are told about him is to risk trivializing the political voice of the poem: however eloquent his words, they are undermined by our sense of the bad faith of their author. Yet entirely to discard the implications of the evidence for the poet's character and milieu may be the first step to inventing Lucan as the romantic republican dissident and herald of freedom which it would be most stirring to believe him to be.

The ancient life of Lucan attributed to Vacca places the ban on recitation after the publication of the first three books of the *Pharsalia*. By the end of the third book, Lucan's account of the civil wars between Caesar and Pompey has advanced as far as Caesar's invasion of Italy, the flight of Pompey and the senatorial forces, the gathering of auxiliaries from the East and Caesar's siege of Massilia *en route* to the Spanish campaign. It is common to claim that these sections of the narrative are free from the hostility to imperial rule which comes to dominate the latter books. This is, however, very largely a fiction. So heavy-handed an interpretation of the poem's content is a good instance of the pernicious impact of biographical evidence. An alternative response to this evidence might be to assume that the 'chill' administered to Lucan by the emperor was in response to some aspect of the first three books and to wonder what it might be.

The proem to the *Pharsalia* is a thirty-two-line lament for the civil wars, their corrosive impact on Roman ethics, and their destruction of a once-great imperial power. At this point, however, Lucan adopts a very different perspective. He turns to the emperor and finds in him a grand consolation for all the sorrows of Rome:

> But if the Fates could find no other way
> for Nero's coming, if eternal kingdoms are purchased
> by the gods at great cost, if heaven could serve its Thunderer
> only after wars with the ferocious Giants,
> then we have no complaints, O gods; for this reward we accept
> even these crimes and guilt; though Pharsalia fill its dreadful
> plains, though the Carthaginian's shade with blood be sated;
> though the final battle be joined at fatal Munda;

> though added to these horrors, Caesar, be the famine of Perusia
> and the struggles of Mutina, the fleets overwhelmed
> near rugged Leucas, and the slave wars under burning Etna,
> yet Rome owes much to citizens' weapons, because it was
> for you that all was done.

(Lucan, Pharsalia 1. 33–45)

Lucan goes on to anticipate the apotheosis of Nero, urges him to occupy the centre of heaven, lest he should overbalance the cosmos or look askance on Rome, begs him to look serenely on the city and finally dismisses Dionysus and Apollo in proclaiming the emperor his muse. The interpretation of all of this is troubled. To many, this is the standard language of imperial panegyric and is evidence, if not of Lucan's sincere admiration for Nero, then at least of his sincere desire to flatter him. Other voices, however, continue to resist this approach. The late-antique commentators on Lucan were the first, claiming that the section urging Nero to occupy the centre of the universe played on his obesity and his squint. I would prefer to emphasize the extreme pressure on Nero to justify the calculation of profit and loss in the passage quoted, the absence of any other reference to this theme in the remorseless pessimism of the rest of the poem, and the scorn heaped on the deification of dead emperors elsewhere in the text. To this approach, any investigation of whether Lucan meant what he said in the dedication must take account of the repeated tendency of the later stages of the poem to comment on and dismiss the consolatory motifs which here he so zealously proclaims.

One might now consider this issue in terms of the audience for the *Pharsalia*. Vacca states that Lucan was banned from recitation in response to the first three books of the poem; Suetonius that he suffered a 'chill' from Nero himself. Let us therefore imagine a situation in which the young poet has completed the first three books of his work and decides that it is time to publicize them by means of recitation. The poet-emperor, his senior by only two years, is certain to be in the audience. Can Lucan possibly have failed to recite his dedication to Nero? Could it not be that it was something in this very dedication which so offended Nero that he responded by freezing out the reciter? Horace in his *Satires* is well aware of the dangers of flattering the young Octavian and fears that his response may be to kick out like a horse. Does Nero administer just such a kick? The poet-emperor was, I suggest, the first reader to see through the posturing of Lucan's dedication.

If the opening of the *Pharsalia* and its encomium of the emperor were enough to provoke displeasure, one can only imagine how Nero might have responded to the content of the rest of the poem. Lucan implicitly invites his reader to engage in this imaginative exercise; and Statius will explore the possibility even further in his dedications to Domitian. Meanwhile, the further development of the *Pharsalia* establishes an alternative ideal audience, and one which refuses to view the civil wars and the subsequent development of Roman history in the same consoling light as the passage quoted above. This pattern emerges most clearly in the seventh book and its account of the crucial conflict of the civil wars: the Battle of Pharsalus. Here, Lucan adopts the strategy of describing what 'we' see or do, and there is the clear sense of his audience thus being drawn into a common political sympathy with the narrator. When, for instance, the Pompeian party foolishly drive their general into an unnecessary and calamitous engagement with the enemy, Lucan asks the gods whether it pleases them 'to add this guilt to our mistakes'. Responding to the same event, he complains that 'We charge to disaster, demanding warfare which will injure us; | in Pompey's camp, Pharsalia is their prayer.' Even when erring, therefore, *we* are clearly Pompeians.

Compare the following passage in which Lucan laments the impact of the battle on his generation:

> From this battle the peoples receive a mightier wound
> than their own time could bear; more was lost than life
> and safety: for all the world's eternity we are prostrated.
> Every age which will suffer slavery is conquered by these swords.
> How did the next generation and the next deserve
> to be born into tyranny? Did we wield weapons or shield
> our throats in fear and trembling? The punishment of others' fear
> sits heavy on our necks. If, Fortune, you intended to give a master
> to those born after battle, you should also have given us a chance
> to fight.

(Lucan, *Pharsalia* 7. 638–46)

Where the dedication to Nero had represented the new Rome of his reign as the happy recompense for all past suffering, now there is just an unbroken continuum of woe. Moreover, the issue is not just the destruction of the nation but the political enslavement of the people. The group which Lucan represents in the first-person plural straddles the time of Pharsalus, in which it is laid low, and the time of Nero, in which its servitude endures. The complaint which Lucan expresses therefore is that *we* did not betray ourselves through cowardice, and that *we* did not have the chance to continue the fight against the monarchy into which *we* were born.

Lucan speaks here for a partisan community. That that community consists of the poet and his audience is further suggested by some further famous lines from the same seventh book. Lucan here is rounding off a lengthy catalogue of the omens which foretold the disaster of the day ahead:

> O mightiest of men—your Fortune gave displays
> throughout the world, on your destiny the entire sky was intent!
> Even amongst later races and the peoples of posterity, these events—
> whether they come down to future ages by their own fame alone
> or whether my devotion also and my toil can do anything
> for mighty names—will stir both hopes and fears together
> and useless prayers when the battle is read;
> all will be stunned as they read the destinies as if
> to come, not past and, Magnus, still they will side with you.
>
> (Lucan, *Pharsalia* 7. 205–13)

To read the *Pharsalia* will be to be immersed in the immediacy of the battle, to become a partisan of Pompey and to endure an eternity of frustrated hope. There is a massive sting to the final two claims. The suggestion that a narrative could be so vivid as to make the events recorded seem present and not yet past was a commonplace in ancient historiography. Yet what Lucan offers his audience is not just a vivid narrative. Rather, his achievement as a writer will be to create the temporal space in which they can disavow the consequences of the events he describes, consequences which shape every aspect of their lived political experience. Inseparable from this, however, is the terrible force of the disappointment which he must inflict on them. To discover that Pompey did not win is to remember that Caesar did, and that Caesar begat Augustus and with him the whole Julio-Claudian house right down to Nero himself.

What is the ideal reading audience, then, to which Lucan serves up his terrible cocktail of illusion and disillusion? It is an audience who perceive themselves as defeated, who reject the system which emerged from Pharsalus, but whose defeat enjoys no prospect of reversal as the generations roll on. It is an audience which will learn from the hopelessly compromised figure of Lucan's Pompey its first lesson in the perils of allowing a leader to overtake his cause. It may hear in Cato the Younger the true voice of republican principle, but may also be alienated by his grotesque self-regard and futile shows of virtue.

Lucan grew up and first performed in an ugly and treacherous world. To be the prodigiously talented nephew of the emperor's tutor was a short cut to celebrity but also to misfortune. Many reciters were surely given a 'chill' by their audience, but few can have suffered thus at the hands of Nero himself. Tales of poetic jealousy, of defamatory verses and lavatorial mockery of the ruler's verse are properly colourful but it must be remembered that the consequence of that 'chill' was the denial to Lucan of the right either to perform his verse or to act as an orator. Perhaps it is in this experience of exclusion that the seeds of the *Pharsalia*'s account of the true Rome lost are to be found.

Silius and the poetry of retirement

The longest extant Roman epic of them all is the *Punica* of Silius Italicus (25–100 CE). The theme of the poem is the Second Punic War, Hannibal's invasion of Italy, the disasters of Trasimene and Cannae, then the turning of the tide through the generalship of Q. Fabius Maximus and Scipio Africanus. The great Ennius had already covered the same ground in his *Annales* (cf. Ch. 1, pp. 9–13) and Silius is duly deferential. Seventeen is an unusual number of books for an ancient epic but the figure suggests that Silius aspires to something comparable to the eighteen books of the *Annales* and Ennius himself is pictured fighting in Sardinia. The patron deity of verse, Apollo, is even on hand to protect the poet destined to sing of Roman wars and equal the Greek Hesiod in glory and honour. Another author who had covered these events and whom Silius will have revered was the great historian Livy, like Silius a native of Patavium (cf. pp. 177–9). As we shall see, such affinities mattered to the poet.

An orator, politician, and imperial administrator before he was a poet, Silius enjoyed the rare privilege amongst his contemporaries of a public career free, if not from rebuke, at least from retaliation. Pliny the Younger marks the poet's death with the following summation of his two careers as statesman and as poet:

> The news has just come that Silius Italicus has starved himself to death in his house near Naples. Ill-health was the reason, for he had developed an incurable tumour which wore him down until he formed the fixed resolve to escape by dying; though he had been fortunate in life and enjoyed happiness up to the end of his days, apart from the loss of the younger of his two sons. The elder and more gifted he left well established in his career and already of consular rank. Italicus had damaged his reputation under Nero—it was believed that he had offered his services as an informer—but he had maintained his friendship with Vitellius with tact and wisdom, won fame for his conduct as governor of Asia, and removed the stigma of his former activities by his honourable retirement. He ranked as one of our leading citizens without exercising influence or incurring ill-will; he was waited on and sought after, and spent many hours on his couch in a room thronged with callers who had come with no thought of his rank; and so passed his days in cultured conversation whenever he could spare time from his writing. He took great pains over his verses, though they cannot be called inspired, and frequently submitted them to public criticism by the readings he gave. Latterly his increasing age led to his retirement from Rome; he made his home in Campania and never left it again, not even on the arrival of the new Emperor: an incident which reflects great credit on the Emperor for permitting this liberty, and on Italicus for venturing to

avail himself of it. He was a great connoisseur; indeed he was criticised for buying too much. He owned several houses in the same district, but lost interest in the older ones in his enthusiasm for the later. In each of them he had quantities of books, statues and portrait busts, and these were more to him than possessions—they became objects of his devotion, particularly in the case of Virgil, whose birthday he celebrated with more solemnity than his own, and at Naples especially, where he would visit Virgil's tomb as if it were a temple. In this peaceful atmosphere he completed his seventy-fifth year, surrounded by attentions though not really an invalid. He was the last consul to be appointed by Nero, and the last to die of all the consuls Nero appointed; and also remarkable is the fact that not only did the last of Nero's consuls die in him but it was during his consulship that Nero perished. (Pliny, *Epistle* 3. 7. 1–10, trans. Radice)

The implications of this passage merit consideration; for they offer an intriguing glimpse of the literary world in which the *Punica* was produced.

The public career of Silius is of some significance. Pliny notes that he reached the consulship in 68 CE, the final year of Nero's reign, and that the troubled times of 69 CE saw him side with the third of the four emperors to rule in that year, Vitellius. Tacitus also refers to negotiations carried out on behalf of Vitellius by Silius; and the opening of the fourth book of his *Histories* reveals the unhappy fate which awaited many of those who had taken the same side when the troops of Vespasian entered Rome. Silius came through all of this and his poem exhibits an unusual absence of rancour towards any of the fallen monarchs under whom he had lived. His Jupiter prophesies a glorious Roman future marked out by the achievements of Vespasian, Titus, and Domitian; the narrative of Cannae even depicts a Galba of glorious name, and has him present the same peculiar claim to be descended from Pasiphaë as his namesake who overthrew Nero. Only when the same account introduces an audacious young horseman Claudius Nero descended from the blood of the Spartan Clausus, do things become more complicated. For here it is hard not to think of the Emperor Nero, the adopted son of Claudius. When last seen, this mid-republican Nero is savagely brandishing the head of the noble Carthaginian general Hasdrubal, an event fully attested by Livy and yet oddly appropriate to the reputation of the fallen ruler. Silius will use no more direct means to disavow the memory of a monarch on whom his peers are happy to heap scorn.

Pliny is evidently less than in love with what he regards as the careful but uninspired poetry of Silius. Martial's epigrams (cf. pp. 212–14) repeatedly flatter the poet as the darling of the Muses and the equal of Virgil but there is some suggestion that he too has his tongue buried pretty firmly in his cheek. Twice the epigrammatist speaks of 'deathless Silius' but the adjective used to express the immortality of the poet (*perpetuus*) is also that used by Ovid in the proem to his *Metamorphoses* to describe the continuous single narrative of a long epic poem. To those faced with the ever-expanding masterpiece of the venerable ex-consul, he may truly have seemed 'perpetual'. Would they ever, could they ever get to the end of his poem? Classical scholars still preen themselves on occasion for having read the whole of the *Punica*.

The disingenuous zeal with which Martial celebrates the rhetorical and poetic achievements of Silius may suggest that the public criticism to which he subjected himself at recitations was not the most exacting. Young writers had every reason to flatter Silius because he was one of the great purchasers and consumers of poetry of his day. In one epigram, Martial sends a copy of his poetic trifles to Silius and likens himself to Catullus presenting Virgil with a collection of his poems. In another, Martial celebrates the same poems 'which the bookshelves of deathless Silius deign to hold'. This is consonant with Pliny's description of the villas of the poet which teem with books, statues, and busts: the purchase of literature as much as its study and its composition is the passion of Silius' indulgent old age.

For Silius, life and literature rather blend into each other. That of which he is proud or towards which he feels affection is almost certain to find itself celebrated at some point in his poem. Pliny refers to the honourable manner in which Silius governed the province of Asia, an undertaking which will have followed his consulship and which is normally dated to around 77 CE and the reign of Vespasian. Silius narrates the allegedly clement and restrained sack of Syracuse by the great M. Claudius Marcellus in book 14 of the *Punica*, and closes his account with the following commentary on the abuses which Domitian has had to correct:

> Happy the peoples, if, as was once the way in war,
> now too our peace left cities undespoiled!
> Yet, had not the care of that man who has now given the
> world ease held back the unreined rage to plunder all,
> greedy rapine would have stripped bare land and sea.
> (Silius Italicus, *Punica* 14. 684–8)

Silius is happy to trumpet the example of Marcellus because the verdict of his contemporaries is that he himself is a living model of the right sort of rule. Of this he was evidently rather proud.

Sermons of this sort are rare in the *Punica*. Silius expresses his own nostalgia for the moral greatness of Rome in the Second Punic War, and laments the paradox of a victory in arms which brought only complacency and the corruption of prosperity. But he is no Lucan. There is no condemnation of imperial power or representation of modern Italy as a land in ruin. Rather, the world of Silius, which penetrates the world of the *Punica* manifests itself in allusions to friends and fellow townsmen and in celebrations of those whom he loved most dearly: the authors who sat upon his shelf. An important example of the former category may be related felicitously to one from the latter. The full name of Silius Italicus is revealed by an inscription found in his province of Asia: Titus Catius Asconius Silius Italicus. This should be compared to that of the famous literary scholar and contemporary of the poet, Q. Asconius Pedianus: note that the *cognomen* of Silius is also the *nomen* of the critic, i.e. Asconius. Now the critic Asconius is known to have been of Paduan descent and a number of historians have inferred that this must also be true of Silius. A touching hint at the writers' shared origins is offered by book 12 of the *Punica* and the sudden entry into the fray of a dashing Paduan hero whose only given name just happens to be the *cognomen* of the critic:

> Young Pedianus dressed in Polydamantean arms
> waged war ferociously and proclaimed himself
> of Trojan seed and origin and of Antenor's stock,
> as famous for his family and the holy Timavus
> and a name blessed for his glory on Euganean shores.
> To him father Eridanus and the peoples of the Veneto in turn
> and the race rejoicing in the Aponus—whether he roused wars
> or in calm preferred the Muses and the silence of the learned life—
> proclaimed no peer, nor was any other youth
> more famed in war, or any youth more famed in verse.
>
> (Silius Italicus, *Punica* 12. 212–22)

Silius strings together a number of place-names of significance to the people of ancient Padua and the myth of their origins. The claim that they are Trojans and descended from Antenor is familiar from Virgil and Livy; the association of Polydamas with Antenor is far more recherché, and perhaps appeals not just to a learned reader but in particular to a learned Paduan reader. Moreover, there can be no doubt that the ideal reader to whom this passage is directed above anyone else is none other than Q. Asconius Pedianus, flattered to discover a heroic ancestor and recognizing in the youth's literary pursuits an amiable reflection of his own special gifts.

Asconius was a good twenty years older than Silius. By the time that Silius was of an age to receive his training in poetry and rhetoric, Asconius must already have established himself as one of the leading critics of the day. It is tempting to see in this passage the pupil's tribute to his teacher. The young Silius, eager to establish himself in Roman life and letters, must have found in his famous fellow townsman a model and an important supporter on his arrival in the capital. Asconius is read now for his commentary on the speeches of Cicero, but he was also known in antiquity for his work *Against the Critics of Virgil*. His influence can surely be detected in the signal dedication to both these writers which distinguishes so much of the life and work of Silius. When Martial flatters the oratorical and poetic compositions of Silius, he represents him as the equal of Cicero and of Virgil; in his wealthy later life, Silius famously bought one of the Campanian villas of Cicero, and he worshipped at the tomb of Virgil, celebrating the poet's birthday with more reverence than his own. In the *Punica*, meanwhile, the literary heroes whose works clutter the bookshelves of Silius and whose busts adorn his mantelpiece find ancestors very similar to Pedianus the Paduan. When Silius catalogues the Roman and Italian forces at the Battle of Cannae, Mantua, home of Virgil, is given a signal place amongst the list of troops from the Po valley:

> You too, peoples of the Eridanus, shorn and stripped
> of men, for no god then paid heed to your
> prayers, rushed to a fight doomed to fail.
> Rocked by war Placentia vied with Mutina,
> Mantua with Cremona in sending youths,
> Mantua, home of the Muses, lifted to the stars
> on Aonian song and a rival to Smyrna's lyre.
> (Silius Italicus, *Punica* 8. 588–94)

Smyrna is here to Homer what Mantua is to Virgil. And what of Cicero? Happily, his native town of Arpinum is also represented at the battle and the leader of the contingent is none other than a distant ancestor of M. Tullius Cicero himself:

> But they who live by the Liris as with Fibrenus it joins
> its sulphurous stream and flows over silent shallows to the shore,
> the shaggy men of Arpinum, the youth stirred from
> Venafrum and the right hands of the Lirenates, shake
> their allied arms and drain huge Aquinum of men.
> Tullius snatched the bronze-clad regiments to war,
> descendant of kings and blood of lofty Tullus.
> O youth of such qualities and fated to give so great
> a fellow-citizen to the peoples of Ausonia in time to come!
> He, heard beyond the Ganges and the Indians,
> will fill the lands with his voice and with the
> thunder of his tongue will quell mad wars and then will
> leave to none of his descendants the hope of equal glory in words.
> (Silius Italicus, *Punica* 8. 399–411)

One might think it more plausible for the forces of Arpinum to be led by the ancestor of its other famous son, the great general C. Marius, but that would be to misconstrue the character of the man and of his work. Silius lived amidst possessions, amidst markers of his devotion to writers and to books. His poem collects poets and orators as he himself did in life.

Statius—in and out of the market-place

Publius Papinius Statius (*c*.61–95 CE) represents the other face of the artistic milieu in which Silius Italicus moved. Born into the artistic culture of Campania which Silius adopted, Statius was a professional poet and the recipient, not the distributor, of artistic patronage. He was from a part-Greek, part-Samnite background and inherited his *métier* from his father, who had combined the life of the writer with that of a teacher of language and literature to the young. The father of Statius began his professional life in the still intensely Greek city of Naples and competed in the Neapolitan games, which were instituted as late as 2 CE but soon became a natural part of the circuit which took in the four great festivals of mainland Greece—the Nemean, Olympian, Isthmian, and Pythian games—as well as the Actian games founded by Augustus. In each of these, artists competed for substantial financial rewards. When the father established himself as a teacher at Rome he had the good fortune to acquire as a pupil the future Emperor Domitian. He very likely also made money from various poetic commissions. The artistic life of the son seems to have followed a very similar path. While Statius is perhaps most famous for his epics, the *Thebaid* and the *Achilleid*, he is also the author of a five-book collection of occasional poems, the *Silvae* (cf. Ch. 5, pp. 125–217, 227–9).

Silius is indulged by his critics because he has the money and the instinct to indulge them in return. For those less financially secure the situation can be very different. The seventh satire of Juvenal urges writers to look to the emperor for support at a time when all other forms of patronage have now failed them. This poem evokes all the shady compromises and starveling indignities of his own Grub Street, and depicts the impact of economic circumstances on two of the authors under discussion in this chapter:

> Lucan may well be content with fame, as he lies at ease
> in his marble gardens. What use, however, to the haggard Saleius
> and Serranus is glory, no matter how great, if it's *only* glory?
> When Statius has made the city happy by fixing a day,
> there's a rush to hear his attractive voice and the strains of his darling

> *Thebaid*. He duly holds their hearts enthralled by his sweetness;
> and the people listen in total rapture. But when with his verses,
> he has caused them all to break the benches in their wild excitement,
> he starves—unless he can sell his virgin *Agave* to Paris.
> Paris also confers positions of military power,
> and puts the gold of six months' service on a poet's finger.
>
> (Juvenal, *Satires* 7. 79–89)

Of the poets named in this passage, only Lucan is unconcerned. He is not just dead but dead and rich. His family can afford to bury him in gardens decorated with marble; his widow Polla Argentaria can commission from Statius himself a poem to honour the dead poet (*Silvae* 2. 7). The works of Serranus and Saleius Bassus have not survived, but Quintilian lists them among the great epicists of Rome. The financial circumstances of the latter are also described in the *Dialogue on Orators* of Tacitus, when M. Aper talks of Bassus working all year on his new book of verse, then forced to hire a recitation hall at his own expense and rush round urging friends to attend—and all for the reward of insincere compliments and a little desultory applause. Yet once, as Aper himself goes on to confess, this same Bassus so impressed the Emperor Vespasian that he was presented with the substantial sum of 500,000 sesterces. There was therefore money to be made from poetry, but no security and always the pressure to bow to the market. Hence Juvenal's description of Statius. The image which runs throughout this passage is that of the poet as pimp: the reaction of the crowd to the feminized *Thebaid* that of the lover panting with lust. Yet there is no reward in this. If he wants cash and with it status, Statius must write a new libretto for a performance of the *Agave* by the noted pantomime artist Paris, and concoct some suitable words as an accompaniment for the gestures and gyrations of the dancer. And they had better be new words—Paris is figured as the pernickety client, refusing to sleep with a prostitute without proof of her virginity.

For a poet acting on Juvenal's advice to seek patronage from the new emperor, an obvious opportunity presented itself in the form of the new literary contests which Domitian instituted in the course of his reign. These were surely based on the Greek festivals in which the father of Statius had competed, but their focus seems to be specifically on poetry and not on gymnastics, athletics, or charioteering. The Alban games were held annually at the villa of Domitian in Alba Longa, and Statius is full of pride for his victorious entry on the theme of the emperor's campaigns against the Germans and the Dacians. The Capitoline games were held only every four years from 86 CE onwards and were apparently rather more prestigious. Statius does not disguise his disappointment at his failure to win the contest of 90 or 94 CE.

Two poems from the *Silvae* are particularly valuable for their commentary on the different levels of Statius' artistic career. In 3. 5, Statius describes his wife who was at his side as he won the Alban games, and was a partner in his grief at his defeat in Domitian's Capitoline games, who heard with vigilant ear the lines he murmured all night long, who shared in the great toil of the *Thebaid* and counted the years of its composition. In 5. 3, Statius laments the fact that his father lived only to see him victorious in the Neapolitan games, but was not there to share in the joy of the Alban games or to console him in his later defeat. Here too Statius closes by describing his father's role in urging him to compose the *Thebaid* and giving him his first lessons in heroic narrative and epic topography. In both these cases, therefore, the *Thebaid* constitutes the true summit of the poet's career, and holds a place above all the verse he wrote even for the greatest competitions. The poem on which he claims at its close to have worked through twelve long years is his artistic monument, a world apart from the more ephemeral efforts with which he competed for the prizes which were his income. This too is the implication of Juvenal's passage. Statius treats the people of Rome to snatches of his masterpiece, but in the market-place they have the value of a loss-leader, generating good publicity and bringing in the short-term remuneration of a libretto here, a praise-poem there.

The *Thebaid* is a monstrously dark epic on the rivalry for the throne of Thebes between the sons of Oedipus, Eteocles, and Polynices. It twice makes pious references to the insuperable majesty of the *Aeneid* but its subject-matter and its aesthetic owe far more to Lucan. Quite different is the *Achilleid*, the attempt to tell the entire story of the life of Achilles. Statius devoted much of his later years to this, but never reached beyond the middle of the second book and the departure of Achilles with Ulysses and Diomedes from the island of Scyros where he has been hidden by his mother Thetis. This poem takes a positively Ovidian pleasure in exploring the sexual ambiguities of the young hero still beautiful enough to be disguised as a daughter of King Lycomedes, whose femininity is sufficiently masculine to prompt schoolgirl crushes on the part of his fellow members of the chorus, and whose determination to show himself a man both in battle and in his yearning for the lovely Deidamia finally forces him to reveal his true identity. Yet, for all the features that make the *Thebaid* and *Achilleid* such very distinct works, they do have one fundamental characteristic in common: the adoption of a theme from Greek mythology and therefore the frustration of the ambitions of the very figure to whom they are both dedicated. The *Achilleid*, for instance, opens with a statement of the poem's theme and then turns to the Emperor Domitian with the following words:

> But you at whom the glory of Italy and Greece wonders from
> afar, for whom the twin laurels of general and poet flower
> rivalrously (the one already regrets its defeat), excuse me
> and permit me in my nervousness briefly to sweat in
> this dust. Long in training and still insecure, I shape to
> write of you and great Achilles plays the prelude for you.
>
> (Statius, *Achilleid* 1. 14–19)

Compare the proem to the *Thebaid* which first asks where the narrative should begin and considers the different cycles of destruction overwhelming the royal family of Thebes. As Statius fixes on his proper theme, he simultaneously defers the composition of another:

> Rather at present I'll permit the joys
> and agonies of Cadmus to have passed.
> The troubled house of Oedipus shall set
> the limit to my lay, since I'll not dare
> as yet to hymn the standards of Italy,
> the triumphs in the North, the Rhine reduced
> twice to our yoke, the Danube twice beneath
> our jurisdiction, Dacians hurled down
> from rebel peaks, Jove saved from war's assault
> when boy had scarce reached man, and thee, the grace
> and glory given to the Latin name,
> youthful successor to thy father's fresh
> achievements, prince whom Rome would fain possess
> for ever.
>
> (Statius, *Thebaid* 1. 15–24)

The proem goes on to anticipate the deification of Domitian after the manner of Virgil's dedication of the *Georgics* to Octavian or Lucan's dedication of the *Pharsalia* to Nero, and to promise that some day Statius truly will compose a historical epic on the emperor's exploits. For now, however, he will have to make do with Thebes.

Domitian thus emerges as a form of super-reader for Statian epic. Any other Roman reading the *Thebaid* or the *Achilleid* is invited simultaneously to imagine the experience of the emperor as he reads, and to judge his reaction to the poems as they unfold. The same conceit recurs in the poet's farewell to the *Thebaid* at the close of the final book. Statius prepares to send forth into the world the work of twelve years of toil and wishes it immortality. Already, however, it seems that parts of the poem are in the public domain, for he describes how Caesar deigns to know it and the youth of Italy learn and recite it in their lessons.

One fundamental point about this construction of an audience for the epic must be established from the beginning. The strategy whereby a poet deflects pressure to compose a work on an evidently uncongenial theme—by promising to do so at a later point in his career and then offering something different instead—is familiar from the poetry of the Augustan age. It is the habitual stance of the elegists towards their patron Maecenas with his plans for an epic celebration of the deeds of the emperor. The difference is that Statius actually makes good his promise. For he himself states that his winning entry for the Alban games was on the German and Dacian campaigns of Domitian; and a brief four-line scrap of an epic entitled *On the German War* is preserved for us by an ancient commentator on Juvenal. These two works may not be identical—the Alban games might well have been won with a lyric celebration of victory—but Statius is clearly not shirking the task. Domitian seems finally to have obtained the laudatory account of his military exploits which the poet elsewhere defers. Statius is a poet in the market-place and it would scarcely be wise to frustrate the ambitions of the poet-emperor and greatest patron of them all.

More important still is the impact on interpretations of the *Thebaid* of the poem's construction of Domitian as super-reader of the text. The poem's theme, for all that the action is firmly located in the distant past of Greek mythology, for all that it is one of the great *literary* themes of epic and tragedy, may have something to say to the Rome of the Flavians. Statius' father had composed a notable poem on the Year of the Four Emperors in 69 CE; his son side-steps this contemporary civil war, but one wonders how much of the father's work found its way into that of the son through allusion and imitation.

Statius sets out to describe the conflict of two brothers for the throne. How resonant was this for a Rome which had seen Britannicus dislodged by Nero or heard rumours of tension between Titus and Domitian themselves? In the sixth book of the *Thebaid*, funeral games are held for the dead child Archemorus. Polynices participates in the chariot-race, is the recipient of much wise counsel from his father-in-law Adrastus, but still falls out of his chariot and is led away all in a daze. Nero too had suffered just such a fall when attempting to drive a ten-horse chariot at the Olympic games. Might the reader who is invited to imagine the reaction of the super-reader Domitian pause and form a picture of the emperor stumbling on this allusion to his hapless predecessor? Does a smile pass across his lips? Or does he grimace as he realizes that these Theban tyrants are not so distant from his world as Statius might pretend? The example is trivial, but the underlying principle is not.

The audience of the *Thebaid*, whether Domitian the dedicatee or the chanting pupils in the schoolroom, or the public at a recitation, are not required to find in every episode of the poem a correspondence to recent Roman life as direct as that between Nero and Polynices in their chariots. It is clear from the evidence of the Roman theatre in this period, as well as in the late Republic, that gesture and intonation on the part of the actor could suggest a particular identification to the audience, but texts such as the *Thebaid* are sold short by an approach which sees behind every mythological mask a specific Roman figure of recent history. The eloquence of the poem lies in its ability to depict in grotesque and hyperbolic form the systematic frailties undermining all monarchical power: the jealous paranoia of the ruler, the fear of the counsellor to give advice which will be unwelcome even if just, the violence done to religious observation and the perversion of martial courage in a struggle for the throne. If Lucan had provided Statius with the vocabulary to describe the corrosive impact on religious and martial values in time of civil war, the terrible events of 69 CE had reminded Rome of the relevance of his vision. The Thebes of the *Thebaid* is a cipher. Statius never follows Lucan's example to mourn the grandeur of the city overwhelmed by civil war, and has no room for a Cato who identifies his cause with that of Rome. Rather, the walls of Thebes must be shattered or defended only inasmuch as they encircle and defend the one goal which drives Eteocles' and Polynices' every action: the throne. There is in the raw nakedness of this pursuit more than a little of the Otho and Vitellius whom Tacitus will present in his *Histories*.

An *Argonautica* for imperial conquerors

Of all the writers of epic in the Neronian and Flavian periods, least is known of Gaius Valerius Flaccus (d. *c*.90 CE). Manuscripts of the remaining eight books of his *Argonautica* also call him Balbus Setinus but this only indicates that he came originally from the hilly, vine-clad town of Setia in Latium or from its Spanish namesake. Quintilian's review of Roman epic poets probably refers to him when it states that 'We have recently lost something big in Valerius' but there is no mention of him in Pliny or Martial. Statius seems to rework Valerius' account of the Hypsipyle story in the *Thebaid*, but never names him in the *Silvae*. Valerius does not seem to have been one of the great characters of the Flavian literary world. Though it is not possible to describe his relationship with his Roman audience, something may be said about the significance of the *Argonautica* for the Rome of the period.

Valerius was not the first Roman to tell of the voyage of the Argo to Colchis, the struggle with Aeetes for the golden fleece and the beginnings of the affair between Jason and Medea. Varro of Atax had already achieved great distinction for his *Argonautica*, apparently composed some time in the mid- to late 40s BCE and in the wake of the successful Pontic campaigns of Pompey in the 60s and Caesar in the early 40s BCE. Ethnography is the foster-child of empire and the poetry of Varro pandered to the hunger for information about new worlds and peoples. It is some indication of Varro's concerns that he also composed a poetic geography called the *Chorographia* and an epic on part of Caesar's Gallic Wars entitled the *War with the Sequani*. Valerius too expatiates on the peoples of the Black Sea region and introduces in book 6 a lengthy description of fighting between Aeetes and his brother Perses which leaves him with no choice but to provide a catalogue of all those who came to fight.

The time of Valerius did not quite see the same succession of Pontic campaigns as had that of Varro, but there had been some significant fighting and it has been shown that he is the first Roman writer to give a convincing description of certain native tribes, in particular the Sarmatians. Moreover, there is some evidence that epics of navigation grew in appeal every time the Roman Empire spread across the seas. Varro of Atax wrote soon after Julius Caesar's invasion of Britain; but Valerius could legitimately claim that his dedicatee Vespasian had more truly earned comparison with the Argonauts by his participation in Claudius' permanent subjugation of that island country. Note how the opening lines of the epic emphasize this exploit, and then twist the commonplace of the emperor's future as a god by making him a star surer to guide by than even the pole star:

> I sing of the first seas through which the sons of the gods passed
> and of the prophetic ship, which dared to aim for the shores
> of Scythian Phasis and burst straight through the clashing
> rocks, finally to reach port on flaming Olympus.
> Apollo, counsel me, if there stands in my chaste home a tripod
> which knows the Cumaean priestess, if the laurel's green
> covers a worthy brow. You too, who have the greater glory
> of opening the seas, ever since the Caledonian Ocean
> bore your sails, previously indignant at the Phrygian Julii,
> snatch me from the crowd and the cloudy earth,
> O holy father, and show me favour as I sing of
> the venerable deeds of old-time men. Your offspring tells of Idume
> overthrown—for so he can—and of his brother black with the dust of Solymus,
> brandishing torches and raging at every tower.
> For you he will institute divine honours and for your family
> a shrine, when already, O father, you shall shine from every
> part of heaven, nor shall the pole star be for Tyrian ships

a surer guide or Helice a more trusted marker for the helmsmen of Greece, whether you give the signs or whether Greece and Sidon and the Nile send out ships with you to show the way. Now may you serenely aid my enterprise, that this voice may fill the Latin cities.

(Valerius Flaccus, Argonautica 1. 1–21)

For Vespasian the navigator, for his imperialist people, the time is right for a new *Argonautica*.

The problem with any work on the theme of the Argonauts is that there is no escaping the encounter with Medea, her agency in the winning of the fleece, and the catastrophic consequences of her marriage to Jason. Valerius, like Apollonios before him, peppers his narrative with allusions to what must occur once Jason is back in Greece. Medea then must represent the dark side of advancing into unknown lands. Yet Valerius has a consolation and is sure to give it a specifically Roman coloration. In the first book, Jupiter reveals his long-term plan after the fashion of his speech to Venus in *Aeneid* 1: the Argonauts will open the seas and will bring Asia to blows with Greece. This will lead to the fall of Asia but the supremacy of Greece will finally fail and pass to what must be assumed to be Rome: 'This then is my resolution concerning the end of the Greeks; soon I shall cherish other nations.' The Virgilian trope is almost forced into the narrative and contributes very little to what follows: Jason has no idea of Rome, he undergoes no gradual revelation of his Roman destiny, his fate is not bound up in any meaningful way with that of Rome. Yet the manner in which Valerius ensures that Rome finds a place in his epic of ancient Colchis is as revealing in its own way as the care with which Statius keeps up the pretence that it is nowhere to be seen in his Thebes.

The other difficulty for the historical plan which Jupiter propounds is that it has no obvious end. As with Pythagoras in book 15 of Ovid's *Metamorphoses*, we are left wondering whether other nations in turn will not be cherished in place of Rome. There is nothing here to suggest that Rome is endless or immutable. Moreover, if the one explicit reference to Rome in the main body of the *Argonautica* is anything to go by, then Valerius is no optimist. No contemporary reader will have forgotten how Vespasian the new Jason came to the throne. When the scythe-bearing chariots of Ariasmenus are turned back on his own men by the aegis of Athena, a striking simile reminds us that by now civil war is a specially Roman activity:

> Just as when most savage Tisiphone stirs
> Roman legions and kings, their columns glittering on
> both sides with spears and eagles, their fathers tillers
> of the same lands, sent as recruits by the same sorry

Tiber from all the fields to wars not these,
so men recently united and seeking to slay a foreign foe
panicked to see Pallas, so did chariots turn and rush to
their destruction, though their drivers called them back.

(Valerius Flaccus, *Argonautica* 6. 402–9)

The Flavian audience of the *Argonautica* will not have missed the importance of these lines.

8 | Imperial space and time: The literature of leisure

CATHERINE CONNORS

Leisure time as hard work

Alongside the more formal modes of literary production—epic, tragedy, history, philosophy, and oratory—Roman imperial audiences also enjoyed less formal literary modes. Examples produced during the post-Augustan period include satire, epigram, mixed collections, the versified fables in the style of Aesop composed by the freedman Phaedrus, and Petronius' satirical and inventive novel, the *Satyricon*. These works are generally presented as ones to enjoy in leisure time, *otium*, and their informal qualities can include smallness of scale, a low or everyday subject-matter and style (as opposed to lofty national or mythological themes), or signs of spontaneous (as opposed to laborious) composition.

But leisure is a cultural artefact: how people describe, spend, and pay for their leisure time reveals processes of self-definition and cultural formation. Literary works which describe themselves as light or insubstantial can thus play a significant cultural role in their capacity to define their élite audiences as élite enough to indulge in a literature of leisure. The category 'élite enough' is a broad one, ranging from emperors and their courtiers, to wealthy families possessing substantial libraries and highly educated slaves, on to those who possess only a few books and scarcely enough time to enjoy them. Authors can be born into the élite, or they can use the practice of literature to blur the line between working for a living and sharing in élite literary leisure. Women can be part of the élite audience for literature to the extent that they have access to education and leisure: this seems likely in wealthy families and possible in the upper echelons of the courtesan trade. Above all, membership in Rome's upper social and economic classes enables a man to have time free of what he would call work and to fill that time with literature among other pursuits—filling that time with literature is one element of what enables a man to be numbered among the élite. In its capacity to communicate the social message that 'this man has time and money enough to read for pleasure', the literature of leisure is like the toga, the expensive draped garment for citizen men to wear which with its cumbersome folds proclaims the wearer free from the demands of physical labour.

Only those who have the luxuries of time and books and education have access to literature's lessons and pleasures: there are good reasons why the meanings of the Latin word *ludus* include both 'game' and 'school'—both fall into the category of things one does instead of working. So in one sense all literature is a product of leisure. Yet for ancient authors and audiences there are clear differences between the serious works of epic, history, tragedy, rhetoric, and philosophy on the one hand and the frivolity of epigram, satire, or otherwise light poetry and fictional prose on the other. Roman epic poetry offers its audiences all-encompassing and eternal views of the imperial world order originating in myth and embodied in the physical city of Rome. Historical works record the men and events that brought the Empire into being. Philosophy and rhetoric offer disciplines of the soul and body and voice, training men to take their appropriate places within Rome's web of social relations. And all of this happens with the full knowledge of authors and audiences: epic poets, historians, philosophers, and rhetoricians are all overtly instructive, passing on Rome's traditions to form the next generation of imperial citizens and subjects. By contrast, the light works to be considered here leave aside the instructive project of the formal, serious genres to present themselves as amusing diversions for their audience's leisure time.

We can explore Roman thinking about the social and cultural meanings of leisure by considering the term *otium*. This word can be translated as 'peace' or 'leisure' but its meaning is best revealed by exploring the other terms against which Romans could define it. *Otium* is space and time from which the obligations of an élite man have been emptied out: *otium* is time free from work (*labor*), from business dealings (*negotium*), from the performance of duties (*officia*), or from political, administrative, or military service. But it is also defined by the élite in relation to how the non-élite are thought to spend (or indeed waste) their free time: a wise man's *otium* is empty of work and other obligations but full of purposeful and productive contemplation, rest, or literary activity. So Cicero can record in his *On Duties* that according to Cato, Scipio Africanus was never so busy as when he was at leisure (3. 1–4). Seneca too emphasizes the purposeful and productive use of *otium* in his *On Leisure*, arguing that the contemplation and investigation of the nature of the world made possible during *otium* can contribute to the greater good of humanity. By contrast, the *otium* of the unwise is taken up with meaningless frivolities such as games, races, jokes, gossip, extravagant meals, and long afternoons at the baths. These definitions of productive as opposed to wasteful leisure form just one part of a larger élite practice of denigrating the work of those whose labour made Rome function: the privileged élite who live off the labour of others prove that they deserve their freedom from work because of the good use they make of their leisure. Poets producing the literature of leisure take their bearings from this opposition between productive élite *otium* and wasteful popular *otium*.

The elder Cato (cf. pp. 8, 29–30) is introduced to begin many a version of Roman literary history. Here, though, we start with his dramatic exit. At a celebration of the Floralia, games in honour of Venus, the female performers hesitated to perform their usual strip-tease. Cato realized that he was the reason for their hesitation and departed so that the show could go on. Authors use the anecdote of Cato's famous departure to characterize their works as frivolous entertainment, not worthy of a Cato's productive *otium*. Martial (see p. 212 below) uses it in the preface to book 1 of his epigrams:

> Epigrams are written for people who go to the Floralia. Let Cato not come into my theatre, or, if he does come in, let him stay to watch. I think I am within my rights if I end this preface with a poem.
>
> > Since you knew about bawdy Flora's charming festival,
> > the holiday shows and the crowd's outrageous behaviour,
> > why, stern Cato, did you enter the theatre?
> > Or had you come just so you could make an exit?

The narrator of Petronius' (see p. 218 below) racy *Satyricon* programmatically rejects serious Catonian readers in the same way:

> > You Catos, why do you wear that frosty look?
> >   Why slate my new and unpretentious book?
> > The language is refined, the smile not grave,
> >   My honest tongue reports how men behave.
> > For mating and love's pleasures all will vouch;
> >   Who vetoes love's hot passion on warm couch?
> > Hear Epicurus, father of truth, proclaim:
> >   'Wise men must love, for love is life's true aim'.
> >   (132. 15, trans Walsh)

These dismissals of Cato dissociate literary works from serious literature and from productive leisure and align them with popular entertainments. When Martial describes his epigram book as 'my theatre' the outdoor, popular mime-attending audience is imaginatively identified with the private, indoor, book-buying audience. But this identification can go only so far: simply by being written works Martial's and Petronius' books reach only a fraction of the popular audiences. This simultaneous sense of identification with and distance from popular entertainment seen in dismissals of Cato from a text's audience is one strategy available to producers and consumers of Rome's literature of imperial leisure.

Others embrace the idea of productive leisure, where literary entertainment prepares a man to return to his administrative or political work with renewed vigour. We see this productive vision of literature and *otium* in Phaedrus' collection of verse fables.

Gaius Iulius Phaedrus, born a slave sometime around 15 BCE and freed by the Emperor Augustus, wrote during the reigns of Tiberius, Caligula, and Claudius and died around 50 CE; under Tiberius he offended the emperor's associate Sejanus somehow and received an unspecified punishment. Following the model of Aesop, he uses short episodes (often animal tales) with funny punchlines to provide gentle moral instruction: 'I don't mean to single out individuals but to represent life itself' (3. prologue 49–50). He locates the origin of this discourse in the language of slavery:

> the slave, subject to punishment
> expressed his true feelings in stories
> because he did not dare to say what he wished
> and so by using invented jokes he escaped punishment for his speech.
>
> (3. prologue 34–7)

Though Phaedrus situates the origins of fable discourse in the slave experience, he frames his own verse fables as requiring leisure from their élite audiences, and indeed providing an opportunity for relaxation that is necessary for the resumption of productive work. Phaedrus traces such relaxation back to his model Aesop with this story. Upon noticing Aesop playing with nuts in a group of boys, an Athenian laughs at him. Aesop shows him an unstrung bow and eventually explains:

> 'You will quickly break your bow if you always keep it strung;
> but if you loosen it, it will be ready for use when you want it.
> In the same way the mind should be allowed some relaxation
> so that it may be better at thinking when it returns to work.'
>
> (3. 14. 10–13)

Even Martial can embrace the notion of productive *otium* when it suits him. Though, as we have seen, Martial excludes 'Catos' at the outset of book 1, in a poem designed to flatter the younger Pliny (cf. pp. 158–60, 173–4 above) he includes 'Catos' among his potential audience. Here is Pliny's painstakingly defensive account of his own practice of sometimes writing and performing light verse, an activity which might seem insufficiently constructive to be worthy of a man's leisure (see also p. 174 above):

> you say that there were some who did not find fault with the poems themselves but still blamed me in a friendly and candid way for writing and performing them. . . . I grant that I sometimes compose verse that is not serious; and I listen to comedies, I watch mimes, I read lyric poetry, and I make sense of Sotadic verse; moreover sometimes I laugh, make jokes and enjoy myself; to deal with all these kinds of harmless relaxations in brief, I am a man. (*Epistles* 5. 3. 1–2)

Martial in his turn flatters Pliny's seriousness and his productive *otium* when he directs his book of epigrams ('not very polished and not very serious, but still not boorish') to go to Pliny's house not during the day, when he is hard at work writing speeches comparable to Cicero's, but 'you'll go more safely late when lamps are lit: this is your hour, when Bacchus goes wild, when the rose rules, when hair is damp: then may even unbending Catos read me' (*Epigrams* 10. 20. 18–21).

This flattering strategy worked to Martial's advantage. Born in Bilbilis in Spain sometime within the years 38–41 CE, Marcus Valerius Martialis arrived in Rome in 64 CE and enjoyed some contact with his fellow countrymen Seneca and Lucan before they were forced to commit suicide by Nero in the aftermath of the failed conspiracy to assassinate Nero in 65 CE. Martial's first widely circulated work was his book of epigrams on the games celebrating the dedication of the Colosseum in 80; in the years 84–5 he published *Xenia* ('guest gifts', now book 13) and *Apophoreta* ('presents for guests to take home', now book 14). Twelve books of epigrams followed at intervals from 86. He retired to his birthplace in Spain in 98 and died in approximately 104. A letter of Pliny's (3. 21. 2) informs us that Pliny made a gift towards Martial's travelling expenses to return the favour Martial had done him by mentioning him in verse, as we have seen above.

But this vision of Martial's epigrams as part of a productive 'Catonian' *otium* is a one-off. More often, he flaunts the frivolity of his epigrams. At the opening of his eleventh book, he flatters his addressee Parthenius by saying that as he is too busy to read Martial, his book must settle for 'lesser' hands, the hands of those who use *otium* wastefully and idly in betting and gossiping about chariot-racing as they loiter in various places in Rome:

> Book with no work to do [*otiose*], dressed in holiday purple,
> where, where are you going?

You aren't going to see Parthenius are you? But of course.
You'd come and go unopened.
He reads petitions to the emperor, not books;
and he is too busy for the Muses, or else he would have time for his own literary
    pursuits.
Or do you think you are fortunate enough
if you fall into less important hands?
Go to the Portico of Quirinus nearby.
Neither the Portico of Pompey, nor the Portico of Europa
nor the Portico of the Argonauts
has a crowd with more time on its hands.
There will there be two or three to
unroll the bookworms in my frivolous works,
but only after they have tired of betting and gossip
about the chariot racers Scorpus and Incitatus.

(Epigrams 11. 1)

The best spot for this anti-Catonian *otium* is the portico associated with the temple of Quirinus, near Martial's own house on the Quirinal. In the next poem, an implicit contrast then emerges between the easy walk to these haunts of leisure and more rigorous journeys when Martial says, 'Harsh readers, study rugged (*salebrosum*) Santra [a grammarian of the late Republic]; I have nothing to do with you. This book is mine' (*Epigrams* 11. 2. 7–8); the word for 'rugged' is a metaphor drawn from descriptions of paths which are rough and hard to travel (cf. *Epigrams* 11. 90. 2). Still, Martial boasts in the next epigram that his poems *do* find audiences among soldiers at arduous distances from Rome—but only to frame his complaint that his books' capacity to amuse on the chilly and hardworking fringes of Empire does not actually make him any money:

My poetry doesn't divert just Rome's free time
    nor do I give it only to ears that aren't busy.
Amid Getic frosts by the standards of Mars
    a hardened centurion wastes his time on my book
and Britain is said to recite my verses.
    What good is that? My wallet knows none of it.
What enduring pages could I pen,
    What great battles I could sound on a Pierian horn,
if, when the holy gods restored Augustus to earth [in the person of the emperor
    Nerva],
    they had also given a Maecenas to you, Rome.

(Epigrams 11. 3)

Martial here blames his failure to write lofty verse on the absence of a generous patron who could provide him with necessary funds. Instead he is practically forced to write a multitude of epigrams which can be exchanged for gifts from lesser patrons, and which can be collected to be sold to the general public, though apparently such sales do not yield a direct financial benefit for the author. Elsewhere he admits that even with a Maecenas as his patron he would not be a Virgil (8. 55). That he was not as needy as he sometimes makes himself sound is clear from his possession of a villa at Nomentum, about thirteen miles north of Rome, where he can relax and sleep peacefully, away from the noise of the city, for as he says self-deprecatingly, 'in Rome a poor man's got no place to think or rest' (12. 57. 3–4). Paradoxically, the poet whose works are to be enjoyed at leisure constructs his career as constant hard work analogous to the duties performed by clients for their patrons. He makes the point that he sends poems to his friends instead of getting up early to perform the early morning greeting, the *salutatio* (1. 70, 108). And from retirement in Spain, Martial looks back on the constant busyness of a poet's life at Rome, contrasting the pleasant 'work' of his leisure with his friend Juvenal's hectic schedule:

> Juvenal, while you perhaps go here and there restlessly
> in the noisy Subura,
> or waste time on mistress Diana's Aventine hill
> while your sweaty toga flaps around you
> on powerful men's thresholds
> and the Greater Caelian hill and the Lesser wear you out as you wander,
> [my hometown] Bilbilis, proud of its gold and iron,
> which I've sought after many Decembers
> has welcomed me back and made me a country fellow.
>
> . . . .
> I enjoy disgracefully long sleep
> which often not even the third hour [9 a.m.] marks the end of,
> and I pay myself back in full for thirty years of vigils . . .
>
> (*Epigrams* 12. 18. 1–9, 13–16)

Martial flaunts the frivolous, time-wasting side of his poetry in rejecting the Catos as readers, but when it suits him, he stresses the ways in which his poems are like work. In general, the relations between *otium*, literature, work, and social and economic class are not fixed and definite but shifting, flexible, and available for opportunistic use by authors and audiences. A man can disdain frivolous literature and claim the moral high ground with Cato, or can be furtive or flamboyant in the pursuit of literary pleasure. An author can flirt with the possibility that his poems have the wide appeal of mime and other shows, but his verbal craftsmanship and technical expertise allow his audience to distinguish their educated leisure from the pleasures of the masses.

Otium and the bay of Naples

The space most closely associated with élite Roman leisure is not at Rome at all, but in luxurious villas dotted along the bay of Naples, especially in the vicinity of the resort town of Baiae. For those who could afford such getaways, Rome was for work while Baiae was for pleasure. Martial entertainingly reverses this conceit when he contrasts a friend's non-productive Roman estate with a paradoxically productive farm near Baiae, one not given over to 'leisured myrtles':

> But you Bassus have a property near Rome, lovely but totally unproductive.
> Your view from a high tower takes in only laurels,
> and you are carefree, for your Priapus fears no thief.
> You feed your vineyard workers with city flour
> and when you go to your painted villa on vacation you bring
> vegetables, eggs, chickens, apples, cheese, new wine.
> Should this be called a country place or a city home out of town?
>
> (*Epigrams* 3. 58. 45–51)

Statius, Juvenal, and Petronius each describe the pleasures available on the bay of Naples in ways which suggest different understandings of relations between work and pleasure and literature.

Statius, like Phaedrus, aligns his informal verse with an understanding of *otium* as a productive and purposeful relaxation which can restore an imperial official for the rigours of his duties, or ready a poet for the demands of the higher literary forms. Born Publius Papinius Statius around 45 CE at Naples and educated at first by his father, who was both teacher and poet, Statius won favour with Domitian upon making his way to Rome. A lost poem *On the German War* praised Domitian's triumphal celebrations in 89. His epic *Thebaid* was published around 91 CE; and the five books of his *Silvae* began to appear in 92 (the title designates a 'miscellaneous collection' from the word *silva*, whose meaning ranges from 'uncultivated woodland' to 'raw material'). He died in Naples in 96, leaving another epic, the *Achilleid*, unfinished (see also pp. 199–204). Although Statius is a professional poet, he often contrives to represent his poetic work as *otium*. He stresses the informality of the *Silvae* and the rapidity of their composition in prefaces attached to the individual books. One effect of this is to blur the boundary between the work he does as a poet and the leisure of his aristocratic audience. The *Silvae* depict a world of imperial *otium*: by praising men for achieving a peaceful refuge from their obligations, Statius celebrates the magnitude of those obligations. In a verse epistle to Vitorius Marcellus, for example, Statius urges him to stop working over the summer at

Rome and take a holiday: his excellent qualities will be greater after relaxation (*maior post otia virtus, Silvae* 4. 4. 34). The poem combines various manifestations of *otium*. Statius writes to Vitorius at Rome from his own leisured retirement on the bay of Naples, and sends his letter by way of the Via Domitiana. This recently constructed road makes access to the pleasures of the area more convenient from Rome; Vitorius is charged with overseeing the road, so his work facilitates Roman pleasures. Statius meanwhile is pausing to relax from his own labours between finishing his long epic poem the *Thebaid* and starting work on the *Achilleid* (he describes the *Thebaid* as a 'long labour' at 3. 5. 35). He had already made the relation between epic and lighter poetry clear in the preface of his first collection of *Silvae*, asserting that all great poets write works of a lighter sort:

> I have long hesitated a great deal about whether I should gather together these pieces which welled up in me with a sudden burst of feeling mixed with some pleasure in their quick composition and issued from me one by one. Why indeed should I take trouble over producing an edition at a time when I am still worried about my *Thebaid*, though it has already left me? Why, we read the 'Gnat' [a mock epic attributed to the youthful Virgil] and we acknowledge the 'Battle of Frogs and Mice' [a mock-epic attributed to Homer], and there is no great poet who has not produced preliminary work in a lighter style.

Like Cato, Hercules is a figure so associated with labour that it is exceptional when he does relax and embrace *otium*. The god appears as a paradigm of the renunciation of labour and the embrace of *otium* in *Silvae* 3. 1, which celebrates the restoration of a temple of Hercules on the bay of Naples near Surrentum by Pollius Felix:

> Come here and bring your presence to the newly-founded shrine.
> Dangerous Lerna does not require you, nor the plains of poor Molorchus,
> nor the dreaded land of Nemea nor the Thracian caves,
> nor the Pharian ruler's desecrated altars,
> but a blessed and straightforward household, unskilled in evil deceit
> a spot worthy of even divine guests.
> Put aside your fierce bow and your quiver's savage horde,
> and your club, stained with much royal blood,
> take off the enemy stretched across your unyielding shoulders.

(3. 1. 28–36)

In withdrawing to a refuge on the bay of Naples, Hercules follows the example of Pollius himself, whose pursuit of undisturbed peace is described in *Silvae* 2. 2, a celebration of his villa near Surrentum:

Live, richer than Midas' treasure or Lydian gold,
fortunate beyond the crowns of Troy and the Euphrates,
whom neither changeable political power nor the fickle mob
nor laws nor military camps trouble, who with a magnificent heart
overcomes hope and fear, transcending every desire,
freed from the limits of Fate, proving resentful Fortuna wrong;
the last day will overtake you not beset by a storm of unresolved business
but having had your fill of life and ready to depart.

(2. 2. 121–9)

Hercules' withdrawal to the bay of Naples follows the example of many wealthy Romans, whose luxurious villas dotted the shores of the bay, making it the place most associated with the Roman experience of *otium*. In *Silvae* 3. 5, Statius writes of his own plans to retire to Naples; the poem is addressed to his wife, who apparently was reluctant to go on the grounds that she was preoccupied with the marriage prospects of her daughter from a previous marriage. Statius describes the area as an escape from all that keeps men busy at Rome:

There is undisturbed peace there, and the leisure of an idle life
undisturbed rest and uninterrupted sleep.
There is no madness in the forum, or laws drawn in disputes . . .

(3. 5. 85–7)

On the bay of Naples by contrast there are plenty of amusements for his wife to enjoy: theatres, baths, temples, and so forth, 'the pleasures of a varied life are all around' (3. 5. 95).

The poet Juvenal (born Decimus Iunius Iuvenalis in approximately 67 CE; his first poem was written after 100 and his fifteenth after 127) makes the Roman desire for peace and quiet on the bay of Naples the framework of his third satire. Satire, the only Roman literary form thought to be wholly Roman in origin, prides itself on representing Rome's seamier side without flinching. Like his predecessor Horace (above pp. 375 ff.), Juvenal mocks excess, hypocrisy, and bad taste, though he tends to be boisterously extreme where Horace is subtle and rather moderate. Here, in the third satire, the poet-narrator goes to Rome's Capena gate to meet a friend named Umbricius who has decided to withdraw to the peaceful isolation of Cumae, 'gateway to Baiae' (Juvenal, *Satires* 3. 4). According to Umbricius it is impossible for a man who does not know how to lie to make his way at Rome. Instead, Umbricius—whose name plays on the associations of *umbra*, 'shadow' or 'ghost'—turns away from the struggle of living at Rome towards quiet Cumae, which is more famously a gateway not to Baiae but to the underworld presided over by the Sibyl. So the poet describes the ghostly Umbricius as 'thus providing the Sibyl with a solitary fellow townsman' (Juvenal, *Satires* 3. 3, trans. Rudd). Direct mention of the Sibyl invites readers to recall her role as Aeneas' guide in the underworld in the sixth book of the *Aeneid*. Indeed, Juvenal has evoked the parade of heroes before Aeneas in Virgil's underworld at the very end of the immediately preceding poem when he imagines what the shades of Rome's republican heroes would feel about the arrival in the underworld of the ghost of an imperial degenerate:

> What does Curius feel,
> or the Scipios twain? What do Fabricius and the shade of Camillus,
> and Cremera's legion and the valiant lads who fell at Cannae
> and the dead of all those wars—when a ghost like this descends
> from the world above? They'd insist on purification . . .
>
> (Juvenal, Satires 2. 153–7, trans. Rudd)

Umbricius' move from Rome to Cumae reverses Aeneas' foundational journey from Cumae to Rome. Juvenal has to stay behind if he is to continue to produce satire: Satire would die if the satirist too abandoned Rome for the restful pleasures of the bay of Naples.

Another satirical treatment of the pleasures available on the bay of Naples forms the framework of the best-preserved sections of the fragmentary *Satyricon* (by Petronius—see below). The surviving sections of the *Satyricon* (mostly from books 14–16, apparently) recount the adventures of a hapless hero Encolpius and his friends as they wander on the bay of Naples, and in the aftermath of shipwreck near Croton in southern Italy. Encolpius is convinced that his difficulties in general, and with sex in particular, result from being pursued by the wrath of the phallic guardian god Priapus. The novel combines parody of epic and of Greek idealizing romantic fiction (perhaps via a tradition of racy Greek fiction which had already mocked the chaste and noble heroes and heroines of Greek romance). It also enthusiastically exploits motifs familiar from verse satire such as extravagant parties, dissolute women, and legacy hunting, and expands farcical situations which seem to have been popular in mime. The prose narrative is interrupted at various points by outbursts of verse. A literary form known as Menippean satire had combined verse with prose in short satirical pieces on various subjects; the satirical account of the aborted deification of the Emperor Claudius attributed to Seneca and known as the *Apocolocyntosis* (*Pumpkinification*) is the only surviving Classical Latin example (see p. 172 above). Petronius' use of verse is more complex and sophisticated than what survives in the Menippean tradition. The surviving fragments of the *Satyricon* include some thirty short poems and two longer poems performed by a character who is a professional poet: sixty-five verses in tragic style on the Fall of Troy, and 295 epic verses on the civil war between Caesar and Pompey.

MOMENTO MORI. *A silver beaker, made about the turn of BCE/CE and found at Boscoreale near Pompeii, shows a Hamlet-like fascination with the great figures of the past reduced to skeletons. Trimalchio in Petronius shows a similarly macabre imagination.*

On the bay of Naples, as they alternately cadge hospitality and try to escape those they have antagonized, Petronius' main characters Encolpius, Ascyltos, and Giton live alienated from the world of work and from the secure pleasures of *otium*. When they wangle a dinner invitation to the home of the fabulously wealthy freedman Trimalchio, his extravagant entertainment takes Roman amusements to outrageous extremes. Trimalchio is obsessed with death in all its forms, from the cooking and eating of meats to ghost stories to the orders for the carving on his own tomb. His house is described in terms which recall the labyrinthine paths to and from the underworld. Add to this his memories of seeing the Sibyl at Cumae shrivelled up in a bottle, and the whole dinner with Trimalchio parodically recalls Aeneas' heroic encounter with the Sibyl at Cumae and his harrowing journey to the underworld.

So, Statius, Juvenal, and Petronius all shuffle the same pack of cards and deal different hands. Petronius' bay of Naples is a land of excess and unmaking the heroic past; Statius' is peaceful and restorative, free from the troubles of Rome; Juvenal's, centred on Umbricius in lonely Cumae, is a sterile place where satire cannot thrive.

Otium and a good nose

It is harder to speak about the life of Petronius than about the other authors we have seen so far. He is probably to be identified with the Petronius described by Tacitus as Nero's 'arbiter of elegance' at *Annals* 16. 17–19, in which case he served as consul in 62 and was forced by Nero to commit suicide in 66. In Tacitus' account, which mentions nothing about the *Satyricon*, Petronius is represented as a master of the amusements of *otium* as well as the business of Empire:

> He spent his days sleeping, his nights in work and life's amusements. Where others earned fame through hard work, he earned it through idleness, and, unlike others who waste their resources, he was not considered a wastrel or spendthrift, but regarded as a man of extravagantly refined tastes. His unconstrained and apparently unselfconscious words and actions were welcomed for their appearance of candour. Nevertheless as proconsul of Bithynia and then as consul, he showed himself to be active and suited for business. (Tacitus, *Annals* 16. 18)

This same theme of finding the middle ground between excessive luxury—as evidenced by sleeping late—and too much hard work is taken up by the satirist Persius. Born into a wealthy Etruscan equestrian family in 34 CE, Aulus Persius Flaccus was educated at Rome and knew the poet Lucan (on whom see above, pp. 188–93 and who, we are told in an ancient biographical notice, admired his works) as well as Thrasea Paetus, a Stoic who took the stern morality of Cato the Younger as his model. Persius' surviving works are six satires and a short prefatory poem; after his death from natural causes in 62, the collection was published by the Stoic Cornutus, who had been Persius' teacher, and another literary friend, Caesius Bassus. In his fifth satire, Persius praises his friend and teacher Cornutus for helping him to understand that true freedom comes from the wisdom not to pursue money or luxury to excess. With a physical concreteness that is typical of his compressed and arresting style, Persius constructs a dialogue to describe a man being roused from sleep by Greed only to be rebuked for his pursuit of profit by Luxury:

In the morning you sleep in and snore. 'Get up,' says Greed, 'hey,
get up!' You refuse. She insists, 'Get up,' she says. 'I can't.' 'Get up.'
'To do what?' 'He asks! Look, import salt fish from Pontus,
beaver-musk, oakum, ebony, frankincense, slippery Coan silk.'

Greed succeeds in persuading the narrator to prepare to embark on a commercial trip, when Luxury interrupts to discourage him:

You dash aboard! Nothing prevents you from
hurrying across the Aegean on a huge ship unless Luxury shrewdly first
gives you a private warning: 'Madman, where oh where are you rushing off to?
...What do you want? Is it that the money that you've cultivated here at a modest
    five per cent should
end up sweating out a greedy eleven per cent?
Do yourself a favour. Let's snatch our pleasures while we can. That you live well is
    in my purview;
you will become ashes, a ghost, a story.
Live with death in mind: time flies, even these words spend it.'

(Persius, *Satires* 5. 132–54)

The poet considers two extremes: sleeping late and doing nothing on the one hand, and working tirelessly for money on the other. The implication is that only some activity such as writing poetry or contemplating philosophy will serve to use *otium* productively. But even writing can pose difficulties. In the third satire a stern friend awakens the poet, rebuking him for sleeping late and telling him to get to work: the poet reaches for parchment and reed pen but complains that the pen doesn't work (Persius, *Satires* 3. 1–14)!

How Persius describes *otium* may have to do with the fact that (according to an ancient biography) he was a member of a wealthy family. He thus has access to the leisure required for writing and has little financial need for a literary patron. He makes an implicit contrast between what will emerge as his private, secretive poetic stance ('Who will read that?' 'Are you asking me? No one at all.' Persius, *Satires* 1. 2) and the derivative productions of poets who depend on winning an audience's approval and financial support, described contemptuously in the poem which serves as a preface to the collection:

Who trained the parrot to say 'hello'?
and who taught the magpie to imitate our speech?
The belly, master of arts and generous source of talent,
ingenious at mimicking words nature denies.
And if the hope of tricky cash should gleam
you'd believe that crow poets and magpie poetesses
were singing Pegasus' sweet song.

(Persius, *prologue* 8–14)

Persius' first satire explodes with outrage as it depicts outlandish literary performances which pander to decadent tastes:

> we write in private, one in metre, one without,
> something big for lungs full of breath to huff and puff over.
> Of course you'll finally read this to a crowd from a raised platform
> all combed, shining in a fresh toga, wearing your birthday sardonyx,
> when you've rinsed out your nimble throat with a luscious trill,
> looking like you're overcome by sexual ecstasy.
> Then you'll see huge Tituses shudder disgracefully with shrill sounds
> when the songs penetrate their loins and
> the trembling verse tickles their most private parts.
>
> (Persius, *Satires* 1. 13–21)

Here Persius positions his private satire which he claims to expect no one to read against the works of those who stir the passions of larger crowds through excessive performances.

Elsewhere, Statius is the target of Juvenal's denunciation of the kind of poetry that is excessively and dramatically appealing to the general public (Juvenal, *Satires* 7. 82–7, see also pp. 199–200 above). The audience loves Statius' epic *Thebaid*, but because they are only a crowd, not a wealthy patron, no financial support is forthcoming unless he sells a text for a pantomime *Agave* to a famous and wildly popular performer Paris (for pantomimes, see p. 210 above). Here too a distinction is being asserted between the 'serious' literature that should be produced under the umbrella of patronage and read reverently, and the literature of popular entertainment. Statius' epic *Thebaid* has a certain popular appeal, but—at least according to Juvenal—only the truly mass-market appeal of a pantomime will keep dinner on Statius' table.

Martial distances his work from the tastes of the general public when he warns his book that in venturing out to booksellers it will expose itself to harsh criticism:

> Would you prefer to inhabit the shops of Argiletum,
> little book, though my boxes have space for you?
> Ah, you don't know Mistress Rome's disdain:
> believe me, Mars' crowd has much too much taste
> Nowhere are there bigger snorts of disdain: young and old,
> even boys have a rhinoceros' nose.
>
> (*Epigrams* 1. 3. 1–6)

Because it plays off of the standard image of the nose as an organ of literary sensibility—Horace for example admiringly calls his satiric predecessor Lucilius a man 'with a clean nose'—Martial's comparison to a rhinoceros mocks the coarse tastes of the sneering public. Elsewhere he self-deprecatingly acknowledges that his own poems are vulnerable to critical sniffs, but again the noses in question are extra-large:

> You may be as big-nosed as you like, you may be completely nose,
>> so big that Atlas if asked would not want to carry it,
> you could mock Latinus himself,
>> but you can't say more against my trivial poems
> than I myself have said.

(Epigrams 13. 2. 1–5)

The notion of the nose as an organ of élite good taste is also central to Martial's mockery of one Caecilius. Caecilius claims to be an urbane wit (like, say, Catullus) but he is instead like a mere vendor who sells his goods indiscriminately to the crowd :

> You think you are a sophisticated wit, Caecilius.
> You aren't, trust me. What then? You are a buffoon.
> You are what the peddler from across the Tiber is,
> one who trades pale yellow sulphur for broken bits of glass,
> you're what the one who sells hot porridge
> to the leisured crowd is,
> what the keeper and master of snakes is,
> what the worthless boys of the salt-fish sellers are,
> what the loudmouthed cook
> who sells smoking sausages in stuffy cook-shops is,
> what the inferior street poet is,
> what the disgraceful show producer from Cadiz is,
> what the sharp tongue of an old catamite is,
> so stop thinking you are
> what only you think you are,
> one who can outdo Gabba with jokes and Tettius Caballus himself.
> Not every one can have a nose;
> someone who jokes with unsophisticated impudence
> is not a Tettius, he's a mere old nag [*caballus*].

(Epigrams 1. 41)

In imperial Rome, the practice of producing and consuming literary works can play an important role in defining the self. In other words, as Martial says, 'It is not given to everyone to have a nose,' not everyone has taste enough to sneer at the right things. In fact, most people (the *turba*) sneer ignorantly through a rhino's nose. *Producers* position their works anywhere along a spectrum from the disgracefully and obscenely frivolous to the pleasantly refreshing to the purposefully contemplative. *Consumers* could encounter the literature of leisure at a relatively open public performance, or at a more private invitation-only gathering. One could purchase a book from a bookseller, or receive a poem or a book of poems as a gift, from a friend, or from the author himself, with the reciprocal obligations that would entail. Each literary transaction marks the consumer as the sort of person who partakes of literature in that particular way: as part of an exclusive and discerning circle of friends, or as one of an indiscriminate crowd, or as something in between.

Those who read Statius can congratulate themselves that his praises of escape from the demands of Empire will refresh them too; they can imagine that they share the wealth that makes leisure possible and the skill that makes literature successful. Those who read Persius and Juvenal can share the satirists' indignant and mocking detachment from everyday Rome. Enjoying what we could call the anti-Catonian literature of leisure of Martial and Petronius allows audiences to partake imaginatively of several experiences at once: to laugh at mime with the masses, to smile alone in the study, or to exchange jokes with friends at a dinner party. Ostensibly those who read Martial and Petronius abandon—at least while they are reading—the obligation to use *otium* in a productive, Catonian way. But these literate and well-crafted works allow the audience to have it both ways—to go slumming in the world of popular amusements while keeping a firm grip on the education and culture that mark them as élite.

Surely a number of Roman readers did relax at readings by these authors, or with texts of their works. The social and cultural importance of these texts extends beyond a narrowly recreational understanding of *otium*. In acquiring and consuming the literature of leisure, as in acquiring and consuming other luxury goods, individuals define themselves. They define not just the dimensions of their own critical noses but the cultural norms which structure society as a whole.

Orbis and *urbs*: Maps in marble

Martial addresses an epigram to one Sextus, apparently Domitian's librarian of the Palatine library:

> may there be a spot somewhere for my books,
>   where Pedo, Marsus, and Catullus are.
> Put the great work of buskin-shod Virgil
>   beside the divine poem on the Capitoline War
>   (*Epigrams* 5. 5. 5–8)

In other words, the books on lighter subjects are kept separate from those on national themes, in this case from Virgil's *Aeneid* and what was apparently a poem by Domitian on the siege of the Capitol in 69. Yet however far apart Romans might keep the literature of *otium* from the hefty tomes of national epic, what Roman men did at leisure was never wholly separate from what they did while carrying out the business of Empire. Even informal works 'in a lighter vein' participate in the discourses which create imperial culture, reflecting and extending their authors' and audiences' experiences of Empire. In informal works, audiences find not the universalizing perspectives of epic nor the carefully marshalled details of history, but fleeting glances at Empire, snatched amid the complicated business of finding one's way through Rome's crowds. The background of myth that authenticates epic's visions of Empire is not absent, but glimpsed from unfamiliar oblique angles. Imperial power is manifest not so much in accounts of campaigns and conquests as in representations of the people and objects streaming into Rome from all over the world (cf. also pp. 41–2, 204–5 above).

Satire and epigram perpetrate, then, mainly through negative example, their own versions of the disciplines of the soul, body, and voice which define the appropriately male and Roman citizen of Empire. Informal works enjoyed at leisure reinforce their audience's status as educated men and contribute to their sense that Rome is the centre of Empire. Into the city money, imported goods, and newcomers pour in torrents, and from it administrators and orders are sent out. Informal literary works help constitute and illuminate the imperial dimensions of the experiences of *otium* along two axes: the spatial experience of Empire extending from its centre at Rome to its distant frontiers, and the temporal experience of Empire, from its legendary Trojan origins through the Republic to the institution of the principate under Augustus and his successors.

A long-standing punning juxtaposition of *orbis* (world) and *urbs* (city) enacts a Roman fascination with measuring the city of Rome against the world. The *orbis* is conceived of as a space which is mastered through military, administrative, and commercial work. This active hard-won imperial mastery gets talked about in the literature of leisure in various ways: work in the world feeds *otium* in the city; the city serves as an archive or epitome of the world. Inhabitants of the city (at least some of them—and the emperor most of all) need go nowhere besides Rome to consume the spoils of all the world. Imperial Rome was a cosmopolis of consumption, and the spoils of Empire adorning its houses, temples, and tables are reproduced in its literature from the elder Pliny's encyclopaedia to Martial's epigrammatic gift labels (books 13 and 14). The imported luxuries are often 'tagged' with their origins. The geographical 'footnoting' of these spoils implicates texts in the physical, objectively real, world.

Yet, though geographical terms of reference have this objective quality (the places referred to really do exist), at Rome, as elsewhere, geographical information is at the same time an imperial product constructed by the mechanisms of travel, trade, and military campaigns, and authenticated by myth. As such, it is never only an objective report of the world. It is always an utterance in the discourses that animate and uphold Empire: geographical stories communicate imperial aspirations. Transgressive geographical communication can be fatal: the historian Dio records that during the reign of Domitian a certain Mettius Pompusianus was put to death for habitually reading the speeches of kings and other leaders in Livy (presumably in a pointed way) and for having a map of the world painted on his bedroom walls (Dio, 67.12.2–4). A man so interested in figures who once wielded power in Rome and in the far reaches of Rome's Empire evidently made Domitian uneasy.

Mastery of the unimaginably vast spaces of Empire is asserted in written, spoken, or implicit narratives of acquiring and transporting luxury goods to Rome. Luxurious imported food and its trappings—whether actually served or described in literature—become part of narratives of imperial ascendancy. Juvenal's account of the huge turbot offered to Domitian overtly maps Empire onto the dinner table:

> In the days when the last of the Flavian line was tearing to pieces
> the half-dead world [*orbem*], and Rome was slave to a bald-headed Nero [i.e. to Domitian],
> off the temple of Venus, which stands above Doric Ancona,
> an Adriatic turbot of wonderful size was caught.
>
> (Juvenal, *Satires* 4. 1–4, trans. Rudd)

The fish is so huge that no dish is big enough to serve it; a council of advisers is summoned. A later commentator's note tells us that this episode parodies a council scene in Statius' poem (now lost) on Domitian's campaigns on the German frontiers. Satire transforms the business of conquest into the culinary amusements of *otium*, while the fish takes on the configurations of the Empire and its border defences :

> 'So what do you recommend? Cut him in pieces?'
> 'Ah, spare him that indignity!' pleaded Montanus, 'Make him a platter
> fit to encircle his massive bulk [*spatiosum . . . orbem*] with its thin defences—'
>
> (Juvenal, *Satires* 4. 130–2, trans. Rudd)

But the emperor is not the only one who consumes the world (*orbis*): a wealthy man dines unsociably alone in Satire 1, 'chewing his way through the finest produce of sea and woodland. Yes off all those antique tables [*orbibus*], so wide and stylish . . . ' (Juvenal, *Satires* 1. 135–8). The wide circles of the tables

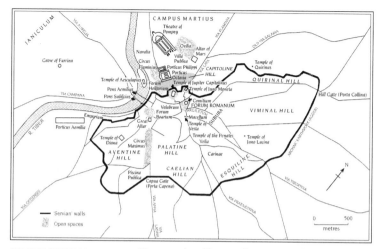

THE URBS THAT RULED THE ORBIS. Many works of Roman literature, including poetry, are informed by an awareness of the urban topography and layout of the great city of Rome.

replicate in miniature the wide spaces of the imperial world. In a similar fashion, Petronius' Trimalchio has himself served a tray of hors-d'oeuvres that replicates the zodiac (*Satyricon* 35). According to Statius (*Silvae* 1. 6) Domitian's celebration of games in honour of Saturnus on the first of December gathers tasty foods, lovely women, and birds from the world over into the Roman amphitheatre in a demonstration of Domitian's cosmos-ordering position as emperor. Statius' poetic account of this spectacle renders the popular experience of the amphitheatre 'safe' for the élite man's *otium*.

In the literature of leisure too we can find the same strategies of measuring the city of Rome against the world at large. To take one arresting example, Martial's epigram (2. 14) on Selius' frantic circuit of the Campus Martius in an attempt to obtain a dinner invitation maps a journey of leisure through the Campus Martius against a series of world-mastering journeys represented by monuments there. Selius begins and ends his trip at what Martial calls 'Europa'; this refers to a painting of Europa's abduction by Jove in the form of a bull. The painting seems to have been near or even within the Porticus Vipsania. This building housed a monumental map of the world produced using a geographical commentary by Marcus Vipsanius Agrippa, the close associate of Augustus. The map served as a memorial to Agrippa's mastery of the sea under the sponsorship of Augustus. The myth of Europa would have been an obvious candidate for a decorative counterpart to the Agrippan map: Jove's abduction of Europa in a sense brings the Western world into being because she becomes the mother of Minos, king of Crete, the first dominant sea power in the Aegean. And the voyage of the Argonauts depicted in the nearby Portico of the Argonauts likewise could offer a mythical foil to the story of sea mastery told by the Agrippan map. Now while there is no reason to doubt that these porticoes really were the scene of much leisured relaxation and trawling for dinner invitations, Martial's account of Selius' movements through the Campus Martius is not solely representational. In a move comparable to Juvenal's equation of Domitian's fish with the Empire, Martial implicitly juxtaposes Silius' search for dinner throughout the Campus Martius with the mythical map of Europa's abduction and Agrippa's imperial map of the world. The hard work of urban leisure is mapped against the hard work of winning—and representing—the world.

There were numerous 'maps' of the world at Rome. Even great buildings lavishly decorated with coloured marble served the knowledgeable élite as imperial maps, because the colour of the various marbles signalled their geographical origins. A certain greenish marble came from near Sparta, a greyish-blue from Carystos, a reddish one from Phrygia and so forth. When poets describe such buildings, the audience no doubt expected them to catalogue the marbles on display. In his *Silvae*, Statius tests his audience's connoisseurship of stone and poetry by combining standard information about the colour and source of the stone with vocabulary that is specially chosen to suit the particular building he is describing. In *Silvae* 4. 2, on Domitian's palace, as Kathleen Coleman has shown, the imported stones are described in words which emphasize rivalry and striving for pre-eminence: the Libyan and Phrygian marbles are modified with the adjective 'emulous' (*aemulus*, 26), and the blue marble of Carystos is described by saying that the stones are 'contesting with' (*certantia*, 28) the blue sea nymph Doris.

In a description of one particularly beautiful sea-view room in Pollius' villa at Surrentum Statius (*Silvae* 2. 2) uses terms which reflect the construction of the villa itself: some imported stones are said to come from Greek mines, some to have been dug up by Phrygian axes, and marble 'which is green and imitates the soft grass with its crags' was 'cut from' (*caesum*, 90) a mountain in Sparta. All of this is designed to reflect the construction of the villa which has already been described as a vast mountain-moving project. In the account of Violentilla's house in 1. 2, the terms in which the stone is described are chosen to allow comparisons with Violentilla's emotional shift in the course of the poem: at Venus' persuasion she has softened her resistance and yields to the overtures of her suitor, a man named Stella. The hard stone silex, and the 'hard stones' of Spartan marble correspond to Violentilla's rejections of Stella. The 'winding pattern' (*flexus*) of onyx prefigures Violentilla's change of heart: 'And now she begins gladly to bend [*flectere*] her stubborn heart and now to account herself hard' (1. 2. 199–201). And the sea-blue stone of Carystos shows the trace of Violentilla's reconciliation to Stella: instead of the terms of rivalry associated with it elsewhere there is a notion of agreement when Statius describes it as 'the vein that matches the deep sea's blue' (lines 149–50). Precisely because the shared geographic lore of stone connoisseurship was so detailed and conventional—everyone was no doubt already expecting reddish Phrygian, bluish Carystian, and greenish Laconian stone to be mentioned—Statius can flatter his audience with the craftsmanship of his 'installations'.

The literature of leisure encourages its audience to imagine the world as storehouse for treasures to be transported to and consumed by Romans. These works thereby contribute to the geographical knowledge that is part of the experience of imperial subjects who even in their amusements can enjoy or reflect on their position as global citizens and rulers. Unlike the dangerous map of Empire on Pompusianus' bedroom wall, the private 'maps' which unfold in the literature of leisure make the pleasures of imperial mastery safe for ordinary mortals to enjoy.

Memories of republican Rome

Though the literature of leisure does not aim primarily to tell historical stories, it taps into veins of memory which run through Roman culture at large: memories of the Republic, memories of Troy, and memories of earlier emperors. Think again of Pompusianus reading the speeches of kings in Livy and mapping the Empire on his bedroom walls: if the literature of leisure makes the scope of Empire safe to enjoy, it also makes the past safe to remember.

The literature of leisure incorporates memories of Rome's rise to Empire when it contrasts imperial luxury with republican simplicity and hard work. In his second satire, Persius decries the influx of luxuries into Rome, saying that it is pointless to waste money on lavish offerings to the gods when simple grain will do just as well; he complains that gold vessels have replaced traditional votive objects:

> Gold has pushed out Numa's vessels and Saturn's bronzes,
> and has changed the Vestals' urns and Tuscan earthenware.
> (Persius, *Satires* 2. 59–61)

For Juvenal too, imperial luxury has displaced republican simplicity when he promises his friend Persicus a simple dinner of kid, asparagus, eggs, chicken, and fruit:

> That was the kind of dinner, quite lavish by then, which the senate
> would eat in days gone by. Curius picked his greens
> in his plot and cooked them himself on his tiny hearth. Such a menu
> is now despised by a filthy labourer digging a ditch
> in chains (he remembers the taste of tripe in a stuffy tavern).
>
> (Juvenal, *Satires* 11. 77–81, trans. Rudd)

The idealized self-sufficiency in the vignette of Curius is parodied by Petronius in an account of Trimalchio's vast estates. One of Encolpius' fellow guests says that 'You shouldn't think that he purchases anything. Everything originates at home: mastich, cedar resin, pepper'—a list of trees believed to grow only in their native lands, not throughout the world (Petronius, *Satyricon* 38.1).

In his own way, Juvenal has as much fun with the idealization of republican simplicity as Petronius does:

> When people trembled before the Fabii and stern old Cato,
> and before such men as Scaurus and Fabricius, when even a censor
> feared the harshness that might result from his colleague's austerity,
> nobody thought it a matter for grave and serious attention
> what kind of turtle, swimming then in the ocean's waves,
> might make a splendid and noble prop for our Trojan élite.
> Couches were small, their sides were plain, and only the headrest
> was bronze; it showed the garlanded head of a common donkey;
> beside it the lively country children would romp and play.
> The soldier was rough, and untrained to admire the art of Greece.
> When, after the sack of a city, he found in his share of the spoil
> cups produced by famous artists, he would break them up
> to give his horse the pleasure of trappings, and to set designs
> on his helmet, so that the foe might see at the moment of death
> Romulus' beast grown tame, as imperial destiny ordered,
> the Quirinal twins within the cave, and the naked image
> of Mars, as, grasping his shield and sword, he swooped from above.
> And so they would serve their porridge on plates of Tuscan ware.
> What silver they had would shine on their weapons and nowhere else.
>
> (Juvenal, *Satires* 11. 90–108, trans. Rudd).

In this vision of republican Rome, people eat off of earthenware not simply because they have yet to be corrupted by the spoils of conquest, but because they are capable of resisting such corruption, and elaborate metalware is broken up to decorate helmets and to give a war horse 'the pleasure of trappings'. Juvenal is pointedly reversing accounts of Corinthian bronze: when the city of Corinth was sacked by Rome in 146, metal statues of Corinth were allegedly melted down for tableware and luxurious statuettes (Pliny, *Natural History* 34. 6). Petronius for his part parodies the connoisseurship of Corinthian bronze in Trimalchio's garbled account of his bronzes, genuine 'Corinthian' because they were made by a slave named Corinthus (*Satyricon* 50). The theme that increasing luxury marks a rupture between the republican past and the imperial present also appears in the *Satyricon*: the poet Eumolpus launches into an epic treatment of the civil war between Caesar and Pompey and begins (using a strategy modelled on the opening of Lucan's epic on the civil war) with the assertion that Rome turned to civil war as desires for luxuries became insatiable (119. 1–38).

Statius' *Silvae* 4. 6 also distils republican history into luxurious dining accessories. Statius reports being invited to dinner by one Novius Vindex, who eschews all imported gourmet luxuries but shows off his collection of Greek art-works, including a statue of Hercules 'epitrapezios' ('at table'). The statue, we are told, once belonged to Alexander the Great, who took it with him on campaign. Then Hannibal owned it; he too took it on campaign, but this only inflamed Hercules' anger, especially on behalf of the citizens of Saguntum (founded under his patronage) when Hannibal laid siege to the city. Subsequently it came into the possession of Sulla. Unlike the warrior owners who boasted to Hercules of their own campaigns, Novius Vindex inhabits a world of *otium*, undertakes no military campaigns, and sings to the statue only of the legendary labours of Hercules himself. The opening scene of the poem, in which Statius receives the dinner invitation while spending his leisure time (*otia*) in the Saepta Julia, implicitly goes over the same historical ground. This enclosure (*c*.300 × 95 metres) in the Campus Martius, planned by Julius Caesar and eventually completed by Agrippa, had once been used for electoral assemblies. As its electoral purpose became obsolete under the emperors, it was used as the site of gladiatorial displays before the opening of the Colosseum in 80. After a fire the site was rebuilt and used as a market known for its luxurious goods. In the Saepta, Romans once gathered for elections, then gladiatorial spectacles, then finally up-market shopping: it is the perfect space from which to enter upon the tale of the Hercules statue.

Again and again in the literature of leisure the public story of historical transformation from republican to imperial Rome is scaled down to a private story of dining. Another set of memories of the Republic centres on conceptions of freedom (*libertas*) and language: here too what was public becomes private as republican civic practices give way in the face of imperial realities. As was the

HERCULES IN MINIATURE. This Roman miniature sculpture is a copy of a famous Greek sculpture Herakles Epitrapezios (i.e. at the table).

case for Roman literature of the Republic and Augustan periods, the production of literary works during the first and second centuries CE continued to be by and for men who had acquired a rhetorical education. Rhetoric continued to be a focus for defining Romanness around ideals of masculinity, mastery of language, and placing oneself in the right spot along the spectrum which led from rustic native Italianness on the one hand, through a cosmopolitan Romanness at the centre, on towards a corrupt and effeminate otherness variously categorized as Greek, Eastern, or Egyptian. But between the end of the Republic and the Neronian period, since most power now rested overtly or covertly in the hands of the emperor, the social role of oratory had moved away from a direct connection to governance and had become a site for virtuosic display.

Persius inserts himself as a young and resisting participant into this story of republican excellence subsiding into imperial mimicry:

> I remember that as a young boy I often smeared my eyes with olive oil
> if I didn't want to recite Cato's last words,
> words much praised by my mad teacher
> as my father listened, sweating, with friends he'd invited.

> (Persius, *Satires* 3. 44–7)

The younger Cato, who struggled to defend the institutions of the Republic against the dangers of the civil strife between Caesar and Pompey, is the exemplary exponent of republican *libertas*. Lucan represents him as a spirited defender of freedom (cf. p. 186) and Seneca pictures Cato in ringing terms: 'He speaks with the voice of freedom [*vocem liberam*] and urges the Republic not to fail in the defence of liberty but to try everything possible, saying that it is more honourable to fall into servitude by chance than to proceed toward it of their own will' (Seneca, *Epistles* 95. 70). Persius takes up the topic of freedom explicitly in his fifth satire, in praise of his teacher the Stoic Cornutus, and rejecting civic and political definitions of freedom, he defines it in solely philosophical terms. A student asserts:

> Is anyone free, except the man
> who can spend his life as he pleases?
> I can live as I like, am I not
> freer than Brutus?
> <div align="right">(Persius, <i>Satires</i> 5. 83–5)</div>

Cornutus corrects the student on 'able' and 'choose', asserting that to be truly free one must have insight into what are the truly useful and worthy things in life:

> When you can truly say 'These are mine, I own them',
> then you are free and wise, with the blessing of Jove and the praetors.
> <div align="right">(Persius, <i>Satires</i> 5. 113–14)</div>

In this exchange, republican freedom of political speech, as exemplified in the public speeches of the first Brutus, the man who brought the Republic into being by expelling the tyrant Tarquinius Superbus, is reconfigured as a private freedom, independent of political and social structures. The other Brutus, the assassin of Julius Caesar, is reduced from national figure to private diversion, when in Statius' witty verses to his friend Plotius Grypus he rebukes Plotius for giving him Brutus' tedious works (probably speeches) as a gift instead of something more enjoyable (*Silvae* 4. 9.20–2). In each case, public republican discourse exemplifying *libertas* is reduced and reconfigured to be the stuff of private diversion in an imperial framework.

The notion of an assertive republican freedom of speech dissolving into the stuff of private imperial entertainment also operates in accounts of the history of satire itself, as we can see in Persius' comparison of his satires with those of his predecessors Lucilius (see pp. 24–5 above) and of Horace (see above pp. 91 ff.):

> Lucilius tore up Rome
> and you Lupus and Mucius, and broke his molar on them.
> Sly Horace mentions every fault while his friend laughs;
> once welcomed in he plays on the feelings,
> clever at dangling the public from his well-blown nose.
> Is it forbidden to me to whisper? not even in secret? in a ditch? nowhere?
> Nevertheless I'll dig a hole for it here: I have seen it, seen it myself, little book.
> Who does not have ass's ears? That is my secret,
> my joke. Though it's small, I wouldn't sell it for any
> *Iliad*.

(Persius, Satires 1. 114–23)

Juvenal too voices a paradoxically outspoken discretion. Although he writes during the time of Trajan (98–117) and Hadrian (117–38), he writes mainly about the time of Domitian (81–96). His first satire describes Lucilius' outspoken attacks on his contemporaries:

> Whenever, as though with sword in hand, the hot Lucilius
> roars in wrath, the listener flushes; his mind is affrighted
> with a sense of sin, and his conscience sweats with secret guilt.
> That's what causes anger and tears.

Juvenal, Satires 1. 165–8, trans. Rudd)

Juvenal adds that by contrast he will write only about the dead: 'I'll try what I may against those whose ashes are buried beneath the Flaminia and the Latina' (*Satires* 1. 171–2). According to Persius and Juvenal, Lucilius and Horace gave readers front-row seats for satire's relatively public attacks on its targets: Persius and Juvenal themselves frame satire as private, marginal, and secretive. So here too, as in its stories of dining, the literature of leisure keeps telling the same imperial story. What had been public (military conquest, freely uttered mockery) has become private (lavish dining, wary and secretive mockery).

Although the works I have been describing as Rome's literature of imperial leisure make few claims to be consequential, they offer us important points of access to the world of ancient Rome. They showcase strategies for defining oneself as an inhabitant of Rome and of Rome's Empire. The trajectories from public to private traced in these works may reflect a questioning of Empire's institutions or an endorsement of them. Either way, we should listen carefully to Rome's literature of leisure to hear the stories it tells of imperial space and time while claiming to leave Empire's work aside.

9 | Culture wars: Latin literature from the second century to the end of the classical era

MICHAEL DEWAR

Small town boys (made good)

Sex sells, as any publisher knows. That much was true in the second century too, though it seems a little magic and a lot of learning could be usefully added to the mix. The proof of this contention may be found in *The Golden Ass*, the celebrated novel of (?Lucius) Apuleius (*c.*125–70 CE) who came from Madaura in the province of Africa. Known formally as *The Metamorphoses*, this is the only Latin novel to survive complete from antiquity, and a remarkable piece of work it is (cf. pp. 218–20). Our hero, a young man by the name of Lucius, is travelling in Thessaly, in northern Greece, a part of the world famous for its witches. Lucius' character is distinguished by a rampant curiosity about, on the one hand, the illicit knowledge of magic and, on the other, a young maid-servant who is privy to many of the secrets of her mistress, a sorceress with a nice line in corporeal transformation. The maidservant's skills are corporeal too, but not quite in the same way. Eager to experiment, Lucius attempts to reproduce the witch's spells, but instead of becoming, as he hoped, a bird, he is transformed into a shaggy old ass. Luckily, there is an antidote: all he has to do is munch on a few rose petals, and all will be as good as new. But of course, if he were to do that straight off, there would be no novel, so poor Lucius in his grotesque inhuman form is subjected to a series of misadventures that take him from one end of Greece to the other, and see him repeatedly stolen, sold, beaten, humiliated, owned by all kinds of unpleasant characters, and threatened by all kinds of even more unpleasant deaths, before eventually being scheduled for a performance in the arena at Corinth. His role is intended to be a central one, fitting to his, as it were, assets: he is to copulate with a woman condemned to death, and thus provide the instrument of her execution.

What was the literary purpose of such a scandalous composition? Apuleius himself explains in the prologue (1. 1):

Now, in this Milesian style, I shall string various tales together for you, and caress your kindly ears with pleasurable murmurings, if only you are not too proud to take a look at Egyptian paper inscribed with the sharpness of a Nile reed-pen—to make you marvel at the shapes and fortunes of men changed into other forms and then turned back once more in due sequence into their own. Time to begin. 'But who is this fellow?', I hear you ask. I can tell you in a few words. Attic Hymettos and the Isthmus of Corinth, and Spartan Taenarus, blessed lands made famous for ever in books more blessed still, are my ancient ancestry. There I did my boyhood service in the tongue of Athens. After that, I came to the city of the Latins as a stranger, and with pain-filled labour, but with no teacher to coach me, I tackled and mastered the native tongue of Roman scholarship. And so I ask first for your indulgence, if, as an unpolished speaker of the strange language of the courts, I give any offence. But as a matter of fact, this very change of speech is appropriate to the kind of writing I am taking on—an art like that of an acrobat, leaping from one horse's back to another. It is a Greek tale that I begin. Reader [*lector*], pay attention: you will enjoy some fun [*laetaberis*].

Having fun, then, would appear to be the dominant motive, and readers who had casually picked up this particular papyrus scroll might think that what they had in their hands was just a literary romp of no great moral pretensions. Indeed, quite the reverse, since Apuleius also makes it clear that his 'novel' is, as much as anything, a compendium of tales in the 'Milesian style'. Such tales got their name from Aristeides of Miletos, who, in about 100 BCE, wrote a collection of saucy stories translated into Latin soon after by Sisenna. These originals have long since vanished, but their disreputable nature is commemorated in Plutarch's story that copies were found in the baggage of Roman officers who shared the defeat of the legions commanded by Crassus at the disastrous Battle of Carrhae in 53 BCE. When they found them, the victorious Parthians were duly scandalized, and passed censorious (though gleeful) comments on the moral character of their humiliated opponents. A fine lot they were to talk, observes Plutarch in his *Life of Crassus*, given that their own royal family was descended in part from Milesian prostitutes; but we get the picture.

Apuleius' prologue encourages us, however, to make a few more deductions about the kind of readership he expected to attract. And 'readership' is here the key word. True, he promises to caress 'kindly ears', but that is because, in accordance with ancient practice, the reader was not expected to read silently, with lips tight shut. Indeed, those who failed to voice the words would be denying themselves most of the marvellous pleasures of Apuleius' sonorous and incantatory narrative. At any rate, as the prologue continues, it is made clear to us that Apuleius expects that we will be encountering his works through the medium of Egyptian papyrus and Nile-reed pen, and if the last word is 'fun', it shares its sentence with a direct address to the 'reader'. This addressee is the ancestor of the 'gentle reader' of eighteenth-century novels, just as Apuleius' characters are the spiritual and cultural ancestors of many of the eccentric figures who litter the pages of Boccaccio, Fielding, and Voltaire. But do the links between Apuleius' implied readers and those undisciplined Roman soldiers show that nothing much had changed in the last two centuries since Carrhae?

The scrolls at Carrhae were Aristeides' Greek originals. Like Virgil and Cicero before him, Apuleius has played a part in the great process of adapting Greek literature into Latin: now the Latin West had its own high-grade pornography, just as it had its own epic poetry and rhetoric. But note that this is the product of the provinces, not of Rome herself. Indeed, it is the product of that very part of the world which, as Livy was at pains to stress, almost won out over Rome for mastery of the world. Apuleius completed his literary studies at Carthage, and it seems to have been there that he spent most of his adult life, and there that he wrote *The Metamorphoses*. Latin literature no longer belonged solely to Rome and Italy; careers in Latin letters now lay open to educated men throughout the Western world. As the Roman Peace encouraged the spread of the Roman tongue, there developed a larger middle class to administer the economy and bureaucracy of the empire, a class with the money to buy such scrolls, the leisure to read them, and the education to appreciate their literary and stylistic values, and their hidden meanings. This was the Empire's glorious high summer, from the accession of Nerva in 98 CE to the death of Marcus Aurelius in 180 CE, the age that Gibbon famously called 'the period in the history of the world during which the condition of the human race was most happy and prosperous'. The borders were secure, the economy flourishing, and the emperors just and mild. For once, the Roman world seemed less concerned with wars than with building and beautifying, with buying and selling, and even with a little reading and writing.

The question of the level of education that Apuleius expected in his readers is almost as important as the fun he provided them. *The Metamorphoses* is a work of Roman literature that, as so often, is more than it pretends to be. It takes the form of a pseudo-biography, and in the last book Lucius, having finally found some roses while on his way to perform his terrible duties in the arena at Corinth, has resumed his human shape. What follows is an account, less racy but no less remarkable, of the hero's spiritual salvation through initiation into the mysteries of the goddess Isis. Those of his contemporaries who knew about Apuleius' other interests might not have been all that surprised after all: he was also the author of a number of treatises on philosophy, such as *On Plato and his Teaching* and *On Socrates' God*. And at the very heart of the novel is a long tale that can hardly be called 'Milesian' at all, though it does share all kinds of elements with folk-tales from many cultures. It is told by an old crone to cheer up a pretty girl (obligatory in ancient novels, as in most modern ones) who has been kidnapped by a group of wicked bandits (obligatory in ancient novels, though optional in modern ones). In this tale, a princess with the by no means insignificant name of Psyche ('Soul') is offered up in sacrificial marriage to a mysterious monster whose identity she is sworn not to try to discover. Promises in fairy stories are made to be broken, and this one is no exception. Driven by a mixture of fear and curiosity for illicit knowledge, she sneaks a look one night, only to wake her mysterious lover up by accidentally dripping candle wax on him as she gazes in awe at his astounding beauty. For her 'monster' husband turns out to be a beautiful young god, albeit one with wings and a bit of a temper—none other, in fact, than Cupid, whose name in Latin ('Cupido') means 'Love'. Love is accordingly what she immediately feels, and she tries to make amends for her misdeeds. She is eventually purified by a number of terrible trials imposed on her by Venus. These prove her love, but once again her curiosity gets the better of her. Venus commands her to bring back from the world of the dead a mysterious jar, and on no account to look into it. Although she therefore has to endure a kind of death in order to enter the underworld, Psyche succeeds in completing her quest, only to make the terrible error of violating the goddess's prohibition once she has safely returned to the world of the living. The jar, in keeping with its provenance, contains a death-like trance, to which Psyche immediately succumbs. Only the love of divine Love himself is able to revive her, and, when he has done so, she is raised to heaven, in the story's last scene, as a goddess. There she is accepted as Cupid's bride and granted the true happy-ever-after ending we already knew to expect. The tale is plainly a Platonic allegory of sorts, and, although scholars argue about its exact meaning, the experiences of Psyche surely mirror and predict those of Lucius. Like Psyche, he is made to undergo a number of thoroughly dehumanizing trials to punish him for his impious curiosity, and like Psyche, too, he is eventually saved, not by his own merits, but by the intervention of a divine being whose power is matched only by her benevolence. We are not told if the pretty girl kidnapped by the bandits got the message, but it is clear that Apuleius was counting on the likelihood that his readers would, if only—as instructed in that prologue—they remembered to 'pay attention'.

Some two centuries or more later, around 400 CE, another African small-town boy who had made big in Carthage and abroad, and who, indeed, had been to school in Apuleius' home town of Madaura, wrote another long, novel-like story of a young man's misdeeds and unmerited salvation. He began, though, with an appeal to a reader who could be guaranteed to pay attention, and he made no promises of fun of any kind:

> Great are you, Lord, and much to be praised; great is your power, and of your wisdom there can be no reckoning . . . Grant me to know and understand, Lord, whether I should first call on you, or praise you, and whether I should first know you or call upon you . . . My faith, Lord, calls upon you, which you have given to me, which you have inspired in me by the humanity of your Son, and by the ministry of your preacher. (Augustine, *Confessions* 1. 1)

The third century had been a dark time of economic, political, and military crisis, of plague and depopulation, of usurpers and emperors who were assassinated almost before the news of their elevation to the purple had been announced in the more distant corners of the Empire: a grim end indeed to Gibbon's vaunted time of happiness and prosperity. The Empire came close to collapse, and reached a terrifying new low in 260 CE, when King Shapur I of Persia captured the Emperor Valerian alive in battle. According to the gloomier accounts preserved for us, poor Valerian spend the rest of his natural lifetime serving Shapur as a footstool whenever the victorious king wanted to mount his horse, and, when he had finally gone to his rest, he was stuffed and put on display as a trophy. By the end of the century, however, the situation had been turned around by such stern and uncompromising rulers as Aurelian (reigned 270–5 CE), who restored the frontiers and was known to everyone by the nickname 'Manus ad Ferrum' ('hand on steel'), and Diocletian (284–305 CE), a visionary bureaucrat with a good sense of military strategy and an even better sense of civil administration. By this time, Africa and many other parts of the West were more than ever a part of the Roman cultural world, with knowledge of the Latin language and respect for education firmly established. Those with social and literary ambitions could study in peace in smaller provincial centres, then go on to the grander schools in the provincial capital. The most gifted could even hope to emulate Augustine (Aurelius Augustinus, 354–430 CE), and make for the bright lights and smart social circles of old Rome. Or better still, if they had an eye to real success, they would go to the new imperial capitals closer to the frontiers which it was now more important than ever to defend.

Augustine headed for Milan, where the Christian emperors of the late fourth century held court, and there won himself enough admirers to be appointed Public Orator. His duties included the official celebration of the emperor's virtues as well as the instruction, in the hallowed style, of young aspirants in search of a proper grounding in traditional élite culture and the elegant rhetoric that was its hallmark. But though the Empire itself must have seemed as much a part of the natural order as the sun that shone down upon it and the taxes it collected, those opening words (quoted above) from his *Confessions* show that the world had changed for ever. The official faith of the court and state was now an Eastern salvation-cult, and not the one that Apuleius had trumpeted in the last book of *The Metamorphoses*. In Milan, Augustine came within the orbit of one of the most forceful and influential characters in the history of the Latin West, the city's irascible bishop, Ambrose (Ambrosius, 339/40–397 CE). A hard man to argue with, Ambrose had given his life to combatting heretics and, when he had the time to spare, those recalcitrant pagans who stubbornly clung to the old ways. He had even once forced the Emperor Theodosius to do public penance in his cathedral for ordering a massacre in the Greek city of Thessalonike.

Augustine never stood a chance. He looked around him, he looked inside him, and he did not much like what he saw. What on earth was the point, he wondered, of this traditional public display literature he was paid to profess? One day, when he was due to recite yet another elegant panegyric to the emperor, he saw something that led him to ruminate on the state of his soul, and came to the conclusion that all his aspirations to worldly happiness were utterly insubstantial and ephemeral:

> That same day, the one when I was preparing to recite to the emperor praises in which I would tell many a lie, and would, as I lied, win favour from people who knew I was lying . . . I saw a poor beggar, already, I think, drunk and happy. And I groaned and spoke to the friends who were with me about all the sorrows that come from our own madness . . . we wanted nothing but to achieve the carefree happiness which that beggar had achieved before us, and at which we might perhaps never arrive. (*Confessions* 6. 6)

What the beggar had achieved with a few pennies, Augustine had been seeking to achieve with much labour and much roundabout effort: 'the joy of a *temporary* felicity.'

It might be felt that it tells us a lot about Augustine that the sight of someone having a good time made him miserable. But that is, in a way, the whole point about the *Confessions*. They are one of the most astoundingly original creations of ancient literature—not a pseudo-biography, like that of Lucius, but the authentic record of a soul in search of peace. They are part autobiography, part theological treatise, part prayer—or perhaps mainly prayer. Although Lucius' salvation seems assured, Augustine feels that his is not only unmerited, but almost as precarious as it is inexplicable, a mystery of God and God's mercy. His

is a mind that cannot relax, and just as Apuleius' work might be said to reflect the settled serenity of his age, so Augustine's belongs to a more unsettled time, when the old world was crumbling away, when Rome itself would not be safe from the barbarians, but when, even so, the battles for civilization were as nothing compared to the war that raged in each man's soul between darkness and light.

Who were the *Confessions* written for? Not, it seems, other mortals, whom Augustine assumes to be hostile, mocking, and worldly:

> And yet allow me to speak before your mercy, me that am but dust and ashes, allow me yet to speak, since behold, it is your mercy, not man, my mocker, to whom I speak (1. 6)

But later this initial impression is modified. We discover that in part, at least, they were written with an eye to the faithful, for whom Augustine, in his role as bishop of Hippo in his home province of Africa, was obliged to provide such guidance as he could from his own spiritual journey and self-examination:

> Upon my return from Madaura . . . the expenses for a further journey to Carthage were being got ready for me, in keeping rather with my father's high spirit than with his resources, since he was only a citizen of middling standing at Thagaste. But to whom am I telling all this? Not to you, at any rate, my God, but in your presence I tell it to my own race, the human race, to whatever small part of it chances upon my writings. And to what end do I do this? Plainly so that I and anyone who reads this may reflect, how deep are the depths from which we must cry to you. (2. 3)

With that readership in mind, a readership that probably knew the psalms better than they knew their Virgil, Augustine writes in a loose but hymnic Latin that is new and fresh, and full of the resonances of a cultural and literary tradition that would have been inexplicably alien to the world of Cicero or Augustus. They are sometimes, with justice, thought of as the first work of medieval literature. But above all, to call them by a title that more accurately reflects the sense of the Latin word *Confessiones*, they are 'Acknowledgements', acknowledgements of the truth of Christian salvation and of the unworthiness of any human individual to earn that salvation, which came of God's mercy, and not of man's deserving. Augustine writes for himself, as a kind of therapy, to adopt the modern view, or as a kind of prayer and examination of conscience, if we try to see things as he himself must have done. His audience includes that greater public to which classical authors traditionally directed their words, but first and foremost he speaks to his own soul and, through his own soul, to the God who made it. It is hardly a purely 'classical' work: but the world of late antiquity was no longer a classical world. It was one of extremes and accommodation, and perhaps Augustine exemplifies both. The *Confessions* could not have been written without the Bible. But neither, one imagines, could they have been written without that rhetorical education Augustine received, and passed on to his pupils, before his conversion under the influence of Ambrose. At any rate, a degree of continuity is discernible amidst the strangeness. And Augustine's addressee might even be said to be the ideal Roman audience, despite His regrettable foreign origins. After all, He was learned to the point of omniscience, and so select that not even the most generous arithmetic could make Him number more than three.

Fighting the good fight

From the late second to the late fourth centuries, traditional pagan Latin literature, especially poetry, was in decline. But so, over the same lengthy period, was paganism itself. Our view of things is no doubt skewed by the relative dearth of traditional literature surviving from, above all, the troubled third century. There is little worth recording, apart from a learned didactic treatise on hunting and some graceful bucolic poems by one Nemesianus, a few poems in light genres from the *Latin Anthology*, a learned hotch-potch of geographical and ethnographical data by Solinus, some handbooks of medicine and traditional moralizing, and a whimsical parody of legal language called *The Piglet's Last Will and Testament*.

Instead, the real innovation and creativity seem to be found overwhelmingly in the pages of Christian authors, both those whose purpose was to attack pagans or attract them to the new faith, and those whose aim was literally to preach to the converted. The readership and audience these Christian writers had before them included many who were excluded from traditional élite culture, and conscientious efforts were made to respond to their needs. A symbolic break here was the preference Christian authors had for the new codex, the direct ancestor of the modern book. Made of sheets of papyrus, and later parchment, bound together, the codex was far easier to read than the cumbersome conventional papyrus roll, which had to be rewound again on its rods when the reader had finished. Duly uplifted by the Word of God, or the writings of His servants, the Christian simply had to slam the codex shut. In addition, the codex was far easier to consult for a particular passage, and this was of the greatest utility when it came to looking up the correct scriptural text needed to quote against heretics and heathens. It was also cheaper, and held much more. Christian authors and Christian readers were creating an entire alternative literary culture, just as they were creating an alternative society.

Similarly, great ingenuity was shown in adapting traditional modes of writing, and whole new genres were in effect being created. The taste for narrative that could not be met among the faithful by such racy works as Apuleius' *Metamorphoses* was satisfied instead by exuberant prose lives of the martyrs, where sex was replaced by titillating accounts of sexual advances repulsed by girls who, though desirable, were pure. These were not tempted into curiosity about illicit knowledge at all, but they were just as attractive, and, if any lack of excitement was still to be felt, then the increase in the component of violence might perhaps serve as adequate compensation. Violence of another kind was visible in the more aggressive works of such Christian apologists as Tertullian of Carthage (*c*.160–*c*.240 CE). Tertullian, who was almost as suspicious of pretty girls as he was of pagans, wrote, for example, treatises *On Veiling Virgins* (he was in favour), *On Chastity* (in favour), *On The Games* (against), and *On The Worship of Idols* (very much against). Not to put too fine a point on it, Tertullian was an intransigent fanatic, obsessed with purity and opposed to the whole structure and outlook of the society that surrounded him. But he helped create a whole new literature that had to be taken seriously on its own terms, one made up of rhetorically magnificent and logically persuasive diatribes against pagan folly and hypocrisy, while his passionate exhortations to those facing persecution also served to hearten the faithful.

A different line was taken by Minucius Felix (*fl.* 200–40 CE), who wrote a Ciceronian-style philosophical dialogue entitled *Octavius*, in which a Christian of that name debates with a pagan apologist called Caecilius. This gentlemanly respondent obligingly excuses the judge—Minucius himself—from having to make a formal adjudication when, with old-fashioned aristocratic courtesy, he confesses himself beaten by Octavius' transparently superior arguments. Minucius, no doubt, was writing for pagans of traditional education whom he thought more inclined to listen to reason than invective. Not all Christian authors, however, were likely to be taken so seriously by their sophisticated pagan opponents in the religious debate. Probably in the third century—though the date is by no means certain—an obscure but sharp-tongued poet from Palestine by the name of Commodian wrote a poem with the title *Against the Jews and Greeks*, which offers more in the way of blistering denunciation of its unhappy targets than it does of doctrinal or literary subtlety. It does, though, give us a clear indication of the extent to which some Christian authors were prepared to adapt—one might say, travesty—the old literary forms in their quest to reach out to their audience. Nominally written in hexameters, the prestigious six-foot quantitative metre of Homer and Virgil, Commodian's poem effectively ignores the rules of classical metrics, with their careful variation of long and short syllables. In their place, he substitutes metrical lines of roughly equal length, where the rhythm is carried instead by the beat of the natural stress of the words in speech, much as in modern English poetry. It is not certain whether Commodian even knew the traditional rules of metre: what is reasonably clear is that he assumed his audience would not. There was a war on, and Commodian was rallying the troops.

The century or so that followed the death of Tertullian saw first the Great Persecutions of Decius and Diocletian, then Constantine's Edict of Milan of 313 granting religious toleration to the Christians, and finally the establishment, through Constantine himself and his quarrelsome sons, of a Christian imperial establishment. In short, Christianity came to be considered acceptable, and even became the preferred faith for those seeking a career in the state bureaucracy. Accordingly, the social rank of converts was now often higher than before. This brought into the faith men—and women too—well educated in the traditional classics. Since the faith was no longer under the same kind of threat, and since there was consequently a less compelling need to keep the faithful uncontaminated by contact with pagan ideas, many of these new converts were less inclined to anathematize the authors and genres they had been brought up to revere. True, the battle was far from over. The real and present danger that the temptations of pagan literature could offer to an insecure soul concerned for its eternal welfare is famously summed up in the dream that afflicted the aristocratic scholar and translator of the Bible Jerome (Eusebius Hieronymus, *c*.347–420 CE) one night on his first visit to the Holy Land. He had gone there to live the life of a monk and learn Hebrew so that he could understand the Bible better. But he was still in some ways a scholarly Roman gentleman of the old school, and had taken along to his desert retreat some light reading, both classical works and religious texts. These he read in alternation, until he fell asleep and was visited by God in His aspect as Divine Judge. Asked to identify himself, the saint replied, 'I am a Christian.' 'You mean a Ciceronian [*Ciceronianus*], not a Christian [*Christianus*],' God thundered back.

But the trend, even so, was towards compromise. Jerome himself, in his seventieth letter, continued to maintain that pagan literature could serve a useful purpose if only its power and its rhetorical beauty could be harnessed to the faith's purpose of saving souls and glorifying God. What he recommended, some upper-class Christians were already doing, and sometimes in quite remarkable ways. A noble lady called Proba composed, some time in the middle of the fourth century, a *cento* from scraps of Virgil (the word *cento* means, in Latin, 'patchwork cloak'). What Proba did was to take innumerable phrases and part-lines from the poems of the most prestigious author of classical Latin literature, and ingeniously stitch them together again in such a way as to create a completely new poem on the Old and New Testaments. Classical literature was thus literally being recycled into a new Christian form so as to provide a devotional text for an audience that wanted to combine the prestige of the old learning with the new faith. Proba's success was so great that Pope Gelasius, in 494 CE, was apparently obliged to give a formal warning to the faithful that it ought not to be treated as a canonical work inspired directly by the Holy Spirit.

POWER OF THE POET. *This late mosaic of Orpheus found in Palestine is now in Istanbul. It seems to reflect the figure of the pagan poet still singing and surviving in an uncultured and barbarous world.*

The restoration of peace and economic prosperity after the chaotic decades of the third century also permitted the building of many new schools throughout the Roman world, not least in Gaul, to train up the men needed to administer and run the renewed Empire. Perhaps the most spectacular and most successful of its polished products was Decimus Magnus Ausonius of Bordeaux (c.310–c.394 CE), who made such a hit as a teacher of rhetoric in his native city that he was summoned by the Emperor Valentinian to his capital at Trier on the Moselle, a city conveniently placed to keep guard over the Rhine frontier. There he acted as tutor to Valentinian's son Gratian, an office he filled so well that he was eventually promoted to the position of Governor of Gaul in 378 CE, and given the supreme honour of the consulship the following year. Emperor, prince, and professor were all three Christians, but the atmosphere of the court was not the atmosphere of the discreet and secluded world inhabited by well-born pious ladies like Proba. Valentinian himself was a soldier through and through, and has been well described as the last Western emperor who systematically patrolled the borders of his Empire. But he was also a man well grounded in the traditional *paideia* ('education') that was still the hallmark of the social élite. His respect for that *paideia* is seen not only in his determination to ensure that his son acquired it from the best teacher available, but in his readiness to engage in competition with that self-same teacher in composing showpiece poems, and in particular a Virgilian *cento* on a theme that might have made Proba blush: the celebration and consummation of a marriage.

In a cover letter to his friend Paulus, Ausonius explains what happened:

> For I am sorry to have disfigured the dignity of Virgil's verse with so frivolous a theme. But what was I do? It was written to order, and the order was of the most powerful kind, for it was requested by one who could impose the request, namely the blessed Emperor Valentinian—a man of great learning, in my opinion. He had once described a wedding in a playful composition of the same kind, with appropriate lines and amusing juxtapositions. Then, since he wanted to see how much it surpassed my own efforts in composition, he ordered me to fashion something similar on the same subject. Just how delicate a task this was for me, you will understand; I wanted neither to beat him nor to be beaten myself, since, if I let him win, my clumsy flattery must be obvious to the judgement of others, and, if I rivalled and surpassed him, my discourtesy would be equally obvious. So I took on the job as if I was reluctant, but met with success, and, since I was deferential in my manner, I kept his favour and managed to give no offence when I won. (*Nuptial Cento*, preface)

Ausonius is concerned to explain to Paulus the difficulty that he was put in by the emperor's challenge: courtesy required that he lose, professional pride that he win. He therefore did his best, but showed as much modesty as he could in earning the palm of victory. But he is also embarrassed—or rather, affects to be—by the subject-matter. And so he might. Virgil, for example, had described the Cyclops Polyphemus with the line

> a terrifying monster, shapeless, huge . . .

Ausonius uses the phrase to describe the bridegroom's penis. Virgil had spoken of the Italian hero Turnus on the battlefield as

> the young man borne hither along the path he knew so well.

Ausonius applies the same line to the new husband as he prepares to insert the aforementioned monster into a place described with words applied by Virgil to the entrance to the underworld. And the exertions that follow, up to and including the moment of climax, are vividly brought before the reader's eyes by a concatenation of lines and phrases used by Virgil in his lofty epic to describe various battles and athletic competitions. The end result is quite a *tour de force*.

Ausonius is at pains to stress that there is a great difference between a dissolute poem and a dissolute author. 'Be satisfied, my friend Paulus | With my page's being naughty: | All I want is to raise a laugh', he says in a postscript, before justifying himself for his actions by learnedly referring Paulus to the precedents set by the likes of Apuleius and Cicero, Plato and Virgil—pagans all. Ausonius, in other words, seems to have achieved a compromise that suited him between the faith he professed and the raunchier but also more urbane culture he had inherited. And it must be noted that his attitude is shared by the emperor himself, and presumed to be equally acceptable to Paulus and the other Gallo-Roman nobles Ausonius addresses through him, by publishing this *cento* and its cover letter. The 'culture wars' are not quite over, but they are no longer being fought to the death as Tertullian thought they should.

Ausonius wrote for the court, for his fellow bureaucrats, for those who, like him, continued to value the poetry, rhetoric, and learning of the world they had inherited as well as the new world that Christianity was promising them. His poems include some that, to modern taste, seem arid and dusty in their academic preoccupations: versifications, for example, of elaborate lists, such as the names of the Muses, the Seven Sages, or the chief cities of Gaul; or ingenious verse disquisitions, not without humour, on the kind of problem of grammar and metre than furrowed the brows of those who earned their bread as Ausonius did. His other works have specialized readerships in mind. *The Daily Round* describes the activities of a high-ranking imperial bureaucrat from morning to sunset: it was written for other bureaucrats, and for those who wanted to know how they spent their time, with a view to advertising the usefulness of a dedicated public servant. *The Professors of Bordeaux* was a work of local civic patriotism, no doubt written principally for the circles in which the great man moved before he was summoned to Trier and glory, though it gives us a rare and welcome look into the high level of sophistication to be found in provincial centres of literary activity. A few others seem to reach out to a wider audience, above all the beautiful *Moselle*, a hexameter description of the poet's journey down that river, through an idyllic world of settled, peaceful cultivation, of lavish villas on the river's banks, of trees drooping over waters full of half-exotic fish, of vines mirrored in the river's calm surface so that land and water can hardly be told apart:

> That is a sight a man may freely enjoy, when the grey-green river
> reflects the shady hill, the waters of the stream
> seem to be in leaf, and the flood thick-planted with vines.

What a colour the shallows have when the Evening Star
has driven forwards his late-coming shadows and drenched
the Moselle—with green mountains!
Whole hillsides float upon the ruffling eddies, and the vine
that is not there ripples, and in the glassy waves the budding vintage swells!
The boatman, fooled by nature, counts up the green shoots,
the boatman who floats in his little barge out over the watery plain,
out in midstream where the image of the hill is blended
with the river and the river joins the edges of the shadows.

(Moselle 189–99)

Such passages are relatively rare in Ausonius. But pedantic though it must often seem to us, his poetry is primarily designed to preserve and celebrate the learning and achievements of the pagan world that was passing, or being transformed for ever, before the professor-consul's very eyes.

'Where your treasure is, there will your heart be also'

Not everyone regretted the passing of this old world. Another local celebrity, and a former pupil of Ausonius', seemed set for a career even more glittering. Paulinus of Nola (Meropius Pontius Paulinus, 353/4–431 CE) was originally Paulinus of Bordeaux. He was a well-connected young man, who beat his tutor to the consulship by one year, and was then sent off to govern the rich and peaceful province of Campania, around the bay of Naples. But this was the age of Ambrose as well as Ausonius, and of those like Augustine who were sickened by the emptiness of the world's glory. Paulinus married a rich Spanish lady whose influence seems to have encouraged his own ascetic inclinations. He abandoned his career, became a priest, and settled in the Campanian city of Nola, where he eventually became bishop. There he wrote poems in epic language for the yearly festivals of the local saint, Felix, and adapted the subject-matter and style of classical poetry to Christian thought. A 'consolation' poem in the old style, for example, turns into a half-logical, half-passionate demonstration of the foolishness of men who insist on lamenting one who has been taken out of the miseries of a fallen world and carried to glory by the intercession of Christ. Indeed, many of Paulinus' poems were primarily designed to lift up the spirits of his congregation, and to confirm them in their faith. They tend, more or less, to turn into sermons, but are distinguished by vivid descriptions of the town and its festival, the saint and his basilica, the priest and his people. More interesting to us, perhaps, because more personal in nature, are the verse letters Paulinus exchanged with other luminaries of the age, Jerome and Augustine among them.

He received letter after letter from his respected old tutor too, but a great gap had opened up between the wordly author of the *cento* and the secluded ascetic and future devotee of St Felix. Ausonius begged Paulinus to come and visit him, and when his repeated requests were met with silence, he burst out in invective against Therasia, Paulinus' wife, that was at best only half-joking:

You stand firm by the law of silence.
Are you ashamed to have a friend still living who claims the right of a father? . . .
Or is it that an informer is treading on your heels,
and what you fear is an inquisitor's over-stern rebuke? . . .
Write your letters in milk, then, and as it dries the paper will keep them
permanently invisible, until the writing is brought forth to view by a scattering of
    ashes! . . .
I can show you countless kinds of concealment
and unbar the ancients' ways of writing secret messages.
If, Paulinus, you fear betrayal and live in dread of being
charged with friendship with me, your harridan of a wife need know nothing of it.
Scorn others if you must, but do not disdain to address a few words to one
who is a father to you. I am your old foster-father and your tutor,
the first to lavish on you the honours of the ancients,
the first to introduce you into the Muses' guild!'

(Ausonius, *Epistle* 28)

It was the wrong tack to take. More silence followed, and then finally a letter full of affection as well as hurt, but not one that can have given much comfort to Ausonius. Paulinus would not, could not join in the kind of game that Ausonius had enjoyed with Valentinian, not even if the subject-matter were less salacious. The break, the definitive repudiation of that classical learning which had raised Ausonius to glory and to which he had given the whole of his life finally came:

Why do you bid the Muses, whom I have rejected,
to return once more into my affections, father?
Hearts dedicated to Christ refuse the Camenae (Muses)
and are closed to Apollo.
Once I had with you this shared purpose—though we were not equals
in skill, we were equals in our zeal—
to summon deaf Apollo from his Delphic cave,
and call the Muses goddesses . . .
But now another power inspires my mind, a greater God,
who demands of us another way of life, claiming back for himself from man the
    gift he gave us,

that we may live for the Father of Life.
To spend our time on idle things, whether for leisure or for work,
and on a literature made of myths, he does forbid.

(Paulinus to Ausonius: Epistle 31)

'Idle things', 'a literature made of myths': these were not, to Paulinus' purit-anical way of thinking, a proper occupation for a servant of Christ. And with these lines he condemned not only the traditional pursuit of classical literature and all those who read it, but the whole career and being of the old tutor who regarded himself as a kind of father to him. But though the tide was strong, it was not all one way. Or at least, not yet.

Rearguard action

The most important sign of an incipient pagan backlash in the fourth century was the accession to the imperial throne of Julian, whose sobriquet 'the Apos-tate' trumpets his challenge to the new Christian establishment just as much as it records the scandalized hostility of those who gave it to him. Julian's reign (361–3 CE) was too short to undo the work of Constantine and his successors, but his aggressive stance towards his enemies gave comfort and inspiration to the traditionalists who clung both to the old gods and to the old ways in literature. Particularly significant in this regard was the ban he promulgated against Christians' holding official positions as teachers of classical literature and rhetoric. Had that held in place, it would have prevented the rise of Ausonius and men like him, since, now that access to traditional literary culture seemed in danger of being cut off, it became clear to everyone that mastery of these skills remained essential for those who aspired to positions of authority in the imperial bureaucracy, in law, and in administration.

Moderate Christians at least were thus growing more willing to come to an accommodation between pagan culture and the demands of life in a Christian empire. That, needless to say, was not the same thing as tolerating pagan wor-ship, or pagans in person. The reign of Theodosius the Great (379–95 CE) was distinguished for such acts of cultural warfare as the prohibition of all pagan sacrifice, the banning of the Olympic games, and the closing or even outright destruction of pagan temples in many parts of the Eastern Empire. The most spectacular casualty was the temple of Serapis, the main centre of pagan culture in Alexandria, still the Roman world's major literary centre. But in the Latin-speaking West, the senatorial aristocracy, which was still largely pagan, retained enormous wealth and social influence. Its last-ditch political resist-ance ended with the defeat of the usurper Eugenius, yet another teacher of rhetoric, at the Battle of the river Frigidus (394 CE). But even after this victory Theodosius and his son Honorius sought to conciliate rather than browbeat these old 'Romans of Rome'. One major result of this toing and froing on the political level was a certain renaissance in pagan literature over the half-century or so from the time of Julian to that of Honorius, especially under the ascendancy of Honorius' chief general and father-in-law, Stilicho. That renaissance, too, was sometimes aggressive, but more usually conciliatory. And not the least of its fruits was the impetus it gave in its turn to magnificent new works by Christians who sought to complete the work of purifying the old canons.

To an admirer of Julian's, albeit one with his eyes open as well as his mind, we owe the last great work of classicizing Latin historiography. Ammianus Marcellinus (c.330–c.400 CE), a Greek-speaking soldier from Antioch, took upon himself the task of completing the *Annals* and *Histories* of Tacitus by recounting the *Deeds* of the Roman emperors from the accession of Nerva in 98 CE to the death of Valens at the hands of the Goths in the catastrophic Battle of Adrianople in 378 CE. Like Tacitus, Ammianus took as his themes decline and its close link with immorality and corruption among the ruling class. He offers us a famous description of the idle rich of the old capital, with their extravagant banquets and odious affectations, their arrogant cruelty towards their slaves and their utter 'provinciality' and ignorance of the affairs of the wider empire. There might thus seem to have been little hope of a cultural renewal spearheaded by these senatorial lightweights, some of whom

> loathing learning like poison, read with care and enthusiasm Juvenal and Marius Maximus, but in the depths of their idleness never touch any volumes at all save these; though why that should be so lies beyond our poor power to judge. (28. 4. 14)

The satires of Juvenal contained plenty to amuse those avid for salacious reading, and the biographies of the Caesars from Nerva to Elagabalus by Marius Maximus were infamous for their uncritical reporting of court gossip. If Ammianus is telling us the truth, their choice of reading material hardly redounds to the credit of these noble heirs of the energetic and cultured senators of the republic and high empire. But then, who was Ammianus writing for? That last bit about his 'poor power to judge' may possibly conceal his pique at the failure of the senators to show much interest in public readings from his own lofty but dour work, to the early parts of which, indeed, Marius Maximus could be thought of as a rival. The very fact that we still have them shows that Ammianus' *Deeds* must have reached a contemporary audience of some kind. But at times, obsessed with his tale of decline, he seems more concerned to write for himself, to help make sense of the deplorable changes he saw in the world around him, with Rome fallen victim to barbarian invaders on the one hand and to unscrupulous courtiers and military thugs on the other. But occasionally he almost seems to be writing for the approval less of his contemporaries or posterity than of the revered past he is trying in some way to save: the approval of those ancient ghosts who light his way, Thucydides and, above all, Tacitus himself.

Honest and literate, patriotic and independent-minded, Ammianus may be said to be himself a good advertisement for the renewed bureaucracy and education system of the fourth century and for the chance of cultural renewal it presented. He is even fair-minded enough to admit that only 'some' of the Romans of Rome were failing their ancestors and their dependants in this shameful way. And he would, one imagines, have felt more kindly towards some of those who come to prominence in the last two decades of the century. Girding their loins for battles both physical and ideological, such men as Nicomachus Flavianus, consul in 394 CE and praetorian prefect under the usurper Eugenius, ostentatiously celebrated pagan rites once more in the old capital. Flavianus indeed set out from Milan for the Frigidus after boasting that, when he returned in victory, he would turn Ambrose's cathedral into stables and conscript his clergy into the army. Ambrose, as usual, had the last laugh, and for Flavianus, defeat could be followed only by honourable suicide. But there was a more peaceful side to Flavianus' activities. He wrote *Annales*, no doubt another historical work designed to complete the labours of Tacitus— and he is one of the stars of Macrobius' *Saturnalia*. This work, which may be more or less contemporary with the events it describes (but which, according to some scholars, may have been composed in the fifth century) is a fictional dialogue set in the holiday season of December 384 CE. It narrates how three leaders of the pagan revival movement, Vettius Agorius Praetextatus, Flavianus himself, and the orator Quintus Aurelius Symmachus act as host on successive days to gatherings of pagan intellectuals who discuss such matters as Roman priestly law and the oratory and philosophy of Virgil. The families of Symmachus and Flavianus in particular also made great efforts to gather and emend the texts of the authors who featured so prominently in the pagan canon. It is largely to their scholarship that we owe the preservation of the works of such authors as Martial, Apuleius, and above all Livy. Also Juvenal, but not, however, Marius Maximus—though whether that was a deliberate response to the censures of Ammianus lies beyond our poor power to judge.

Among these public-spirited men, the best known is Symmachus (Quintus Aurelius Symmachus Eusebius, *c*.340–402 CE). Although they have been castigated as nothing more than elegant if verbose visiting-cards, his *Letters* serve much the same purpose as those of Pliny the Younger (cf. Ch. 6, pp. 173–4) almost three centuries before, putting before our admiring eyes the busy and bustling life of an aristocrat devoted to the service of the state. To that extent, they are also similar to the poems his Christian friend Ausonius wrote under the title *The Daily Round*. Symmachus kept out of trouble during the revolt of Eugenius that claimed the life of his other friend Flavianus, and he even kept up a correspondence with Ambrose, though he was much too polite to allude directly to their religious differences, or even to acknowledge familiarity with Ambrose's episcopal dignity, treating him instead as just another leisured Roman aristocrat.

Though equally courteous, his most celebrated exchange with the feisty bishop of Milan, however, was indirect. The Emperor Gratian, Valentinian's son and Ausonius' pupil, refused to accept the Senate's traditional offer of the robes of the Pontifex Maximus, the head of the ancient priestly colleges of the city. And by an edict of 382 CE he formally disestablished the ancient cults, such as those of the Vestal Virgins, and deprived them of their state endowments. A concomitant result was the removal from the Senate House of the altar to the goddess of Victory which had kept a benevolent eye on the deliberations of that august assembly since time immemorial. Symmachus, as Prefect of the City, made a graceful but powerful plea to Gratian for their restoration, appealing in his *Third Referral* to tradition, to the services the old gods had performed in preserving Rome and in raising her to her state of glory, and to the spirit of religious toleration. In what may well be the most famous phrase of the century he observed of religious truth that 'it is not by one path alone that man can arrive at so great a secret'. But his rival for Gratian's ear was Ambrose, who was as victorious then as he would later prove against Flavianus.

It should be noted that, on both sides of the religio-political fence, the purpose of 'literature' was still more often pragmatic than purely aesthetic. Symmachus' elegance was deployed for a definite aim that had implications for the use of public money as well as for symbolic ideology. Editing Livy was intended to preserve for the education and inspiration of contemporaries the great story of Roman republican *pietas* and the reward it had earned from the gods. On the other side, Jerome was commissioned to replace a wide range of sometimes inaccurate, if much-loved, current translations of the Bible, and he conscientiously applied himself to the study of Hebrew before presenting the world with the Vulgate version that became the standard sacred text of the Catholic Church down to modern times. Pope Damasus (reigned 366–84 CE) wrote short poems to accompany and explain his work in renovating and beautifying the churches and shrines of the martyrs in a city now thought to belong as much to the Apostles Peter and Paul as to Jupiter and the Olympians. Prudentius (Aurelius Prudentius Clemens, 348–*c*.405 CE), a retired Spanish civil servant, was inspired by some of these, and by the cult of the martyrs of his native land, to compose longer hymns celebrating the victories of these champions of the faith. He seems to have consciously set out to replace the patriotic odes of Horace with Christian ones, celebrating martyrs whose virtues outstrip those of Regulus and the other pagan heroes of antiquity.

In this he was to some extent emulating the activity of Ambrose, who hated heretics even more than he hated pagans. The biggest bugbear of the early years of his time as bishop was the Arian heresy, whose followers obstinately refused to accept that the Son was the equal of the Father. They had until quite recently made up almost half the population of the city of Milan, but their protectress, the Empress Justina, outraged him by seeking to secure for their use a single church in the capital, the Basilica Portiana. 'Jezebel', as Ambrose called her with his customary restraint, obviously had to be made to back down. So the bishop shut himself up inside the disputed church with a large army of his supporters until, fearing a massacre and massive civil unrest, she did. Ambrose's Catholic shock-troops—among them, it seems, Augustine's mother Monica—may well have felt some hesitation in the face of the empress's soldiers. To strengthen their resolve Augustine wrote some of the earliest known Latin hymns 'in the manner of the East, so that the people would not grow faint through the weariness of their sorrow' (Augustine, *Confessions* 9. 7).

Pragmatic compositions aimed at defying imperial authority were, however, far less common than those whose purpose was to celebrate and justify it. Prose orations delivered for such occasions as the arrival of an emperor in a particular city or on the anniversary of his accession were composed in vast numbers. Inevitably ephemeral, they have almost all disappeared, but a few were preserved by accident, or thanks to the fame of their author or the admiration won for their style. A collection of a dozen such speeches, known as the *Latin Panegyrics*, appears to have been assembled in the late fourth or early fifth century in Gaul. It comprises the model *par excellence* of the genre, Pliny the Younger's thanksgiving speech to Trajan for his consulship (cf. pp. 159 ff.), and a mixture of others by authors named or anonymous, delivered to emperors from Constantine to Theodosius—and, in one case, to a governor of Gaul. Useful for the information they preserve on contemporary history, albeit often obliquely, they also reveal much about the ceremonial nature of such public literature and about the audiences who dutifully attended to hear them recited. Invariably elegant and invariably laudatory, their function is primarily to celebrate the virtues of those they honour and to display the loyalty of those on whose behalf they were delivered. Nonetheless, they often do a careful job of presenting to the all-important governing classes the emperor's policies, while also—though more rarely—serving on occasion to give the emperor a discreet reminder of his subjects' needs and an indication of their concerns. In short,

CHRISTIAN CONQUEST. These ivory portraits of the young Emperor Honorius were made in 406 CE. In the left-hand panel he holds an inscription which says 'In the name of Christ may you always be victorious'. The abbreviation for 'Christ' uses Greek letters (as in our modern 'Xmas').

though they may seem to modern eyes the emptiest and most distastefully adulatory compositions to survive from classical antiquity, their social function, to help cement the bond between ruler and ruled in the interests of social harmony, was of enormous importance.

Since so much of what the panegyrists say is obscured by the conventions of praise, and since so much of the historical circumstances that provided the backdrop to individual speeches can no longer be recovered, a detailed understanding of the circumstances of their recitation, and therefore of their effect on a given audience, is often impossible. A partial exception to this rule is provided by the panegyrics delivered by Claudian of Alexandria (Claudius Claudianus, *c.*370–*c.*404 CE) over a period of some ten years in the early part of the reign of Honorius (394–404 CE). Claudian is an exception in other ways too: his panegyrics are in verse, and he, like Ammianus, was a Greek-speaking easterner. He belongs to a distinct class of poets who cannot be thought of in quite the same terms as men like Ausonius, men of high birth and high position. Claudian is a highly succesful example of the 'wandering poets', professional authors who moved from city to city and earned their keep by putting their talents at the service of the city government or of individual wealthy patrons. He is sometimes called 'the last of the classical poets', not just because of his strictly pagan themes and idiom, but also because of the superb technical accomplishment of his verse and his thorough familiarity with the classical authors of the canon. He also had a glorious style that, were it not for his contemporary subject-matter, might trick one into thinking his poems had been composed under Nero or Domitian rather than under Honorius and the power behind his throne, Stilicho. Most of Claudian's poetry was explicitly designed to serve Stilicho's purposes. The career of Stilicho offers a spectacular example of the cultural changes Rome was currently undergoing. His mother was a Roman, but his father belonged to a German tribe called the Vandals. In time the Vandals would give the Romans a great deal of trouble; indeed, they later conquered Africa and even sacked Rome itself in 455 CE with such horrifying violence that their name has come into English as a word for any barbarous thug who wilfully destroys property of any kind. In the late fourth century, however, some of them, including Stilicho's father, were serving as mercenaries in the Roman army against other barbarians and were becoming assimilated. Stilicho himself rose to such prominence that Honorius' father, the Emperor Theodosius, chose him as a husband for his niece and adopted daughter Serena, and after Theodosius' death he exercised a kind of semi-official regency over the young Honorius.

It would be simplifying matters too far to speak of Claudian merely as a vehicle for broadcasting Stilicho's propaganda, but his poetry, for all its sophistication, clearly serves practical political purposes. He not only celebrates, for example, the young emperor's consulships and his marriage to Stilicho's daughter Maria, but also denounces Stilicho's political opponents in satirical invective worthy of Juvenal. Pity Eutropius, chief minister of Honorius' brother, the Eastern Emperor Arcadius. Eutropius had dared, though a eunuch, to accept a consulship and, worse still, had had the audacity to have a real man, the brave and noble Stilicho, declared an 'enemy of the people' by the Senate at Constantinople:

What a fine sight he made, as he strained to move his feeble limbs
beneath the weight of the toga, borne down by the consular garb,
an old man made to look more repulsive still by the gold he had donned!
Like an ape that imitates human form, decked out
by some mocking lad in precious Chinese silks,
his back and buttocks left uncovered,
something for the supper-guests to howl at . . .

(Against Eutropius 1. 300–6)

That no doubt answered to all the prejudices of the Milanese courtiers against effeminate Easterners in general, let alone the ones who aspired to lead armies and govern the state when they lacked the full complement of manly assets. On other occasions, Claudian's brief was to smooth down ruffled feathers closer to home. In 401 CE Alaric the Visigoth led his people on to Italian soil, and threw the whole country into a panic. It took months to get him out again, and though Stilicho finally achieved a comprehensive victory at Pollentia in the Po valley on Easter Day 402 CE, resentment was felt against the general by the senators, who had seen their estates burned, their slaves conscripted, and the very walls of Rome threatened. Worst of all, Stilicho had struck some kind of bargain with an enemy who surely ought simply to have been dealt with in the Roman way, not by treaty but by brute military force. Nothing to worry about, Claudian assured them some eighteen months later, when Honorius made a rare, conciliatory visit to the old capital to inaugurate his sixth consulship. In Claudian's epic-style account Alaric himself is made to explain how Stilicho had it all worked out in advance:

With what cunning, with what skill,
did Stilicho, always my doom, entrap me! While pretending to spare me,
he blunted the edge of my warlike spirit and found the power to carry the war
back over the Po I had crossed once before! A curse on that treaty,
worse than the yoke of slavery! Then it was that the power of the Goths was
                                                            extinguished,
then for my own self, then did I bargain death!'

(On The Sixth Consulship of Honorius 300–5)

It is not recorded whether the senators found this explanation acceptable, though one imagines that they quite liked hearing themselves called 'a host worthy of worship, gods!' in the preface to the poem with which Claudian began his recitation on the Palatine Hill on that first day of January, 404.

Whistling in the wind

Within seven years, Claudian was dead, Stilicho had fallen from grace and been beheaded, and Alaric was back. Rome fell to a foreign army for the first time since the Gauls had taken the city after the Battle of the Allia eight centuries before (390 BCE.). From far Palestine, Jerome let out a cry of anguish: true to both his Christian and his Ciceronian selves, he compared the dreadful calamity to the destruction of Moab and to the fall of Troy, quoting from the second book of Virgil's *Aeneid* (*Letter* 127). Augustine, more thoughtful and more methodical, applied his vast erudition and his powerfully original mind to propounding a new understanding of the very nature of history and of civilization in his *City of God*, demonstrating that all cities fall, save only the holy Jerusalem carried by the faithful in their hearts, exiled as they are in this fallen world from that heavenly state.

Pagan authors had no such consolation, their very existence being bound up with the fate of the earthly city that Christians and barbarian spies like Stilicho had destroyed. That, at least, was the view of Rutilius Claudius Namatianus, who has left us an elegiac poem recording his journey home to his estates in Gaul through an Italian countryside shattered by war. Namatianus vented his spleen against Christians in general, and especially monks, a tribe that hid themselves in dark monasteries instead of doing their duty and fighting. He also inveighed passionately against Jews and corrupt officials, but most of all Stilicho. It is a diatribe against what could not be changed, written, it seems, for a dwindling band of marginalized pagan aristocrats whose powerlessness was now painfully visible.

The Western Empire limped on for most of the next century, but, though there were hopes of renewal under Honorius' energetic general Constantius and, later, the Emperor Valentinian III's able first minister Aetius, who defeated Attila the Hun in 451 CE, all such hopes proved transitory. Imperial control contracted, as first Britain was given up, and then Gaul and Spain partitioned among the Visigoths, the Burgundians, and the Vandals. Paganism lingered among the peasants of the more remote country areas, but it was no longer a force worth considering among the embattled Gallo-Roman élite.

Men like Gaius Sollius Modestus Appollinaris Sidonius of Clermont-Ferrand in Gaul (*c*.431–*c*.486 CE) still aspired to both literary and political success, but they were too busy dealing with the urgent matters of the present to refight the battles of the past. Sidonius was a local aristocrat, who rose, like Ausonius before him, to be Prefect of the City of Rome and who, like Claudian, wrote verse panegyrics of reigning, if short-lived, emperors; and, again like Claudian, won a reward in the form of an honorary statue in the Forum of Trajan. In

Sidonius' hands poetry remained pragmatic in aim as well as ceremonial. So, for example, in his laudation of the brutal Majorian, we see Sidonius pleading with the new emperor to pardon the city of Lyons its sin in rising in revolt after the murder of his predecessor Avitus, and to relax the harsh conditions imposed upon it. The task cannot have been to Sidonius' taste: Avitus was his father-in-law. But he was carrying on the ancient tradition of *noblesse oblige*, putting his learning and his oratorical skills at the service of his countrymen. His other poems comprise marriage-songs and descriptions, in the manner of Statius, of the villas of rich men like himself. It is hard to see who else would have read them. Sidonius' world was shutting down around him. His poetry served to preserve *Romanitas*, Roman culture, in a country that had passed under the authority of its barbarian invaders.

The main cultural divide was now between, not pagan and Christian, but Catholic Roman and Arian German. The Church now represented the only effective arm of Roman power in Gaul, and men like Sidonius came under pressure to protect their countrymen with such means as it afforded them. So, though stronger on classical mythology than on the Scriptures, he accepted the role of bishop, and largely gave up the luxury of poetry. Diplomacy and administration now took up much of his time, but when not tactfully losing at backgammon to the king of the Burgundians, he wrote letters to other embattled Gallo-Roman nobles and bishops, letters that still attempted to do what Pliny's had done (cf. pp. 173–4), and show for the world—or for that small part of it that could understand their self-consciously elaborate Latin—a good man whose varied and dutiful life was spent in the service of his country.

However classicizing their motivation, the extraordinary style and diction of Sidonius' letters reveal very clearly that the pursuit of Latin literature in the classical mode was swiftly turning into an elevated kind of whistling in the wind. The rhetoric schools were closing, since the new rulers had less need of their products, and the cities they served were shrinking. And the very language was rapidly undergoing that massive shift in its pronunciation that made the old metrical rules of classical verse more and more alien to the spoken word. To attempt to pin down the precise moment and the cause of the death of classical Latin literature would result only in an arid debate—more arid than anything in the works of Ausonius. There is a good case for saying that it lingered for some time longer in quieter parts of the West still under the control of the Empire or of barbarian kings with aspirations to be accepted. Dracontius recited part of his mythological *Romulea* in the presence of the proconsul Pacideius around the year 480 CE, apparently in a concert-hall attached to the Baths of Gargilius in Carthage. As late as 544 CE, Arator read his two-book adaptation, in the hexameters traditionally associated with heroic poetry, of *The Acts of the*

Apostles to an appreciative audience, including Pope Vigilius, in the Church of S. Pietro in Vincoli in Rome. And twenty years later at the Eastern court of Constantinople, the African poet Corippus celebrated in dazzling hexameters, modelled on those of Claudian, the accession of the Emperor Justin II. But by the end of the fifth century, Latin, as Cicero or Virgil would have understood it, was for practical purposes no longer a living language in most of the West. The schools had retreated from the forum to the cloister; and the audience was gone. The literature that had come to maturity amidst the clamour of the law-courts and the rough-and-tumble of the wooden theatres of the Republic (cf. p. 22 above) was shivering to its death in the chilly silence of Sidonius' study.

But it would be neither fair nor sensible—indeed, one might say hardly Christian—to blame Sidonius, who, after all, had a lot on his plate. These were complex times, and the combination of aloof protestations of cultural superiority with outrageous xenophobic simplification seemed, no doubt, the best means for preserving sanity in a world that was ceasing to be Roman and was gradually edging its way into the Middle Ages. At any rate, it was in a spirit of humorous self-knowledge as much as of cultural arrogance that Sidonius responded when he was asked by the senator Catullinus for a wedding-song in the traditional mode. He could not write cheerful songs in hexameters (six-foot verse), he said, obliged as he was to listen instead to the songs of the great clumping brutes who were his new masters (*Poems* 12. 1–11):

Why, even supposing I had the power, do you bid me compose a poem
of Venus, who loves the wedding-songs of old?
I find myself placed in the midst of long-haired hordes,
enduring the sound of German words,
and, time and time again, praising with a straight face
the compositions of some Burgundian glutton who gels his hair with rancid butter.
Shall I tell you what breaks the power of song?
My Muse has been driven away by barbarian strummings,
and has spurned six-foot verse ever since she saw
that her only patrons were seven feet tall.

Further Reading

1. THE BEGINNINGS OF LATIN LITERATURE

W. S. Anderson, *Barbarian Play* (Toronto and London, 1993).

E. Fraenkel, *Elementi plautini in Plauto* (Florence, 1960).

S. Goldberg, *Epic in Republican Rome* (New York and Oxford, 1995).

—— 'Plautus on the Palatine', *Journal of Roman Studies*, 88 (1998), 1–21.

A. S. Gratwick, 'Drama', in *The Cambridge History of Classical Literature*, vol. ii: *Latin Literature*, ed. E. J. Kenney and W. V. Clausen (Cambridge, 1982), 77–132.

E. S. Gruen, *Culture and National Identity in Republican Rome* (London 1993).

—— *Studies in Greek Culture and Roman Policy* (Berkeley and London, 1996).

R. L. Hunter, *The New Comedy of Greece and Rome* (Cambridge, 1985).

D. Konstan, *Roman Comedy* (Ithaca, NY, 1983).

E. Segal, *Roman Laughter* (Oxford, 1987).

O. S. Skutsch (ed.), *The Annals of Ennius* (Oxford, 1985).

L. R. Taylor, 'The Opportunities for Dramatic Performances in the Time of Plautus and Terence', *Transactions and Proceedings of the American Philological Association*, 68 (1937), 284–304.

Translations

Plautus, trans. P. Nixon, 5 vols. (Loeb Classical Library: Cambridge, Mass., 1916–38).

Terence, trans. J. Sargeaunt, 2 vols. (Loeb Classical Library: Cambridge, Mass., 1912).

Naevius, Ennius, Pacuvius, Accius, Lucilius, trans. E. H. Warmington, '*Remains of Old Latin*', 4 vols. (Loeb Classical Library: Cambridge, Mass., 1935–40).

2. PROSE LITERATURE DOWN TO THE TIME OF AUGUSTUS

E. Badian, 'The Early Historians', in T. A. Dorey (ed.), *Latin Historians* (London, 1966).

M. Beard and M. H. Crawford, *Rome in the Late Republic* (London, 1985).

E. Fantham, *Roman Literary Culture: From Cicero to Apuleius* (Baltimore and London, 1996).

E. J. Kenney, 'Books and Readers', in *The Cambridge History of Classical Literature*, vol. ii: *Latin Literature* (Cambridge 1982), 3–32.

M. Winterbottom, 'Literary Criticism', in *The Cambridge History of Classical Literature*, vol. ii: *Latin Literature* (Cambridge 1982), 33–50.

Translations

Caesar: Civil War, trans. J. Carter (Oxford World's Classics: Oxford, 1997).

Caesar: Gallic War, trans. C. Hammond (Oxford World's Classics: Oxford, 1996).

Cato and Varro: De re rustica, trans. W. D. Hooper and H. B. Ash (Loeb: Cambridge, Mass., 1935).

Cicero: Defence Speeches, trans. D. H. Berry (Oxford World's Classics: Oxford, 2000).

Cicero: Republic, trans. N. Rudd (Oxford World's Classics: Oxford, 1998).

Cicero: Letters to Atticus and to his Friends, trans. D. R. Shackleton-Bailey (Penguin: London, 1999).

Cicero: on the Nature of the Gods, trans. P. G. Walsh (Oxford World's Classics: Oxford, 1998).

Sallust, trans. J. C. Rolfe (Loeb: Cambridge, Mass., 1931).

3. POETRY OF THE LATE REPUBLIC

J. H. Gaisser, *Catullus and his Renaissance Readers* (Oxford, 1993).

Monica Gale, *Myth and Poetry in Lucretius* (Cambridge, 1994).

David West, *The Imagery and Poetry of Lucretius* (Edinburgh, 1969).

T. P. Wiseman, *Catullus and his World* (Cambridge, 1985).

Translations

Catullus: The complete poems, trans. G. Lee (Oxford World's Classics: Oxford, 1990).

Lucretius: On the nature of the Universe, trans. R. Melville (introduction and notes by D. and P. Fowler) (Oxford, 1997).

4. POETRY BETWEEN THE DEATH OF CAESAR AND THE DEATH OF VIRGIL

S. H. Braund, *Roman Verse Satire* (Oxford, 1992).

Francis Cairns, *Virgil's Augustan Epic* (Cambridge, 1989).

Emily Gowers, *The Loaded Table* (Oxford, 1993).

P. R. Hardie, *Virgil* (Oxford, 1998).

Duncan Kennedy, *The Arts of Love* (Cambridge, 1993).

R. O. A. M. Lyne, *Further Voices in Virgil's Aeneid* (Oxford, 1987).

—— *The Latin Love Poets* (Oxford, 1980).

P. White, *Promised Verse: Poets in the Society of Augustan Rome* (Cambridge, Mass., 1993).

G. Williams, *Horace* (Oxford, 1972).

Translations

Virgil: the Eclogues, the Georgics, trans. C. Day-Lewis (Oxford World's Classics: Oxford, 1983).

Virgil: the Aeneid, trans. C. Day-Lewis (Oxford World's Classics: Oxford, 1986).

Virgil: the Aeneid, trans. R. Fitzgerald (Oxford World's Classics: Oxford, 1983).

Virgil: the Eclogues, trans. Guy Lee (Penguin: London, 1984).

Propertius: the poems, trans. Guy Lee (Oxford World's Classics: Oxford, 1994).

Tibullus: Elegies, trans. Guy Lee (Leeds, 1990).

The Satires of Horace and Persius, trans. Niall Rudd (Penguin: London, 1979).

Horace: the complete Odes and Epodes, trans. David West (Oxford World's Classics: Oxford, 2000).

Virgil's Aeneid: A New Prose Translation, trans. David West (Penguin: London, 1991).

Virgil's Georgics, trans. L. P. Wilkinson (Penguin: London, 1982).

5. POETRY OF THE LATER AUGUSTAN AND TIBERIAN PERIOD

On individual authors and works

Horace Epistles

E. Fraenkel, *Horace* (Oxford, 1957).

R. S. Kilpatrick, *The Poetry of Friendship* (Edmonton, Alberta, 1986).

Horace Odes 4

M. C. J. Putnam, *Artifices of Eternity. Horace's Fourth Book of Odes* (Ithaca, NY, and London, 1986).

Ovid. General

A. Barchiesi, *The Poet and the Prince. Ovid and Augustan Discourse* (Berkeley and Los Angeles, 1997).

G. K. Galinsky, *Ovid's Metamorphoses: An Introduction to the Basic Aspects* (Oxford, 1975).

N. Holzberg, *Ovid. Dichter und Werk* (Munich, 1997) (Eng. trans. to be published by Cornell U.P. in 2001).

H. Jacobson, *Ovid's Heroides* (Princeton, 1974).

R. Nagle, *The Poetics of Exile: Program and Polemic in the Tristia and Epistulae ex Ponto of Ovid* (Brussels, 1980).

C. Newlands, *Playing with Time: Ovid and the Fasti* (Ithaca, NY, 1995).

J. B. Solodow, *The World of Ovid's Metamorphoses* (Chapel Hill, NC, and London, 1988).

F. Verducci, *Ovid's Toyshop of the Heart: Epistulae Heroidum* (Princeton, 1985).

L. P. Wilkinson, *Ovid Recalled* (Cambridge, 1955).

G. D. Williams, *Banished Voices. Readings in Ovid's Exile Poetry* (Cambridge, 1994).

Translations

There are translations of all the works discussed in this chapter, of varying readability, in the Loeb Classical Library.

In the Oxford World's Classics series there are translations of the following:

Horace: The Complete Odes and Epodes, trans. David West (1997)

Propertius: The Poems, trans. Guy Lee (1994).

Ovid: The Love Poems, trans. A. D. Melville (1989).

Metamorphoses, trans. A. D. Melville (1986).

Sorrows of an Exile (Tristia), trans. A. D. Melville (1995).

Ovid's Fasti: Roman Holidays, trans. B. R. Nagle (Bloomington, Ind., 1995).

6. PROSE LITERATURE FROM AUGUSTUS TO HADRIAN

E. Fantham, *Roman Literary Culture: From Cicero to Apuleius* (Baltimore and London, 1996).

D. C. Feeney, '*Si licet et fas est*: Ovid's Fasti and the Problem of Free Speech under the Principate', in A. Powell (ed.), *Roman Poetry and Propaganda in the Age of Augustus* (London 1992), 1–25.

K. Galinsky, *Augustan Culture* (Princeton, 1996).

N. Horsfall, 'Empty Shelves on the Palatine', *Greece and Rome*, 40 (1993), 58–67.

Translations

Livy: The Rise of Rome: Books 1–5, trans. T. J. Luce (Oxford World's Classics: Oxford, 1998); the rest of his history—various translators, in Penguin or Loeb.

Pliny, Letters, and Panegyricus, trans. B. Radice (Loeb: Cambridge, Mass., 1969).

Seneca the Elder: Declamations, trans. M. Winterbottom (Loeb: Cambridge, Mass., 1974).

Seneca the Younger: Tragedies, trans. D. R. Slavitt (Baltimore, 1992–5).

Tacitus: Agricola and Germania, trans. A. R. Birley (Oxford World's Classics: Oxford, 1999).

Tacitus: The Histories, trans. W. H. Fyfe, rev. D. S. Levene (Oxford World's Classics: Oxford, 1997).

Tacitus: The Annals of Imperial Rome, trans. M. Grant (Penguin: London, 1989).

7. EPIC OF THE IMPERIAL PERIOD

F. M. Ahl, *Lucan: An Introduction* (Ithaca, NY, 1976).
—— 'Statius' Thebaid: A Reconsideration', *ANRW*, 2. 32. 5 (1986), 2803–912.
—— M. A. Davis and A. Pomeroy, *'Silius Italicus'*, *ANRW*, 2. 32. 4 (1986), 2492–561.
W. J. Dominik, *The Mythic Voice of Statius. Power and Politics in the Thebaid* (Leiden, 1994).
D. C. Feeney, *The Gods in Epic* (Oxford, 1991).
P. Hardie, *The Epic Successors of Virgil* (Cambridge, 1993).
D. Hershkowitz, *The Madness of Epic* (Oxford, 1998).
—— *Valerius Flaccus' Argonautica* (Oxford, 1998).
G. O. Hutchinson, *Latin Literature from Seneca to Juvenal* (Oxford, 1993).
M. G. L. Leigh, *Lucan: Spectacle and Engagement* (Oxford, 1997).
J. H. W. G. Liebeschuetz, *Continuity and Change in Roman Religion* (Oxford, 1989).
J. Masters, *Poetry and Civil War in Lucan's 'Bellum Civile'* (Cambridge, 1992).
W. C. Summers, *A Study of the Argonautica of Valerius Flaccus* (Cambridge, 1894).
D. W. T. C. Vessey, *Statius and the Thebaid* (Cambridge, 1973).
—— 'Flavian Epic', in *Cambridge History of Classical Literature*, ii. 558–96 (Cambridge, 1992).
M. Wilson, 'Flavian Variant: History, Silius' Punica', in A. J. Boyle (ed.), *Roman Epic* (London 1993), 218–36.

Translations

Lucan, trans. J. D. Duff (Loeb Classical Library, 1928); S. Braund (Oxford World's Classics, 1999).
Silius Italicus, trans. J. D. Duff (Loeb Classical Library, 1934).
Statius, trans. J. H. Mozley, 2 vols. (Loeb Classical Library, 1928).
Statius: Thebaid, trans A. D. Melville (Oxford World's Classics: Oxford, 1995).
Valerius Flaccus, trans. J. H. Mozley (Loeb Classical Library, 1934).

8. THE LITERATURE OF LEISURE

J. C. Bramble, *Persius and the Programmatic Satire: A Study in Form and Imagery* (Cambridge, 1974).
S. Braund, *Beyond Anger: A Study in Juvenal's Third Book of Satire* (Cambridge, 1988).
—— (ed.), *Satire and Society in Ancient Rome* (Exeter, 1989).
M. Coffey, *Roman Satire* (2nd edn., Bristol, 1989).
K. M. Coleman, *Statius Silvae IV, edited with an English Translation and Commentary* (Oxford, 1988).
C. Connors, *Petronius the Poet: Verse and Literary Tradition in the Satyricon* (Cambridge, 1998).

D. P. Fowler, 'Martial and the Book', *Ramus*, 24 (1995), 31–58.

E. Gowers, *The Loaded Table: Representations of Food in Roman Literature* (Oxford 1993).

A. Hardie, *Statius and the Silvae* (Liverpool, 1983).

J. Henderson, *Figuring out Roman Nobility: Juvenal's Eighth Satire* (Exeter, 1998).

—— *A Roman Life: Rutilius Gallicus on Paper and in Stone* (Exeter, 1998).

H. Hofmann, *Latin Fiction: The Latin Novel in Context* (London, 1999).

D. M. Hooley, *The Knotted Thong: Structures of Mimesis in Persius* (Ann Arbor, 1997).

G. L. Schmeling, *The Novel in the Ancient World* (Leiden, 1996).

N. W. Slater, *Reading Petronius* (Baltimore, 1990).

J. P. Sullivan, *Martial the Unexpected Classic* (Cambridge, 1991).

J. Tatum, *The Search for the Ancient Novel* (Baltimore, 1994).

J. P. Toner, *Leisure and Ancient Rome* (Oxford, 1995).

P. White, 'The Presentation and Dedication of the Silvae and Epigrams', *Journal of Roman Studies*, 64 (1974), 40–61.

—— 'The Friends of Martial, Statius, Pliny and the Dispersal of Patronage', *Harvard Studies in Classical Philology*, 79 (1975), 265–300.

—— 'Amicitia and the Profession of Poetry in Early Imperial Rome', *Journal of Roman Studies*, 68 (1978), 74–92.

Translations

Petronius: Satyricon, trans. P. G. Walsh (Oxford, 1997).

Juvenal: The Satires, trans. N. Rudd, ed. W. Barr (Oxford, 1992).

Persius: The Satires, trans. G. Lee, introduction and commentary W. Barr (Liverpool 1987).

For translations of Phaedrus, Statius' *Silvae*, and Martial's *Epigrams*, see the editions of the Loeb Classical Library.

9. LATIN LITERATURE FROM THE SECOND CENTURY TO THE END OF THE CLASSICAL ERA

General

P. Brown, *Augustine of Hippo* (London, 1967).

—— *The Cult of the Saints* (Chicago, 1981).

—— *Religion and Society in the Age of St Augustine* (London, 1972).

—— *The World of Late Antiquity: From Marcus Aurelius to Muhammad* (London, 1971).

A. Cameron, *Claudian: Poetry and Propaganda at the Court of Honorius* (Oxford, 1970).

T. Hägg, *The Novel in Antiquity* (Oxford, 1983).

Robin Lane Fox, *Pagans and Christians* (London, 1986).

F. J. E. Raby, *A History of Christian Poetry* (Oxford, 1953).

P. G. Walsh, *The Roman Novel* (Cambridge, 1970).

Translations

Ammianus Marcellinus: The Later Roman Empire (A.D. 354–378), selected and trans. Walter Hamilton (Penguin, 1986).

Apuleius: The Golden Ass, trans. and ed. P. G. Walsh (Oxford World's Classics, 1999).

Augustine: The Confessions, trans. Henry Chadwick (Oxford World's Classics, 1991).

Ausonius, with an English trans. by Hugh G. Eveleyn-White, 2 vols. (Loeb Classical Library) (repr. Cambridge, Mass., and London, 1988).

Claudian, with an English trans. by Maurice Platnauer, 2 vols. (Loeb Classical Library) (repr. Cambridge, Mass., and London, 1972).

Sidonius: Poems and Letters, with an English trans., introduction, and notes by W. B. Anderson, 2 vols (Loeb Classical Library) (repr. Cambridge, Mass., and London. 1980).

Chronology

This chronology was compiled for *Literature in the Greek and Roman Worlds*, which includes the material in this edition.

Date	Historical Events	Literary and Related Developments
BCE	Traditional date of first Olympic Games (776) Traditional date of foundation of Rome (753) Age of Greek settlement in Italy, Sicily, and East	Development and dissemination of Greek alphabet on Phoenician model (800–750)
750	Development of heavy 'hoplite' armour and emergence of polis society	
700	Spartan expansion (from *c.*730)	Homer and Hesiod active about now Archilochos active as poet (675–640)
650	Greeks begin to penetrate Egypt	Terpander, Kallinos, Semonides, Tyrtaios, Mimnermos, Alkman active as poets
600	Earliest Greek coins minted (*c.*595) Solon archon at Athens: social and political reforms (594) Greek mercenaries carve their names on the Abu Simbel inscription (591)	Sappho and Alkaios active as poets (610–575) Solon active as poet (600–560)
575	Age of 'Tyrants' in major Greek states other than Sparta	Thales predicts eclipse of the sun (585) Rise of panhellenic festivals (Pythia 582, Isthmia 581, Nemea 573) Anaximander active as philosopher (570–550) (570–475) lifetime of Xenophanes (philosopher-poet)
550	Croesus king of Lydia (560–546) Cyrus the Great founds Persian empire (559–530) Cyrus' conquest of Lydia and Ionian Greeks— *'The year the Mede arrived'* (546) Carthaginians and Etruscans check Greek expansion in western Mediterranean	Stesichoros, Theognis, Hipponax, and Ibykos active as poets Anaximenes active as philosopher

Date	Historical Events	Literary and Related Developments
525	Darius seizes the Persian throne (521)	Anakreon active as poet (535–490) City Dionysia festival established at Athens (by 534) Pythagoras active as philosopher Simonides active as poet
500	Foundation of Roman Republic (traditional date) (509) 'Democratic' reforms of Kleisthenes at Athens (508) Ionian Revolt against Persian rule (499, defeated with Battle of Lade and sack of Miletos 494) First Persian expedition to mainland Greece: Battle of Marathon (490) Persian and Carthaginian invasions of Greece and Sicily: Battles of Artemision, Thermopylai, Salamis (480); Plataia, Mykale (479); Himera (480)	Alkmaion (doctor), Hekataios (historian), Herakleitos, Parmenides (philosophers) active Earliest surviving poem of Pindar (498) Phrynichos prosecuted for his play *The sack of Miletos* (494) First comedy performed at the City Dionysia at Athens (480s) Bakchylides active as poet First victory of Aischylos (active 499–456)
475	Foundation of Delian league against Persia under leadership of Athens (478) Battle of Eurymedon effectively ends Persian threat (467) Radical reforms and murder of Ephialtes at Athens Perikles' supremacy begins (461–429)	First victory of Sophokles (active 468–406) Anaxagoras (philosopher) arrives in Athens
450	Athenian expedition to Egypt ends in disaster Treasury of Delian League moved from Delos to Athens—regarded as beginning of 'Athenian empire' (454) 'Peace of Kallias' ends hostilities between Athens and Persia (449)	First production by Euripides (active 455–406) Zeno and Empedokles active as philosophers Work begins on Parthenon in Athens Herodotos active as historian (445–426) Publication of the Laws of the Twelve Tables at Rome
425	Peloponnesian War between Athenian and Spartan alliances (431–404) First Athenian expedition to Sicily 427 'Peace of Nikias' between Athens and Sparta and their allies (421) Disastrous Athenian expedition to Sicily (415–413)	Thoukydides begins his *History* (431–404) Demokritos (atomist philosopher), Hippokrates (doctor), Sokrates and Protagoras (philosophers), Hellanikos (historian) active

Date	Historical Events	Literary and Related Developments
425 *cont.*		Embassy of Gorgias to Athens also begins the formal art of rhetoric *Acharnians* of Aristophanes (active 420s–380s) Hippias (antiquarian and polymath) active
400	Oligarchic coup of 'the 400' at Athens (411) Democracy restored at Athens (410) Spartans destroy Athenian fleet at Battle of Aigospotamoi; Siege of Athens (405) Capitulation of Athens; installation of regime of 'the Thirty' (404) Fall of 'the Thirty'; democracy restored at Athens (403) Sack of Rome by the Gauls	Andokides and Lysias active as speech-writers (410–387) Antisthenes (cynic), Aristippos (hedonist), and Euklides, pupils of Sokrates, active (400–360) Trial and execution of Sokrates (399) Isokrates (writer and educator) active (397–338) Plato (philosopher) active (396–347); founds the Academy (387) Antimachos, epic poet, active Xenophon (historian and essayist) active (390–354)
375	Following Corinthian War (395–386), Peace of Antalkidas ('King's Peace') imposes Persian-backed control by Sparta on Greece (386) Thebes destroys Spartan power at Battle of Leuktra (371) Domination of Greek world by Thebes under Pelopidas and Epaminondas (371–362)	Diogenes (cynic philosopher) active (360–323)
350	Philip II becomes king of Macedon (359) Phokians seize Delphi and provoke Sacred War, bringing Philip into central Greece against them (356–352) Philip defeats Athens and Thebes at Chaironeia: end of Greek independence (338)	Theatre at Epidauros built Literary and political careers of Demosthenes (d. 322) and Aischines (left Athens 330) begin Theopompos (historian) active (350–320) End of *History* of Ephoros (340)
325	Death of Philip: accession of Alexander (336) Alexander crosses into Asia: Battle of Granikos and conquest of Asia Minor (334) Foundation of Alexandria in Egypt (331) Conquest as far as Punjab (327) Death of Alexander, aged 32; regency of Perdiccas (323) and period of 'the successors'	Aristotle begins teaching at Athens and founds the Lykeion (Peripatetic school) (335) Pyrrho (sceptic) active as philosopher Career of Menander (321–289); *Dyskolos* performed 317

Date	Historical Events	Literary and Related Developments
300	Peace between the successors recognizes in effect the division Antigonos (Asia), Cassandros (Macedon/Greece), Lysimachos (Thrace), Ptolemy (Egypt), and by omission Seleukos (the Eastern domains) (311) Battle of Ipsos: destruction of power of Antigonos and Demetrios; Antigonos killed (301)	Klearchos (Peripatetic philosopher) visits Ai Khanum in Afghanistan (310) Zeno of Kition establishes Stoic school in *Stoa Poikile* at Athens (310) Philitas of Kos (scholar and founder of Alexandrian poetry) appointed tutor to future Ptolemy II Epikouros establishes his philosophical school at Athens (307) Ptolemy I founds Mouseion of Alexandria Zenodotos royal tutor and first head of the Library Euclid (mathematician) active
275	Pyrrhos of Epeiros crosses into south Italy to aid the Greek cities: is defeated by the Romans (280–275) Earliest Roman coinage Antigonos Gonatas, son of Demetrios, defeats Gauls; becomes king of Macedon, founding Macedonian dynasty (276) Ptolemy unsuccessfully supports Greek independence from Macedon (267–262)	Douris of Samos (leading exponent of 'tragic history') active
250	First Punic War between Rome and Carthage, ending in Roman victory (264–241) Eumenes I founds independent power at Pergamon (263–241) Diodotos establishes independent Greek kingdom in Bactria (239–130)	Kallimachos, Theokritos, Lykophron, Aratos, Poseidippos active as poets Manetho (historian and Egyptian priest) lays foundations of Egyptian history Hieronymos of Kardia (historian of the Successors) dies aged 104; Timaios of Tauromenion (historian of the West) dies aged 96 (260) Apollonios of Rhodes writes the *Argonautika* Herodas (author of Mimes) active
225		Livius Andronikos (earliest Roman poet and playwright) active (240–207) First play of Naevius produced (236) Chrysippos succeeds Kleanthos as head of Stoic school (232)

Date	Historical Events	Literary and Related Developments
200	Second Punic ('Hannibalic') War—Hannibal invades Italy (218–201) First war between Rome and Macedon (214–205) Scipio Africanus defeats Hasdrubal in Spain: Spain divided into two provinces (211–206) Scipio defeats Hannibal at Battle of Zama; Carthage becomes a dependent of Rome Roman conquest of Cisalpine Gaul (202–191) Second Macedonian (200–197)	Career of Plautus (204–184); *Miles Gloriosus* performed (204) Ennius active at Rome as poet and teacher (204–169) Q. Fabius Pictor writes first prose history of Rome, in Greek (202)
175	Battle of Pydna: end of Antigonid kingdom of Macedon; Rome divides territory into 4 republics (167)	Polybios the historian arrives in Rome (167) Plays of Terence produced (166–159)
150	Macedonia becomes a Roman province (149–148) Carthage destroyed by Romans; Africa becomes Roman province (149–146) Achaian War: sack of Corinth (146)	Karneades (head of the Academy) comes to Rome on an embassy (155) Publication of Cato's *Origines* or history of Rome Panaitios (Stoic philosopher, *c.*185–109) arrives in Rome (144)
125	Attalos of Pergamon bequeaths his kingdom to Rome (133) War against Jugurtha in Numidia (122–106)	Calpurnius Piso (Roman historian) consul Lucilius (Roman satirist) active
100	Gaius Marius consul for first of six times; he reforms the army (107) Social War in Italy over citizenship (91–88)	Meleagros of Gadara (poet and collector of earliest epigrams in *The Greek Anthology*) active Aristeides of Miletos' 'Milesian Tales' translated into Latin by Sisenna
75	Sulla appointed dictator of Rome: Sullan reforms (87) Slave Revolt of Spartacus (73–71) Pompey's reorganization of East: end of Seleucid monarchy, and of independent kingdom of Judaea; Bithynia, Cilicia, Syria, Crete, organized into provinces; client kingdoms established elsewhere (66–64)	Poseidonios (philosopher, historian, polymath) active at Rhodes (87–51) Cicero's earliest extant speech (81) Philodemos (poet, Epicurean philosopher) active at Rome (75–35)

Date	Historical Events	Literary and Related Developments
50	Caesar campaigns in Gaul (58–49) Civil War between Caesar and Pompey (49) Dictatorship of Caesar (47–44; murdered 15 March 44) Octavian seizes consulate (43) Defeat of Republicans at Philippi by Octavian and Mark Antony	Diodoros of Sicily, Dionysios of Halikarnassos (historical writers) active Sallust (historian and moralist) active Catullus active as poet (59–54) Caesar writes his account of the *Gallic Wars* (58–52) Death of Lucretius: posthumous publication of his poem *On the Nature of the Universe* (55) M. Terentius Varro (antiquarian) active (49–27) Virgil's *Eclogues* published (38) Horace's *Satires* written (37–30)
25	Octavian defeats Antony and Kleopatra at Actium: annexation of Egypt by Rome (31–30) 'The Republic Restored'—first constitutional settlement; Octavian takes name 'Augustus' (27)	Strabon (geographer and historian) active (44–21 CE) Propertius' *Elegies I* published (29) Vitruvius' *On Architecture* (28–23) Ovid begins his *Amores* Death of Tibullus and of Virgil (19)
1CE	Final dynastic settlement: Tiberius given tribunician power (2–4)	End of Livy's history of Rome (9 BCE) Death of Horace and of Maecenas (8 BCE) Ovid banished to the Black Sea (8 CE)
25	**The Julio-Claudians**: reign of Tiberius (14–37) Reign of Gaius Caligula (37–41)	Philo (Jewish writer) active Death of Elder Seneca (writer on oratory) (37)
50	Reign of Claudius (41–54) Reign of Nero (54–68) Pisonian conspiracy against Nero (65) Jewish Revolt (66–73)	St Paul's *Letter to the Corinthians* (58) Younger Seneca's *Letters* (62) Lucan (epic poet) and Persius (satirist) active Suicides of Seneca and Lucan (65) Josephus, rebel leader in Judaea and future author, deserts to the Romans (67) Chariton, Heliodoros, Achilles Tatius, Longus (Greek novelists) active (precise dates uncertain)

Date	Historical Events	Literary and Related Developments
75	'The Year of the Four Emperors': Galba, Otho, Vitellius, Vespasian struggle for power (69) **The Flavians**: reign of Vespasian (69–79) Reign of Titus (79–81) Eruption of Vesuvius: destruction of Pompeii and Herculaneum (79) Reign of Domitian (81–96) Campaigns of Agricola in Britain	Frontinus (administrator and technical writer) active Death of Elder Pliny (administrator, naturalist, and encyclopedist) investigating eruption (79) Statius, Silius Italicus, Martial (poets), and Quintilian (writer on rhetoric) active
100	**The Antonines**: reign of Nerva (96–8) Reign of Trajan (98–117): under him, Roman Empire reaches its greatest geographical extent Trajan conquers Dacia; annexes Armenia and Mesopotamia (101–17) Jewish Revolt (115–17)	Dio Chysostom (Greek orator), Epiktetos (moralist), and Plutarch (essayist and biographer) active in Greek literature Pliny the Younger (orator and letter-writer) consul and governor of Bithynia (100–11) Tacitus writes *Histories* and *Annals*
125	Reign of Hadrian (117–38) Hadrian's visit to Britain; Hadrian's Wall from Tyne to Solway (122–7) Final dispersal of Jews following Bar Kochba's revolt (132–5)	Appian (historian), Arrian (philosopher and historian), Lucian (satirist), and Ptolemy (astronomer) active in Greek literature; Suetonius (biographer) and Juvenal (poet) in Latin
150	Reign of Antonius Pius (138–61)	Pausanias writes his description of Greece Herodes Atticus (Greek orator) and Fronto (Latin orator) active Aelius Aristides, Dion (orators) active Apuleius (poet) and Galen (doctor and polymath) active
175	Reign of Marcus Aurelius (161–80) Reign of Commodus (180–92)	*Meditations* of Marcus Aurelius (174–80) Athenaios writes *Deipnosophistai*
200	**The Severans**: reign of Septimius Severus (193–211) Severus campaigns in Britain and dies at York (208–11) Reign of Caracalla (212–17) *Constitutio Antoniniana* grants citizenship to all inhabitants of the Empire (212) Reign of Elagabalus (218–22)	Philostratos (literary biographer), Herodian (historian), Marius Maximus (biographer), Sextus Empiricus (Sceptic philosopher), Alexander of Aphrodisias (commentator on Aristotle), Tertullian, Clement, and Origen (Christian writers) active

Date	Historical Events	Literary and Related Developments
225	Reign of Alexander Severus (222–35)	Cassius Dio (historian), Plotinos (Neoplatonist philosopher), Nemesianus (Latin poet), Minucius Felix (philosophical writer) active
250	Period of military anarchy, with almost twenty emperors, problems on frontiers and with bureaucracy and economy (235–84)	
275	**The Late Empire**: Diocletian re-establishes central power and founds the Tetrarchy (284–306) Roman Empire partitioned into Eastern and Western portions	
300	Career of Constantine the Great (306–37) Christianity declared official state religion at Rome (312) Constantine reunites Empire Last persecution of Christians in Rome (303–11) Edict of Milan: Constantine establishes toleration of Christianity (313)	
325	Foundation of Constantinople (324) Seat of Empire moved to Constantinople	
350	Rome splits into two Empires again under sons of Constantine (340) Reign of Julian the Apostate (360–3)	Gregory of Nazianzus (Bishop and letter-writer) active Ausonius (teacher of rhetoric, poet) active (c.310–94)
375	Reign of Theodosius the Great (378–95) Roman legions begin to evacuate Britain Visigoths cause trouble on eastern frontiers Theodosius reunites the Empire for the last time (392–5)	Ambrose (bishop) active Ammianus Marcellinus (Latin historian) active Symmachus (letter-writer) active Prudentius (composer of hymns) active
400	Division of Empire between sons of Theodosius Sack of Rome by Alaric the Visigoth (410)	Saint Augustine's *City of God*, following sack of Rome (411) Jerome (Christian writer) active (c.347–420) Paulinus (bishop, poet) active (c.353–431) Claudian (poet and panegyrist) active

Date	Historical Events	Literary and Related Developments
425	Barbarians settle in Roman provinces – Vandals in southern Spain, Huns in Pannonia, Ostrogoths in Dalmatia, Visigoths and Suevi in Portugal and northern Spain	*Digest* of Roman law is compiled (439) (?)Macrobios (Intellectual writer) active
450	Vandals sack Rome (455)	Proklos (neoplatonist philosopher), Nonnos (Greek poet), Sidonius Apollinaris (Gallic prelate and Latin writer) active
475	End of Roman Empire in the West: German Odovacar deposes the derisively titled Emperor Romulus Augustulus and is proclaimed king of Italy (476)	
500	Clovis, king of the Franks, founds Merovingian power; is converted to Christianity Conquest of Italy by Theodoric the Goth: he founds the Ostrogoth kingdom of Italy (493)	Boethius (scholar, philosopher, theologian) active Stobaios' *Anthology of Greek literature*
525	Justinian, Eastern emperor, seeks to reconquer Italy and Africa (527–65)	Justinian orders the closure of the Academy at Athens (529)

Acknowledgements

Museum of the Aquila. Photo: Soprintendenza per I Beni Ambientali Architettonici Artistici e Storici — p. 14

The Louvre, Paris. Photo: © RMN – Chuzeville — p. 36

Postmuseum, Berlin. Photo: AKG London — p. 42

Photo: German Archaeological Institute, Rome — p. 49

© Egyptian Museum of Antiquities. Photo: Egypt Exploration Society — p. 53

The Metropolitan Museum of Art, New York, Rogers Fund, 1911. (11.90) — p. 56

Museum of Roman Civilization, Rome. Photo: Fototeca Unione — p. 105

National Museum, Naples. Photo: Archivi Alinari — p. 109

Somerset County Museum, Taunton. Photo: © University of London, Warburg Institute — p. 117

The Metropolitan Museum of Art, New York, Rogers Fund, 1920. (20.192.16) — p. 142

American Academy in Rome. Photo: Fototeca Unione — p. 162

National Museum, Naples. Photo: Sopritendènza Archeologica delle Province di Napoli e Caserta — p. 169

Drawing by Richard H. Abramson — p. 180

The Louvre, Paris. Photo: © RMN — p. 219

© British Museum — p. 232

Civici Musei d'Arte e Storia di Brescia. Photo: Fotostudio Rapuzzi — p. 241

Archaeological Museum, Istanbul — p. 246

Collezione dell' Accademia di Sant' Anselmo. Photo: Archivi Alinari — p. 256

Index

NOTE: Figures in italics denote illustrations.

For Quinctius, 29; *For Sestius*, 33; *For the Manilian Law*, 159; *On Duties*, 124, 209; *On Old Age*, 4, 160; *Orator*, 37–8, 161; *Philippics*, 155, 157, 164; *Republic*, 12, 39–40, 41
Cinna, Gaius Helvius, 54, 66–7, 68, 70, 72, 75
civic culture and society: local patriotism, 248
civil wars, 54–5, 75, 76, 77, 78, 204, 206; Horace and, 89–90, 93, 103; Virgil and, 85–6, 86–7, 110, 113, 114
Claude Lorrain, 118
Claudian of Alexandria, 257–8, 259
Claudius, Emperor, 167, 172, 173, 176, 218
Claudius, Appius, the Blind, 29
codices, *169*, 243
coinage, *162*
Colleges, Roman artistic, 10
Columella, Lucius Junius Moderatus, 28, 35, 171
comedy
    OLD (Athenian political), 7; audience, 18; *parabasis*, 18
    NEW, 7, 18; audience, 18; Roman adaptation, 15–16, 18
    ROMAN, 15–24; adaptation of New Comedy, 15–16; audience, 15–16, 17–20; costumes, 16, 18, 19; performance context, 13–4, 19–20; palliate, 15–6; prologues, 18, 21–23; *see also* Terence
commentaries: Roman historiography, 44, 48–51
Commodian, 244
competitions, literary, 200–1
conservatism, 155, 171
Constantine I, Emperor, 245
context of genesis of art: effect of distance, 73
contiones, 32
controversiae, 161–2, 164
Corinth, 38, 231
Corippus, Flavius Cresconius, 261
Cornutus, Lucius Annaeus, 220, 233
corona (Roman crowd), 33–5, 158
Cossutianus Capito, 185
costume, theatrical, 16, 18, 19

courts, 158
Crassicus Pansa, 67
Cremutius Cordus, Aulus, 169, 176, 186–7, 190
cultus, 134, 135, 138
Curiatius Maternus, 184–5, 188

dactylic rhythms, *see also* hexameter
Damasus, Pope, 254
Dante Alighieri; *Divine Comedy*, 82
death, 219, *219*; Lucretius on, 57, 62, 63, 65
declamation, 160–6
dedications, 78–9; *see also* patronage
Demetrios (Cynic philosopher), 186
Demokritos, 57
dialogue form: philosophical, 172, 244
didactic poetry: Ovid's *Art of Love* as, 137, 138–9; *see also* Lucretius; Virgil (*Georgics*)
Dio Cassius, 226
Diogenes of Babylon, Stoic, 27
Dionysios of Halikarnassos, 177
Diphilos, 15
Domitian, Emperor, 166, 200, 226, 229; poem by, 224, 225; Statius and, 191–2, 199, 201–2, 203
Dracontius, 260
drama: one-off and repeat performances, 14; performance context, 18; political role, 16, 24–5, 26, 164–5, 184–5; Roman, 13–17, 184–5; *see also* comedy; costume; mime; tragedy
Dryden, John, 17, 133

ecphrasis, 127, 146
education: Christian influence, 245, 251; in rhetoric, 161, 239–40, 242; Roman world, 28, *36*, 54, 161, 237–8, (Late Empire), 239, 245, 246, 247, 251, 260; school books and exercises, 10–1, 116, 123; *see also* literacy; *paideia*
Egypt *see* Alexandria; papyri
eighteenth century, 88, 93
elegiac metre, 94, 132
elegy, 93–100; *recusatio*, 130; *see also* individual poets
Elizabeth I of England, 82

231, 233; *Thebaid*, 199–200, 201, 202, 203–4, 206, 215, 216, 222
Stilicho, 252, 257, 258, 259
Stoicism, 58; adherents, 29, 172–3; suicides, 182
stone, conoisseurship, 228–9
Strabo, 1, 9
stress, metrical, 260
style, appropriateness of, 42, 43
suasoriae, 161, 162–3, 186, 187
Subrius Flavus, 189
Successors of Alexander, 28–9
Suetonius Tranquillus, Gaius, 69, 163–4, 165, 171
Sulla, Lucius Cornelius, 29, 48
Sulpicia, 99–100
Sulpicius Rufus, Servius, 38–9
Symmachus Eusebius, Quintus Aurelius, 253–4

Tacitus, Cornelius, 28, 160, 179–83, 220; *Agricola*, 182–3; *Annals*, 110, 157–8, 179, 181–2, 185–6; *Dialogue on Orators*, 160–1, 166, 184–5, 188, 189, 200; *Germania*, 176; *Histories*, 179
Taras/Tarentum, 28, 29
techne (technical manual) genre, 35–6
Terence (Publius Terentius Afer), 15, 19, 20–3, 23–4; life, 9, 23, 28; patronage, 9, 23–4; prologues, 18, 21–3; *Brothers*, 15, 23; *Eunuch*, 15, 20–1; *Girl from Andros*, 15; *Hecyra* or *Mother-in-law*, 15, 21–3; *Phormio*, 23; *Self-Tormentor*, 15, 20
Tertullian, 244, 248
theatres, 25, 81, 82; *see also* drama
Theodosius the Great, Emperor, 240, 251–2, 257
Theokritos, 76–7
Thrasea Paetus, 184, 185–6, 189, 220
Tiberius, Emperor, 150, 154, 158, 166–7, 168, 176
Tibullus, Albius, 98–100, 104, 106, 131, 135, 136
time: imperial concept of, 225, 229–34
Torquatus, Titus Manlius, 12–13
tragedy, 16, 132, 145, 165–6, 184–5; *see also individual tragedians*

tragicomedy, 17
Trajan, Emperor, 167, 168; Column of, Rome, *49*; Pliny's panegyric, 159–60, 173, 174, 255
transmission of classical texts, 66, 253; *see also* papyri *and under individual authors*
Trier, 246–7
triumphs, 14
triumviral period, 75–93

urbanitas, 43, 133–4
urbs and *orbis*, 225, *227*

Vacca; life of Lucan, 189, 190
Valentinian, Emperor, 246–7, 248
Valerius Flaccus, Gaius, 204–7
Valerius Maximus, 25, 171, 175
Valerius Poplicola, Publius, 29
Vandals, 257, 259
Varius Rufus; *Thyestes*, 79, 145
Varro, Marcus Terentius, 37, 40, 41, 168; antiquarianism, 4, 37, 40, 149; *On Rural Matters*, 37, 41, 83
Varro of Atax, 205
Varus, Alfenus, 79–80
Velleius Paterculus, 177
Verona, Renaissance, 73
Vespasian, Emperor, 166, 168, 205–6
Vettius Agorius Praetextatus, 253
Virgil, allusiveness, 76–7, 84, 114, 115, 120; and Augustus, (*Aeneid*), 108, 110, 112, (*Eclogues*), 77–8, 79, (*Georgics*), 83, 85–6, 87, 202; birthplace, 28; Caligula on, 169; *cento*s, Virgilian, (Ausonius', on consummation of marriage), 247–8; Christian interest in, 82, 245, 247–8, 259; civil war references, 76, 77, 78, 85–6, 86–7, 110, 114; ecphrasis, 127; and Homer, 107–8, 114, 120; inimitability, 132–3; Juvenal's evocation of, 218; and Kallimachos, 84, 115; and Maecenas, 79, 80, 83, 85; metrics, 132–3; and neoterics, 113; and Ovid, 120, 132–3, 136, 143–4; Parthenios' influence on, 54; Petronius parodies, 219; recitations, 80, 81, 83, 112; Silius Italicus